Jenn –
To the best chef
ever,
Marcia Wilhelm

MOLTO ITALIANO

OTHER BOOKS BY MARIO BATALI

Simple Italian Food
Holiday Food
The Babbo Cookbook

MOLTO ITALIANO

327 SIMPLE ITALIAN RECIPES TO COOK AT HOME

MARIO BATALI

Photography
BEATRIZ DA COSTA

Art Direction
LISA EATON *and* **DOUGLAS RICCARDI**

An Imprint of HarperCollinsPublishers

THIS BOOK IS DEDICATED TO

Susi and Benno and Leo

the true lights in my always well-lit sky

MOLTO ITALIANO: 327 SIMPLE ITALIAN RECIPES TO COOK AT HOME

Copyright © 2005 by Mario Batali.

"Adventures in Italian Wine" copyright © 2005 by David Lynch.

All rights reserved. Printed in the United States of America.

No part of this book may be used or reproduced in any manner whatsoever without written permission except in the case of brief quotations embodied in critical articles and reviews.

For information, address HarperCollins Publishers Inc., 10 East 53rd Street, New York, NY 10022.

HarperCollins books may be purchased for educational, business, or sales promotional use.

For information, please write: Special Markets Department, HarperCollins Publishers Inc.,

10 East 53rd Street, New York, NY 10022.

FIRST EDITION

Designed by Memo Productions

Photography by Beatriz Da Costa

Additional photography by Ralph Del Pozzo, High Design NYC (pages 6, 33, 93, 165, 307, and 349)

Illustrations by Elayne Sears

Library of Congress Cataloging-in-Publication Data has been applied for.

ISBN 0-06-073492-2

03 04 05 06 ❖/RRD 10 9 8 7 6 5 4 3 2 1

ACKNOWLEDGMENTS

Special thanks to the Italian community in America, whose devotion to good food and family makes Italian the lingua franca in great kitchens and dining rooms everywhere.

I would like to give special thanks to the following people, for their individual and invaluable contributions that made it possible for me to create a book like this in the middle of everything else.

To my partner Joe Bastianich, who reaches further to test us and makes more sense than I do.

To all of the great people who work with me in the restaurants, particularly Frank Langello, Elisa Sarno, Gina DePalma, Alfredo Ruiz, David Lynch, Jim Logan, Jeremy Nouye, Zach Allen, Ryan Tarpey, Morgan Rich, Dennis Mullaly, Meredith Kurtzman, and Howard Howarth, all of whom manage the teams with aplomb and style and make the real experience something special every day.

To my other partners, Jason Denton, Mark Ladner, Dave Pasternack, Simon Dean, Lidia Bastianich, Andy Nusser, and Nancy Selzer, whose work is often overlooked but who are the real thing.

To my assistant, Pamela Lewy, for getting me to, and keeping me in, the right place, as well as for incredible focus and constant intelligence.

To Sarah LaGrotteria, for true clarity and a lot of vocabulary.

To food artists Anne Burrell and Cristina Cain, for cooking the food for the images in this book.

To Lisa Eaton and Douglas Riccardi, who made the book look good enough to eat and easy to use.

To Beatriz da Costa, prop stylist Betty Alfenito, and Lara Robby, for creating such beautiful images.

To Judith Sutton, for making order out of chaos.

To Food Network, for continuing to give me a soapbox.

To Jim Gandolfini, Mitch Burgess, Robin Green, Michael Imperioli, and David Chase, for making Sunday night Italian night and a joy and challenge to watch.

To my Mom and Dad, for keeping food and love a priority.

To my editor and publisher, Daniel Halpern, for pushing it to the edge, and his team for helping him.

To my agent, Tony Gardner, and my lawyer, Cathy Frankel, for fighting the good fight.

To Jim Harrison and Michael Stipe, for a constant source of poetry and truth.

To Guy de la Valdene, for the birds and the French stuff.

To Bobby Flay, Wolfgang Puck, Emeril Lagasse, Michael Schlow, Lee Hefter, Cesare Casella, and Tom Valenti, for constantly showing me what a chef can be.

To all of the cooks, amateur and professional, who constitute the only club I'd ever join.

Each of my previous three cookbooks was assembled as a kind of snapshot representing specific times in my life, a life in the world of food—

progressing from my apprenticeship in Borgo Capanne, a little town outside of Bologna, through my formative years in New York City, to the present. I remain a student of Italian cooking, but by now I have seen a lot of different types of cooking. I have worked hard to learn and understand everything that happens in a kitchen—from purely regional cooking, as found in the micro-regions of the entire Italian peninsula, to the variations Italian-American cooking has morphed into throughout the United States. I can safely say that today the state of Italian cuisine is in top form. Americans are cooking with more awareness of the importance of seasonal and local ingredients, as well as a better sense of the regional variations in techniques and styles, than ever before. I believe this to be true of American cooking with respect to all the cuisines of the Western world, but most important the cooking of Italy, France, and Spain.

This book is a collection of my all-time favorite simple recipes drawn from my travels in Italy and my cooking here in America, on TV and at home, and it represents the best cooking of classic Italian dishes both here and in their place of birth.

Italians approach each meal with a certain reverence for seasonality—because they have to. Although in the dozen or so big Italian cities with fancy international grocery stores you can find asparagus in December and cherries in February, Italy is, for the most part, still a pretty rural place. The majority of the population lives in smaller towns, with only the occasional visit to the big city for shopping or night life. The shops in these small towns sell local, seasonal products, which dictates a seasonal diet, peppered with *primizie*, or the first-of-the-season excitement that still occurs in Italy. It's a gastronomical cycle, in which spring onions beget asparagus, and asparagus begets porcini mushrooms, and porcini mushrooms beget tiny overwintered cardoons, and so on, right through cherries and into apricots and then onto strawberries and peaches, and eggplants and tomatoes, and acorn squash, and grapes, olives, and apples. And so goes the food of most Italians, whether they live in Amalfi, the Abruzzi, or the Veneto. Because of this natural progression, Italians always seem so excited about the next meal—everything is new and fun when there is a new vegetable or fruit in the kitchen or on the shelves of the *alimentaria*.

The most important step you will take in the creation of any meal is the first one, the shopping. With the best products, it is much easier to prepare a perfect meal. With adequate products, it is easy to produce an adequate meal. Ninety percent of the success of your meal has already been determined when the food has been packed into your car at the grocery store or farmers' market. I can guarantee that if you know the name of the person who picked your salad greens, or apples, or herbs, or cut your meat, or caught your fish, you will have a meal that is significantly better than if you do not. Limiting the number of people in your own personal food chain is a way of maximizing and guaranteeing the quality of the products that find their way to your table.

Italians and Italian Americans know this already, as do others who are in tune with the rhythm of the planet and the goods derived from it that nourish us and make us happy. But this book is not a manifesto for an ideology we should all subscribe to by now. It is a reference and handbook to guide you, to help you create delicious food to serve to your friends and family,

food to make others happy. One of the big differences between Italy and America is the appreciation of home cooking. In Italy, people tend to go out to eat for social reasons, for business meetings, for special occasions, for sacramental parties. The last reason people go to a restaurant in Italy is for better food: everyone knows that the truly best plate of lasagne is served at grandma's house on Sunday, and that the perfect osso buco is made at Aunt Somebody-or-Other's house, not in a restaurant. I feel the same way when I am near my mom and dad's house in Seattle. I enjoy going out to restaurants, but when I am hoping for the "pinnacle of pasta," or a truly spectacular multicourse meal, it will be at their house. Americans tend to place their trust in the unknown, mysterious kitchens of the newest restaurant to open. In fact, in recent years we seem to care more about the opening of a new restaurant than we do the opening of a new play or a new version of *Don Giovanni* by the local opera company. This makes me happy, but at the same time, it makes me just a little sad.

There is no greater joy for me than cooking something and placing it on the table before this new breed of American eaters—no greater satisfaction than to see the pleasure on their faces as they truly enjoy the food. It should be love and joy and music and art and dance and being together that drive us to cook, to eat, and to share. That is the way the citizens of Italy have been doing it for centuries—and they seem to be doing a great job. If this book offers anything at all, I want it to give you a passage into this place I refer to, where the love of food and the joy of coming together operates as one thing at your table, all of the time.

ACB 07563816
CHIANTI CLA
DENOMINAZIONE DI ORIGINE
CONTROLLATA E GARANTITA

ADVENTURES IN ITALIAN WINE · BY DAVID LYNCH

Let's face it: Italian wine is not a simple field of study. In the same way that Italians can find new and creative places to park their cars (ever been to Palermo?),

they've planted vineyards on just about every available parcel on the peninsula. Anyone who has seen the dizzying terraces of the Cinque Terre or the gnarled vines of Vesuvius can appreciate the lengths to which Italians will go to make wine. In all, there are better than three hundred wine appellations in Italy and close to four hundred different grape varieties in regular use, so don't kid yourself into thinking this is going to be easy.

That said, there is an easy way to start: just look closely at a map of Italy, and familiarize yourself with its twenty-one regions. Even after almost two centuries as a "unified" country, Italy is hardly a coherent whole, physically or politically. An Italian's allegiance is to his local province first, Italy second, and where wine is concerned, each region of Italy is its own little wine nation. Take it a region at a time, as you do with the food, and Italian wine starts to make sense in a hurry.

Look at the southern region of Puglia, for example: the "heel" of the boot. It juts out into the sea and is one of the few relatively flat stretches of land in Italy. When you taste the red wines of Puglia, regardless of which local grapes they're made from, you taste the heat of the Adriatic sun: you taste super-ripe, almost sun-baked fruit flavors, warm alcohol, and a dash of southern Italian spice.

Then you look at the northwestern region of Piemonte, home to the famous reds of Barolo and Barbaresco, and you see the great ring of Alps walling the region off from most of its neighbors (note: the map needs to be a topographical one for this). The feel of a typical Piemontese red is a little more nervous, acidic, and tannic in comparison to the plump and juicy reds of Puglia. Cooler sub-Alpine air occasionally blows through the vineyards of Piemonte, where they wait until

October or even November to harvest some of their reds. The Puglians can pick red grapes as early as August.

When you taste the crisp, aromatic white wines of Trentino-Alto Adige, where the vineyards hug steep slopes in the shadow of the Dolomites, it's hard not to imagine little rivulets of ice-cold minerally mountain runoff. Drink the coastal white wines of Liguria, and you pick up a definite brininess from the nearby sea. Ditto for the whites of Naples and the Amalfi Coast.

A regional approach to Italian wine takes on even more resonance when you factor food into the equation. Maybe you've heard the expression "If it grows together, it goes together" and thought it either mere cliché or incomprehensible, but in reality, if you've traveled much in Italy, you've experienced it firsthand: In Piemonte, for example, over a plate of tiny beef-filled agnolotti dressed with butter and truffles, where the glass of Barolo you're drinking is filled with many of the same earthy, heady aromas of the dish. Or in Amalfi, where the zippy, briny, lemony insalata di mare you are eating is perfectly complemented by the zippy, briny, lemony Greco di Tufo sweating in the nearby carafe. You could go to a wine class to learn this kind of stuff, or you can simply leaf through this cookbook, prepare one of Mario's recipes, and seek out a wine from the same region to go with it. So, for the Clams Genovese (named for the Ligurian city of Genoa), for example, you might go for a Ligurian white from the local Vermentino grape—it doesn't matter which one. When you try the food and the wine together, you are re-creating the experience of actually being there. And for his Cuttlefish with Chickpeas, which to

me summons images of the little osterie of Venice, a fleshy white from either a Soave, from about a half-hour away in the Veneto, or a Tocai Friulano, from the northeastern enclave of Friuli-Venezia Giulia.

Know your Italian regions, and you will surprise yourself with your Italian wine erudition. As you sip your Tocai Friulano, you may note to your companion that its fragrance and delicate balance owes to the vineyard's proximity to the Alps. Swirl your glass of supple Sicilian Nero d'Avola and remember that the southeastern end of Sicily, where this grape originated, lies at a more southerly latitude than Tunisia—no wonder the wine is so fat, dark, and ripe!

Okay, fine, maybe this is all getting a little highminded. You want simple? I'll make it simple. On the white side, start in what was traditionally called the Tre Venezie ("three Venices"): the northeastern regions of Trentino-Alto Adige, Veneto, and Friuli-Venezia Giulia. Drink mountain-cooled whites from grapes such as Pinot Bianco (an Alto Adige specialty), Garganega (the grape in Veneto's Soave), and the above-mentioned Tocai Friulano. These are typically clean, fragrant, lightly oaked, yet substantial whites that will go with all sorts of foods. Stated bluntly, Friuli-Venezia Giulia and Trentino-Alto Adige are Italy's premier white wine regions. If you're short on time and patience, stick with them.

On the red side, there are three "noble" grapes to start with: Nebbiolo, Sangiovese, and Aglianico. Nebbiolo is the thinking-person's red grape, giving the wines of Barolo and Barbaresco the earthy, perfumy complexity of great red Burgundy. The woodsy black cherry flavors of Sangiovese are, in a word, incomparable, whether you're drinking a great Brunello di Montalcino or a simple Chianti Classico. And then there's the dark and brooding Aglianico, the spicy southerner, which in wines such as Campania's Taurasi unleashes an almost tobacco-like savor on the palate.

From these humble beginnings, you will soon be hounding your local wine retailer for a good Falanghina or Fiano di Avellino to go with Mario's Scungilli alla Sorrentina. You will pester him further for a dry Lambrusco to go with the Prosciutto with Baked Stuffed Figs. The adventure of Italian travel, food, and ultimately, wine, is trying to truly fit in with the locals, to be a *vero italiano*, not a *brutto americano*.

WINE NOTES

Barolo and *Barbaresco* are wine villages near the city of Alba in southeastern Piedmont. Barolo and Barbaresco wines are made from the Nebbiolo grape, which may be Italy's most noble red variety. Nebbiolo, often compared to Pinot Noir, is an extremely aromatic grape that yields complex, earthy, long-aging wines. Barolos and Barbarescos are considered the Burgundies of Italy and are wines to seek out when you're building a cellar. *Five Great Names*: Conterno, Gaja, Giacosa, Pio Cesare, and Rocche dei Manzoni. *Recommended Dishes*: Agnolotti, Pork Spareribs with Red Wine.

Brunello di Montalcino is Tuscany's most prestigious red wine, made from 100 percent Sangiovese grapes in the village of Montalcino, southwest of Siena. In Montalcino, the Sangiovese variety is referred to as Sangiovese Grosso or Sangiovese Brunello, and the grape is a larger-berried, thicker-skinned version than the Sangiovese used elsewhere in Tuscany. Brunello di Montalcino is dense, dark, and smoky, with a deep black cherry fruitiness. There are many great recent vintages, including 1997, 1999, 2000, and 2001. *Five Great Names*: Argiano, Castello Banfi, Col d'Orcia, Mastrojanni, and Talenti. *Recommended Dishes*: Pici with Lamb Sauce, Chicken Hunter's-Style.

Chianti Classico is the wine region located between Florence and Siena in Tuscany. Within central Tuscany there are actually a number of different appellations incorporating Chianti in their name, but Chianti Classico is the most famous. Chianti Classico wines are crafted using a predominance of Sangiovese, the most-planted red grape in all of Italy. A wine labeled simply Chianti Classico is likely to have lots of cherry fruit, bright acid, and a woodsy aroma, great for simple pastas or pizzas. A Chianti Classico with the Riserva designation is typically fuller-bodied, as it has been aged for several years in wood and bottle before release. The wines of Chianti Classico have improved dramatically in recent years and are fantastic values. *Five Great Names*: Antinori, Brolio, Fattoria di Felsina, Fontodi, and Querciabella. *Recommended Dishes*: Quail with Artichokes, "Weeds" with Sausage.

Vino Nobile di Montepulciano is a wine made in and around the village of Montepulciano in Tuscany. As with Chianti Classico and Brunello di Montalcino, it is made predominantly from the Sangiovese grape. Stylistically, it falls somewhere between Chianti and Brunello. Montepulciano is a beautiful town southeast of Siena, and it should not be confused with the grape variety called Montepulciano, which is grown in Abruzzo and elsewhere. *Five Great Names*: Avignonesi, Boscarelli, Poliziano, Salcheto, and Valdipiatta. *Recommended Dishes*: Guinea Hen with Vinegar, Pork Loin in the Style of Porchetta.

Prosecco is a grape variety grown in northeast Italy, particularly the region of Veneto. Just outside Treviso, in the villages of Conegliano and Valdobbiadene, Prosecco is fashioned into a light, fruity sparkling wine that is especially popular in the bars and restaurants of Venice. These sparklers are made in the "tank method," meaning that their carbonation comes from a second fermentation in a pressurized tank, rather than in the bottle. Prosecco is typically lighter and faintly sweeter than Champagne. It makes an excellent aperitif. *Five Great Names*: Bisol, Mionetto, Nino Franco, Ruggeri, and Zardetto. *Recommended Dishes*: Fritto Misto of Calamari, Sea Scallops, and Lemon, Jumbo Shrimp Marsala Housewife–Style.

Soave is a town just east of Verona as well as the famous white wine appellation. The wines of Soave are made in and around the village of Soave, using a predominance of Garganega grapes. Although Soave's reputation suffered from decades of mass production, today it is a much-improved wine with a legion of great young producers. Look especially for wines labeled Soave Classico, as they are from more prized vineyards. These are fragrant, fleshy white wines that go well with many dishes. *Five Great Names*: Gini, Inama, Monte Tondo, Pieropan, and Graziano Prà. *Recommended Dishes*: Octopus and Potato Salad, Goat Cheese and Scallion Ravioli.

Tocai Friulano may be the most noteworthy native white grape in Italy. A distant relative of Sauvignon Blanc, Tocai is indigenous to Friuli-Venezia Giulia, in northeast Italy. The grape makes bright yet substantial white wines with lots of floral, citrus, and mineral flavors. Like other white wines of Friuli, Tocai is both crisp and aromatic and substantial in body. Great for cheeses and prosciutto, and other *salumi*, as well as seafoods. Look especially for Tocai Friulano from the Collio and Colli Orientali del Friuli appellations. *Five Great Names*: Bastianich, Felluga, Schiopetto, Venica, and Zamò. *Recommended Dishes*: Italian Fennel Salami with Braised Fennel Salad, Trenette with Pesto, Beans, and Potatoes.

Orvieto is a town in southern Umbria that lends its name to the wine region around it. The crisp, minerally white wines of Orvieto are made from a blend of local grapes, including Trebbiano and Grechetto. Typically these are light, simple whites that are best with a good chill and served with seafood. *Five Great Names*: Bigi, Castello della Sala, Mottura, Palazzone, and Salviano. *Recommended Dishes*: Rigatoni with Sheep's Milk Cheese and Pepper, Monkfish Scalloppine with Chianti and Sage.

Valpolicella and *Amarone* are wines made in the hills of Valpolicella, north of Verona in the region of Veneto. A basic Valpolicella is a dry, spicy red made mostly from the local Corvina grape, while Amarone della Valpolicella is, most simply, a Valpolicella made from dried grapes. Amarone is a very intense, alcoholic, and faintly sweet red, since the process of drying the grapes before fermentation heavily concentrates their fermentable sugars. Amarone is a classic red for the cheese course, while Valpolicella is decidedly lighter, well suited to tomato-based pastas and those with cheese sauces. *Five Great Names*: Begali, Masi, Le Ragose, Quintarelli, and Zenato. *Recommended Dishes*: Radicchio Tortelloni with Parmigiano Cream, Chicken with "Cooked Wine."

Aglianico is the premier red grape variety of southern Italy. It is used most famously in the wines of the Taurasi appellation, in central Campania, as well as in northern Basilicata for the wines labeled Aglianico del Vulture. You will see many wines labeled simply Aglianico along with some type of geographical designation, with the best ones hailing from Campania and Basilicata. Aglianico is an extreme grape: dark and smoky, chunky and spicy, a great red for rustic pastas or grilled meats. *Five Great Names*: Feudi di San Gregorio, Mastroberardino, Molettieri, Paternoster, and Terredora. *Recommended Dishes*: Potato Croquettes, Braised Veal Rolls in Tomato Sauce.

Montepulciano d'Abruzzo is a wine made from the Montepulciano grape in the region of Abruzzo. Montepulciano the grape—a plump, juicy red that has a lot of similarities to Merlot—is not to be confused with Montepulciano the place, which is in Tuscany. Although traditionally Montepulciano d'Abruzzo was thought of as a soft, simple quaffing wine, producers in Abruzzo are elevating this supple red to new heights, yet it still remains a great value. *Five Great Names*: Cataldi Madonna, Illuminati, Masciarelli, Nicodemi, and Valentini. *Recommended Dishes*: Ricotta Gnocchi with Sausage and Fennel, Roman-Style Baby Lamb.

Gavi is the name of a village in southeastern Piedmont, as well as the name of the wine appellation in and around it. A white wine made from the Cortese grape, it has a decidedly chalky, mineral edge: a classic light Italian white with loads of acidity. *Five Great Names*: Broglia, La Scolca, Valditerra, Vigne Regali, and Villa Sparina. *Recommended Dishes*: Pansotti with Walnut Sauce, Marinated Sole Venetian-Style.

VEGETABLE
ANTIPASTO

Antipasto can be as basic and yet sublime as a few slices of prosciutto or salami on a plate all by themselves,

ringing in my head and on my tongue like a guitar solo by Jimi Hendrix, or a plate of olives and some pecorino cheese drizzled with great olive oil, transporting my brain to a sunny autumn day in Umbria. It might mean a plate of anchovies with some slices of warm bread and an icy glass of bone-dry white wine on a hot summer day. Often a soupy vegetable or grain dish is served as the first course, rather than an antipasto course, and the pasta course is nixed, but then the soupy dish is called a *primo*. In fact, one is free to place all these things on the table. As the seasons change, so do the colors or paints on the cook's palette, leading to inevitable movement through the culinary year, with change as the main event.

One of the most important things about any great meal is the fact that it is generally a *series* of courses. It does not matter so much whether it is two courses or five, what matters is that each course has its own standing and weight. In other words, the critical element is balance, which in turn makes for a harmonic experience. A great meal is like a global concert performed by the planet, which unfolds to reveal its different components— various weather systems, a cast of seasons, alternating landscapes—all working together to form a heightened experience. And the antipasto course is the first movement.

Vegetables are presented in infinite ways: sometimes raw, sometimes just dressed with oil and lemon, sometimes fried, grilled, or roasted—but almost always not too far from the way the vegetable looked when it was picked. Salads are dressed with good oil and lemon juice or vinegar and that is all, just enough accompaniment to allow their own true flavors to dance ethereally on the palate.

Seafood antipasti are simply cooked, marinated very lightly, or served raw, with the intention of maintaining the fresh, just-out-of-the water flavor that is the hallmark of all Italian seafood ideology.

The variety of cured meats, *salumi*, is ever increasing, with the artisan butcher's craft enjoying a true renaissance in the last ten years. Almost all cured-meat antipasti are presented as a selection of several of the current favorites on the plate, simply and unadorned.

As for cheese, there are as many cheeses in Italy as there are towns. One easy way to serve a good cheese antipasto is to choose a selection from one region of cow's milk, sheep's milk, and goat's milk cheeses. In that way, you can get a sense of the flavor variations from milk to milk within one geographic locale.

Each one of the following dishes can easily stand on its own as a single course in a meal. You could also choose two or three of them and make a light meal, served together or in separate courses of smaller plates. Or you might choose to serve a plate of pasta as the first course and follow with one or two of these antipasto dishes for a small, lighter main course. This book is not intended to be the road map to a single great meal or two, it is intended to serve as your inspiration, your muse. You are the artist here, these are merely your tools.

15

CAULIFLOWER FRITTERS

Bigne Salate

These salty wine accompaniments are traditional to the Neapolitan kitchen and are very much part of the party scene in chic Napoli during the Christmas holidays. The batter is very similar to pâte à choux in the cooking of France, where they use it for savory gougères—cheese puffs—as well as for desserts like profiteroles and croquembouche.

MAKES 15 TO 20 FRITTERS

1 cup WATER

1 teaspoon SALT

8 tablespoons (1 stick) UNSALTED BUTTER

1 cup ALL-PURPOSE FLOUR

6 large EGGS

1 large head CAULIFLOWER (about 2½ pounds), cut into 1-inch florets, including core and lower green leaves

8 salt-packed ANCHOVIES, filleted, rinsed, and finely chopped

8 cups EXTRA-VIRGIN OLIVE OIL, for deep-frying

1. Combine the water, salt, and butter in a 2-quart saucepan over medium heat and bring to a boil, stirring until the butter melts. Have a whisk and a wooden spoon ready. Remove from the heat and dump the flour in all at once, whisking until smooth. Return the pan to the heat and cook, stirring constantly, until the dough starts to pull away from the sides of the pan and form a ball, about 3 minutes. Remove from the heat and stir until tepid, 6 to 8 minutes.

2. Add the eggs one at a time, stirring until each one is completely incorporated before adding the next. Pour the batter into a large bowl and cover with plastic wrap, placing the plastic wrap directly on top of the batter. Set aside.

3. Bring 4 quarts of water to a boil in a medium pot. Set up an ice bath next to the stove. Plunge the cauliflower into the boiling water and cook until tender (not al dente), 8 to 10 minutes. Drain the cauliflower and immediately place in the ice bath to stop the cooking. Drain the cauliflower, pat dry with a kitchen towel, and set aside in a bowl.

4. Preheat the oven to 200°F.

5. Add the anchovies to the batter, stirring well. Toss the cauliflower into the batter, and stir gently to coat.

6. In a 6- to 8-quart pot, heat the olive oil to 375°F. Line a baking sheet with several layers of paper towels. Use two tablespoons to form the fritters, lifting up one cauliflower floret at a time, with a generous amount of batter adhering to it, and then carefully drop them into the hot oil. Cook 6 or 7 florets at a time, flipping them occasionally with a slotted spoon, until golden brown, then transfer to drain on the paper towel–lined baking sheet and keep warm in the oven. Serve hot.

CAULIFLOWER PANCAKES
Fritelle di Cavolfiore

This antipasto is particularly appropriate in mid-fall, when cauliflower is at its peak. The pancakes do not need to be served hot out of the pan—room temp is fine—but do not chill or try to reheat them, so delicate are they.

MAKES 6 SERVINGS

½ cup EXTRA-VIRGIN OLIVE OIL

1 large head CAULIFLOWER, leaves removed, cored, and cut into ½-inch pieces

4 salt-packed ANCHOVIES, filleted, rinsed, and finely chopped

9 large EGGS, beaten

½ cup FRESH BREAD CRUMBS

¼ cup ALL-PURPOSE FLOUR

¼ cup freshly grated PECORINO ROMANO

4 ounces RICOTTA SALATA, in one piece

1. In a 10- to 12-inch sauté pan, heat ¼ cup of the olive oil over medium-high heat until smoking. Add the cauliflower and anchovies, reduce the heat to medium, and cook, stirring frequently, until the cauliflower is very soft yet still holds its shape, 15 to 20 minutes. Remove from the heat and allow to cool.

2. Place the cauliflower in a large bowl, add the eggs, bread crumbs, flour, and pecorino, and stir very gently to mix, leaving distinct lumps and whole bits of cauliflower.

3. In a 10- to 12-inch nonstick sauté pan, heat 2 tablespoons of the olive oil over medium heat until smoking. Drop the cauliflower batter by the tablespoon into the pan, without crowding the pancakes, and cook, turning once, until golden brown, about 3 minutes on each side. Transfer to paper towels to drain, then transfer to a serving platter and continue cooking the pancakes, adding the remaining oil to the pan as necessary.

4. Coarsely grate the ricotta salata over the pancakes, and serve.

THE BRASSICA FAMILY

Cauliflower, broccoli, cabbage, mustard greens, turnips, and Brussels sprouts are all members of the same family of high-sulfur and iron-rich vegetables, the brassicas. Each of these possesses any number of volatile oils called mustard oils (actually isothiocyanates) that are not noticeable when the plant is whole but can cause your eyes to tingle when cut or broken. Cooking the vegetables causes these oils to break down and release smelly derivatives, which is why you can always tell when someone is cooking these class clowns of the school of vegetables. The less you cook them, the less of the smelly stuff they release; I have noticed that cooking them in oil, rather than water, tends to limit the odiferous activity as well.

EGGPLANT BRUSCHETTA

Bruschetta di Melanzane al Fungo

It is very Emilian to cook eggplant "in the style of mushrooms," sautéed with garlic and oil. I first had this preparation at the excellent restaurant Da Lancellotti in Soliera, in the land of true aceto balsamico, run by brothers Emilio and Francesco with love and attention to every detail.

MAKES 4 SERVINGS

6 tablespoons EXTRA-VIRGIN OLIVE OIL

1 medium RED ONION, halved lengthwise, then sliced lengthwise into ½-inch-wide strips

4 cloves GARLIC, thinly sliced

4 long, thin medium ITALIAN EGGPLANT, halved lengthwise and cut into ¼-inch-thick half-moons

SALT and freshly ground BLACK PEPPER

8 slices ITALIAN PEASANT BREAD

½ cup finely chopped ITALIAN PARSLEY

1. In a 10- to 12-inch sauté pan, heat the olive oil over medium-high heat until smoking. Add the onion and cook until just softened, 6 to 7 minutes. Add the garlic and cook until soft, about 2 minutes. Add the eggplant and cook, stirring frequently, until soft and golden brown, about 7 minutes. Remove from the heat, season with salt and pepper, and allow to cool.

2. Meanwhile, preheat the grill or broiler.

3. Toast the bread on the grill or under the broiler until golden brown on both sides.

4. Stir the parsley into the eggplant mixture, spoon the mixture onto the toasts, and serve.

RAW VEGETABLES *with* GARLIC-ANCHOVY BATH

Bagna Cauda

This is a very traditional Piemontese antipasto, often served as a snack in the early evening, particularly during white truffle season in the fall, when the sauce is enhanced with truffles. Its name means, literally, "warm bath," and if there's any left over, I like to crack an egg or two into the dregs of the garlicky bath, mix them together, and pour the scented eggs into a waiting hot frying pan—scrambled eggs! Then I grate some white truffle over the whole thing and eat spoonful after loving spoonful.

MAKES 4 SERVINGS

¼ cup WHOLE MILK

12 cloves GARLIC, sliced paper-thin

1 cup EXTRA-VIRGIN OLIVE OIL

8 tablespoons (1 stick) UNSALTED BUTTER

¼ cup ANCHOVY FILLETS, rinsed and drained

Freshly ground BLACK PEPPER

1 FENNEL BULB, trimmed, cored, and cut into thick strips

4 CARDOON STALKS, peeled and blanched in boiling water for 10 minutes

1 RED BELL PEPPER, cored, seeded, and cut into bite-sized squares

1 YELLOW BELL PEPPER, cored, seeded, and cut into bite-sized squares

1 loaf ITALIAN PEASANT BREAD, cut into chunks

1. Combine the milk and garlic in a small saucepan over medium heat and bring to a boil, then lower the heat and simmer for 10 minutes. Strain the milk into a small bowl, and reserve the garlic.

2. Combine the olive oil and butter in a medium saucepan and heat over medium heat until the butter is melted. Add the garlic, 2 tablespoons of the garlic cooking milk, the anchovy fillets, and pepper to taste. Use an immersion blender to blend until well combined, or transfer to a regular blender and blend well, being careful with the hot oil. (The sauce will not remain emulsified very long—that would not be very Italian.)

3. Pour the bagna cauda into a warmed fondue pot and place over a flame to keep warm. Serve with the vegetables and bread for dipping.

EGGPLANT INVOLTINI *with* RICOTTA *and* SCALLIONS

Involtini di Melanzane

These are spectacularly simple and yet will look as if you've been cooking all day. Just one thing: it would be better to overcook them by five minutes than to undercook them by one.

MAKES 4 SERVINGS

2¼ cups EXTRA-VIRGIN OLIVE OIL

3 medium EGGPLANT, sliced lengthwise into ⅓-inch-thick slices

1 cup fresh RICOTTA

1 large EGG

2 SCALLIONS, thinly sliced

¼ teaspoon freshly grated NUTMEG

SALT and freshly ground BLACK PEPPER

2 cups BASIC TOMATO SAUCE (page 71)

¼ cup whole PARSLEY LEAVES

1. In a 10- to 12-inch sauté pan, heat 2 cups of the olive oil over medium-high heat until it reaches 370°F. Add the eggplant slices 3 or 4 at a time and fry, turning once, until soft and light golden brown, about 2 minutes. Transfer to paper towels to drain.

2. Preheat the oven to 375°F.

3. In a medium bowl, combine the ricotta, egg, scallions, and nutmeg and mix well. Season with salt and pepper. Lay the eggplant slices out on a work surface and place 1 table-spoon of the ricotta filling at the base of each slice. Roll the eggplant up around the filling to form a neat roll and set seam side down on the work surface.

4. Lightly oil a baking dish just large enough to hold the eggplant roll-ups. Pour the sauce into the dish and place the rolls seam side down in the sauce.

5. Bake until the cheese starts to melt out of the rolls, about 15 minutes. Drizzle with the remaining ¼ cup olive oil, sprinkle with parsley, and serve.

EGGPLANT PARMIGIANA
Melanzane alla Parmigiana

Baking the eggplant instead of frying it makes this dish a lot lighter and tastier. It also makes it possible to serve it at room temperature, with no fear of cold, greasy bread crumbs wrecking your day.

MAKES 2 TO 4 SERVINGS

¼ cup EXTRA-VIRGIN OLIVE OIL

2 large EGGPLANT (about 1 pound each)

SALT and freshly ground BLACK PEPPER

3 cups BASIC TOMATO SAUCE (page 71)

1 bunch BASIL, leaves removed and cut into chiffonade

1 pound fresh MOZZARELLA, cut into ¼-inch-thick slices (you need 12 slices)

½ cup freshly grated PARMIGIANO-REGGIANO

¼ cup lightly TOASTED BREAD CRUMBS

1. Preheat the oven to 450°F. Oil a baking sheet with olive oil.

2. Cut each eggplant into 6 slices. Lightly season each disk with salt and pepper, and place on the oiled sheet.

3. Bake for 12 to 15 minutes, until deep brown on top. Transfer to a large plate or a platter and let cool. Lower the oven temperature to 350°F.

4. Arrange the 4 largest eggplant disks in a 9-by-12-inch baking pan, spacing them evenly. Spread ¼ cup of the tomato sauce over each disk, and sprinkle each with a teaspoon of basil. Place 1 slice of mozzarella over each and sprinkle with 1 teaspoon Parmigiano. Top with 4 more slices of eggplant and repeat the layering with the cheeses, tomato sauce, and basil, then repeat again, using all the remaining basil and Parmigiano, to make 4 medallions. Sprinkle the toasted bread crumbs over the top.

5. Bake, uncovered, for 20 minutes, or until the cheese is melted and tops are lightly browned. Serve hot, warm, or at room temperature.

FRIED EGGPLANT

Melanzane Fritte

This is the Modenese version of a simple fry that is popular all over Italy, as evidenced by the use of butter and rare balsamic vinegar as the condiment of choice. The key to the recipe is the youth of the eggplant. As they mature, eggplants develop deep seed pockets that can be bitter.

MAKES 6 SERVINGS

½ cup ALL-PURPOSE FLOUR

3 large EGGS

1 cup TOASTED BREAD CRUMBS

2 pounds small young EGGPLANT, halved lengthwise and cut into ⅓-inch-thick half-moons

¼ cup EXTRA-VIRGIN OLIVE OIL

1 tablespoon UNSALTED BUTTER

SALT and freshly ground BLACK PEPPER

2 tablespoons AGED BALSAMIC VINEGAR

1. Spread the flour on a plate. Lightly beat the eggs in a shallow bowl. Spread the bread crumbs on another plate. Dredge the eggplant in the flour and bat it against your hand to remove any excess, then dip in the eggs, turning to coat completely, and dip in the bread crumbs, coating completely. Set aside on a sheet of parchment or wax paper.

2. In a 10- to 12-inch sauté pan, heat the olive oil over medium-high heat just until smoking. Add the butter and heat until it foams and subsides. Add the eggplant, in batches, and cook, turning occasionally, until both sides are dark golden brown. Remove from the pan, season with salt and pepper, and drain on a plate lined with paper towels.

3. Transfer to a platter, drizzle with the vinegar, and serve immediately.

FRYING WITH OLIVE OIL

The smoking point of an oil is the temperature at which it will start to smoke and turn harsh or bitter. The oils typically recommended for deep-frying have smoke points of around 440°F to 450°F—peanut, corn, and safflower oil are at the high end, grapeseed and canola are slightly lower. The smoking point of olive oil is quite a bit lower, around 375°F. According to logic, then, and a whole lot of "food science experts," it would seem that frying in extra-virgin olive oil would result in burnt flavor or soggy undercooked foods. But anyone who has ever eaten an artichoke "alla Giudia" in Rome knows this not to be the case, and olive oil is my oil of choice for deep-frying.

MIXED CROSTINI
Crostini Misti

MAKES 12 SERVINGS

1 pound PORCINI or PORTOBELLO MUSHROOMS, stems removed if using portobellos

½ cup EXTRA-VIRGIN OLIVE OIL

4 fresh SAGE LEAVES, cut into chiffonade

2 cloves GARLIC, thinly sliced

SALT and freshly ground BLACK PEPPER

1 small RED ONION, cut into ¼-inch dice

2 RED BELL PEPPERS, cored, seeded, and cut into ⅛-inch dice

1 teaspoon fresh THYME LEAVES

1 teaspoon fresh OREGANO LEAVES

1 bunch CAVOLO NERO (black kale) or other KALE (about 1 pound), tough stems removed and sliced crosswise into ½-inch-wide ribbons

1 teaspoon HOT RED PEPPER FLAKES

4 ounces sliced PROSCIUTTO DI PARMA, cut into ¼-inch dice

2 LEEKS, white and light green parts only, cut into ¼-inch-thick rings and thoroughly rinsed

1 bunch MINT, leaves only

1 *STIRATO* (long thin Italian bread) or BAGUETTE, cut on the bias into ½-inch-thick slices

1 LEMON, halved

1. Preheat the oven to 450°F.
2. Place the mushrooms on a baking sheet and drizzle with 2 tablespoons of the olive oil. Roast for 20 minutes. Remove from the oven and allow to cool on the baking sheet.
3. Chop the mushrooms into ½-inch pieces and place in a medium bowl, along with their juices. Add the sage and garlic, season, and set aside.
4. In a 10- to 12-inch sauté pan, heat 2 tablespoons of the olive oil over medium heat. Add the onion and cook until soft and translucent, about 5 minutes. Add the red peppers, thyme, and oregano, increase the heat to high, and sauté until the peppers and onions are very soft, about 5 more minutes. Transfer to a bowl, season with salt and pepper, and set aside.
5. Heat 2 tablespoons of the olive oil in the same pan over medium heat until smoking. Add the cavolo nero and red pepper flakes and cook, stirring, until the kale is wilted and soft, 4 to 5 minutes. Add ¼ cup water and stir quickly as it steams and softens the kale, cooking until the water has completely evaporated. Transfer the cabbage to a bowl, stir in the prosciutto, and set aside. Wipe the pan clean.
6. Heat the remaining olive oil in the pan over medium heat until smoking. Add the leeks and cook, stirring occasionally, until very soft and translucent, 8 to 9 minutes. Transfer to a bowl and allow to cool. Tear the mint leaves into small pieces and add to the leeks. Season with salt and pepper and set aside.
7. Grill or toast the bread, until browned.
8. Moisten any pieces that seem dry with a little olive oil and a squeeze of lemon. Top each with a heaping tablespoon of one of the mixtures, and serve immediately.

NEAPOLITAN CROSTINI

Crostini Napoletani

Adding cream to ricotta, though not at all Italian, makes American ricotta almost as good as the Neapolitan version.

MAKES 8 SERVINGS

2 cups fresh RICOTTA

¼ cup HEAVY CREAM

3 tablespoons freshly ground BLACK PEPPER

1 teaspoon HOT RED PEPPER FLAKES

3 tablespoons fresh MARJORAM

16 small slices CRUSTY BREAD (baguette size) or 8 large slices country ITALIAN PEASANT BREAD

3 cloves GARLIC

16 marinated fresh ANCHOVY FILLETS or salt-packed ANCHOVY FILLETS rinsed

3 tablespoons EXTRA-VIRGIN OLIVE OIL

1. Preheat the broiler. In a small bowl, mix the ricotta with the cream, black pepper, red pepper flakes, and marjoram. Set aside.
2. Place the bread on a baking sheet and toast under the broiler, turning once, until light golden brown on both sides. While the toast is still hot, rub each slice with a garlic clove. Spread some of the ricotta over each slice of bread. Top each with an anchovy (2 each if using peasant bread) and return to the baking sheet.
3. Place the crostini back under the broiler until the cheese just oozes, about 1 minute. Transfer to a serving platter, drizzle with the olive oil, and serve immediately.

MARINATED OLIVE SALAD

Insalata di Olive

You can use any of your favorite olives in this recipe, but try to choose a medley of different colors and sizes.

MAKES 4 SERVINGS

½ cup PICHOLINE OLIVES

½ cup NIÇOISE OLIVES

½ cup GAETA OLIVES

½ cup cracked SICILIAN OLIVES

5 tablespoons chopped fresh OREGANO

1 FENNEL BULB, trimmed

Grated zest and juice of 1 ORANGE

1. In a medium bowl, combine the olives, toss in the oregano, and set aside.
2. Using a mandoline or other vegetable slicer (or a very sharp knife), shave the fennel as thin as possible.
3. Add the fennel to the olives and toss well. Add the orange zest and juice and toss again.

SAUTÉED BLACK *and* GREEN OLIVES *in* TOMATO SAUCE

Olive col Pomodoro

This is a great antipasto that transcends an already perfect existence, a bowl of olives. Heated through, olives become more meaty, more vivid, more visceral, more Nigella Lawson—in short, more of what we want and need when we are hungry.

MAKES 2 CUPS

¼ cup EXTRA-VIRGIN OLIVE OIL

2 cloves GARLIC, chopped

8 ounces small BLACK BRINE-CURED OLIVES, such as Gaeta, rinsed and patted dry

8 ounces small GREEN BRINE-CURED OLIVES, such as Arbequina or Nyons, rinsed and patted dry

1 cup BASIC TOMATO SAUCE (page 71)

1. In a 10- to 12-inch sauté pan, heat the olive oil over medium-high heat until hot. Add the garlic, increase the heat to high, and cook, stirring, until golden, about 2 minutes. Add the olives and cook for 3 minutes, or until softened.

2. Add the tomato sauce, lower the heat, and simmer for 15 to 20 minutes, occasionally basting the olives with the tomato sauce. Serve warm or at room temperature.

Photograph on page 62.

OLIVES

The olive tree (*Olea europea*), along with its fruit and the oil it produces, is a quintessential symbol of the Mediterranean region. The tree is an evergreen that features distinctive silvery-green foliage. The trees are grown in valley meadows and on terraced hillsides, and even trees more than several hundred years old can still produce a good crop.

Olives are harvested at various stages of ripeness. Green olives are less ripe, with firm flesh and more bitter flavor tones. As the olives mature, they blacken, soften, and begin to release more of their oils, making for a softer, richer-flavored fruit. Olives can be cured in salt, in water, in a brine solution, or in oil, or they may be dry-cured. Brine and oil cures are also enriched with flavorings such as citrus rinds, herbs, and spices.

GRILLED MOZZARELLA SANDWICHES

Mozzarella in Carozza

These are the ultimate elegant snack that makes grilled cheese sammies into performance art. The whole game here is the choice of mozzarella, so do not make these unless you can find, if not real mozzarella from Campania, a comparable high-quality mozzarella *di bufala*. Or, totally change the recipe and use another great cheese, like Taleggio or even a fine American Cheddar.

MAKES 4 SERVINGS

1 pound fresh BUFFALO MOZZARELLA, cut into 4 equal pieces about 3 inches by 4 inches

Eight ½-inch-thick slices firm WHITE SANDWICH BREAD

2 large EGGS

½ cup HEAVY CREAM

1 teaspoon fresh THYME LEAVES

1 teaspoon SALT

A grating of NUTMEG

¼ cup EXTRA-VIRGIN OLIVE OIL

2 tablespoons UNSALTED BUTTER

1. Place the mozzarella on 4 slices of the bread. Cover with the 4 remaining slices to form sandwiches. Trim the crusts off to make perfect 4-inch squares.

2. In a wide shallow bowl, whisk the eggs. Add the cream, thyme leaves, salt, and nutmeg and whisk until well blended.

3. In a 10- to 12-inch nonstick sauté pan, heat 2 tablespoons of the olive oil over medium-high heat until smoking. Add 1 tablespoon of the butter and cook until the sizzling subsides. Dip 2 of the sandwiches into the egg mixture, turning to coat, place in the pan, and cook until golden brown on first side, about 2 minutes. Flip over and brown on the other side. Transfer the sandwiches to individual plates and repeat the process with the remaining 2 tablespoons olive oil, 1 tablespoon butter, and 2 sandwiches. Cut in half, and serve immediately.

WINTER CAPRESE SALAD

Insalata Caprese Invernale

I love this winter version of the Neapolitan classic because it is very easy to do, and the slow-roasted tomatoes are better than any regular tomatoes for all but about three months of the year. The extra pesto keeps well in the fridge for two weeks, provided you cover the top with a half-inch of extra-virgin olive oil.

MAKES 4 SERVINGS

6 PLUM TOMATOES, cut lengthwise in half

¾ cup EXTRA-VIRGIN OLIVE OIL

SALT and freshly ground BLACK PEPPER

1 clove GARLIC

3 tablespoons freshly grated PARMIGIANO-REGGIANO

3 cups fresh BASIL LEAVES, plus a few leaves for garnish

2 tablespoons PINE NUTS

4 large BOCCONCINI (from buffalo mozzarella) or 1 pound BUFFALO MOZZARELLA, cut into quarters

1. Preheat the oven to 200°F.
2. In a medium bowl, toss the tomatoes with ¼ cup of the olive oil and salt and pepper to taste. Place cut side down on a small baking sheet and bake for about 2 hours, or until the tomatoes are softened.
3. Remove the tomatoes from the oven and let cool.
4. Transfer the cooled tomatoes to a colander and set aside to drain while you make the pesto.
5. Combine the garlic and Parmigiano in a blender and pulse until the garlic is roughly chopped. Add the basil and pulse 7 or 8 times, or until the leaves are shredded. With the blender running, slowly add the remaining ½ cup olive oil, blending until smooth.
6. Toast the pine nuts in an 8-inch sauté pan over medium heat, tossing frequently, until golden brown, 3 to 4 minutes. Transfer to a plate to cool.
7. To serve, arrange 3 tomato halves cut side down on each plate. Place a ball of mozzarella in the center and spoon 2 tablespoons of the pesto onto each ball of mozzarella. Sprinkle with the pine nuts and garnish with basil leaves.

CHEESE
(Formaggio)

It should come as no surprise that the Italians are just as particular, just as regional, just as obsessed about their cheeses as they are about their salami, their wine, their pasta, their vegetables, their seafood, and everything else they put in their mouths. Cheese, in its myriad permutations and styles, can easily be a part of every single course, whether in a fancy restaurant or at a daily meal at home, from antipasto all the way through, and including, dessert.

The menu could begin with an antipasto of mozzarella di bufala or scamorza from Campania, or burrata from Puglia, served unadorned or with a few leaves of basil and a drizzle of good olive oil. Then proceed to the pasta course, with fresh ricotta or squaquerone stuffed inside a pasta in Emilia-Romagna, scented with freshly grated nutmeg and a bit of parsley, or grated over the top of the pasta— pecorino romano or Parmigiano-Reggiano for the rookies, or more esoteric regional cheeses such as aged Montasio in Friuli or Castelmagno in Piemonte. As a course on its own, a plate of local fresh and aged sheep's milk cheese is an option in almost every trattoria in the land. And cheese after dinner with a piece of fruit and the rest of the wine on the table is the norm. Dessert? Two words: Italian cheesecake! Following is a list of the thirty DOP cheeses currently produced in Italy. DOP, from *denominazione d'origine protetta,* means that their origins and names are guaranteed; within each of the DOPs, however, there are superior brands and producers. The best way to find out about them is to go to a great cheese shop and taste them with a cheese-monger—and trust your palate.

Asiago

Bitto

Bra

Caciocavallo Silano

Canestrato di Puglia

Casciotta d'Urbino

Castelmagno

Fiore Sardo

Fontina d'Aosta

Formai de Mut

Gorgonzola

Grana Padano

Montasio

Monte Veronese

Mozzarella di Bufala Campana

Murazzano

Parmigiano-Reggiano

Pecorino Romano

Pecorino Sardo

Pecorino Siciliano

Pecorino Toscano

Provolone Valpadana

Quartirolo Lombardo

Ragusano

Raschera

Robiola di Roccaverano

Taleggio

Toma Piemontese

Valle d'Aosta Fromadzo

Valtellina Casera

For more information on how to buy, store, and serve Italian cheeses, pick up a copy of *Italian Cheese* by the Slow Food Editore—they are true masters.

MOZZARELLA SKEWERS *with* ANCHOVY SAUCE

Spiedini alla Romana

This is a classic fry-shop "hero" all over the south of Italy, eaten as often for a mid-morning snack as for lunch or dinner. Most fry shops rev up their vats of oil around nine in the morning and work through to the middle of lunch, around 2 p.m., then close till 6 p.m., when they open for the "home-meal-replacement" crowd.

MAKES 8 SERVINGS

1 loaf day-old ITALIAN BREAD, cut into 2-inch-thick slices and then into 2-inch cubes

1 pound fresh BUFFALO MOZZARELLA, cut into 2-inch cubes

1½ cups EXTRA-VIRGIN OLIVE OIL

3 large EGGS

8 salt-packed ANCHOVIES, filleted, rinsed, and chopped into ⅛-inch pieces

¼ cup finely chopped ITALIAN PARSLEY

16 short BAMBOO SKEWERS

1. Thread 3 cubes of bread and 2 cubes of cheese onto each skewer, beginning and ending with bread, and sandwiching the cheese tightly between the bread cubes. Set aside.

2. In a large deep heavy-bottomed skillet, heat 1 cup of the olive oil over high heat until almost smoking. Meanwhile, lightly beat the eggs in a large shallow bowl. Working in batches, dip each skewer in the eggs, turning to coat, then lift out, letting the excess drip off, and add to the oil. Cook, turning occasionally, until light golden brown on all sides, about 5 minutes. Transfer the skewers to a plate lined with paper towels to drain.

3. In a small saucepan, combine the remaining ½ cup olive oil and the anchovies and bring to a boil over low heat, stirring until the anchovies have fallen apart. Remove from the heat and stir in the parsley.

4. Transfer the spiedini to a platter or individual plates, pour the oil over them, and serve.

FRIGGITORIE

Friggitorie, or fry shops, can be anything from elaborate temples of gastronomy with literally hundreds of fried foods sitting at room temp on long marble counters to little shacks near the beach with whitebait the only item on the menu. One thing is certain, if it is a good one, it will always be crowded. Italians love their fried foods and snack on them relentlessly. They like to eat them right out of the oil and piping hot, but they also buy the goods to eat at home, either as is or reheated in the oven.

FRIED ONIONS
Cipolline Fritte

This dish is traditionally made with the first cipolline, small, squat Italian onions at the end of summer, but I love pearl onions or even trimmed fat scallions for an "upside the head" smack of radiant pungency. The batter comes off feeling like Japanese tempura in its crisp and feather-like delivery. This procedure will also work with lightly cooked vegetables outside the lily family, such as slices of baked sweet potato or blanched Romano beans.

MAKES 6 SERVINGS

2 large EGGS, separated

SALT and freshly ground BLACK PEPPER

¾ cup ALL-PURPOSE FLOUR

½ cup WHOLE MILK

¼ cup freshly grated PECORINO ROMANO

2 cloves GARLIC, crushed

1 pound CIPOLLINE or PEARL ONIONS, peeled

¼ cup finely chopped ITALIAN PARSLEY

4 cups EXTRA-VIRGIN OLIVE OIL, for deep-frying

1. In a large bowl, combine the egg yolks, ½ teaspoon each salt and pepper, and the flour, and whisk to combine. Gradually add the milk, whisking until the batter is smooth. Stir in the pecorino and garlic and let rest for 30 minutes. (Set the egg whites aside in a large bowl.)

2. Meanwhile, bring 2 quarts of water to a boil in a large saucepan, and add 1 tablespoon salt. Set up an ice bath next to the stovetop. Blanch the onions in the boiling water for 2 minutes, then refresh in the ice bath. Drain and pat dry with paper towels.

3. Fold the parsley into the batter. In a large bowl, beat the egg whites to stiff peaks. Fold the egg whites into the batter.

4. In a large deep saucepan, heat the olive oil over high heat to 365°F. Using tongs, and working in batches, dip each onion into the batter, shaking off the excess, and then fry until golden brown on all sides. With a slotted spoon or spider, transfer to a plate lined with paper towels to drain, and season with salt. Serve hot.

SICILIAN CHICKPEA FRITTERS

Panelle

These tasty little fritters are an integral part of the Sicilian snack situation. They are also players at breakfast, lunch, and dinner, filler for sandwiches, and afternoon wine tidbits as well.

MAKES ABOUT 20 FRITTERS

1⅓ cups CHICKPEA FLOUR (see Note)

1 teaspoon SALT

4 cups WATER

¼ cup freshly grated PECORINO SARDO

¼ cup finely chopped ITALIAN PARSLEY

4 cups EXTRA-VIRGIN OLIVE OIL, for deep-frying

1. Lightly oil a 9-by-12-inch baking pan.

2. In a 4-quart saucepan, combine the chickpea flour and salt. Gradually add the water, stirring constantly to prevent lumps. Stir in the pecorino and parsley. Place the saucepan over medium heat and cook, stirring constantly, until the mixture is as thick as hot breakfast cereal, about 10 minutes. Pour the mixture into the oiled baking pan and let cool.

3. Invert the chickpea mixture onto a cutting board. Using cookie or other metal cutters, cut into decorative shapes, and transfer to a plate. Cover and refrigerate until ready to use.

4. In a heavy, deep 4-quart saucepan, heat the olive oil over medium-high heat until it reaches 365°F. Drop the panelle into the oil in batches, 6 or 7 at a time, and cook, turning once or twice, until deep golden brown, about 4 minutes. Transfer to a plate lined with paper towels to drain. Serve warm.

Note: Chickpea flour is available at Italian markets and some specialty grocers. Do not use Indian chickpea flour.

POTATO "PIZZA"

Pizza di Patate

These are traditional to the holiday table in Campania and can be made with any starchy tuber, such as manioc (also called cassava and yuca) or even Jerusalem artichokes. Sweet potatoes are particularly well suited.

MAKES 8 SERVINGS

4 pounds RUSSET POTATOES

1½ cups RICOTTA

1 cup freshly grated HARD PROVOLONE

2 large EGGS

½ cup finely chopped ITALIAN PARSLEY

SALT and freshly ground BLACK PEPPER

2 cups FRESH BREAD CRUMBS

About ¼ cup EXTRA-VIRGIN OLIVE OIL

1. Bring 8 quarts of salted water to a boil in a large pot. Add the potatoes and cook until they are easily pierced with a paring knife, about 25 minutes.

2. Drain the potatoes and let cool slightly.

While they are still warm, peel them and pass them through a food mill into a large bowl. Add the ricotta, provolone, eggs, and parsley, season with salt and plenty of pepper, and mix well.

3. Spread the bread crumbs on a plate. Using wet hands, divide the potato mixture into quarters and form into four 6-inch "pizzas," each about ½ inch thick. Press both sides of each pizza into the bread crumbs to coat. Set aside.

4. Preheat the oven to 450°F. Set a rack on a baking sheet.

5. In an 8-inch nonstick pan, heat 1 tablespoon of the olive oil over medium-high heat until smoking. Place 1 pizza in the pan and cook, turning once, until dark golden brown on both sides, about 4 minutes per side. Transfer the pizza to a tray lined with paper towels to drain, and repeat with the remaining pizzas, adding more oil to the pan as necessary.

6. To serve, place the pizzas on the rack on the baking sheet and heat in the oven for 6 to 8 minutes. Serve in a pile on a platter.

BREAD CRUMBS

Bread crumbs are often used for coating ingredients before sautéing or frying, as well as an ingredient for stuffing vegetables, meat, fish, or poultry. They also act as a binder with egg or oil in stuffings and pastas and they make a nice crust when browned atop a dish or toasted. Make dried crumbs by drying fresh—not stale—bread in an oven at very low temperature and then making crumbs of it in a food processor. For fresh bread crumbs, just grind slices or chunks of bread to the desired size in the processor. Ready-made bread crumbs are available at bakery departments in grocery stores and in specialty markets; they are okay if you do not have time to make them yourself. Bread crumbs sold in canisters in grocery stores are unacceptable in any real kitchen.

SCAFATA *of* FAVA BEANS *and* ESCAROLE

Scafata di Primavera

They do not serve al dente vegetables in Rome, they serve them cooked through, and with maximum flavor. This is not a dish that is brightly colored like the cover of a food magazine. You're looking for the more muted pale green of a true Roman spring.

MAKES 4 SERVINGS

¼ cup EXTRA-VIRGIN OLIVE OIL

2 ounces PANCETTA, cut into ⅛-inch dice

½ medium SPANISH ONION, thinly sliced

1 teaspoon HOT RED PEPPER FLAKES

8 BABY ARTICHOKES, tough outer leaves removed, stems trimmed, and halved

1 cup hot WATER

2 pounds FAVA BEANS, shelled and peeled

2 pounds fresh PEAS, shelled (about 1 cup)

½ head ESCAROLE, cut crosswise into ½-inch-wide ribbons

1 tablespoon freshly ground BLACK PEPPER

SALT

4 fresh MINT LEAVES

1. In a 10- to 12-inch sauté pan, combine the olive oil and pancetta and cook over medium heat until the pancetta is soft and translucent, about 6 minutes. Add the onion, red pepper flakes, and artichokes and cook until the artichokes are just tender, 8 to 10 minutes.

2. Add the water, favas, peas, escarole, and pepper and cook until the escarole is wilted and soft and the peas and beans are tender, about 8 minutes. Season with salt.

3. Tear the mint leaves into pieces, sprinkle over the scafata, and serve. This dish is also good at room temperature.

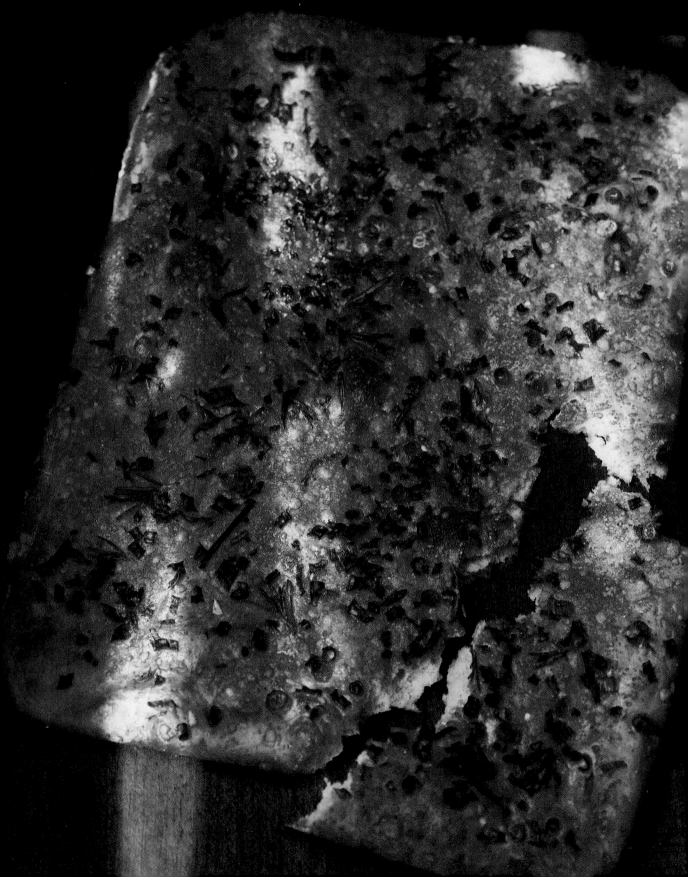

CHEESE BREAD *from* GENOA
Focaccia al Formaggio

I refined my basic recipe for the Genoese bread called focaccia by adding a lot more olive oil for drizzling after a visit to Liguria Bakery in San Francisco's poetic and magnificent North Beach. Many of the original Italian settlers to the Bay Area hailed from Liguria, and the bakery's focaccia was absolutely authentic and perfect.

MAKES 8 SERVINGS

DOUGH

½ cup WARM WATER

1 tablespoon ACTIVE DRY YEAST

1 teaspoon SALT

1 teaspoon SUGAR

4 cups high-gluten PIZZA or BREAD FLOUR, plus more for dusting

¼ cup EXTRA-VIRGIN OLIVE OIL

1 cup freshly grated PECORINO ROMANO

1 cup freshly grated PARMIGIANO-REGGIANO

¾ cup EXTRA-VIRGIN OLIVE OIL

2 bunches SCALLIONS, cut into ⅛-inch-thick slices

2 tablespoons fresh ROSEMARY, chopped

1 tablespoon COARSE SEA SALT

1. Put the warm water in a large warmed bowl, add the yeast, and stir to dissolve. Let stand for 3 minutes, or until foamy.

2. Add the salt and sugar and stir to combine. Add the flour and olive oil and mix, first with the spoon and then using your hands, until the dough comes together into a ball that no longer sticks to your fingers.

3. Wash and dry your hands. Transfer the dough ball to a work surface and knead, occasionally dusting the dough with a teaspoon of flour or so, until you have a smooth, firm ball, about 15 minutes.

4. Place the dough in a lightly oiled large bowl and cover it with a clean kitchen cloth. Place the bowl in a warm area (such as above the refrigerator) and let rise until the dough has doubled in size, about 2 hours.

5. Punch the dough down and divide it into 2 equal pieces. Shape each one into a ball, return to the bowl, cover, and let rise for 30 minutes.

6. Preheat the oven to 450°F. Lightly oil two 11-by-17-inch baking sheets.

7. Place each piece of dough on an oiled baking sheet and, using a rolling pan or your hands, flatten it to fit the baking sheet. Using your fingertips, poke indentations across the entire surface of each bread. Sprinkle with both cheeses, drizzle with the olive oil, and then sprinkle with the rosemary, scallions, and salt. Bake for 14 to 15 minutes, until golden brown on top and bottom. Serve warm.

FRIED ZUCCHINI FLOWERS *with* GOAT CHEESE

Fiori di Zucca Fritti

This is a variation on a dish I have tasted a hundred times in the shadow of Mount Vesuvius, in Campania outside Napoli. There they generally make it with the local ricotta made from water buffalo milk, the same milk that goes into their exquisite mozzarella. I have substituted local goat's milk cheese from New York State, but you could use any soft, creamy, delicate cheese.

MAKES 4 SERVINGS

12 ZUCCHINI FLOWERS

1 cup fresh GOAT CHEESE CURD, preferably from Coach Farm, or soft goat cheese

1 large EGG

2 SCALLIONS, thinly sliced

¼ teaspoon freshly grated NUTMEG

SALT and freshly ground BLACK PEPPER

1 pound GOLDEN or YELLOW TOMATOES or GOLDEN CHERRY TOMATOES, roughly chopped

½ cup plus 2 tablespoons EXTRA-VIRGIN OLIVE OIL

3 tablespoons RED WINE VINEGAR

8 fresh BASIL LEAVES, chiffonade

1. Gently open the zucchini flowers and remove the stamens (and any bugs).

2. In a small bowl, stir together the goat cheese, egg, scallions, nutmeg, and salt and pepper to taste. Using a small spoon, stuff each blossom with about 1½ tablespoons of the filling. Set aside.

3. Combine the tomatoes, ½ cup of the olive oil, the vinegar, basil leaves, and 1 teaspoon salt in a blender and blend until smooth. Pour the mixture through a strainer set over a bowl and set aside.

4. Preheat the oven to 200°F. Line a baking sheet with paper towels.

5. In a 10- to 12-inch nonstick sauté pan, heat the remaining 2 tablespoons olive oil over medium-high heat until smoking. Place 4 flowers into the pan and cook, turning occasionally, until golden brown on both sides, about 8 minutes. Transfer to the baking sheet and keep warm in the oven while you cook the remaining 2 batches.

6. Arrange 3 blossoms on each plate. Drizzle with the tomato dressing and sprinkle with basil. Serve immediately.

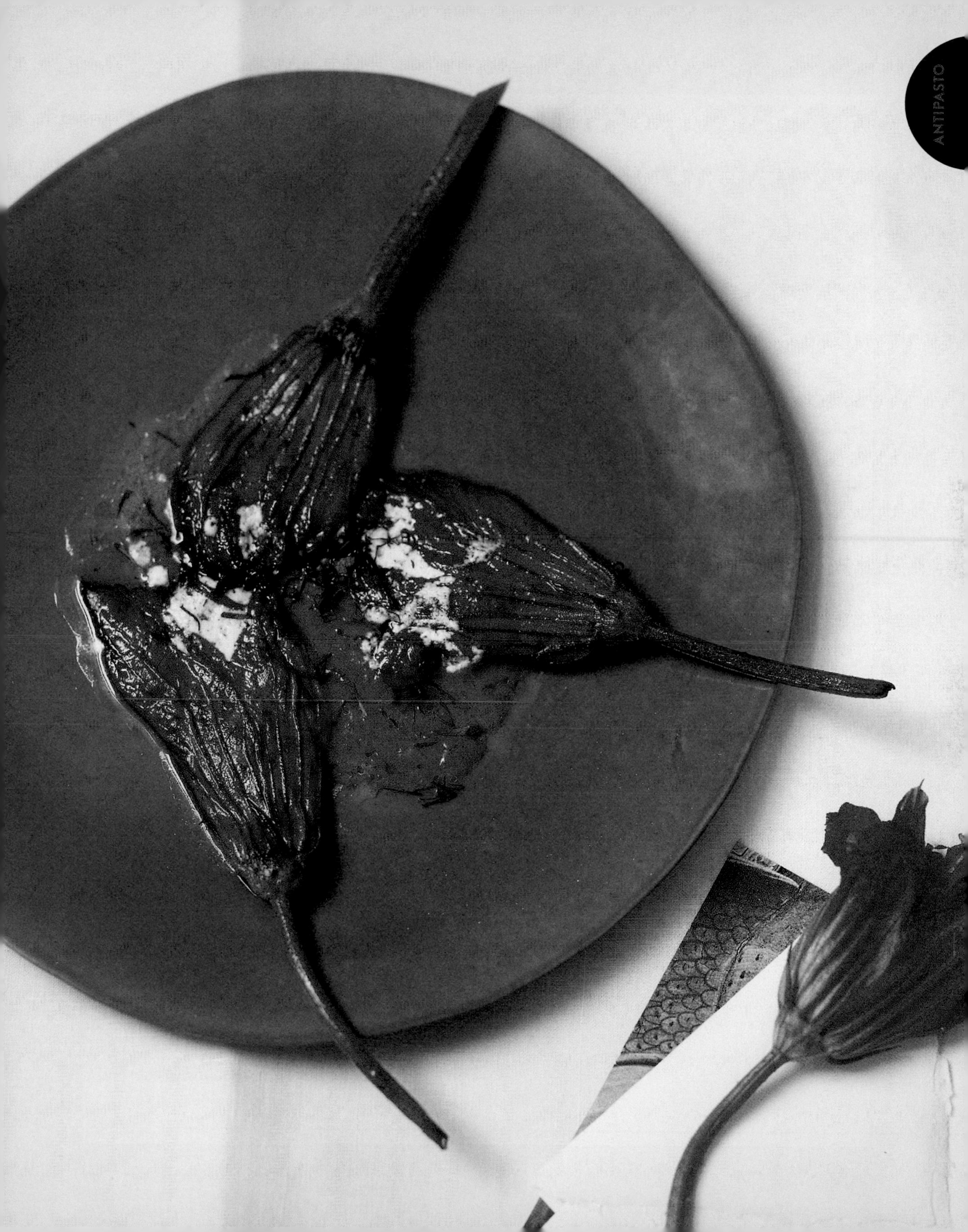

CREPES *with* THREE CHEESES
Crespelle al Formaggio

Crepes like these are often served in place of a pasta course, particularly for large groups at weddings or holiday gatherings. They have the advantage of holding their heat well for the long walk down a hall of three hundred guests.

MAKES 6 SERVINGS

(MAKES ABOUT 18 CRESPELLE)

BATTER

1½ cups ALL-PURPOSE FLOUR

4 large EGGS

½ teaspoon SALT

2 cups WHOLE MILK

FILLING

2½ cups RICOTTA, drained in a strainer lined with cheesecloth for 30 minutes

8 ounces FRESH MOZZARELLA, grated

1 cup grated SOFT SHEEP'S MILK CHEESE (such as cacio or a young pecorino)

8 ounces SALAMI, cut into ⅛-inch dice

½ teaspoon freshly grated NUTMEG

EXTRA-VIRGIN OLIVE OIL

4 tablespoons UNSALTED BUTTER, at room temperature

1. To make the batter, place the flour in a large bowl. Crack the eggs over the flour and whisk them in. Add the salt, then whisk in the milk, a little at a time. Allow the batter to stand for 20 minutes.

2. To make the filling, combine the ricotta, mozzarella, sheep's milk cheese, and salami in a bowl, add the nutmeg, and stir until smooth and well blended. Set aside.

3. Heat a 6-inch nonstick crepe pan or skillet over medium-high heat until hot. Brush with olive oil, reduce the heat to medium, and pour 1½ to 2 tablespoons batter into the pan, swirling to coat the bottom evenly. Cook until pale golden on the bottom, 30 to 40 seconds. Flip over and cook on other side for 20 seconds, then transfer to a plate. Continue the process until all the batter has been used; you should have about 18 crespelle.

4. Preheat the oven to 450°F. Butter a 9-by-13-inch baking dish with some of the butter.

5. Reserve ¼ cup of the filling for the topping. Fill each crespella with 3 tablespoons of the remaining filling and gently fold in half. Arrange the crespelle, overlapping them slightly, in the baking dish. Smear the reserved filling over the top and dot with the remaining butter.

6. Bake for 12 to 15 minutes, until piping hot and crisp on top. Serve hot, or allow to cool and serve at room temperature.

GREEN TOMATO FRITTATA

Frittata ai Pomodori Verdi

MAKES 4 SERVINGS

1 large GREEN TOMATO, cut into ½-inch cubes

SALT

¼ cup EXTRA-VIRGIN OLIVE OIL

8 large EGGS

½ cup freshly grated PECORINO ROMANO

2 tablespoons finely chopped fresh CHIVES

Freshly ground BLACK PEPPER

1. Preheat the oven to 425°F.

2. Sprinkle the tomato generously with salt and let drain in a strainer or colander for 10 minutes.

3. In a 12-inch nonstick ovenproof sauté pan, heat the olive oil over medium-high heat until smoking. Rinse the tomatoes and pat dry in a kitchen towel. Add the tomatoes to the pan and cook, stirring occasionally, until very soft and golden brown, 8 to 10 minutes.

4. Meanwhile, in a medium bowl, beat together the eggs, pecorino, and chives. Season with salt and pepper. Pour the egg mixture into the tomato pan and cook for 3 to 4 minutes, pulling in the sides of the mixture with a wooden spatula to distribute the raw eggs around the pan.

5. Place the pan in the oven and bake until the frittata is just cooked through, about 8 minutes. Invert the frittata onto a serving platter and cut into 8 wedges. Serve immediately, or let cool to room temperature.

Photograph on page 49.

FRITTATA *with* SPINACH *and* CHEESE
Frittata di Spinaci e Cacio

This is a simple antipasto served in the Trastevere section of Rome as one in a series of courses that may include roasted peppers with anchovies, marinated olives, marinated goat cheese, and other such informal dishes. Together the combination would make a great light lunch.

MAKES 4 SERVINGS

2 pounds SPINACH, tough stems removed and rinsed well

2 tablespoons EXTRA-VIRGIN OLIVE OIL

1 ONION, finely chopped

8 large EGGS

¼ cup grated CACIO DI ROMA or other SHEEP'S MILK CHEESE

¼ cup freshly grated PARMIGIANO-REGGIANO

SALT and freshly ground BLACK PEPPER

1. Bring 6 quarts of water to a boil in a large pot, and add 2 tablespoons salt. Set up an ice bath next to the stove. Plunge the spinach into the boiling water and cook for 2 minutes. Drain and transfer to the ice bath until chilled.

2. Remove the spinach from the ice bath and drain in a colander, then place between two plates and squeeze out the excess liquid. Place in a kitchen towel and twist to dry further, then place on a cutting board and finely chop.

3. In a 9-inch nonstick sauté pan, heat the olive oil over medium heat until hot. Add the onion and cook, stirring, until soft, about 5 minutes.

4. Meanwhile, in a medium bowl, beat the eggs to blend. Add the spinach, cheeses, and salt and pepper to taste and mix well to combine.

5. Pour the egg mixture into the skillet and cook until the bottom has set, about 5 minutes. Hold a flat plate over the pan and invert the frittata onto the plate, then slide it back into the pan. Cook until just set, about 5 minutes more, and serve hot.

From top: Green Tomato Frittata (page 47), Frittata with Spinach and Cheese, and Frittata with Herbs (page 51).

FRITTATA *with* HERBS
Frittata alle Erbe

This recipe was inspired by the Friulian spring, when the entire countryside is a verdant explosion of flavors and textures celebrating the rebirth of the soil after a long cold winter. The list of herbs is merely a suggestion; anything green and fresh is used in Friuli.

MAKES 4 SERVINGS

8 large EGGS

SALT and freshly ground BLACK PEPPER

½ cup fresh MARJORAM LEAVES

½ cup ITALIAN PARSLEY LEAVES

½ cup fresh BASIL LEAVES

½ cup chopped FENNEL FRONDS (optional)

½ cup SORREL or ARUGULA, cut into chiffonade

2 SCALLIONS, thinly sliced

1 tablespoon chopped fresh THYME

1 tablespoon chopped fresh SAGE

2 tablespoons UNSALTED BUTTER

1½ teaspoons RED WINE VINEGAR

1½ tablespoons EXTRA-VIRGIN OLIVE OIL

1.   In a large bowl, season the eggs with salt and pepper and beat to blend. Add ¼ cup each of the marjoram, parsley, basil, fennel fronds, if using, and sorrel, the scallions, thyme, and sage and beat until well mixed and slightly frothy.

2.   In an 8- to 10-inch nonstick sauté pan, heat the butter over medium heat until just starting to turn brown. Add the egg mixture and cook until set on the bottom, about 7 minutes. Hold a flat plate over the pan and invert the frittata onto the plate, then slide it back into the pan and cook just until set, 6 to 7 minutes. Slide the frittata onto a plate and allow to cool for 10 minutes.

3.   In a medium bowl, combine the remaining ¼ cup each marjoram, parsley, basil, fennel fronds, if using, and sorrel. Add the vinegar, olive oil, and salt and pepper to taste and toss well.

4.   Serve the frittata cut into wedges, alongside the herb salad.

Photograph on page 49.

MIXED FRIED VEGETABLES

Fritto Misto di Verdura

In Rome, they fry everything in extra-virgin olive oil, much to the disapproval of the fry police you read about in cookbooks who claim that the lower smoking point of the extra-virgin oil leaves an off or slightly burnt flavor—something I have never noticed in any of my meals in the Eternal City, and I always use extra-virgin myself. This dish is a simple introduction to the fritto misto concept, but the variations are up to you. Anything works, as long as you cut the vegetables into pieces that can be cooked through quickly. Romans are down with crisp vegetables in their fritti—but not raw.

MAKES 6 SERVINGS

8 cups EXTRA-VIRGIN OLIVE OIL, for deep-frying

8 ounces small SWEET PEAS in the pod or SUGAR SNAPS

8 ounces GREEN BEANS, ends snapped off

1 head BROCCOLI, cut into small florets

2 bunches SCALLIONS, trimmed to 4-inch lengths

1 ZUCCHINI, cut into ½-inch-thick rounds

1 YELLOW BELL PEPPER, cored, seeded, and cut into ½-inch-wide strips

1 RED BELL PEPPER, cored, seeded, and cut into ½-inch-wide strips

4 LEMONS, 2 cut into thin slices, 2 cut into wedges

2 cups CORNSTARCH

SALT

1. In a large deep saucepan, preferably one with a basket, heat the olive oil over medium-high heat until it reaches 375°F. Meanwhile, in a wide shallow bowl, combine half of the vegetables and half of the lemon slices. Sprinkle with 1 cup of the cornstarch and toss quickly with your hands to coat, then toss into a large strainer and bat it against your hand to remove the excess cornstarch.

2. Carefully drop the vegetables and lemon slices into the hot oil and cook until golden brown and crispy, 3 to 4 minutes. Transfer to a plate lined with paper towels to drain. Repeat with the remaining vegetables and lemon slices; allow the oil to return to 375°F before adding this batch.

3. Season the hot fritto misto with salt and serve immediately with the lemon wedges.

SHAVED FENNEL *with* BLOOD ORANGES, PECORINO *and* POMEGRANATES

Finocchi e Tarocchi

Shaved fennel is a cliché in Italian restaurants here, but when done correctly, it's dear to my heart. I am a confessed fennel-holic and cannot get enough of its fresh crisp anise flavor. It is nearly epic when matched with winter fruits like pomegranates and blood oranges, but it works with apples in the fall and cherries in the late spring as well.

MAKES 4 SERVINGS

2 large round FENNEL BULBS, trimmed, and SEVERAL FENNEL FRONDS set aside

Juice of 1 LEMON

¼ cup EXTRA-VIRGIN OLIVE OIL

4 large BLOOD ORANGES, peeled and segmented

1 cup POMEGRANATE SEEDS

SALT and freshly ground BLACK PEPPER

An 8-ounce chunk HARD PECORINO, such as sardo or toscano, for shaving

1. Using a mandoline or other vegetable slicer, shave the fennel crosswise into ⅓-inch-thick slices. Place in a bowl and toss with the lemon juice and olive oil. Add the blood orange segments, pomegranate seeds, and fennel fronds and toss gently to mix. Season with salt and pepper.

2. Arrange the fennel salad on four individual plates. Shave the pecorino in long shards over each plate, and serve.

SEGMENTING CITRUS

Using a paring knife, cut off the top and bottom of the fruit to expose the flesh. Stand the fruit upright on the work surface and, with your knife, carefully remove the skin and bitter white pith, working vertically from top to bottom and following the natural round shape of the fruit, turning it as you go. Carefully trim away any remaining pith.

To segment, hold the fruit over a bowl to catch the juices, and cut down along either side of the membrane to free each section of fruit. Then, if the recipe also calls for the juices, squeeze the membranes over the bowl to extract the remaining juices.

ROASTED PEPPER ROLL-UPS

Peperoni Ripieni

These simple Sicilian classics are great all by themselves, but the lily can be gilded with the addition of some thin strips of young pecorino or provolone.

MAKES 4 SERVINGS

3 medium BELL PEPPERS—a mixture of red and yellow

7 tablespoons EXTRA-VIRGIN OLIVE OIL

1½ tablespoons chopped CAPERS

1½ tablespoons PINE NUTS, lightly toasted

1½ tablespoons RAISINS, soaked in warm water for 15 minutes and drained

2 salt-packed ANCHOVIES, filleted, rinsed, and finely chopped

⅓ cup TOASTED BREAD CRUMBS

1 heaping tablespoon minced ITALIAN PARSLEY

SALT and freshly ground BLACK PEPPER

1. Preheat the grill or broiler.

2. Rub the peppers all over with 3 tablespoons olive oil. Grill or broil, turning often, until the skin is blackened all over. Let cool, then peel the peppers, rubbing the skin gently to remove all the charred bits. Cut into quarters, and remove the stems and seeds. Set aside.

3. Preheat the oven to 425°F.

4. In a small bowl, combine the capers, pine nuts, drained raisins, anchovies, bread crumbs, and parsley. Season with a little salt if necessary and pepper to taste, and stir in the remaining 4 tablespoons of olive oil.

5. Lay out the pepper slices, peeled side down. Divide the stuffing among them, placing it at the wide end of each slice, then roll up each slice and secure with a toothpick. Place on a baking sheet.

6. Bake the peppers for 15 minutes, or until they are warmed through and beginning to color lightly. Serve hot or at room temperature.

MARINATED ROASTED PEPPERS *with* GOAT CHEESE, OLIVES *and* FETT'UNTA

Antipasto di Peperoni

Perhaps the most misunderstood and misinter-preted antipasto in Italian-American restaurants, this is actually a classic example of shopping versus cooking. Bottled or jarred roasted peppers are okay—but nothing compares to the ones you do at home over the grill, or even under the broiler, with that evanescent quality of just done and handmade that is the hallmark of great cooking anywhere. Obviously, locally grown peppers picked at the peak of season, from midsummer on through late fall, are better than the beautiful yet flavorless harlequins available from Holland all the year round. I love to toss in a couple of roasted jalapeños or cayenne peppers to mix it up a bit (much to the chagrin of the wine geeks).

The word *fetta* means sliced, and *unta* means greasy, so *fett'unta* is a greased slice—or a shiny, happy piece of bread.

MAKES 6 SERVINGS

4 large RED or YELLOW BELL PEPPERS, or a combination

7 tablespoons EXTRA-VIRGIN OLIVE OIL

6 ANCHOVY FILLETS, rinsed, patted dry, and finely chopped

2 tablespoons salt-packed CAPERS or CAPER BERRIES, rinsed and drained

10 giant cracked SICILIAN OLIVES

1 tablespoon RED WINE VINEGAR

1 teaspoon finely chopped fresh ROSEMARY

8 ounces FRESH GOAT CHEESE from a log (preferably Coach Farm), cut into twelve ⅓-inch-thick rounds

Six 1-inch-thick slices ITALIAN PEASANT BREAD

2 cloves GARLIC

1. Preheat the grill or broiler.

2. In a large bowl, toss the whole peppers with 2 tablespoons of the olive oil to coat evenly. Place the peppers on the grill or on a baking sheet under the broiler and grill, turning often, until the skin is evenly blackened all over. Set aside to cool.

3. Peel the peppers, rubbing the skin gently to remove all charred bits. Cut the peppers in half and remove and discard the seeds and stems. Slice into 1-inch-wide strips and place in a medium bowl.

4. Add the anchovies, capers, olives, vinegar, rosemary, and 2 tablespoons of the olive oil to the peppers and toss to mix well. Divide the mixture evenly among six plates. Place 2 goat cheese rounds in the center of each one.

5. Toast the bread on the grill or under the broiler until light brown on both sides. Lightly rub each toast with a garlic clove and drizzle each one with ½ tablespoon olive oil. Place one toast on each plate and serve.

MARINATED VEGETABLES
Verdure in Scapece

Preserving the bounty of the harvest is the habit of all great food cultures, starting as necessity and blossoming into artisanal craftwork as the society becomes richer and more food savvy. This recipe comes from Campania, and it represents their faves of late-summer garden riches.

MAKES 4 SERVINGS

2 EGGPLANT (about 1 pound total), cut into ½-inch-thick rounds

2 medium ZUCCHINI (about 1½ pounds total), cut into ½-inch-thick rounds

3 tablespoons COARSE SEA SALT

¼ cup EXTRA-VIRGIN OLIVE OIL, plus more for brushing the vegetables

2 RED and 2 YELLOW BELL PEPPERS, cored, seeded, and cut into quarters

¼ cup WHITE WINE VINEGAR

2 cloves GARLIC, thinly sliced

½ cup small GREEN OLIVES

½ cup small BLACK OLIVES

1 salt-packed ANCHOVY, filleted, rinsed, and chopped

2 tablespoons finely chopped fresh OREGANO or MINT

1. Sprinkle the eggplant and zucchini slices with the salt and arrange on a baking sheet in a single layer. Cover with a second baking sheet, weight the sheet with cans or other heavy weights, and let sit for 2 hours.

2. Preheat the grill or broiler.

3. Pat the eggplant and zucchini slices dry with paper towels and brush them on both sides with olive oil. Place on the grill or on a baking sheet under the broiler and cook, turning once, for 5 minutes on each side, or until dark golden brown. Transfer to a bowl and cover to keep warm. Brush the pepper wedges with olive oil, place skin side down on the grill or skin side up on the baking sheet, and cook until blackened and blistered, 5 to 6 minutes. Transfer to the bowl and cover again.

4. In a small bowl, combine the ¼ cup olive oil, the vinegar, garlic, olives, anchovies, and oregano and mix well. Pour the mixture over the hot vegetables and immediately cover with aluminum foil. Set aside at room temperature to marinate overnight before serving.

Note: To store, pack the vegetables tightly into a widemouth jar and cover with the marinade. Cover and refrigerate; they should keep for several weeks in the fridge if you can keep your hands out of the jar. Serve at room temperature.

PORCINI SALAD *with* ARUGULA

Insalata di Porcini

This is the most luxurious salad in the entire book, one that in the hills of Emilia-Romagna represents the excellent relationship between the forager and the cook. Lucky for us, we can now buy fresh porcini in the spring and fall. Some come from Croatia, some from South America, but the best come from Italy. They grow under chestnut and oak trees in Emilia and Toscana and are easy to recognize, with their fat rotund stems and their deep brown caps, often stained with bits of oxidized chestnut leaves. As with many epic Italian recipes, it is the quality of the ingredients more than the technique of the cook that makes the dish great.

MAKES 4 SERVINGS

4 large fresh PORCINI (about 1 pound)

2 bunches ARUGULA, washed and spun dry (about 3 loose cups)

½ cup EXTRA-VIRGIN OLIVE OIL

Grated zest and juice of 1 LEMON

SALT and freshly ground BLACK PEPPER

An 8-ounce chunk of PARMIGIANO-REGGIANO, for shaving

COARSE SEA SALT

1. Preheat the grill or broiler.

2. Carefully cut each mushroom in half. Place on the grill or on a baking sheet under the broiler and cook, turning often, until charred and softened, 8 to 10 minutes.

3. In a large bowl, place the arugula, ¼ cup of the olive oil, and the lemon zest and juice. Season to taste with salt and pepper and toss to mix thoroughly. Divide the salad equally among four plates.

4. Remove the hot mushrooms from the grill or broiler and place over the center of each salad. Using a vegetable peeler, shave Parmigiano onto each salad, right around the mushrooms. Spoon 1 tablespoon of the remaining olive oil over each salad, sprinkle with coarse sea salt, and serve immediately.

FIRE-ROASTED SWEET *and* HOT PEPPERS *with* ANCHOVIES

Peperoni e Alici

This dish is also an excellent *contorno* for any grilled whole fish or big steak.

MAKES 6 SERVINGS

½ cup plus 3 tablespoons EXTRA-VIRGIN OLIVE OIL

4 BELL PEPPERS—a mixture of red, yellow, and/or green

1 HOT CHILE PEPPER, such as cayenne or jalapeño

16 marinated fresh ANCHOVY FILLETS (page 76) or 8 salt-packed ANCHOVIES

1 LEMON, halved (if using salted anchovies)

2 tablespoons fresh OREGANO LEAVES

12 cloves GARLIC, thinly sliced

1 teaspoon SEA SALT

½ teaspoon freshly ground BLACK PEPPER

2 LEMONS, peeled, seeded, and finely chopped

2 teaspoons HONEY (optional)

BASIL OIL

½ cup BASIL LEAVES

½ cup EXTRA-VIRGIN OLIVE OIL

1 teaspoon SALT

1. Preheat the grill.
2. Rub 3 tablespoons olive oil all over the peppers and place directly onto the hot coals if using hardwood charcoal or on the grill rack. Cook the peppers, turning occasionally, until charred on all sides, 10 to 15 minutes.
3. While the peppers char, if you are using whole salt-packed anchovies, fillet them; soak the fillets in warm water for 10 minutes, then drain and rinse with cool water. Place the rinsed fillets in a small bowl, squeeze the juice of the halved lemon all over them, and stir well. Let sit for 5 minutes.
4. When the peppers are done, remove from the grill and let stand until cool enough to handle. Remove the charred skin, core and seed the peppers, and slice into 1-inch-wide strips. Place in a serving dish and allow the peppers to cool to room temperature. Stir in the oregano, ¼ cup of the olive oil, and the anchovy fillets.
5. In a small sauté pan, heat 2 tablespoons of the olive oil over medium-high heat. Add the garlic and cook until softened and golden brown, about 1 minute. Transfer the garlic and oil to a small bowl and let cool.
6. Add the remaining 2 tablespoons olive oil, the sea salt, pepper, and chopped lemons to the garlic and whisk to combine. If desired, add the honey, bit by bit, to sweeten to taste. Add to the pepper and anchovy mixture, and stir to distribute evenly.
7. To make the basil oil, place ingredients in blender and blend until smooth. Serve peppers with a drizzle of the basil oil on the side.

From top: Fried Celery (page 65), Sautéed Black and Green Olives in Tomato Sauce (page 28), and Fire-Roasted Sweet and Hot Peppers with Anchovies.

STUFFED CELERY

Sedani Ripieni

Although it sounds like a dish out of the '50s, it is pure and simple Roman cooking that reminds me of the Trastevere in the spring.

MAKES 4 SERVINGS

1 bunch CELERY HEARTS

1 slice DAY-OLD BREAD, soaked in ¼ cup MILK and squeezed dry

1 pound lean GROUND BEEF

3 large EGGS

2 tablespoons finely chopped ITALIAN PARSLEY

SALT and freshly ground BLACK PEPPER

1 cup ALL-PURPOSE FLOUR

½ cup plus 3 tablespoons EXTRA-VIRGIN OLIVE OIL

1 clove GARLIC, finely chopped

1½ cups peeled and coarsely chopped ripe TOMATOES

1. Separate the celery stalks and remove the stringy fibers with a peeler or sharp paring knife. Cut into thirty-two 2½-inch-long pieces.

2. Put the celery in a medium saucepan, add 1 teaspoon salt and water to cover, and bring to a boil. Cover and cook until tender, 12 to 15 minutes. Drain and let cool.

3. Place the soaked bread in a medium bowl. Add the beef, 1 egg, 1 tablespoon of the parsley, 1 teaspoon salt, and ⅛ teaspoon pepper, and mix well to combine. Shape into 16 small balls.

4. Put ½ cup of the flour in a small bowl. Place 1 meatball between 2 pieces of celery and press so that they hold together. Roll in the flour and lay on a tray. Repeat with the remaining celery and meatballs.

5. In a small bowl, beat the remaining 2 eggs with a pinch of salt. Put the remaining ½ cup flour in another small bowl. Heat ½ cup olive oil in a large heavy-bottomed skillet over medium-high heat until very hot. Dip each piece of the stuffed celery in the beaten eggs, letting the excess drop off, then dredge in the flour, and place in the hot oil. Fry, turning occasionally, until golden on all sides.

6. Transfer the celery to a large skillet that holds it in a single layer. Add the garlic, tomatoes, the remaining 3 tablespoons olive oil, the remaining 1 tablespoon parsley, and salt and pepper to taste. Place over medium heat and cook, covered, for 25 to 30 minutes. Serve hot.

FRIED CELERY
Sedani Fritti

This simple fry, very much part of the Roman antipasto scene, is such a breeze to do that it has become my template recipe for all southern Italian–style fried vegetables.

MAKES 8 SERVINGS

10 ribs CELERY, cut on the bias into 2-inch lengths

1 cup EXTRA-VIRGIN OLIVE OIL

½ cup ALL-PURPOSE FLOUR

½ cup CORNSTARCH

2 large EGGS

SALT and freshly ground BLACK PEPPER

1. Bring 4 quarts of water to a boil in a medium pot, and add 2 tablespoons salt. Add the celery and cook until tender but not mushy, 12 to 15 minutes. Drain and spread on paper towels to cool.

2. In a large heavy-bottomed skillet, heat the olive oil over medium-high heat until it is almost smoking. Meanwhile, place the flour on one plate and the cornstarch on another plate. Lightly beat the eggs in a shallow bowl. Working in batches, dredge the cooled celery pieces in the flour, then dip them in the eggs, letting the excess drip off, and then dredge in the cornstarch. Place the celery in the hot oil and fry, turning occasionally, until a deep golden brown on all sides. Use a slotted spoon to transfer the fried celery to a plate lined with paper towels.

3. Season to taste with salt and pepper and serve immediately.

Photograph on page 63.

BESCIAMELLA
MAKES ABOUT 3½ CUPS

5 tablespoons UNSALTED BUTTER

¼ cup ALL-PURPOSE FLOUR

3 cups WHOLE MILK

2 teaspoons SALT

½ teaspoon freshly grated NUTMEG

1. In a medium saucepan, melt the butter over medium heat. Add the flour and stir until smooth. Cook, stirring, until light golden brown, 6 to 7 minutes.

2. Meanwhile, in another medium saucepan, heat the milk to just under a boil. Add the milk to the butter mixture about 1 cup at a time, whisking constantly until very smooth, and bring to a boil, whisking. Cook, whisking, until thickened, about 10 minutes; remove from the heat. Season with the salt and nutmeg. Transfer to a bowl and let cool, then cover and refrigerate until ready to use. *(See page 66.)*

CARDOON CUSTARD

Sformato di Cardi

Savory custards are very sexy, very impressive, and, best of all, very easy to make. Two other variations on the theme follow this recipe. They can be served at room temperature with a little salad for an elegant antipasto or as a vegetable side to a simple roast, thus dressing up the whole meal. Cardoons are my favorite member of the cynar family of thistles that also includes the artichoke in its lineage. They look a lot more intimidating than they really are, but be sure and wear gloves when you clean them, or your hands will look rusty all week.

MAKES 8 SERVINGS

5 CARDOONS, about 15 inches long (1 to 1½ pounds total)

¼ cup EXTRA-VIRGIN OLIVE OIL

1 medium RED ONION, cut into ¼-inch dice

½ cup FRESH BREAD CRUMBS

3 cups BESCIAMELLA (page 65)

3 large EGGS

2 large EGG YOLKS

½ cup RICOTTA

½ cup freshly grated PARMIGIANO-REGGIANO

Freshly grated NUTMEG

SALT and freshly ground BLACK PEPPER

¼ cup TOASTED BREAD CRUMBS

¼ cup FENNEL fronds or fresh DILL

1. Bring 6 quarts water to a boil in a large pot, and add 2 tablespoons salt. Meanwhile, peel the fibrous part off the cardoon stalks and cut each stalk on the bias into ¼-inch pieces. Drop the cardoons into the boiling water and cook until tender, about 15 minutes. Drain and allow to cool.

2. In a 10- to 12-inch sauté pan, heat the olive oil over medium heat until smoking. Add the onion and cook until soft and light golden brown, 7 to 9 minutes. Add the cardoons and cook until very soft, about 10 more minutes. Remove from the heat and let cool.

3. Preheat the oven to 350°F. Butter a small Bundt pan (or eight 6-ounce soufflé cups) and sprinkle with the fresh bread crumbs to coat.

4. Transfer the cooled cardoon mixture to a medium bowl and add the besciamella, eggs and yolks, ricotta, and ¼ cup of the Parmigiano. Season with nutmeg, salt, and pepper.

5. Pour the cardoon mixture into the prepared pan and place it in a roasting pan. Pour enough water into the roasting pan to come 3 inches up the sides of the Bundt pan, and place it in the oven. Bake for 1 hour, or until a toothpick poked into the sformato comes out clean. Allow to rest for 15 minutes.

6. Run a thin knife around the edges of the sformato and the center tube and turn it out onto a serving plate. Sprinkle with the toasted bread crumbs and the remaining ¼ cup Parmigiano. Garnish with fennel fronds, and serve.

Photograph on page 69.

SAVORY CHESTNUT CUSTARD

Sformato di Castagne

MAKES 8 SERVINGS

1 pound dried peeled CHESTNUTS, soaked overnight in cool water and drained

2 cups WHOLE MILK

½ cup FRESH BREAD CRUMBS

5 large EGGS, separated

3 cups BESCIAMELLA (page 65)

4 ounces FONTINA, grated

½ cup freshly grated PARMIGIANO-REGGIANO

1¼ cups TOASTED BREAD CRUMBS

Several gratings of NUTMEG

SALT and freshly ground BLACK PEPPER

4 tablespoons UNSALTED BUTTER

¼ cup whole PARSLEY LEAVES

1. Place the chestnuts in a 2-quart saucepan, add the milk, and bring to a boil over medium heat. Lower the heat and simmer until the chestnuts are tender, about 1 hour. Remove from the heat.

2. Preheat the oven to 375°F. Butter a small Bundt pan (or eight 6-ounce soufflé cups) and sprinkle with the fresh bread crumbs to coat.

3. Drain the chestnuts and mash with a fork, or process in a food processor, to a smooth puree. Transfer the puree to a large bowl and add the egg yolks, besciamella, Fontina, Parmigiano, toasted bread crumbs, and nutmeg. Season to taste with salt and pepper.

4. In a large bowl, whip the egg whites to soft peaks. Carefully fold the whites into the chestnut mixture.

5. Pour the mixture into the prepared pan and place it in a roasting pan. Pour enough water into the pan to come 3 inches up the sides of the Bundt pan and place in the oven. Bake for 40 to 45 minutes (30 to 35 minutes if using soufflé cups), until a toothpick inserted into the sformato comes out just clean. Allow to cool for 5 minutes.

6. Run a sharp knife thin around the edges of the sformato and the center tube, and invert onto a serving plate. Garnish with parsley and serve.

From top: Savory Chestnut Custard, Cardoon Custard (page 66), Fennel Custard (page 70).

FENNEL CUSTARD

Sformato di Finocchio

MAKES 8 SERVINGS

2 FENNEL BULBS (1 to 1½ pounds), trimmed, cored, and cut into ½-inch dice

¼ cup EXTRA-VIRGIN OLIVE OIL

1 medium RED ONION, cut into ¼-inch dice

½ cup FRESH BREAD CRUMBS

3 cups BESCIAMELLA (page 65)

4 large EGGS

3 large EGG YOLKS

½ cup RICOTTA

½ cup freshly grated PARMIGIANO-REGGIANO

Freshly grated NUTMEG

SALT and freshly ground BLACK PEPPER

¼ cup TOASTED BREAD CRUMBS

2 BLOOD ORANGES, cut into segments

¼ cup BLACK OLIVES, pitted

1. Bring 6 quarts water to a boil in a large pot, and add 2 tablespoons salt. Drop the fennel into the water and cook until tender, about 10 minutes. Drain and allow to cool.

2. In a 10- to 12-inch sauté pan, heat the olive oil over medium heat until smoking. Add the onion and cook until soft and light golden brown, 7 to 9 minutes. Add the fennel pieces and cook until very soft, about 10 more minutes. Remove from the heat and let cool.

3. Preheat the oven to 350°F. Butter a small Bundt pan (or eight 6-ounce soufflé cups) and sprinkle with the fresh bread crumbs to coat.

4. Transfer the fennel mixture to a medium bowl and add the besciamella, eggs and yolks, ricotta, and ¼ cup of the Parmigiano, mixing well. Season with nutmeg, salt, and pepper.

5. Pour the mixture into the prepared pan and place it in a roasting pan. Pour enough water into the roasting pan to come 3 inches up the sides of the Bundt pan, and place in the oven. Bake for 1 hour, or until a toothpick poked into the sformato comes out clean. Allow to rest for 15 minutes.

6. Run a thin knife around the edge of the sformato and the center tube and turn it out onto a serving plate. Sprinkle with the toasted bread crumbs and the remaining ¼ cup Parmigiano, top with blood oranges and olives, and serve.

Photograph on page 69.

MOCK TRIPE *in* TOMATO SAUCE
Trippa Finta al Pomodoro

This is a great antipasto, as well as an excellent brunch dish—one that holds well served warm or at room temperature. You could substitute your herb of choice for the oregano in the omelets, or add cooked vegetables cut into small pieces.

MAKES 4 SERVINGS

8 large EGGS

1 tablespoon fresh OREGANO LEAVES

SALT

½ teaspoon HOT RED PEPPER FLAKES

4 tablespoons UNSALTED BUTTER, cut into 4 pieces

1½ cups BASIC TOMATO SAUCE (see sidebar)

½ cup freshly grated PECORINO ROMANO

1. In a large bowl, whisk the eggs to blend. Season with the oregano, salt to taste, and red pepper flakes.

2. In a medium nonstick sauté pan, heat 1 tablespoon of the butter until it foams and subsides. Pour one-quarter of the egg mixture into the pan and cook until it has set and slides easily in the pan (like a crepe), about 2 minutes. Flip over and cook for 1 minute on the other side, then transfer to a plate to cool. Repeat the procedure with the remaining butter and egg mixture to make 3 more omelets.

3. When the omelets are cool, cut into ¼-inch-wide strips.

4. In a medium heavy-bottomed saucepan, bring the tomato sauce to a boil, then reduce the heat to a simmer. Add the egg strips and simmer for 10 minutes. Transfer to a deep platter, top with the pecorino, and serve.

BASIC TOMATO SAUCE
MAKES 4 CUPS

¼ cup EXTRA-VIRGIN OLIVE OIL

1 SPANISH ONION, cut into ¼-inch dice

4 cloves GARLIC, thinly sliced

3 tablespoons chopped fresh THYME

½ medium CARROT, finely shredded

Two 28-ounce cans whole TOMATOES

SALT

1. In a 3-quart saucepan, heat the olive oil over medium heat. Add the onion and garlic and cook until soft and light golden brown, 8 to 10 minutes. Add the thyme and carrot and cook until the carrot is quite soft, about 5 minutes.

2. Add the tomatoes, with their juice, and bring to a boil, stirring often. Lower the heat and simmer until as thick as hot cereal, about 30 minutes. Season with salt. The sauce can be refrigerated for up to 1 week or frozen for 6 months.

SEAFOOD
ANTIPASTO

FLATBREAD *with* FENNEL, FRESH ANCHOVIES *and* CACIOCAVALLO

Tarongia

The name *tarongia* is probably a modification of the word *tarocco*, which is Sicilian for blood orange, because of the dark orange color these spectacular fried "pizzas" turn when finished under the broiler. Whatever the derivation, they are as mysterious and inviting as the Sicilian people—who sometimes seem more northern African than Italian in their brooding silence, as well as in their exotic and exquisite cooking.

MAKES 4 SERVINGS

16 marinated fresh ANCHOVY FILLETS (page 76) or 8 salt-packed ANCHOVIES, filleted and rinsed

½ cup MILK (if using salted anchovies)

1½ cups plus 3 tablespoons EXTRA-VIRGIN OLIVE OIL

DOUGH (see page 43), prepared through the first rise

About 2 tablespoons freshly ground BLACK PEPPER

1 FENNEL BULB, fronds reserved, bulb trimmed, cored, and sliced ⅛-inch thick

1 cup freshly grated CACIOCAVALLO or other SHEEP'S MILK CHEESE

2 tablespoons FENNEL SEEDS

1. If using salt-packed anchovies, soak the fillets in the milk for 30 minutes; drain well.

2. Pour the 1½ cups olive oil into a large deep frying pan and heat over medium-high heat until it reaches 375°F. Meanwhile, divide the dough into 4 pieces and roll each piece into a 10-inch circle. One at a time, fry each circle, turning once, until golden brown, 4 to 5 minutes, and transfer to paper towels to drain; allow the oil to return to 375°F each time. While the flatbreads are still hot, sprinkle generously with the pepper.

3. In a 10-inch sauté pan, heat the remaining 3 tablespoons olive oil over medium-high heat until just smoking. Add the sliced fennel and cook, stirring often, until soft and golden brown, 8 to 10 minutes. Transfer to a bowl and let cool, then stir in the fennel fronds.

4. Preheat the broiler. Spread one quarter of the fennel mixture on top of each tarongia and sprinkle each with 2 tablespoons caciocavallo. Place 4 anchovy fillets on each tarongia and sprinkle with the fennel seeds. Top with the remaining caciocavallo.

5. Place the tarongia on a baking sheet and broil until the cheese is melted and the tops are toasted deep golden brown. Serve warm.

ANTIPASTO

MARINATED FRESH ANCHOVIES

Alici Marinati

If fresh anchovies are hard to find, you can substitute fresh sardines, smelts, or even whitebait in this simple ceviche-style dish. Fresh anchovies are increasingly available from Italy and from Spain, where they are called *boquerones*.

MAKES 8 SERVINGS

2 pounds fresh ANCHOVIES

2 cups WHITE WINE VINEGAR

2 cups EXTRA-VIRGIN OLIVE OIL

2 tablespoons dried OREGANO

2 tablespoons HOT RED PEPPER FLAKES

¼ cup finely chopped ITALIAN PARSLEY

4 cloves GARLIC, sliced paper-thin

2 tablespoons COARSE or FINE SEA SALT

1.   Using scissors, trim the fins off all the anchovies. Using a sharp paring knife, slit each fish open along the belly and gut the fish, removing the gills as well. Rinse the fish and cut off the heads. Slit each one open down the back and carefully remove the spine and pinbones by pulling them out with your index finger and thumb. Separate the two fillets and rinse again.

2.   Arrange a single layer of fillets in a large oval gratin dish or other baking dish and sprinkle with some of the vinegar. Continue with the remaining fish fillets, sprinkling each layer with vinegar, and then pour the rest of the vinegar over the top. Let the anchovies marinate, covered, for at least 4 hours in the refrigerator.

3.   Drain the anchovies, rinse, and pat dry with a kitchen towel. Wash and dry the gratin dish. Layer the cured anchovies back in the dish, seasoning each layer with 2 to 3 tablespoons olive oil, a pinch of oregano, a sprinkle of red pepper flakes, a sprinkle of parsley, a few garlic slices, and a sprinkle of salt. Allow the anchovies to marinate for at least 2 hours in the refrigerator. (The cured anchovies will keep for a week in the refrigerator.)

4.   To serve, bring the anchovies to cool cellar temperature, just about 58°F. Place 8 or 9 anchovies on each plate, draining them first of excess oil.

MARINATED FLUKE

Sfogi in Saor

MAKES 8 SERVINGS

1¼ cups EXTRA-VIRGIN OLIVE OIL

½ cup ALL-PURPOSE FLOUR

SALT and freshly ground BLACK PEPPER

2 pounds FLUKE FILLETS, skin and bones removed

1 SPANISH ONION, cut into ½-inch dice

½ cup dried CURRANTS

2 tablespoons SUGAR

¼ cup PINE NUTS

1½ cups RED WINE VINEGAR

1. In a large deep saucepan, heat 1 cup of the olive oil to 375°F. Season the flour with salt and pepper and spread on a plate. Working in batches, dredge the fillets in the seasoned flour and fry in the hot oil, turning once, until golden brown. Transfer to paper towels to drain.
2. In a 10- to 12-inch sauté pan, heat the remaining ¼ cup olive oil over medium heat. Add the onion and cook until softened and lightly browned, 10 to 12 minutes. Add the currants, sugar, pine nuts, and vinegar and bring to a boil. Cook until the currants are soft, 5 to 6 minutes. Remove from the heat and allow to cool.
3. Choose an earthenware or other baking dish that just holds the fried fillets in a single slightly overlapping layer, and arrange them in the dish. Top with the onion mixture, cover, and refrigerate for at least 24 hours.
4. Serve at room temperature.

OCTOPUS and POTATO SALAD

Insalata di Polpo

One of the tricks to good cooked spuds is to keep them out of the fridge. Once they have gone below 45 degrees, they turn mealy.

MAKES 6 SERVINGS

1 pound medium WAXY POTATOES, such as Yukon Gold or Yellow Finn

1 pound cooked OCTOPUS TENTACLES, cut into ½-inch-thick slices

2 SCALLIONS, thinly sliced

¼ cup finely chopped ITALIAN PARSLEY

½ cup EXTRA-VIRGIN OLIVE OIL

3 tablespoons fresh LEMON JUICE

½ RED ONION, sliced paper-thin

SALT and freshly ground BLACK PEPPER

1. Bring 6 quarts of water to a boil in a large pot, and add 2 tablespoons salt. Add the potatoes and cook until tender but not falling apart. Drain and allow to cool for 10 minutes, then peel the potatoes and cut into ½-inch slices.
2. Mound the octopus slices attractively in the center of a platter and arrange the warm potato slices around the edges. Sprinkle with the scallions and parsley.
3. In a small bowl, whisk together the olive oil, lemon juice, onion, and salt and pepper to taste. Pour the dressing over the octopus and still-warm potatoes. Cover with foil and set aside in a cool place to marinate for an hour before serving.

WARM SEAFOOD SALAD

Insalata Tiepida di Mare

This is a variation on a classic dish of the Adriatic Sea, spiced up with the American touches of crayfish, jalapeños, and mint. I hope the Italians do not mind, but it is sooo good . . .

MAKES 4 SERVINGS

¼ cup RED WINE VINEGAR

12 MUSSELS, scrubbed and debearded

12 BABY OCTOPUS, cooked in a pot of boiling water with a cork for 45 minutes (see page 261), drained, and cooled

12 extra-large SHRIMP (16 to 20 count), peeled and deveined

4 small cleaned CALAMARI

12 CRAYFISH, cooked in boiling water for 2 minutes, drained, and shelled

2 SCALLIONS, thinly sliced

½ cup EXTRA-VIRGIN OLIVE OIL

2 red or green JALAPEÑOS, thinly sliced

¼ cup fresh MINT LEAVES

SALT and freshly ground BLACK PEPPER

2 cups WILD BITTER GREENS or BABY MUSTARD GREENS, washed and spun dry

2 LEMONS, cut into wedges

1. Bring 2 quarts of water to a boil in a large saucepan, and add 1 teaspoon salt and 1 tablespoon of the vinegar. Add the mussels, octopus, and shrimp and boil until the shrimp start to turn pink and the mussels start to open, about 1 minute. Add the calamari and crayfish and cook until the squid is just translucent, about 1 minute. Drain immediately and transfer to a large bowl.

2. Add the scallions, the remaining 3 tablespoons vinegar, the olive oil, jalapeños, mint, and salt and pepper to taste and toss to coat. Add the greens, toss again, and serve warm, with the lemon wedges.

Photograph on page 84.

FRITTO MISTO *of* CALAMARI, SEA SCALLOPS *and* LEMON
Fritto Misto

There is no real trick to great fried food, other than perfect primary ingredients. The simplicity and crispness of the cornstarch crust is something that will change your opinion about batters and cooking-school fry-station setups. And heed not the advice of those who claim that extra-virgin olive oil burns at the required temperature, for they have never eaten an artichoke in the Jewish ghetto of Rome.

For another amazing antipasto, anchovy *beccafichi*, wrap salted anchovies around bay leaves, coat them in cornstarch, and deep-fry as indicated below. *(Photograph page 89).*

MAKES 4 SERVINGS

8 cups EXTRA-VIRGIN OLIVE OIL, for deep-frying

1 pound CALAMARI, cleaned and drained

8 ounces diver (dry) SEA SCALLOPS, cut horizontally in half

4 LEMONS, 2 cut into ⅛-inch-thick slices, 2 cut into wedges

2 cups CORNSTARCH

SALT and freshly ground BLACK PEPPER

1. In a large deep saucepan, preferably one with a basket, heat the olive oil over medium-high heat until it reaches 375°F. Meanwhile, in a wide shallow bowl, combine half the calamari, half the scallops, and half the lemon slices. Sprinkle with 1 cup of the cornstarch and toss quickly with your hands to coat, then toss into a large strainer and bat it against your hand to remove the excess cornstarch.

2. Carefully drop the seafood and lemon slices into the hot oil and cook until golden brown and crispy, about 1 minute. Transfer to a plate lined with paper towels to drain.

3. Immediately repeat with the remaining calamari, scallops, and lemon slices; allow the oil to return to 375°F before adding this second batch. Season the fritto misto with salt and pepper and serve immediately with the lemon wedges.

Photograph on page 81.

CLAMS OREGANATO

Vongole Origanate

A dish of baked clams seems like the ultimate retro '60s kind of bad Italian-American antipasto, right out of *Leave It to Beaver*, but when done right, with the right clams, it is actually stellar. The briny breath of sea air is the first thing you taste, followed by the delicate and sweet enhancement of the minimalist accompaniments.

MAKES 6 SERVINGS

¼ cup EXTRA-VIRGIN OLIVE OIL, plus extra for drizzling

1 medium RED ONION, cut into ⅛-inch dice

4 cloves GARLIC, thinly sliced

1 RED BELL PEPPER, cored, seeded, and cut into ⅛-inch dice

1 cup FRESH BREAD CRUMBS

SALT and freshly ground BLACK PEPPER

24 medium LITTLENECK CLAMS, scrubbed

About 3 cups KOSHER SALT

2 tablespoons chopped FRESH OREGANO or MARJORAM or 1 teaspoon DRIED OREGANO

1. In a 10- to 12-inch sauté pan, heat the olive oil over medium heat until smoking. Add the onion, garlic, and bell pepper and cook until softened and light golden brown, 6 to 7 minutes. Add the bread crumbs and cook, stirring, until they are light golden brown, about 3 minutes. Remove from the heat, season with salt and pepper, and let cool.

2. Meanwhile, carefully open the clams with a clam knife, discarding the top shells and leaving the clams in the bottom shells. Drain the clam liquid into a small bowl; set aside. Loosen the clams from the bottom shells but do not remove them.

3. Spread the kosher salt on a baking sheet so that it is at least ½ inch deep, and nestle the clams in their half-shells in the salt. Set aside.

4. Preheat the broiler. Stir the oregano and the reserved clam liquid into the bread crumb mixture. Pack about 2 teaspoons of the crumb mixture loosely over and around each clam. (The clam, not the stuffing, is the most important part of the dish, so the stuffing should surround and enhance the clams, not overpower them.) Place under the broiler and heat just until the crumb mixture is deep golden brown, 1½ to 2 minutes; you're not really cooking the clams.

5. Drizzle the clams with a few drops of olive oil, and serve.

From left to right: Clams Oreganato, Clams Genovese (page 82), and Clams Casino (page 83).

CLAMS GENOVESE

Vongole Genovese

I never ate these in Genoa, but the floral and herby pesto plays perfect pinochle with the elusive salty sweetness of our dreamy East Coast mollusks, flying high on a broiler buzz.

MAKES 6 SERVINGS

24 medium LITTLENECK CLAMS, scrubbed

About 3 cups KOSHER SALT

1 SCALLION, thinly sliced

4 cloves GARLIC, thinly sliced

1 cup loosely packed fresh BASIL LEAVES

1 teaspoon PINE NUTS

¼ cup freshly grated PECORINO ROMANO

½ cup EXTRA-VIRGIN OLIVE OIL

2 tablespoons FRESH BREAD CRUMBS

SALT

A LEMON WEDGE or two

1. Carefully open the clams with a clam knife, discarding the top shells. Loosen the clams from the bottom shells but leave them in the shells.

2. Spread the kosher salt on a baking sheet so it is at least ½ inch deep, and nestle the clams in the salt. Set aside.

3. Combine the scallion, garlic, basil, and pine nuts in a food processor and pulse until finely chopped; do not process to a paste. Add the pecorino and olive oil and pulse for 10 seconds, or just until the pesto thickens. Transfer to a small bowl and season with salt.

4. Preheat the broiler. Place a scant ½ teaspoon of pesto next to each clam in its shell and sprinkle with bread crumbs. Place under the broiler and cook just until the clams are starting to curl at the edges. Squeeze a few drops of lemon juice over, and serve warm.

Photograph on page 81.

CLAMS CASINO

Vongole al Casino

The combination of the sweet and hot peppers with the briny salinity of the sea brings me closer to heaven, and the Jersey Shore, and the Ligurian Coast, all at the same time.

MAKES 4 TO 6 SERVINGS

8 slices PANCETTA (about 3 ounces), cut into ¼-inch dice

2 tablespoons EXTRA-VIRGIN OLIVE OIL

1 ONION, cut into ¼-inch dice

2 large cloves GARLIC, thinly sliced

1 RED BELL PEPPER, cored, seeded, and cut into ¼-inch dice

1 GREEN BELL PEPPER, cored, seeded, and cut into ¼-inch dice

½ teaspoon dried OREGANO, crumbled

2 teaspoons RED WINE VINEGAR

2 tablespoons freshly grated PARMIGIANO-REGGIANO

SALT and freshly ground BLACK PEPPER

24 CHERRYSTONE CLAMS, scrubbed

4 to 5 cups KOSHER SALT

1. Preheat the oven to 400°F.

2. In a 10- to 12-inch heavy-bottomed sauté pan, cook the pancetta over medium heat, stirring, just until it begins to brown and render its fat. Transfer the pancetta to a plate lined with paper towels, and drain the fat from the pan.

3. Add the olive oil to the same pan and heat over medium-low heat until hot. Add the onion and garlic and cook until soft but not colored, about 5 minutes. Add the bell peppers and oregano and cook, stirring, until the peppers are tender but still a retain a bit of bite, about 6 minutes.

4. Transfer the mixture to a small bowl and stir in the pancetta, vinegar, and Parmigiano. Season to taste with salt and pepper.

5. Carefully open the clams with a clam knife, discarding the top shells. Loosen the clams from the bottom shells, but leave them in the shells.

6. Make a ½-inch-thick bed of kosher salt an a baking sheet, and nestle the clams in the salt. Using a small spoon, divide the bell pepper mixture among the clams. Bake until just cooked through, 12 to 15 minutes.

7. To serve, arrange the clams on a platter lined with a bed of coarse salt.

Photograph on page 81.

MIXED FISH FRY

Gran Fritto di Pesce

For pieces of seafood that are bigger than bite-size, I like to add Wondra flour to the cornstarch mix, as its high percentage of barley flour causes it to form a crisper crust with the longer fry time and higher moisture content.

MAKES 4 SERVINGS

8 cups EXTRA-VIRGIN OLIVE OIL, for deep-frying

1 pound CALAMARI, cleaned and drained

12 OYSTERS, shucked

8 ounces diver (dry) SEA SCALLOPS, cut horizontally in half

4 ounces WHITEBAIT or other TINY FISH (for eating whole)

8 ounces ROCK SHRIMP

4 tiny SOLE, skinned and gutted

4 BLOWFISH tails

4 LEMONS, 2 cut into ⅛-inch-thick slices, 2 cut into wedges

2 cups CORNSTARCH

2 cups WONDRA

SALT and freshly ground BLACK PEPPER

1. In a large deep saucepan, preferably one with a basket, heat the olive oil over medium-high heat until it reaches 375°F. Meanwhile, in a wide shallow bowl, combine half the calamari, shellfish, fish, and lemon slices. In a medium bowl, whisk together the cornstarch and Wondra. Sprinkle half the cornstarch mixture over the fish and shellfish and toss quickly with your hands to coat, then toss into a large strainer and bat it against your hand to remove the excess cornstarch mixture.

2. Carefully drop the seafood and lemons into the hot oil and cook until golden brown and crisp, 1½ to 2 minutes. Transfer to a plate lined with paper towels to drain.

3. Immediately repeat with the remaining seafood and lemon slices; allow the oil to return to 375°F before adding this second batch. Season the fritto di pesce with salt and pepper and serve immediately with the lemon wedges.

From top: Warm Seafood Salad (page 78), and Mixed Fish Fry.

TUNA *and* RICOTTA FRITTERS

Polpette di Tonno e Ricotta

Once you have fried these and they have cooled, you could reheat them in a light, simple tomato sauce and serve them as a hot main course. You could also toss them with a little spaghetti—kind of like a tuna meatball.

MAKES 6 SERVINGS

2 pounds RUSSET POTATOES

Two 6- to 7-ounce cans ITALIAN TUNA packed in olive oil

1 cup fresh RICOTTA, drained in a sieve lined with cheesecloth for an hour

1 bunch MARJORAM, leaves only

SALT and freshly ground BLACK PEPPER

3 large EGGS, separated

3 cups EXTRA-VIRGIN OLIVE OIL, for deep-frying

1 cup ALL-PURPOSE FLOUR

1 cup FRESH BREAD CRUMBS

2 tablespoons chopped ITALIAN PARSLEY

1 tablespoon LEMON ZEST

1. In a large pot, bring 8 quarts of salted water to a boil. Add the potatoes and cook until easily pierced with the point of a paring knife, about 25 minutes; drain.

2. Peel the potatoes and, while they are still warm, pass through a food mill into a large bowl. Immediately add the tuna, ricotta, marjoram, and salt and pepper to taste. Add the egg yolks and mix well to combine. Using two tablespoons, or your moistened hands, form the mixture into golf ball–sized balls and set on a baking sheet.

3. In a large deep saucepan, heat the olive oil over medium-high heat until it reaches 370°F. Meanwhile, place the flour in a shallow bowl. Lightly beat the egg whites in another bowl. Put the bread crumbs and parsley in a third bowl. Working in batches, dredge the tuna balls in the flour, then dip in the egg whites, letting the excess run off, and dredge in the bread crumbs. Carefully drop the balls into the hot oil and fry, turning occasionally, until golden brown on all sides, about 4 minutes. Using a slotted spoon, transfer to a plate lined with paper towels to drain. Sprinkle with lemon zest. Serve hot.

HOT POLENTA-ANCHOVY SANDWICHES

Rebecchini

I first tasted these little heroes in a tiny fry shop in Rome, along with some baccalà, some amazing fried chicory called *torzelli*, and a glass of stingingly cold Frascati. The combination of the four, in my brain and on my palate on a hot June afternoon, illuminated the ceiling of the Sistine Chapel in a way Michelangelo could never have foreseen.

MAKES 4 SERVINGS

5 cups WATER

1 teaspoon SALT

1 cup quick-cooking POLENTA or fine CORNMEAL

¼ cup EXTRA-VIRGIN OLIVE OIL

4 cloves GARLIC, thinly sliced

12 salt-packed ANCHOVIES, filleted, rinsed, and patted dry

2 tablespoons CAPERS, rinsed, drained, and roughly chopped

About 4 cups EXTRA-VIRGIN OLIVE OIL, for deep-frying

½ cup ALL-PURPOSE FLOUR

3 large EGGS

1. Brush a large baking sheet with olive oil and set aside.

2. In a medium saucepan, bring the water to a boil and add the salt. Whisking vigorously, slowly pour in the polenta in a thin stream and return to a boil, then cook, stirring constantly, until as thick as porridge, about 1 minute, switching to a wooden spoon (or a polenta stick) to stir as the polenta thickens. Pour the polenta out onto the baking sheet and spread it evenly into a rectangle about 10 inches by 16 inches and ⅛ to ¼ inch thick. Allow to cool for 1 hour. (The polenta can be made up to 1 day ahead, covered, and refrigerated.)

3. Meanwhile, in a small saucepan, combine the ¼ cup olive oil and garlic and cook over medium heat until the garlic is just light brown. Add the anchovies and capers and stir until the anchovies dissolve into a paste. Remove from the heat and set aside.

4. Pour 3 inches of olive oil into a deep heavy saucepan and heat over medium-high heat to 370°F. While the oil is heating, spread the flour on a plate. Lightly beat the eggs in a shallow bowl. Using a cookie cutter or grappa glass, cut the polenta into 2-inch rounds; you should have about 40 rounds. Place ¼ teaspoon of the anchovy mixture on one polenta disk and make a sandwich by covering it with a second polenta disk. Repeat with the remaining polenta and anchovy filling.

5. Working in batches of 6 or 7, dredge each sandwich in the flour, then dip into the eggs, letting the excess drop off, and fry until golden brown, about 3 minutes per batch. Transfer to a paper towel–lined plate to drain, and serve hot.

Left to right: Fried Stuffed Olives (page 105), Anchovy Beccafichi (see headnote page 79), Hot Polenta-Anchovy Sandwiches.

CONCH STEW *from* SORRENTO

Scungilli alla Sorrentina

Scungilli always sounds like a dish the Sopranos should be serving at their Sunday supper. In fact, it is easier to find these fresh in Chinatown than in Little Italy, where they are often precooked and out of the shell. If it is up to you to get them out of their homes, a simple blanch will pry them loose.

MAKES 8 SERVINGS

2 pounds shelled fresh SCUNGILLI or CONCH or large WHELKS

2 tablespoons RED WINE VINEGAR

¼ cup EXTRA-VIRGIN OLIVE OIL

1 medium RED ONION, cut into ¼-inch dice

2 YELLOW BELL PEPPERS, cored, seeded, and cut into ¼-inch dice

1 tablespoon fresh THYME LEAVES

1 cup DRY WHITE WINE

3 PLUM TOMATOES, cut into ¼-inch dice

SALT and freshly ground BLACK PEPPER

2 LEMONS, cut into wedges

HOT RED PEPPER FLAKES

1. Place the scungilli in a pot and cover with water. Add the vinegar and a cork (the cork helps tenderize the scungilli), bring to a boil, and boil for 1 hour, or until tender. Drain and let cool.

2. Slice the scungilli into ¼-inch-thick rounds and set aside.

3. In a 6- to 8-quart pot, heat the olive oil over medium heat until hot. Add the onion, bell peppers, and thyme and cook until the vegetables are softened, 8 to 10 minutes. Add the wine, tomatoes, and scungilli and bring to a boil. Lower the heat to a simmer and cook for 15 minutes. Season to taste with salt and pepper.

4. Serve in shallow bowls, with the lemon wedges and red pepper flakes on the side.

CUTTLEFISH *with* CHICKPEAS

Seppie in Zimino di Ceci

Cuttlefish have an undeserved "stepchild" reputation in America, and I rarely see them outside of "Guido"-style restaurants in Little Italys around the country. They are found in sizes from as small as my pinky fingernail to as big as my fist. I prefer them the size of my thumb, but the most important factor is freshness. They should smell like cucumbers and sea breezes and shimmer in milky iridescence.

MAKES 4 SERVINGS

6 tablespoons EXTRA-VIRGIN OLIVE OIL

1 medium SPANISH ONION, sliced into ¼-inch-thick rounds

3 ribs CELERY, cut into ¼-inch-thick slices

4 cloves GARLIC

1 cup cooked CHICKPEAS, rinsed and drained if canned

2 DRIED HOT CHILE PEPPERS

4 ANCHOVY FILLETS, rinsed and patted dry

1 cup BASIC TOMATO SAUCE (page 71)

3 pounds CUTTLEFISH or CALAMARI, cleaned and cut into ½-inch-wide pieces

1 cup DRY WHITE WINE

2 tablespoons WHITE WINE VINEGAR

2 medium WAXY POTATOES, peeled and cut into ¼-inch dice

4 ounces BABY SPINACH, washed and spun dry

SALT and freshly ground BLACK PEPPER

LEMON WEDGES

1. In a 10- to 12-inch sauté pan, heat the olive oil over medium heat until hot. Add the onion, celery, garlic, chickpeas, chile peppers, and anchovies and cook until the onion and celery are softened and light golden brown, about 10 minutes.

2. Add the tomato sauce, cuttlefish, wine, and vinegar and bring to a boil. Lower the heat, cover, and simmer for 1 hour, or until the cuttlefish is tender.

3. Add the potatoes and spinach and cook until the potatoes are tender, about 8 minutes. Season to taste with salt and pepper and transfer into an earthenware or other serving dish. Serve with the lemon wedges.

MEAT
ANTIPASTO

CHICKEN LIVER CROSTINI

Crostini Toscani

These simple and delicious crostini are almost always part of an antipasto misto in the wine-making regions of Toscana—often served with slices of salami or the local prosciutto, or pickled vegetables. The real zinger here is the use of anchovies and capers for the saline component. As for people who claim to dislike anchovies, do not feel obligated to disclose their presence.

MAKES 4 SERVINGS

3 tablespoons EXTRA-VIRGIN OLIVE OIL

1 medium RED ONION, cut into ⅛-inch dice

1 tablespoon CAPERS

2 tablespoons ANCHOVY PASTE or 4 ANCHOVY FILLETS, rinsed and patted dry

8 ounces CHICKEN LIVERS, rinsed and patted dry

½ cup DRY RED WINE, such as Chianti

2 tablespoons TOMATO PASTE

SALT and freshly ground BLACK PEPPER

Eight 1-inch-thick slices ITALIAN PEASANT BREAD

1. In a 10- to 12-inch sauté pan, heat the olive oil over medium heat until smoking. Add the onion, capers, and anchovy paste (or anchovies) and cook the onion is until golden brown, 8 to 10 minutes.

2. Add the chicken livers and cook, stirring, until lightly browned, 4 to 5 minutes. Add the wine and tomato paste and bring to a boil. Lower the heat and simmer for 15 minutes. Season to taste with salt and pepper.

3. Transfer the chicken livers to a food processor and pulse 5 or 6 times, until chopped to a chunky puree. Transfer to a bowl.

4. Meanwhile, preheat the broiler. Toast the bread, turning once, until golden brown. Spread the liver mixture over the toasts and serve immediately.

ANTIPASTO

CHICKEN LIVERS *with* BALSAMIC VINEGAR

Fegatini alla Modenese

My friend Cesare Casella first made me this dish when he worked at Sapore di Mare in East Hampton, Long Island. It was a cool summer evening, and I was surprised to see chicken livers on the menu. I was also surprised by how the delicate texture and sweet flavor of the leeks and the sweet balsamic vinegar transformed the lowly chicken livers.

MAKES 4 SERVINGS

¼ cup EXTRA-VIRGIN OLIVE OIL

½ cup ALL-PURPOSE FLOUR

SALT and freshly ground BLACK PEPPER

1 pound CHICKEN LIVERS, rinsed and patted dry

2 large LEEKS, white parts only, cut into 2-inch-long strips and thoroughly rinsed

½ cup BALSAMIC VINEGAR

3 tablespoons UNSALTED BUTTER

2 cups trimmed CURLY ENDIVE or CHICORY, washed and spun dry

1. In a 10- to 12-inch sauté pan, heat the olive oil over medium-high heat until smoking. Meanwhile, in a shallow bowl, season the flour with salt and pepper. Dredge the chicken livers in the flour, shaking off any excess, add to the pan, and sauté until crisp and golden brown, 8 to 10 minutes. Transfer to a plate.

2. Add the leeks to the pan and cook until softened, 8 to 10 minutes. Return the chicken livers to the pan, add the vinegar and butter, and cook until the liquid is reduced by half. Add the endive, toss to coat, and serve immediately.

PANCETTA-WRAPPED RADICCHIO

Radicchio in Padella

Although this may seem elaborate, the payoff is huge when the rollicking flavor of the raw onion pickle kicks up a poetic harmony against the muted bitterness of the cooked radicchio and the sweet triumph of Italian pork belly.

MAKES 4 SERVINGS

½ cup RED WINE VINEGAR

½ cup COLD WATER

¼ cup SUGAR

¼ cup SALT, plus more to taste

1 large RED ONION, halved lengthwise and thinly sliced

12 ounces PANCETTA, sliced paper-thin

4 heads RADICCHIO, quartered

Freshly ground BLACK PEPPER

1 cup BALSAMIC VINEGAR

1 tablespoon EXTRA-VIRGIN OLIVE OIL

1 teaspoon fresh ROSEMARY LEAVES

1. In a small bowl, combine the red wine vinegar, water, sugar, and salt. Add the onion and let stand for 1 hour.

2. Unroll the slices of pancetta and wrap 2 pieces of pancetta around each radicchio quarter. Set aside.

3. Heat a 10- to 12-inch nonstick sauté pan over medium heat for 1 minute. Gently place the radicchio in the pan and cook, turning frequently with tongs, until the pancetta is browned and crisp, 6 to 8 minutes. Transfer to a plate. Sprinkle with salt and pepper, cover with foil, and keep in a warm place.

4. Drain any fat from the pan, and add the balsamic vinegar and olive oil. Bring to a boil and reduce by half. Remove from the heat.

5. Drain the onions, discarding the liquid, and arrange one-quarter of the onions in a small pile in the center of each plate. Lean the warm radicchio pieces up against the onions like a teepee, and spoon about 1 teaspoon balsamic sauce over each piece. Sprinkle with rosemary and serve immediately.

ANTIPASTO

COPPA *with* CREMONA-STYLE MUSTARD FRUIT

Spuntino con Mostarda di Cremona

This is a simple variation on the traditional spicy fruit-based condiment from Cremona, often served with bollito misto. I love this stuff as a spicy kick in sandwiches made with mortadella or any other highly spiced snacky snack that I can find in the fridge.

MAKES 8 SERVINGS

4 DRIED FIGS, stemmed and cut into quarters

1 unripe PEAR, peeled, cored, and cut into ½-inch cubes

½ cup DRIED APRICOTS, cut into ½-inch-thick batons

½ cup DRIED CHERRIES

½ cup DRIED CRANBERRIES

½ cup GOLDEN RAISINS

3½ cups DRY WHITE WINE

2½ cups SUGAR

½ cup COLMAN'S MUSTARD POWDER

¼ cup MUSTARD SEEDS

2 tablespoons HOT RED PEPPER FLAKES

1 pound great COPPA—such as one from Armandino's Salami (see Sources, page 504)

1. In a medium saucepan, combine the figs, pear, apricots, cherries, cranberries, and raisins and stir to mix. Add the wine and bring to a boil over medium heat. Lower the heat to a simmer and let cook until the wine is reduced to 1 cup, about 30 minutes.

2. Remove from the heat, add the sugar, mustard powder and seeds, and red pepper flakes, and stir to dissolve the sugar. Allow to cool, then cover and let steep for 24 hours at room temperature.

3. Transfer the mostarda to a jar, seal, and refrigerate.

4. Slice the coppa and serve with the mostarda. (Any remaining mostarda can be refrigerated for at least a week.)

PROSCIUTTO *with* GRILLED FIGS

Prosciutto con Fichi Grigliati

The trick to enjoying real prosciutto is twofold: it must be sliced paper-thin and it must be fresh and moist. Buy only from a place that sells a lot of prosciutto, or you may get something that has oxidized and thus tastes salty, or even dried out. In my dream world, everyone has an industrial deli slicer at home and spends half the day slicing prosciutto for their friends and the other half making lasagne.

MAKES 4 SERVINGS

12 ripe FIGS, cut in half

6 tablespoons EXTRA-VIRGIN OLIVE OIL

4 ounces PROSCIUTTO DI PARMA, sliced paper-thin

1. Preheat the grill or broiler.
2. Place 12 of the fig halves in a small bowl, add 3 tablespoons of the olive oil, and toss to coat. Place the figs cut side down on the grill or cut side up on a baking sheet under the broiler and cook for 3 to 5 minutes, until lightly charred. Transfer the figs to a plate and allow to cool.
3. In a medium bowl, combine the grilled figs, raw figs, and the remaining 3 tablespoons olive oil and use your hands to toss gently so as not to break up the figs.
4. Arrange the prosciutto on four plates. Pile the fig salad on top of the prosciutto, and serve.

FENNEL SALAMI
WITH BRAISED FENNEL SALAD
Finocchiona con Finocchio

MAKES 6 SERVINGS

12 very small FENNEL BULBS, trimmed, or 4 to 6 larger bulbs, trimmed, quartered, and cored

¼ cup EXTRA-VIRGIN OLIVE OIL

3 cloves GARLIC, finely chopped

3 salt-packed ANCHOVIES, filleted, rinsed, and chopped

½ teaspoon HOT RED PEPPER FLAKES

SALT and freshly ground BLACK PEPPER

1 FINOCCHIONA (fennel salami)

1. Bring a large pot of water to a boil. Drop in the fennel, return to a boil, and cook until tender, about 10 minutes. Drain and set aside.

2. In a sauté pan large enough to hold the fennel in a single layer, heat the olive oil over medium-low heat until hot. Add the garlic, anchovies, red pepper flakes, and salt and pepper to taste, and cook gently until the garlic has softened and the anchovies begin to dissolve, about 2 minutes. Add the fennel, stirring to coat with the oil, and cook for 5 minutes to marry the flavors. Remove from the heat and allow to cool to room temperature.

3. Thinly slice the finocchiona and serve the fennel alongside.

PROSCIUTTO
WITH BAKED STUFFED FIGS
Prosciutto con Fichi al Forno

MAKES 4 SERVINGS

12 ripe FIGS

6 ounces GORGONZOLA, at room temperature

2 tablespoons finely chopped WALNUTS, plus ½ cup WALNUT pieces

½ cup finely chopped ITALIAN PARSLEY

4 ounces thinly sliced PROSCIUTTO DI PARMA

1. Preheat the oven to 450°F.

2. Cut an **X** in the top of each fig, leaving them attached at the base. Place on an ungreased baking sheet, and gently open them out with your fingers. In a small bowl, stir together the Gorgonzola, walnuts, and parsley until well mixed. Using a spoon, gently stuff 1 tablespoon of the filling into each fig.

3. Bake the figs for 8 to 10 minutes, until the cheese filling is bubbling out.

4. Meanwhile, lay 3 or 4 slices of prosciutto on each of four plates. Place 3 figs in the center of each plate, sprinkle with the reserved walnut pieces, and serve immediately.

POTATO CROQUETTES
Crocchette di Patate

These may seem little more than baubles, but when made perfectly they sing the same song the sirens used to lure Ulysses and his sailors into the rocks off Sorrento. This is a potato's version of the Amalfi Coast, in a single bite. A note of caution: you will want to be attentive to the quantity consumed.

MAKES 6 SERVINGS

3½ pounds RUSSET POTATOES, peeled and cut into 1-inch chunks

4 large EGGS, separated

4 ounces PROSCIUTTO COTTO (Italian cooked ham), cut into ¼-inch dice

4 tablespoons UNSALTED BUTTER, cut into pieces, at room temperature

¼ cup freshly grated PARMIGIANO-REGGIANO

Several gratings of NUTMEG

SALT and freshly ground BLACK PEPPER

1 cup ALL-PURPOSE FLOUR

1 cup FRESH BREAD CRUMBS

2 cups EXTRA-VIRGIN OLIVE OIL, for frying

1. Bring 8 quarts of water to a boil in a large pot. Add the potatoes and cook until easily pierced with a paring knife, about 15 minutes.

2. Drain the potatoes and, while they are still hot, pass them through a food mill into a large bowl. Immediately add the egg yolks, prosciutto, butter, Parmigiano, and nutmeg and mix well. Season with salt and pepper.

3. With moist hands, divide the mixture into golf ball–sized portions, and form each ball into a 2-inch disk.

4. Place the flour and bread crumbs on two separate plates. Lightly beat the egg whites in a shallow bowl. Dredge each potato disk in the flour, then dip in the egg whites, and finally dredge in the bread crumbs.

5. In a large heavy-bottomed skillet, heat the olive oil until almost smoking. Working in batches to avoid overcrowding the pan, cook the croquettes, turning once, until deep golden brown, about 8 minutes. Transfer to a plate lined with paper towels to drain, and serve hot. (These can be reheated from room temperature in a moderate oven, but they should not be refrigerated.)

FRIED STUFFED OLIVES

Olive all'Ascolana

These are not like the "mcbuggets" of the hip young osterie set in small towns throughout Italy, where they are made by some sharp fast food dudes weaned on and trained by fast food-niks from hell. These are the real thing, like the ones grandma made. Buy great salami from someone like my dad and good olives from someone you know, and fry the stuffed olives in delicious oil from Italy. Careful, you will want to frug with the women in black.

MAKES 30 OLIVES

2 cups EXTRA-VIRGIN OLIVE OIL, for deep-frying

30 jumbo ITALIAN OLIVES from Ascoli

8 ounces Italian FENNEL SALAMI (*finocchiona*), cut into ¼-inch cubes

4 slices CRUSTY BREAD, cut into ½-inch cubes

1 tablespoon finely chopped ITALIAN PARSLEY

½ teaspoon MACE

½ cup ALL-PURPOSE FLOUR

2 large EGGS

½ cup FRESH BREAD CRUMBS

1. Heat the oil in a large deep saucepan to 375°F. While the oil heats, pit the olives, being careful not to tear the flesh (a cherry pitter works best here—don't be afraid).

2. Place the salami, bread cubes, parsley, and mace in a food processor and chop by pulsing for 5 seconds at a time until the mass resembles the texture of wet bread crumbs, 5 or 6 pulses. Transfer to a bowl, and gently stuff 1 teaspoon of the mixture into each olive.

3. Spread the flour on a plate. Lightly beat the eggs in a shallow bowl. Put the bread crumbs on another plate. Roll the olives in the flour, then in the egg, and finally in the bread crumbs. Gently drop the olives into the hot oil, in batches, and fry until golden brown, about 4 minutes. Serve warm with a delicious aperitivo, such as Campari and tonic.

Photograph on page 89.

STUFFED RICE BALLS ROMAN-STYLE
Suppli' al Telefono

Fry shops in Rome and Napoli are like candy shops to a childish food freak like me. There is nothing in these shops that I would not try: everything from mini eggplant parms to savory fried panzerotti to mini calzones filled with molten sheep's milk ricotta. These *suppli'* have a cult that is all their own; you will find us strutting down the streets of the Eternal City, stretching strings of mozzarella from our hands to our gluttonous mouths.

MAKES 6 SERVINGS

¼ cup DRIED PORCINI

1 cup HOT WATER

3 tablespoons EXTRA-VIRGIN OLIVE OIL, plus 4 cups for deep-frying

3 tablespoons UNSALTED BUTTER

1 SPANISH ONION, cut into ¼-inch dice

2 ounces PROSCIUTTO DI PARMA, cut into ¼-inch dice

1 cup ARBORIO RICE

2 large EGGS, beaten

¼ cup chopped ITALIAN PARSLEY

⅔ cup freshly grated PARMIGIANO-REGGIANO

5 ounces MOZZARELLA, cut into ¼-inch dice

1¾ cups DRIED BREAD CRUMBS

SALT and freshly ground BLACK PEPPER

1. In a small bowl, soak the mushrooms in the hot water for 30 minutes.

2. Lift out the mushrooms, reserving the liquid, and finely chop. Strain the soaking liquid through a fine sieve into another small bowl and set aside.

3. In a medium saucepan, heat the 3 tablespoons olive oil and butter over medium heat. Add the onion and prosciutto and cook until the onion is softened, about 7 minutes. Add the rice and cook, stirring until opaque, about 3 minutes. Add 2 cups hot water and the mushroom water, bring to a boil, and cook uncovered, until the liquid is absorbed, about 20 minutes. Turn the rice out into a bowl, and allow to cool for 10 minutes. Stir the eggs, parsley, and Parmigiano into the rice.

4. For the filling, mix the chopped porcini and the mozzarella cubes together in a bowl.

5. Using a tablespoon, make egg-shaped balls of the rice mixture; you should have 12 to 14. Use your thumb to make an indentation in the center of each, insert 1 teaspoon of the filling, and use your palms to round the ball so that the filling is completely enclosed.

6. In a large deep pot, heat the 4 cups olive oil over medium-high heat until it reaches 370°F. Roll each ball in the bread crumbs so that it is completely coated, and set on a plate. Working in batches, fry the balls in the hot oil until golden brown, about 5 minutes. With a slotted spoon, transfer to paper towels to drain, and season with salt and pepper. Serve warm or at room temperature (do not refrigerate).

HERB SANDWICH *from* PARMA
Erbazzone

This is a classic dish of Parma, yet I have never seen it anywhere else. The most traditional stuffed pasta there is filled with nearly the same cast as the erbazzone, with the addition of ricotta and omission of pancetta.

MAKES 6 SERVINGS

DOUGH

2 cups ALL-PURPOSE FLOUR

½ cup CAKE FLOUR

¼ teaspoon SALT

5 tablespoons high-quality LARD or UNSALTED BUTTER, chilled

3 tablespoons EXTRA-VIRGIN OLIVE OIL, chilled

7 to 10 tablespoons COLD WATER

FILLING

5 ounces thinly sliced PANCETTA, minced

3 large cloves GARLIC, minced

1 medium RED ONION, cut into ¼-inch dice

Freshly ground BLACK PEPPER

2 tablespoons EXTRA-VIRGIN OLIVE OIL

2½ pounds SPINACH, BEET GREENS, or SWISS CHARD LEAVES, or a blend, blanched in boiling water until barely wilted, drained, squeezed dry, and chopped

1½ to 2 cups freshly grated PARMIGIANO-REGGIANO

SALT

2 large EGGS, beaten

GARLIC OIL

2 tablespoons high-quality LARD or EXTRA VIRGIN OLIVE OIL

1 clove GARLIC, minced

1. To make the dough, combine the flours and salt in a bowl, make a well in the center, and add the lard and olive oil. Working with your fingertips or a pastry cutter, blend in the fats until the mixture resembles coarse crumbs. Sprinkle with 7 tablespoons of the water and toss with a fork until the dough begins to form clumps. If it is too dry, add more water, a teaspoon or so at a time. Gather the dough into a ball, wrap in plastic wrap, and chill for at least 30 minutes.

2. To make the filling, in a small bowl, combine about ¼ cup of the pancetta with a little of the garlic, about ¼ cup of the onion, and a generous amount of pepper. Set aside.

3. Cook the remaining pancetta in the olive oil in a large skillet over medium-low heat until it has given off much of its fat, about 5 minutes. Add the remaining onion and cook, covered, for 15 minutes, or until the onion has softened. Uncover, raise the heat to high, and cook until the filling is a rich golden brown, about 6 minutes. Add the spinach, reduce the heat to medium, and cook until the greens are tender, about 7 minutes.

4. Stir in the remaining garlic and cook for

another 30 seconds or so, until fragrant. If a brown glaze has formed on the skillet bottom, add a little water and simmer, scraping the browned bits, until the liquid evaporates. Turn the filling into a bowl and let cool.

5. Add 1½ cups of the Parmigiano and the reserved pancetta mixture to the filling. Taste for seasoning, and add up to ½ cup more Parmigiano, if desired. Blend in the eggs.

6. Set a rack as close to the bottom of the oven as possible and preheat the oven to 400°F.

7. For the garlic oil, combine the lard and garlic in a small pan and heat over medium heat until the lard has melted. Remove from the heat.

8. Brush a 14-inch pizza pan with the olive oil. Divide the dough in half. On a lightly floured surface, roll out one piece to about a 14-inch circle, and place it on the pan. Spread the filling over the pastry, leaving about a 2-inch border.

9. Roll out the second piece of dough to a 14-inch round. Dampen the edges of the bottom crust with water, top with the second round of dough, and pinch the edges together. Fold the edges over toward the center of the torta, and crimp. Make a few slashes in the top of the crust for steam to escape.

10. Bake for 20 minutes. Brush the crust with the garlic oil, and bake for another 20 minutes, or until the top is pale gold and very crisp and the edges are golden brown. Cut into narrow wedges to serve.

PARMA

Parma is considered to be one of the gastrocapitals of all of Italy for two main reasons, Parmigiano-Reggiano and prosciutto di Parma. The presence of these two gustatory heroes is no mere happenstance—Parma's geographic position in the upper valley of the Po River creates ideal conditions for the slow curing of perfect ham, and the richness of the soil is paramount in raising the cattle to produce exquisite cheeses. Such excellence extends beyond the world of food: Giuseppe Verdi was born in nearby Roncole in 1813 and Arturo Toscanini was born inside the walls of the city in 1867. One of my favorite places in all of Italy is Parma's Piazza del Duomo, where the original cathedral and octagonal baptistry dating from 1196 still stand in haunting beauty. The Teatro Farnese (1617) in the Palazzo della Pilota is maintained in perfect condition for modern productions and is regularly filled to capacity by sophisticated local music and theater fans. Along Piazza Ghiaia, there is a daily fruit and produce market that is as vibrant and inspirational as any in Italy, which easily translates into great meals anywhere in town.

TRIPE ROMAN-STYLE
Trippa alla Romana

This is a dynasty dish in any great Roman trattoria, and one that can spark fiery debate over the presence of celery, mint, garlic, pecorino, and chiles, all of which should be in here!

MAKES 6 SERVINGS

2 pounds CALF'S TRIPE

½ cup WHITE VINEGAR

1 teaspoon VANILLA EXTRACT

2 tablespoons EXTRA-VIRGIN OLIVE OIL

1 RED ONION, thinly sliced

½ bunch CELERY, stalks thinly sliced, pale leaves from inner stalks reserved

4 cloves GARLIC, halved

2 cups BASIC TOMATO SAUCE (page 71)

½ cup DRY WHITE WINE

½ cup freshly grated PECORINO ROMANO

¼ cup freshly grated PARMIGIANO-REGGIANO

1 bunch MINT, leaves only

1. In a large pot, combine the tripe, vinegar, and vanilla, and add enough water to cover by 2 inches. Bring to a boil, reduce to a brisk simmer, and cook until the tripe is tender, 1 to 1¼ hours, replenishing the water as necessary. Drain the tripe and allow to cool.

2. Slice the tripe into 2-by-1-inch strips, and set aside.

3. In a deep 12-inch skillet, heat the olive oil over high heat until smoking. Add the onion, celery, and garlic and sauté until softened, 8 to 10 minutes. Add the tomato sauce, wine, and tripe and bring to a boil. Reduce the heat to a simmer, cover, and cook for 20 minutes.

4. Meanwhile, in a small bowl, combine the grated cheeses and mint and stir to mix.

5. Divide the tripe among six warmed bowls and top with the cheese and mint mixture. Serve immediately.

TRIPE

Who will join me in a dish of tripe? It soothes, appeases the anger of the outraged, stills the fear of death, and reminds us of tripe eaten in former days, when there was always a half-filled pot of it on the stove.
—GÜNTER GRASS

Tripe is the muscular lining of beef stomach. The stomach has two parts, and there are three types of tripe. Smooth tripe, also called plain tripe, comes from the first belly chamber, and it is best avoided. Honeycomb tripe, from the second stomach chamber, is the best type, with a honeycomb pattern on the inside and a more tender texture. Pocket tripe comes from the far end of the second belly chamber. Tripe must be cooked for at least twelve hours in order for it to be digestible, and it is always sold precooked.

CARPACCIO *with* OLIVE SALAD *and* MUSTARD AÏOLI

Carpaccio con Olive

This is a variation on the Piemontese classic served often in the summer and early fall. The most important component in this dish, of course, is the beef, so find a butcher who sells prime-grade or choice Midwestern beef and who will cut it to order for you.

MAKES 4 SERVINGS

AÏOLI

1 large EGG

Juice of 1 LEMON (grate the zest for the salad before juicing the lemon)

1 clove GARLIC, thinly sliced

2 tablespoons DIJON MUSTARD

1 cup EXTRA-VIRGIN OLIVE OIL

SALT and freshly ground BLACK PEPPER

OLIVE SALAD

½ cup GAETA OLIVES, pitted

½ cup cracked GREEN SICILIAN OLIVES, pitted

Grated zest of 1 LEMON

1 teaspoon fresh MARJORAM LEAVES (or substitute 1½ teaspoons dried OREGANO, toasted under the broiler or in a dry skillet until fragrant)

1 pound boneless BEEF EYE OF ROUND, thinly sliced by your butcher

SALT and freshly ground BLACK PEPPER

1. To make the aïoli, combine the egg, lemon juice, garlic, and mustard in a blender and blend until smooth, about 1 minute. With the machine running, very slowly pour in the olive oil, two drops at a time until the sauce begins to thicken, and then in a thin stream. Season to taste with salt and pepper. The aïoli should be the consistency of heavy cream; if it is too thick, thin with a little cool water, adding a teaspoon at a time and blending between additions. Transfer to a bowl and set aside.

2. To make the olive salad, mix the olives, lemon zest, and marjoram leaves together in a small bowl. Set aside.

3. To make the carpaccio, very lightly oil two 8-inch squares of heavy-duty aluminum foil. Lay a slice of beef on top of one piece and cover with the second piece of foil. Using a meat mallet, pound the meat until it is as thin as construction paper. Lift off the top piece of foil, flip the pieces of beef onto a chilled plate, and repeat with the remaining meat, covering each plate, including the rim, completely.

4. To serve, arrange a mound of olive salad in the center of each plate. Season the beef to taste with salt and pepper. Using a teaspoon, drizzle the aïoli over the meat, and serve. (Any extra aïoli can be covered and refrigerated for up to 2 days.)

AIR-DRIED BEEF *with* RAW ARTICHOKES *and* SHIITAKES

Bresaola con Carciofi

True bresaola from Italy is beef salted and then air-dried like prosciutto, and it can be difficult to find. A good substitute is Bundnerfleisch from Switzerland; a bad one is the commercial American stuff. The traditional accompaniment for the sweet, delicate meat is this slightly bitter salad of raw artichokes (I've added shiitakes, an untraditional touch)—a classic example of a dish exceeding the sum of its components.

MAKES 4 SERVINGS

Grated zest and juice of 1 LEMON

¼ cup EXTRA-VIRGIN OLIVE OIL

8 BABY ARTICHOKES

4 ounces SHIITAKE MUSHROOMS

SALT and freshly ground BLACK PEPPER

4 ounces BRESAOLA, sliced paper-thin

1. In a medium bowl, stir together the lemon juice and zest and olive oil; set aside. Remove the outer leaves of the artichokes and trim the stems. Using a sharp knife, slice each artichoke into paper-thin slices, and immediately toss into the lemon juice mixture.

2. Remove the stems from the shiitakes. Slice the shiitakes into $\frac{1}{16}$-inch-thick slices and toss into the bowl with the artichokes. Gently stir to mix well, and season to taste with salt and pepper.

3. Arrange the bresaola on four chilled plates. Arrange the mushroom mixture on top of the bresaola and serve immediately.

WARM TERRINE *of* SAUSAGE, PEPPERS, POLENTA *and* MOZZARELLA

Terrina di Polenta

MAKES 6 SERVINGS

8 ounces SWEET ITALIAN SAUSAGE

¼ cup EXTRA-VIRGIN OLIVE OIL

12 cloves GARLIC

1 large RED BELL PEPPER, cored, seeded, and cut into ½-inch-wide strips

1 large GREEN BELL PEPPER, cored, seeded, and cut into ½-inch wide strips

10 cups WATER

1 teaspoon SALT

1 teaspoon SUGAR

2 cups POLENTA

8 ounces fresh MOZZARELLA, cut into 3-inch-by-¼-inch-thick strips

¼ cup freshly grated PARMIGIANO-REGGIANO

1. Preheat the oven to 350°F.

2. Prick the sausage, put it in a small baking pan, and bake for 20 minutes. Transfer to paper towels to drain and cool, then remove the casings and crumble the meat. Set aside.

3. In a 10- to 12-inch sauté pan, heat the olive oil over medium heat until smoking. Add the garlic and peppers and sauté until soft and light golden brown, about 8 minutes. Remove from the heat, transfer the garlic cloves to a small plate and the peppers to another plate, and allow to cool.

4. Bring the water to a boil in a large heavy saucepan, and add the salt and sugar. Slowly add the polenta in a thin stream, whisking continuously. Lower the heat and cook, stirring frequently, until the polenta resembles hot cereal.

5. Working quickly, pour about a ¾-inch-deep layer of polenta into a 12-inch-long by 4-inch-wide by 4-inch-deep terrine mold. Sprinkle half of the crumbled sausage over the polenta. Cover the sausage with about 1½ cups of the warm polenta, using a spatula to spread it evenly to the edges of the mold. Layer the peppers over the polenta and scatter the garlic cloves over them. Pour another 1½ cups polenta over the peppers, spreading it evenly to the edges. Lay the mozzarella strips, side by side and lengthwise down the mold, over the polenta, leaving a border all around. Pour another layer of warm polenta over the mozzarella, spreading it evenly to the edges. Lay the remaining sausage over the polenta. Cover the sausage with polenta, filling the terrine, and smooth the top. (There may be a little leftover polenta.)

6. Let cool, then cover and chill the terrine overnight.

7. Preheat the oven to 450°F.

8. To serve, invert the terrine onto a cutting board. Slice into ¾-inch-thick slices. Lay the slices on a baking sheet. Bake for 10 to 12 minutes, until heated through.

9. Sprinkle the slices of terrine with the Parmigiano and serve immediately. Garnish with a fresh mozzarella, tomato, and basil salad.

SWEET-AND-SOUR CALF'S TONGUE

Lingua in Agrodolce

I find it easier to serve things that people do not often eat (read "are hesitant about") as an antipasto course, when they are hungrier and less risk aversive. It has always surprised me that some people are suspicious of offal and yet have no fear of eating an arm, a shoulder, or the fatty muscle just under the rib cage (i.e., the steak).

Calf's tongue was a part of my growing up, though I am not sure whether it was the budget or the diversity, or both, we were looking for. I was never disappointed to find it on the table at suppertime. It was then, and is today, delicious!

MAKES 8 SERVINGS

2 large CALF'S TONGUES (about 3 pounds)

¼ cup EXTRA-VIRGIN OLIVE OIL

1 pound CIPOLLINI or PEARL ONIONS, peeled

2 medium CARROTS, cut into ¼-inch-thick rounds

2 ribs CELERY, cut into ¼-inch-thick slices

Grated zest and juice of 3 ORANGES

¼ cup RED WINE VINEGAR

1 cup BASIC TOMATO SAUCE (page 71)

SALT and freshly ground BLACK PEPPER

¼ cup finely chopped ITALIAN PARSLEY

1. Place the tongues in a pot just large to hold them and cover them with water. Cover the pot and bring to a boil. Lower the heat and simmer for 1½ hours. Remove from the heat and leave the tongues in the liquid until cool enough to handle.

2. Remove the tongues from the pot, peel them, and remove the fatty parts at the base of each one. Slice into ½-inch slices across the grain and set aside. Reserve 1½ cups of the cooking liquid, and discard the remainder.

3. In a heavy-bottomed Dutch oven, heat the olive oil over medium heat until smoking. Add the onions, carrots, and celery and cook, stirring often, until lightly browned, 8 to 10 minutes.

4. Add the orange juice, vinegar, reserved 1½ cups cooking liquid, and tomato sauce and bring to boil. Add the tongue and cook, uncovered, at a brisk simmer until the liquid has reduced by two thirds, about 30 minutes.

5. Season the tongue with salt and pepper and turn out into a shallow platter. Sprinkle with the orange zest and parsley, and serve.

SOUP, RICE
AND
POLENTA

Soup, risotto, and polenta are the true comfort foods of the Italian table. In the traditional vernacular they are referred to as *primi*, or first courses, along with the pastas, but in the real sense they represent the backbone of the diet of an until quite recently nearly completely agrarian society of farmers, hunters, and shepherds.

These are the dishes from a rural Italy with a reliance on simple hearty meals that were not so heavily based on proteins as those of the wealthy society of today. With their roots in the peasant cooking of the countryside, these dishes have now come to reflect a certain nostalgia for times gone by. And recently they have been revisited in even the chicest of places—at the chicest of prices. I suggest serving them as true first courses and skipping the antipasto course on these days, if not just to feel the happy stomach vibe of a traditional meal, but also to keep some of our meals as simple as they were in tradition.

Clearly the idea of hot thick soup, creamy risotto, or a plate of polenta is most appealing in the dead of winter, but they are well served into the warmer months as well. Many of these soups can be served at room temperature or even cool, with just a drizzle of great oil, or a grating of some Parmigiano or pecorino to finish. Polenta becomes lighter when made with finer grinds of cornmeal. A polenta of nearly baby powder texture when raw can become the lightest silken liquid, with a mouthfeel and weight just this side of a light sauce. Risotto is only as heavy as the hand that cooks it. I often eschew a reduced stock or broth for simple vegetable cooking liquid or even plain water in the search for light and truth at the bottom of my rice plate. And instead of finishing all risottos with butter and cheese, I sometimes like to end with a drizzle of fragrant oil, just off the heat.

BREAD SOUP
Zuppa di Pane

This simple soup makes any cook look like a chef. The variations on the minestrone theme are endless, and it really works for a fridge-clean day—or a day when someone forgot to shop. The key is the drizzle of olive oil at the end and the raw herbs on top—the combination adds a remarkably fresh bite to literally anything.

MAKES 6 SERVINGS

1½ cup chopped mixed FRESH HERBS, such as marjoram, thyme, basil, mint, arugula, and Italian parsley

2 medium ZUCCHINI, cut into ½-inch dice

8 ounces GREEN BEANS, tops and tails removed and cut into 1-inch lengths

1 pound RUSSET POTATOES, peeled and cut into 1-inch chunks

2 ripe TOMATOES, peeled and coarsely chopped

1 SPANISH ONION, cut into ¼-inch dice

1 clove GARLIC, crushed

8 cups cold WATER

SALT

Two 1-inch-thick slices thick ITALIAN PEASANT BREAD, crusts removed

½ small DRIED HOT CHILE PEPPER or 1 teaspoon HOT RED PEPPER FLAKES

Freshly ground BLACK PEPPER

½ cup EXTRA-VIRGIN OLIVE OIL

1. In a large pot, combine 1 cup of the herbs, the zucchini, green beans, potatoes, tomatoes, onion, garlic, and cold water. Add salt to taste and bring to a boil over high heat. Reduce the heat to medium-low and cook, covered, until the potatoes are tender, 20 to 25 minutes.

2. Meanwhile, soak the bread briefly in water to cover, then squeeze to get rid of excess liquid.

3. Crumble the bread and add it to the soup, along with the chile pepper. Cook, stirring with a wooden spoon, until the bread has broken down and thickened the soup, about 10 minutes. Season with salt and pepper to taste.

4. Ladle the soup into bowls, drizzle with the olive oil, and sprinkle with the remaining ½ cup chopped herbs.

"COOKED WATER" SOUP
Acquacotta

This is a forager's version of bread soup, with mushrooms taking on a central role. You could easily substitute a good cultivated mushroom, like shiitake. Or for another version, skip mushrooms altogether and substitute another found item: wild dandelion leaves from the backyard, wild scallions, or the baby leeks called ramps. The soup got its name because originally Tuscans would toss whatever was at hand into a pot of simmering water—and end up with dinner.

MAKES 4 SERVINGS

¼ cup EXTRA-VIRGIN OLIVE OIL

1 ONION, cut into ¼-inch dice

4 ribs CELERY, cut into ¼-inch-thick slices

6 cloves GARLIC, crushed

4 cups WATER

2 pounds ripe TOMATOES, peeled, seeded, and finely chopped

½ bunch THYME, leaves only

SALT and freshly ground BLACK PEPPER

8 ounces PORCINI, very thinly sliced

Four 1-inch-thick slices ITALIAN PEASANT BREAD

1 bunch CHIVES, cut into ½-inch lengths

Freshly grated PARMIGIANO-REGGIANO

1. In a large pot, heat the olive oil over high heat until almost smoking. Add the onion, celery, and garlic and cook until softened, about 8 minutes. Add the water, tomatoes, and half the thyme and season with salt and pepper to taste. Bring just to a boil, then reduce the heat and simmer for 20 minutes.

2. Preheat the grill or broiler.

3. Add the mushroom slices to the soup and simmer for 10 minutes.

4. Meanwhile, toast the bread on the grill or under the broiler. Place 1 toast in each of four warm soup bowls.

5. Ladle the soup over the toasted bread and top with the remaining thyme, the chives, and Parmigiano.

BEAN *and* PASTA SOUP
Pasta e Fagioli

Each region has its own version of this classic bean and pasta soup. You can usually tell the bloodline of the dish from the kind of pasta or beans it uses. In this case, the fresh pasta scraps from tortellini making and the borlotti beans link it to Emilia-Romagna.

MAKES 6 SERVINGS

2 tablespoons PORK FATBACK, slightly softened and mashed into a paste

6 tablespoons EXTRA-VIRGIN OLIVE OIL

¼ cup finely chopped ITALIAN PARSLEY

1 medium SPANISH ONION, finely chopped

2 tablespoons TOMATO PASTE

8 cups CHICKEN STOCK (opposite)

3 cups cooked BORLOTTI BEANS or KIDNEY BEANS, rinsed and drained if canned

2 cups DRIED PASTA SCRAPS from making fresh pasta (or broken dried fettuccine)

SALT and freshly ground BLACK PEPPER

1. In a Dutch oven, heat the pork fat and 2 tablespoons of the olive oil over high heat until almost smoking. Add the parsley and onion and cook, stirring, until the onion is browned and soft, 8 to 10 minutes.

2. Stir in the tomato paste, reduce the heat to medium, and cook for 10 minutes. Add the chicken stock and beans and bring to a boil. Lower the heat and simmer for 30 minutes.

3. Add the pasta and simmer for 10 more minutes. Remove from the heat, season with salt and pepper, and allow to rest for 10 minutes.

4. Divide the soup among six serving bowls, drizzle with the remaining ¼ cup olive oil, and serve.

DRIED BEANS

Dried beans have a long shelf life, are simple to prepare, and make for a satisfying meal. They also provide a significant amount of protein as well as vitamins A and D. To begin the softening process, soak dried beans in a copious amount of water for 12 hours. After this good long soak, drain, place the beans in a pot, and cover by at least an inch or two with fresh cold water. Do not add any salt or any acid at this point; even a tomato has enough acid to make the outer skins harden. Bring the water to a boil, then lower to a simmer and let simmer gently until the beans are perfectly tender. Drain and rinse under cold water. At this point, the beans can be dressed or finished as desired.

ROMAN EGG DROP SOUP

Stracciatella alla Romana

This is classic Italian comfort food. It is a soup that kids and adults love equally, and it will cure whatever ails you.

MAKES 6 SERVINGS

6 cups CHICKEN STOCK

3 large EGGS

3 tablespoons SEMOLINA FLOUR

¼ cup freshly grated PARMIGIANO-REGGIANO, plus extra for serving if desired

1 tablespoon finely chopped ITALIAN PARSLEY

Pinch of freshly grated NUTMEG

SALT and freshly ground BLACK PEPPER

1.   If the chicken stock is not cold, measure out 1 cup and refrigerate it until chilled.
2.   Meanwhile, in a large saucepan, bring the remaining 5 cups stock to a boil.
3.   In a small bowl, combine the cold broth, eggs, semolina, Parmigiano, parsley, and nutmeg and whisk until well blended. Whisk the mixture into the boiling stock, reduce the heat to low, and cook, whisking, for 3 to 4 minutes. Season with salt and pepper to taste.
4.   Divide the soup among six warmed bowls and serve, topped with more grated Parmigiano, if desired.

CHICKEN STOCK
MAKES ABOUT 8 CUPS

2 tablespoons EXTRA-VIRGIN OLIVE OIL

BONES, WINGS, and SCRAPS from 3 whole chickens, excess fat removed

3 CARROTS, coarsely chopped

2 ONIONS, coarsely chopped

4 ribs CELERY, coarsely chopped

4 quarts WATER

2 tablespoons TOMATO PASTE

1 tablespoon BLACK PEPPERCORNS

1 bunch PARSLEY STEMS

1.   In a large heavy-bottomed pot, heat the olive oil over medium-high heat until smoking. Add the chicken parts and brown all over, turning frequently. Transfer the chicken parts to a platter and reserve.
2.   Add the carrots, onions, and celery and cook until softened and browned, about 10 minutes. Return the chicken to the pot and add the water, tomato paste, peppercorns, and parsley, and stir to dislodge the browned bits from the bottom of the pot. Bring to a boil, then reduce the heat and cook at a low simmer for 2 hours, or until reduced by half, occasionally skimming the fat.
3.   Remove from the heat and strain into a large bowl, pressing on the solids with the bottom of a ladle to extract all the liquid. Let cool, stirring occasionally. Cover and refrigerate.

CHILLED TOMATO
AND BREAD SOUP
Pappa al Pomodoro

When tomatoes are at their peak in early September but it is still too hot to cook, this recipe will make you look as if you spent a lot of time working in the kitchen. In fact, it is just those crazy tomatoes, doing the work of trenchermen, watching your back.

MAKES 4 SERVINGS

3 to 4 pounds overripe TOMATOES, cored

1½ cups torn DAY-OLD BREAD

¼ cup fresh BASIL LEAVES

1 tablespoon chopped fresh THYME

½ cup EXTRA-VIRGIN OLIVE OIL

½ cup cold WATER

SALT and freshly ground BLACK PEPPER

4 BAGUETTE SLICES, toasted and cooled

2 SCALLIONS, thinly sliced

1. In a food processor, process the tomatoes until liquid. Add the bread, basil, thyme, olive oil, and water and process to blend. Season aggressively with salt and pepper. If the soup is too thick, thin with a little more cold water. Transfer to a bowl, cover, and refrigerate for 30 minutes.

2. Stir the soup well, then divide among four bowls. Place a baguette slice in the center of each, and top with the scallions.

BEET GREEN SOUP
Zuppa di Bietole

MAKES 2 SERVINGS

⅓ cup EXTRA-VIRGIN OLIVE OIL

1 ONION, halved and sliced into ¼-inch-thick half-moons

2 cloves GARLIC, finely chopped

2 medium RUSSET POTATOES, peeled and cut into ½-inch dice

2 teaspoons COARSE SEA SALT

½ teaspoon HOT RED PEPPER FLAKES

4 cups BEET GREENS, sliced into ½-inch-wide ribbons

3 cups WATER

1 small BAY LEAF

SALT and freshly ground BLACK PEPPER

Four ½-inch-thick slices ITALIAN PEASANT BREAD, toasted

Freshly grated PECORINO ROMANO

1. In a large pot, heat the olive oil over high heat until hot. Add the onion and garlic and cook until softened but not browned, about 8 minutes. Add the potatoes, sea salt, and red pepper flakes, then add the greens, stirring well. Add the water and bay leaf and bring just to a boil, then reduce the heat and simmer until the potatoes are tender, about 15 minutes. Season with salt and pepper.

2. Serve in large bowls, with the toasted bread alongside and pecorino sprinkled over the top.

CHICKPEA *and* PASTA SOUP

Minestra di Ceci e Pasta

This is an Abruzzese version of *pasta e fagioli*, using chickpeas as the legume of choice and the traditional saffron from the town of L'Aquila. You can soak your own dried chickpeas (use a scant 1 cup dried beans) and cook them instead of using canned, if you prefer.

MAKES 4 SERVINGS

½ cup EXTRA-VIRGIN OLIVE OIL

6 cloves GARLIC, finely chopped

1 teaspoon finely chopped fresh ROSEMARY

1 teaspoon SAFFRON THREADS

1 cup BASIC TOMATO SAUCE (page 71)

5 cups HOT WATER

One 15.5-ounce can CHICKPEAS, rinsed and drained

SALT and freshly ground BLACK PEPPER

8 ounces dried FETTUCCINE, broken into short lengths

1. In a large pot, heat ¼ cup of the olive oil over medium heat until hot. Add the garlic, rosemary, and saffron and cook until the garlic begins to brown. Add the tomato sauce and 1 cup of the water, stir well, and bring to a boil.

2. Meanwhile, place half of the chickpeas in a food processor and puree. Place the remaining chickpeas in a large bowl and stir in the chickpea puree and the remaining 4 cups hot water.

3. Add the chickpea mixture to the pot and season with salt and pepper to taste. Bring to a boil, add the pasta, and cook according to package instructions. Season to taste with salt and pepper.

4. To serve, divide the soup among four warmed bowls and drizzle with the remaining ¼ cup oil. The soup is even better if allowed to cool to room temperature before serving.

ONION SOUP EMILIA-ROMAGNA–STYLE

Cipollata

This rich dish, almost more stew than soup, makes for a restorative lunch on a chilly autumn day. Italians use *cipollotte*, red onions, with the green stalks still fresh and soft, which add a fragrant bite. If you can find them at the farmers' market in the fall, you should use them too. The eggs stirred in at the end reflect the Emilian love of rich, farm-fresh intensity; you can omit them if you want and just add the cheese for a lighter version.

MAKES 6 SERVINGS

4 tablespoons UNSALTED BUTTER

5 tablespoons LARD or FATBACK

12 RED or WHITE BULB ONIONS, halved and sliced into thin half-moons

¼ cup ALL-PURPOSE FLOUR

½ cup DRY WHITE WINE

½ cup MILK

6 cups CHICKEN STOCK (page 125)

3 large EGGS

¼ cup freshly grated PARMIGIANO-REGGIANO

SALT and freshly ground BLACK PEPPER

6 slices TUSCAN or other COUNTRY BREAD

¼ cup EXTRA-VIRGIN OLIVE OIL

1. In a large heavy-bottomed pot, melt the butter and lard over low heat. Add the onions and cook slowly for 30 minutes, stirring occasionally and allowing them to develop a rich brown color.

2. Add the flour and stir until smooth and lump-free. Cook for 15 minutes, stirring frequently. Gradually add the wine, milk, and stock, stirring gently but constantly. Increase the heat slightly, cover, and cook for 30 minutes at a brisk simmer.

3. Preheat the grill or broiler.

4. Bring the soup to a boil and remove from the heat. Whisk the eggs and Parmigiano together and stir into the soup. Replace the lid and allow to stand off the heat for 5 minutes, then season to taste with salt and pepper.

5. Meanwhile, grill the bread or toast under the broiler. Drizzle with the olive oil and place 1 toast in each warmed soup bowl.

6. Ladle the soup into the bowls, and serve.

CAULIFLOWER SOUP

Minestra di Cavolfiore

Vegetable soups thickened with grains or pasta were originally designed to feed a family with very little for very little, but they now have value beyond nostalgia. This is a great rib-sticker that can just as easily be made vegetarian by substituting water or tomato juice for the chicken stock and seasoning it a bit more assertively right before serving.

MAKES 4 SERVINGS

¼ cup EXTRA-VIRGIN OLIVE OIL

2 pounds CAULIFLOWER, trimmed, cored, and cut into florets

1 medium RED ONION, cut into ⅛-inch dice

4 cloves GARLIC, thinly sliced

2 BAY LEAVES

Pinch of HOT RED PEPPER FLAKES

4 cups CHICKEN STOCK (page 125)

1 cup BASIC TOMATO SAUCE (page 71)

SALT and freshly ground BLACK PEPPER

8 ounces MEZZA ZITI (half-sized ziti)

1. In a large pot, heat the olive oil over medium-high heat until hot. Add the cauliflower florets and cook, stirring frequently, until just beginning to become tender and light golden brown, about 10 minutes. Add the onion, garlic, bay leaves, and red pepper flakes and cook for 5 minutes, stirring often.

2. Add the chicken stock and tomato sauce, stir well, and bring to a boil. Reduce the heat to a simmer and cook until the cauliflower is very tender, about 25 minutes.

3. Add enough water to bring the liquid back to its original level, season to taste with salt and pepper, and bring to a boil. Add the ziti and cook at a low boil for 2 minutes longer than the package instructions call for.

4. Turn off the heat, and adjust the consistency with water if necessary; the soup should be nearly as thick as porridge. Check the seasoning, divide the soup among warmed bowls, and serve.

CHICORY SOUP *with* EGG
Zuppa di Cicoria con l'Uova

I love soup with eggs, especially on a cold autumn day when I am hungry but feeling lazy. This is a great no-work meal that is really jazzed up with the eggs. For an extra bump, grate a little salty pecorino over each bowl at the table.

MAKES 4 SERVINGS

¼ cup EXTRA-VIRGIN OLIVE OIL

2 large SPANISH ONIONS, cut into ¼-inch dice

3 ounces thinly sliced PANCETTA, finely chopped

2 cloves GARLIC, finely chopped

½ teaspoon HOT RED PEPPER FLAKES

2 tablespoons finely chopped fresh MINT

1 pound ripe TOMATOES, coarsely chopped

2 heads CHICORY or CURLY ENDIVE (approximately 2 pounds), trimmed, washed, spun dry, and torn into 1-inch pieces

1 tablespoon SALT, or more to taste

8 cups WATER

4 slices ITALIAN PEASANT BREAD, toasted

4 large EGGS

A piece of PECORINO ROMANO, for grating (optional)

1. In a medium pot, heat the olive oil over medium-high heat until almost smoking. Add the onions, pancetta, garlic, red pepper flakes, and mint and cook for 8 to 10 minutes, until the onions are lightly golden. Add the tomatoes and cook until beginning to soften, about 5 minutes. Add the chicory and salt, stir, and cook for 3 more minutes.

2. Add the water and bring to a boil, then lower the heat and simmer for 30 minutes.

3. To serve, place a slice of toasted bread in each serving bowl and break an egg on top. Ladle the hot soup over to cook the eggs and soak the bread. If desired, grate a little pecorino over the top.

BREAD DUMPLING SOUP

Zuppa di Polpettine di Pane

These little dumplings were probably invented by a thrifty baker's wife. They demonstrate how frugality can result in the creation of something from practically nothing. The nutmeg's natural harmony with the Parmigiano-Reggiano is the melody of this song.

MAKES 4 SERVINGS

6 cups ½-inch cubes DAY-OLD BREAD

2 cups MILK

6 large EGGS, 4 separated, 2 left whole

4 ounces PROSCIUTTO DI PARMA, cut into ⅛-inch dice

1½ cups freshly grated PARMIGIANO-REGGIANO

½ teaspoon freshly grated NUTMEG

¼ cup finely chopped ITALIAN PARSLEY

SALT and freshly ground BLACK PEPPER

2 cups FRESH BREAD CRUMBS

½ cup EXTRA-VIRGIN OLIVE OIL

6 cups CHICKEN STOCK (page 125)

1. In a large bowl, cover the bread with the milk. Allow to sit for 10 minutes.

2. Lightly beat the egg yolks in another large bowl. Squeeze the excess milk from the bread, and transfer the bread to the bowl. Add the prosciutto, 1 cup of the Parmigiano, the nutmeg, the 2 whole eggs, parsley, and salt and pepper to taste and mix well. Roll the mixture into balls about 1 inch in diameter.

3. In a small shallow bowl, beat the egg whites to a froth. Spread the bread crumbs on a plate. Roll each ball in the egg whites, then dredge in the bread crumbs, and set on a plate. In a large heavy-bottomed skillet, heat the olive oil over medium-high heat until almost smoking. Cook the balls, turning them occasionally, until golden. Transfer to a plate lined with paper towels to drain.

4. Meanwhile, heat the stock in a medium saucepan until hot. Season with salt and pepper.

5. Divide the dumplings evenly among four warmed soup bowls, pour the hot broth over them, and sprinkle the remaining ½ cup Parmigiano over the top.

TUSCAN CABBAGE *and* BEAN SOUP
Ribollita

This is the mother of all minestrone, a dish of unending variations. I have had this served to me as a simple room-temperature soup in the summer and as a pancake-thick drift of porridge in the depth of winter. My favorite is the one Cesare Casella's mom makes when she comes to visit his restaurant Beppe in NYC.

MAKES 8 SERVINGS

¾ cup dried CANNELLINI BEANS, soaked overnight in water and drained

¼ cup EXTRA-VIRGIN OLIVE OIL

2 SPANISH ONIONS, cut into ½-inch dice

2 LEEKS, white and light green parts only, thinly sliced and thoroughly rinsed

2 CARROTS, cut into ¼-inch dice

2 ribs CELERY, cut into ¼-inch-thick slices

2 WAXY YELLOW POTATOES, such as Yellow Finn, cut into ½-inch dice

2 cloves GARLIC, 1 thinly sliced, 1 cut in half

2 sprigs THYME

1 sprig ROSEMARY

1 BAY LEAF

1 pound CAVOLO NERO (black cabbage), KALE, or COLLARD GREENS, roughly chopped

8 ounces WHITE CABBAGE, roughly chopped

SALT and freshly ground BLACK PEPPER

2 tablespoons TOMATO PASTE

Eight ½-inch-thick slices ITALIAN PEASANT BREAD

Freshly grated PARMIGIANO-REGGIANO

1. Place the cannellini beans in a medium pot, add water to cover by 2 inches, and bring to a boil over high heat. Lower the heat and let the beans simmer until tender, about 45 minutes.

2. Meanwhile, in an 8-quart pot, heat the olive oil over medium-high heat until very hot but not smoking. Add the onions, leeks, carrots, celery, potatoes, sliced garlic, and herbs and cook, stirring occasionally, until the vegetables begin to soften, about 5 minutes. Add the cabbages and cook until they have softened and wilted a bit, about 10 minutes. Season with salt and pepper, add the tomato paste, and stir until it is well distributed. Reduce the heat to low and cook for 10 minutes.

3. Drain the beans and add to the pot with the vegetable mixture. Add enough cool water to cover by 2 inches. Bring to a boil, then lower the heat, cover, and simmer for 45 minutes.

4. Preheat the grill or broiler.

5. Just before serving the soup, grill the bread or toast under the broiler, turning once, until golden brown. Rub the toasted bread with the cut sides of the remaining garlic clove.

6. Serve the soup hot in warmed bowls with the garlic bruschetta on the side. Garnish with a sprinkling of Parmigiano.

PORCINI SOUP *with* MASCARPONE CROSTINI

Zuppa di Porcini

Fresh porcini mushrooms are available in the spring and fall and are worth the splurge for a special occasion. That said, this soup is nearly as good with plain old button mushrooms. You could also serve the mascarpone crostini for a quick appetizer.

MAKES 4 SERVINGS

1 tablespoon EXTRA-VIRGIN OLIVE OIL

1 tablespoon UNSALTED BUTTER

1 small ONION, finely diced

1 pound PORCINI, stems roughly chopped, caps cut into thin strips (or substitute trimmed PORTOBELLOS or BUTTON MUSHROOMS)

¼ cup finely chopped ITALIAN PARSLEY

5 cups CHICKEN STOCK (page 125)

SALT and freshly ground BLACK PEPPER

CROSTINI

½ cup MASCARPONE

1 teaspoon finely chopped fresh ROSEMARY

½ teaspoon SALT

1 teaspoon freshly ground BLACK PEPPER

12 thin BAGUETTE SLICES, toasted

1. In a large pot, heat the olive oil and butter over medium-high heat until the butter foams and subsides. Add the onion, porcini stems, and parsley, reduce the heat to medium, and cook, stirring often, until the mushrooms are very soft, about 10 minutes. Add the stock and bring to a boil. Add the sliced porcini caps and simmer for 20 minutes. Season to taste with salt and pepper.

2. Meanwhile, to make the crostini, in a small bowl, mix the mascarpone with the rosemary, salt, and pepper. Smear the mascarpone mixture onto the baguette slices.

3. Place 3 crostini in each of four bowls, ladle the soup over the crostini, and serve immediately.

ANCHOVY *and* ALMOND SOUP
Zuppetta di Alici

This simple Calabrese soup can be made with salt-packed anchovies from a can rather than fresh and will be delicious in its own way. The herb punch added at the end makes for an explosion of flavor on the first bite, and is a good lesson to keep in mind for other soups.

MAKES 4 SERVINGS

¼ cup EXTRA-VIRGIN OLIVE OIL, plus extra for drizzling

½ medium RED ONION, finely chopped

4 JALAPEÑOS, seeded and finely chopped

¼ cup SLICED ALMONDS

1 cup DRY WHITE WINE

1 cup BASIC TOMATO SAUCE (page 71)

3 cups HOT WATER

1 pound fresh ANCHOVIES or SARDINES, cleaned, gutted, and filleted, or 8 ounces salt-packed ANCHOVIES, filleted and rinsed

4 slices ITALIAN PEASANT BREAD

2 SCALLIONS, thinly sliced

10 fresh BASIL LEAVES, cut into chiffonade

10 fresh MINT LEAVES, cut into chiffonade

1. In a 10- to 12-inch sauté pan, heat the olive oil over high heat until smoking. Add the onion, jalapeños, and almonds and cook until the onion is softened and lightly browned, 5 to 7 minutes. Add the wine, tomato sauce, and hot water and bring to a boil. Add the anchovies, return to a boil, and boil until the liquid is reduced by one quarter. Lower the heat to a gentle simmer and cook for 8 to 10 minutes.

2. Meanwhile, preheat the grill or broiler.

3. Grill the bread or toast under the broiler until lightly golden.

4. Divide the soup among four warmed serving bowls, and sprinkle with the scallions, basil, and mint. Serve with the grilled bread drizzled with olive oil.

ANCHOVIES

There are many species of anchovies, but perhaps the most prized is the one found in the Mediterranean, *Engraulis encrasicholus*. Regarded by many diners as salty pizza killers, fresh anchovies have recently become very popular with the cognoscenti because of their delicate oily flesh and magnificent rich flavor when fried or cooked on the grill. Historically in the West, anchovies were preserved whole in salt barrels, but in more contemporary times they have been most often found filleted in cans, covered in mediocre oil and heavily salted to boot. Happily, there are now several great producers of salt-packed whole anchovies, the Rolls Royce of anchovy products; my favorite is an Italian company called Recca. And marinated fresh anchovies in the style of Spain, called *boquerones*, are increasingly available in specialty markets—at the seemingly high price of $20 per pound, but they are well worth the money. Served in small portions in antipasto they are sublime.

MUSSEL SOUP *with* SAFFRON

Cozze allo Zafferano

Mussels pack such an intense flavor that they make their own stock as they cook. Add saffron, the king of spices, to the mix and all you need is water and wine for a deeply satisfying light lunch or heartwarming winter starter.

MAKES 8 SERVINGS

1 teaspoon SAFFRON THREADS

1 cup DRY WHITE WINE

2 pounds MUSSELS, preferably Prince Edward Island, scrubbed and debearded

1 ONION, finely chopped

3 sprigs ITALIAN PARSLEY

1 sprig THYME

1 BAY LEAF

Freshly ground BLACK PEPPER

1 cup HOT WATER

2 tablespoons EXTRA-VIRGIN OLIVE OIL

1. In a small cup, dissolve the saffron in ¼ cup of the wine.

2. In a 10- to 12-inch sauté pan, combine the mussels, onion, parsley, thyme, bay leaf, pepper, the remaining ¾ cup wine, the water, saffron mixture, and olive oil and bring to a boil over high heat. Cover and cook, shaking the pan occasionally, until all the mussels have opened. Remove from the heat and, using tongs, transfer the mussels to a bowl. Reserve the cooking liquid.

3. Once the mussels are cool enough to handle, place the mussels in the shell in another bowl and then in the refrigerator to chill, reserving the juices from the bowl.

4. Strain the mussel juices and the cooking liquid into another pan, bring to a boil over high heat, and reduce by two thirds.

5. Divide the mussels among eight serving bowls, drizzle the broth over, and serve.

FREGULA SOUP *with* CLAMS
Fregola con Vongole

Fregula, the Sardegna version of couscous, has a distinct, nutty flavor. Often served as a side dish in place of rice or grain, it has a particular affinity for seafood, as in this simple, earthy soup.

MAKES 4 SERVINGS

1 pound dried SAFFRON FREGULA

¼ cup EXTRA-VIRGIN OLIVE OIL

1 medium RED ONION, thinly sliced

4 cloves GARLIC, thinly sliced

2 ounces PROSCIUTTO DI PARMA, cut into ⅛-inch dice

1 pound TINY CLAMS, such as Manilas or cockles, scrubbed

1 cup DRY WHITE WINE

1 cup CHICKEN STOCK (page 125)

Pinch of SAFFRON THREADS

½ cup BASIC TOMATO SAUCE (page 71)

1 tablespoon HOT RED PEPPER FLAKES

1 bunch ITALIAN PARSLEY, leaves only

1. Bring 6 quarts of water to boil in a large pot, and add 2 tablespoons salt. Add the fregula and cook for 20 minutes, or as directed on the package.

2. Meanwhile, in a 10- to 12-inch sauté pan, heat the olive oil over medium-high heat until smoking. Add the onion, garlic, and prosciutto and sauté until the onion is softened, about 5 minutes. Add the clams, wine, stock, saffron, and tomato sauce and bring to a boil.

3. Drain the fregula, add to the pan, and cook until the consistency resembles risotto. Add the red pepper flakes and parsley and stir well.

4. Divide the soup among warmed bowls and serve.

CLAM *and* MUSSEL SOUP
Brodetto di Cozze e Vongole

I am particularly fond of Latin American chiles such as jalapeños and serranos, for alternative heat sources in my zippy Italian dishes, and I use a couple of habanero chiles in place of the red pepper flakes when I make this for myself, but the result is too hot for most of my friends. I will leave it up to you to turn it up as much as you like.

MAKES 4 SERVINGS

½ cup EXTRA-VIRGIN OLIVE OIL

2 SCALLIONS, thinly sliced

4 cloves GARLIC, thinly sliced

1 teaspoon HOT RED PEPPER FLAKES

20 LITTLENECK CLAMS, scrubbed

20 MUSSELS, preferably Prince Edward Island, scrubbed and debearded

1 cup DRY WHITE WINE

½ cup BASIC TOMATO SAUCE (page 71)

4 slices ITALIAN PEASANT BREAD

1 tablespoon chopped fresh BASIL

1 tablespoon chopped fresh CHIVES

1 tablespoon chopped fresh MARJORAM

COARSE SALT

¼ cup finely chopped ITALIAN PARSLEY

1. Preheat the grill or broiler.

2. In a 10- to 12-inch sauté pan, heat ¼ cup of the olive oil over medium-high heat until smoking. Add the scallions, garlic, and red pepper flakes and cook until the scallions and garlic are soft and light golden brown, about 1 minute. Add the clams and mussels, stirring to mix. Add the wine and tomato sauce, cover, and cook until all the clams and mussels are open, 5 to 6 minutes.

3. Meanwhile, to make the bruschetta, grill or toast the bread until quite dark. Combine the basil, chives, and marjoram and mix well. Drizzle the toasted bread with the remaining ¼ cup olive oil, and sprinkle with the chopped herbs and some coarse salt.

4. Add the parsley to the clams and mussels and stir well. Divide the broth, clams, and mussels among four bowls. Top with the bruschetta, and serve immediately.

CLAM *and* CHORIZO STEW

Zuppa di Vongole e Chorizo

The Portuguese have served clams and pork for all of time, and for good reason: there is a natural affinity between the briny, succulent bivalves and the rich, unctuous meat of chorizo—or pancetta. Here the sweetness of the vermouth works with the tomato sauce to create a heady perfume reminiscent of late summer, even if there's a chill in the air.

MAKES 4 SERVINGS

½ cup EXTRA-VIRGIN OLIVE OIL

1 medium RED ONION, cut into ½-inch dice

8 ounces cooked CHORIZO, thinly sliced

½ cup CINZANO BIANCO (sweet white vermouth)

1½ cups BASIC TOMATO SAUCE (page 71)

½ cup DRY WHITE WINE

24 LITTLENECK CLAMS, scrubbed

1 BAGUETTE

¼ cup DRY RED WINE

6 cloves GARLIC, thinly sliced

1 bunch MARJORAM, leaves only, finely chopped

1. Preheat the oven to 450°F.

2. In a medium heavy-bottomed pot, heat ¼ cup of the olive oil over medium-high heat until smoking. Add the onion and chorizo and cook until the onion is softened, about 8 minutes. Add the vermouth and bring to a boil. Add the tomato sauce, white wine, and clams, cover, and cook until all the clams are open, about 10 minutes.

3. Meanwhile, split the baguette lengthwise in half. Brush the bottom half of the bread with the red wine, then with the remaining ¼ cup olive oil. Sprinkle with the garlic and marjoram and replace the top of the bread.

4. Place the bread on a baking sheet, unwrapped, and heat in the oven for 5 minutes. Remove and cut into quarters.

5. Divide the clams and broth among four warmed bowls and serve immediately, with the bread on the side.

RED WINE RISOTTO *with* RADICCHIO *and* ASIAGO

Risotto al Bardolino

This makes an excellent simple first course in the fall, when the late-season radicchio has developed a pleasantly bitter taste that really sings with the Asiago.

MAKES 4 SERVINGS

¼ cup EXTRA-VIRGIN OLIVE OIL

1 medium ONION, cut into ¼-inch dice

1½ cups ARBORIO RICE

1 cup DRY RED WINE, such as Bardolino or Valpolicella

8 cups CHICKEN STOCK (page 125), heated until hot

1 head RADICCHIO, cut crosswise into ½-inch-wide ribbons

4 tablespoons UNSALTED BUTTER

¼ cup freshly grated PARMIGIANO-REGGIANO, plus more for serving

½ cup freshly grated ASIAGO

1. In a 10- to 12-inch sauté pan, heat the olive oil over medium heat until almost smoking. Add the onion and cook until softened and translucent but not browned, 8 to 10 minutes. Add the rice and stir with a wooden spoon until toasted and opaque, 3 to 4 minutes.

2. Add the wine, then add a 4- to 6-ounce ladleful of stock and cook, stirring, until the liquid is absorbed. Add enough stock to just cover the rice and bring to a boil. Add the radicchio and stir well, then cook, stirring, until the stock is absorbed. Continue stirring and adding the stock a ladleful at a time, waiting until the liquid is absorbed each time before adding more, until the rice is tender and creamy yet still a little al dente, about 18 minutes (you may have a little stock left over).

3. Remove the pan from the heat, add the butter and both cheeses, and stir vigorously until well mixed, about 25 seconds. Divide the risotto among warmed plates, and serve with additional Parmigiano.

SAFFRON RISOTTO

Risotto alla Milanese

This is the classic accompaniment to Osso Buco (page 363), but it stands up well as a *primo* when the antipasto or main course is highly spiced or very rich. The delicate flavor combination of the saffron and cheese is calming on the palate.

MAKES 4 SERVINGS

1 teaspoon SAFFRON THREADS

8 cups CHICKEN STOCK (page 125), heated until hot

¼ cup EXTRA-VIRGIN OLIVE OIL

1 medium ONION, cut into ¼-inch dice

1½ cups ARBORIO RICE

½ cup DRY WHITE WINE

4 tablespoons UNSALTED BUTTER

½ cup freshly grated PARMIGIANO-REGGIANO, plus more for serving

1. Add the saffron to the hot stock, stirring to infuse.

2. In a 10- to 12-inch sauté pan, heat the olive oil over medium heat until almost smoking. Add the onion and cook until softened and translucent but not browned, 8 to 10 minutes. Add the rice and stir with a wooden spoon until toasted and opaque, 3 to 4 minutes.

3. Add the wine, then add a 4- to 6-ounce ladleful of the stock and cook, stirring, until the liquid is absorbed. Continue stirring and adding the stock a ladleful at a time, waiting until the liquid is absorbed each time before adding more, until the rice is tender and creamy yet still a little al dente, about 18 minutes (you may have a little stock left over).

4. Remove the pan from the heat and stir in the butter and Parmigiano until well mixed. Divide the risotto among four warmed plates, and serve with additional Parmigiano.

RISOTTO *with* BAROLO
Risotto al Barolo

Some of the simplest and most satisfying dishes come from the great wine-growing areas, like this relatively plain risotto, the pure expression of the noble nebbiolo grape.

MAKES 4 SERVINGS

¼ cup EXTRA-VIRGIN OLIVE OIL

1 medium ONION, cut into ¼-inch dice

1½ cups ARBORIO RICE

1 cup BAROLO or other DRY RED WINE

8 cups CHICKEN STOCK (page 125), heated until hot

4 tablespoons UNSALTED BUTTER

½ cup freshly grated PARMIGIANO-REGGIANO, plus more for serving

1. In a 10- to 12-inch sauté pan, heat the olive oil over medium heat until almost smoking. Add the onion and cook until softened and translucent but not browned, 8 to 10 minutes. Add the rice and stir with a wooden spoon until toasted and opaque, 3 to 4 minutes.

2. Add the wine, then add a 4- to 6-ounce ladleful of stock and cook, stirring, until the liquid is absorbed. Continue stirring and adding the stock a ladleful at a time, waiting until the liquid is absorbed each time before adding more, until the rice is tender and creamy yet still a little al dente, about 18 minutes (you may have a little stock left over).

3. Remove the pan from the heat and stir in the butter and Parmigiano until well mixed. Divide the risotto among four warmed plates, and serve with additional Parmigiano.

RISOTTO *with* MUSHROOMS *and* VIN SANTO

Risotto con Funghi e Vin Santo

If you cannot find the vin santo, the Italian dessert wine, a dry sherry would be a fair substitute, as both have a lot to say when around meaty mushrooms. If fresh porcini are not available, double the amount of shiitakes and add a couple of tablespoons of well-rinsed dried porcini when the rice goes into the pan; they will rehydrate during the cooking process.

MAKES 4 SERVINGS

¼ cup EXTRA-VIRGIN OLIVE OIL

½ medium RED ONION, finely chopped

8 ounces PORCINI, sliced

8 ounces SHIITAKE MUSHROOMS, stems removed, caps sliced

1½ cups ARBORIO RICE

8 cups CHICKEN STOCK (page 125), heated until hot

1 cup VIN SANTO

4 tablespoons UNSALTED BUTTER

½ cup freshly grated PARMIGIANO-REGGIANO

SALT and freshly ground BLACK PEPPER

1. In a 10- to 12-inch sauté pan, heat the olive oil over medium heat until almost smoking. Add the onion and cook until softened and translucent but not browned, 8 to 10 minutes.

2. Add the mushrooms and sauté until lightly browned. Add the rice and stir until thoroughly coated and opaque, about 3 minutes.

3. Add a 4- to 6-ounce ladleful of the stock and cook, stirring, until the liquid is absorbed. Continue stirring and adding the stock a ladleful at a time, waiting until the liquid is absorbed each time before adding more, until the rice is tender and creamy but still al dente, about 18 minutes.

4. Add the vin santo and cook until the alcohol smell is gone, about 2 minutes. Remove from the heat, add the butter and Parmigiano, and stir vigorously for 25 seconds. Season with salt and pepper, divide the risotto among four warmed plates, and serve.

VENETIAN-STYLE RISOTTO *with* PEAS
Risi e Bisi

This is classic springtime fare everywhere in the Veneto, but I'll say right now that it depends entirely on the quality of the peas—the younger and smaller, the better.

MAKES 4 SERVINGS

¼ cup EXTRA-VIRGIN OLIVE OIL

4 SHALLOTS, finely chopped

2 ribs CELERY, finely chopped

2 ounces PROSCIUTTO DI SAN DANIELE, cut into ⅛-inch dice

1½ cups ARBORIO RICE

8 cups CHICKEN STOCK (page 125), heated until hot

2 pounds fresh PEAS, shelled (1½ cups)

4 tablespoons UNSALTED BUTTER

½ cup freshly grated PARMIGIANO-REGGIANO

SALT and freshly ground BLACK PEPPER

1. In a 10- to 12-inch sauté pan, combine the olive oil, shallots, celery, and prosciutto and cook over medium heat until the shallots and celery are softened but not browned, 8 to 10 minutes.

2. Add the rice and stir for 2 minutes, until it is almost opaque. Add enough stock to just cover the rice, turn the heat up to high, and bring to a boil. Cook, stirring, until the stock begins to be absorbed, then add another ladleful. As the level of stock dips below the level of the rice, continue to add stock one ladleful at a time, to keep the rice covered, stirring constantly. After 15 minutes, taste the rice; it should still be quite hard.

3. Add the peas and continue to cook for about 4 more minutes, adding a little more stock if necessary, until the rice is tender and creamy yet still al dente. The risotto should be quite moist, but not swimming (even so, you may have a little stock left over).

4. Remove from the heat, add the butter and Parmigiano, and stir vigorously for 25 seconds. Season with salt and pepper, divide the risotto among four warmed plates, and serve immediately.

RISOTTO *with* ACORN SQUASH

Risotto con Zucca

The first taste of acorn squash every fall is an exciting reminder of the rich and complex flavors and real cooking that follow the simplicity of summer tomatoes and mozzarella.

MAKES 4 SERVINGS

¼ cup EXTRA-VIRGIN OLIVE OIL

1 medium ONION, cut into ¼-inch dice

1 small ACORN SQUASH, peeled, seeded, and cut into ¼-inch dice

1½ cups ARBORIO RICE

½ cup DRY WHITE WINE

8 cups CHICKEN STOCK (page 125), heated until hot

4 tablespoons UNSALTED BUTTER

½ cup freshly grated PARMIGIANO-REGGIANO, plus more for serving

SALT and freshly ground BLACK PEPPER

1. In a 10- to 12-inch sauté pan, heat the olive oil over medium heat until almost smoking. Add the onion and squash and cook until the onion is softened and translucent but not browned, 8 to 10 minutes. Add the rice and stir with a wooden spoon until toasted and opaque, 3 to 4 minutes.

2. Add the wine, then add a 4- to 6-ounce ladleful of stock and cook, stirring, until the liquid is absorbed. Continue stirring and adding the stock a ladleful at a time, waiting until the liquid is absorbed each time before adding more, until the rice is tender and creamy yet still al dente, about 18 minutes.

3. Remove the pan from the heat, add the butter and Parmigiano, and stir vigorously until well mixed, about 25 seconds. Season with salt and pepper. Divide the risotto among four warmed plates, and serve with additional Parmigiano.

BLACK RISOTTO *with* CUTTLEFISH
Risotto Nero colle Seppie

The technique of using the blanching liquid of the main event as the cooking liquid for the risotto yields a very delicate and sophisticated flavor. This also works well when making a risotto with vegetables like asparagus and fennel.

MAKES 4 SERVINGS

½ ONION, roughly chopped, plus 1 ONION, finely chopped

½ CARROT, roughly chopped

1 BAY LEAF

1 pound cleaned CUTTLEFISH, with its ink sac if possible

¼ cup EXTRA-VIRGIN OLIVE OIL

2 packets SQUID INK (if cuttlefish ink is unavailable)

1½ cups ARBORIO RICE

1 cup DRY WHITE WINE

SALT and freshly ground BLACK PEPPER

4 tablespoons UNSALTED BUTTER

¼ cup finely chopped ITALIAN PARSLEY

1. Bring 3 quarts of water to a boil in a large saucepan, and add the roughly chopped onion, carrot, and bay leaf. Prepare an ice bath. Plunge the cuttlefish into the boiling water and cook for 30 seconds. With a skimmer or tongs, remove the cuttlefish and submerge in the ice bath for 1 minute, then drain and set aside. Keep the cooking liquid warm over low heat.

2. In a deep 10- to 12-inch skillet, combine the olive oil, finely chopped onion, and squid ink and cook over medium heat until the onion is softened but not browned, 8 to 10 minutes. Add the rice and cook, stirring constantly, until opaque, 2 to 3 minutes. Add the wine, then add a 4- to 6-ounce ladleful of the cuttlefish cooking liquid, and cook, stirring constantly, until the liquid is absorbed. Continue stirring and adding the liquid a ladleful at a time, waiting until the liquid is absorbed each time before adding more, for 15 minutes.

3. Meanwhile, chop the cuttlefish into 1-inch pieces. Toss the cuttlefish into the rice and continue cooking, adding more liquid if necessary, until the rice is tender and creamy but still al dente, about 4 more minutes. Season with salt and pepper.

4. Remove from heat, add the butter and parsley, and stir vigorously for 25 seconds. Divide the risotto among four warmed plates and serve immediately.

LOBSTER RISOTTO

Risotto con Aragosta

I prefer spiny lobsters for risotto, as well as for grilling. Their flavor is sweeter and they are easier to use because you do not have to mess with the legs and claws. But our market lobsters are excellent as well—and far easier to find still alive.

MAKES 4 SERVINGS

½ ONION, coarsely chopped, plus 1 ONION, finely chopped

1 CARROT, coarsely chopped

1 BAY LEAF

Two 1½-pound LOBSTERS

¼ cup EXTRA-VIRGIN OLIVE OIL

2 tablespoons TOMATO PASTE

1½ cups ARBORIO RICE

1 cup DRY WHITE WINE

SALT and freshly ground BLACK PEPPER

2 tablespoons UNSALTED BUTTER

¼ cup finely chopped ITALIAN PARSLEY

1. Bring 3 quarts of water to a boil in a large pot, and add the coarsely chopped onion, carrot, and bay leaf. Prepare an ice bath. Plunge the lobsters into the boiling water and cook for 2 minutes. Remove and submerge in the ice bath for 1 minute, then drain and set aside. Keep the lobster cooking liquid warm over low heat.

2. In a deep 10- to 12-inch skillet, combine the olive oil, finely chopped onion, and tomato paste and cook over medium heat until the onion is softened but not browned, 8 to 10 minutes. Add the rice and stir with a wooden spoon until toasted and opaque, 3 to 4 minutes. Add the wine, then add a 4- to 6-ounce ladleful of the lobster cooking liquid and cook, stirring constantly, until the liquid is absorbed. Continue stirring and adding the liquid a ladleful at a time, waiting until the liquid is absorbed each time before adding more, for 15 minutes.

3. Meanwhile, remove the lobster meat from the shell, leaving the claws whole, and chop the tail into 1-inch pieces. Toss the lobster into the rice and continue cooking until the rice is tender and creamy but still al dente, about 2 minutes. Season with salt and pepper.

4. Remove from the heat, add the butter and parsley, and stir vigorously. Divide the risotto among four warmed plates and serve immediately.

BLACK OLIVE POLENTA *with*
SHIITAKES, GARLIC AND ROSEMARY
Polenta con Funghi

The polenta could just as well be grilled, to add a smoky flavor. Or the whole thing could be baked in a 375-degree oven, spooning the mushrooms over the cooled polenta still in the baking pan and adding a little grated Parmigiano-Reggiano.

MAKES 8 SERVINGS AS AN APPETIZER, 4 AS AN ENTRÉE

5 cups WATER

1 cup quick-cooking POLENTA or fine CORNMEAL

1 cup OLIVE PASTE

SALT

¼ cup EXTRA-VIRGIN OLIVE OIL

6 cloves GARLIC, thinly sliced

2 pounds SHIITAKE MUSHROOMS, stems removed and caps cut into ¾-inch slices

1 cup DRY WHITE WINE

1 tablespoon chopped fresh ROSEMARY

SALT and freshly ground BLACK PEPPER

¼ cup coarsely chopped ITALIAN PARSLEY

1. Bring the water to a boil in a 4-quart saucepan. Add the polenta in a thin stream, stirring constantly, then lower the heat to a simmer. Stir in the olive paste and salt to taste and cook, stirring, until the consistency of thick oatmeal, 5 to 7 minutes.

2. Pour the polenta out into an ungreased 8-by-12-inch baking pan, and smooth the top with the back of a spoon. Set aside to cool.

3. Preheat the broiler. Cut the polenta into 4 rectangles, then cut each one diagonally in half, and remove from the pan. Arrange on a baking sheet, and set aside.

4. In a 10- to 12-inch sauté pan, heat the olive oil over moderate heat until almost smoking. Add the garlic and sauté until just lightly browned. Add the shiitakes and, stirring quickly so the garlic doesn't burn, cook until lightly browned, 3 to 4 minutes. Add the wine and rosemary, bring to a boil, and reduce by half. The mixture should still be loose but not as thin as a sauce.

5. Meanwhile, place the polenta under the broiler and cook, turning once, until hot but not colored, about 3 minutes per side.

6. Place a wedge of polenta on each plate and spoon the shiitakes over the top. Season with salt and pepper to taste. Sprinkle with the parsley. Serve immediately.

POLENTA *with* CAPOCOLLO, ROBIOLA *and* RAMPS

Polenta alle Cipolle e Formaggio

Ramps are wild baby leeks, and the season usually starts around the second week of April in New York. We usually load up the truck and head upstate to pick them by the bucketful, then invite people over for a "rampage," a meal based entirely on these sweet little buggers. If you cannot find them, tiny scallions are a fine substitute.

MAKES 4 SERVINGS

5 cups WATER

1 cup quick-cooking POLENTA or fine CORNMEAL

2 tablespoons fresh THYME LEAVES

1 tablespoon HONEY

8 ounces CAPOCOLLO, sliced paper-thin (you need 24 slices)

1½ cups (about 12 ounces) ROBIOLA CHEESE

3 tablespoons EXTRA-VIRGIN OLIVE OIL

20 RAMPS, trimmed, rinsed, and patted dry

1. Bring the water to a boil in a 4-quart saucepan. Add the polenta in a thin stream, stirring constantly. Lower the heat to a simmer, add the thyme and honey, and cook, stirring, until the polenta is as thick as porridge, 5 to 7 minutes.

2. Pour the polenta into an ungreased 10-by-15-inch baking pan and smooth the top with the back of a spoon or a spatula. Allow to cool.

3. Preheat the oven to 375°F. Butter four 5-inch round gratin dishes.

4. Invert the polenta onto a cutting board and cut into six 5-by-9-inch rectangles. Cut each rectangle lengthwise in half. Lay 1 piece of polenta in a gratin dish. Lay 1 slice of capocollo over the polenta, and follow with 2 tablespoons robiola cheese over the capocollo. Repeat the layering process twice so that you have 3 layers of polenta topped with capocollo and robiola, then repeat the process in the remaining three gratin dishes.

5. Place the gratin dishes in oven and bake for about 20 minutes, until heated through and golden brown on top.

6. Meanwhile, in a 10-inch sauté pan, heat the olive oil over high heat until smoking. Sauté the ramps until softened, 2 to 3 minutes. Keep warm.

7. Remove the polenta from the oven. Place three polenta rectangles on each plate. Arrange the ramps on each plate and serve immediately.

POLENTA *with* CLAMS
Polenta con Vongole

MAKES 4 SERVINGS

5 cups WATER

1 cup quick-cooking POLENTA or fine CORNMEAL

¼ cup EXTRA-VIRGIN OLIVE OIL

1 medium RED ONION, chopped into ¼-inch dice

4 cloves GARLIC, thinly sliced

1 teaspoon HOT RED PEPPER FLAKES

20 LITTLENECK or MANILA clams, scrubbed and rinsed

1 cup DRY WHITE WINE

¼ cup finely chopped ITALIAN PARSLEY

1. Bring the water to a boil in a 4-quart saucepan. Add the polenta in a thin stream, whisking constantly. Lower the heat to a simmer and cook, stirring, until the polenta is as thick as porridge, 5 to 7 minutes. Remove from the heat and cover the pan tightly with a lid or plastic wrap to keep the polenta warm.

2. In a 12-inch sauté pan, heat the oil over medium heat. Add the onion, garlic, and red pepper flakes and cook until the onion is softened and translucent, 3 to 5 minutes. Add the clams and wine, cover, bring to a boil, and cook until all the clams have opened.

3. Add the parsley and cook, stirring, for about 20 seconds.

4. Divide the polenta among four plates and spoon five clams over each puddle of polenta. Spoon the cooking juices over the clams and serve immediately.

POLENTA *with* SALT COD
Polenta con Baccalà

This dish was my grandma's absolute favorite on Christmas Eve. Even the kids loved pungent salt cod prepared this way.

MAKES 8 SERVINGS

1 pound BACCALÀ or STOCCAFISSO (see page 295), any bones and skin removed, soaked in cold water in the refrigerator for 3 days (change the water daily)

¼ cup EXTRA-VIRGIN OLIVE OIL

½ medium RED ONION, cut into ¼-inch dice

3 cloves GARLIC, thinly sliced

1 cup DRY WHITE WINE

2 cups BASIC TOMATO SAUCE (page 71)

2 tablespoons FENNEL SEEDS

1 tablespoon HOT RED PEPPER FLAKES

5 cups WATER

1 cup quick-cooking POLENTA or fine CORNMEAL

FRESH HERBS for garnish (optional)

1. Drain the baccalà and cut into 1-inch cubes; set aside.

2. In a 4-quart saucepan, heat the olive oil over medium-high heat until smoking. Add the onion and garlic and cook until softened and light golden brown, 8 to 10 minutes.

3. Add the baccalà and stir until well mixed. Add the wine, tomato sauce, fennel seeds, and red pepper flakes and bring to a boil. Lower the heat and simmer for 15 minutes, or until the liquid is reduced by one-third. Remove from the heat, and cover to keep warm.

4. Meanwhile, bring the water to a boil in a 4-quart saucepan. Add the polenta in a thin stream, whisking constantly. Lower the heat to a simmer and cook, stirring, until the polenta is as thick as porridge, 5 to 7 minutes. Remove from the heat.

5. To serve, reheat the baccalà if necessary. Divide the polenta among eight plates and spoon the baccalà over it. Garnish with fresh herbs, if desired, and serve immediately.

DRIED
PASTA

Dry pasta made in factories throughout Italy is eaten by Italians everywhere—in Italy and beyond. If there is one thing that defines the entire Italian gastronomic culture, it is spaghetti with tomato sauce, arguably one of Italy's top one hundred contributions to the world.

Why? Because it is quite simply one of the most satisfying things ever to be put in front of a couple of hungry kids, or grandmas, or teenagers, or college professors. Everybody loves pasta—even in the age of Atkins, people eat more pasta than any other type of dish in all of my restaurants.

Italian dry pasta is made using durum wheat flour and water. It is mixed in large mixers and extruded through various metal dies to form the shapes. It is passed slowly through long ovens to dry, and then packaged. Each of the tools or steps affects the quality, from the metal of the die to the length of the drying time (the longer and slower, the more al dente the pasta will remain during cooking). It is definitely worth it to buy slightly more expensive brands like De Cecco, Martelli, or Rustichella d'Abruzzo. The only trick to making great pasta is to cook it in 6 quarts of well-salted water for each pound of pasta; I add 2 tablespoons of sea salt to that water, and I don't subscribe to the idea of adding oil or anything else. I cook the pasta about a minute short of the package instructions, quickly drain it, and then toss it immediately into the pan with the sauce and cook them together for just a minute or two. If at this point the dish seems a little dry, I splash a little of the pasta cooking water into the pan to loosen it a bit and continue the process. Then I add any cheese or herbs, remove the pan from the heat, add a little extra-virgin olive oil, and serve it. This is the only way I do it.

Keep in mind that Italians like their pasta just barely sauced: it is all about the pasta, with a balance between the pasta and the sauce. Oversaucing has traditionally been the most heinous error American cooks make. Try it the next time with a little less of everything and see if it tastes better and feels better in the mouth. Italians are also very specific about which shapes go with which types of sauce. Long thin noodles go best with light oil- or vegetable-based sauces, like clam sauce with wine and some parsley or pesto. Thicker spaghetti goes handily with tomato sauces and other long-cooked vegetable sauces. Really thick noodles like bucatini are good with thicker sauces that contain chunks of pancetta or sausage. Short tubes are good at holding onto thicker meat-based sauces, as well as vegetables or creamy butter-based sauces. Bigger tubes, shells, and twists like fusilli can hold sneaky amounts of chunky, rich ragus in their nooks or holes, and are really good with cheese grated a little less fine than usual. Fresh pasta is another thing altogether, and I deal with it in the next section.

PASTA

PASTA SHAPES

STRANDS OR SPAGHETTI-LIKE PASTA

BAVETTE: thin ribbons

BUCATINI: thick spaghetti strands with a hole in the center

CAPELLINI or **ANGEL HAIR:** "fine hairs," thin, delicate strands

FETTUCCE: "ribbons," the widest of the fettuccine family

FETTUCCINE: flat ribbons about ¼ inch wide

LASAGNETTE: ¾-inch-wide flat ribbons with curly edges

LINGUINE: "little tongues," very narrow ribbons

PAPPARDELLE: 1½-inch-wide flat noodles, similar to fettuccine

SPAGHETTINI: thin spaghetti

SPAGHETTONI: the thickest spaghetti

TAGLIARINI: narrow ribbons, ⅛ inch wide or less

TAGLIATELLE: flat ribbons similar to fettuccine

TRENETTE: thick, narrow ribbons

VERMICELLI: very fine spaghetti

OTHER SHAPES

AGNOLOTTI: "priests' caps," stuffed pasta filled with meat or cheese

CAVATELLI: narrow shell shapes, used for pasta salads or with meat sauces

CONCHIGLIE: tiny "conch shells" (the larger ones are called *conchiglioni*); ridged shells

CRESTE DI GALLI: "cockscombs," a medium shape with the appropriate ridges to grab onto sauces

FARFALLE: "butterflies," also called bow ties

FUSILLI: corkscrew pasta, short spiral shapes; longer fusilli are called *fusilli col buco* or *fusilli lunghi*

GEMELLI: "twins," double strands—short, thick spirals twisted together

GNOCCHETTI: small, curved pasta shapes that look like gnocchi

GRAMIGNE: "weeds," narrow curls of hollow pasta that somewhat resemble the first stalk of a green flower curling its way out of the earth

LUMACHE: "snails," shell shapes, best with chunky sauces; the larger version, *lumaconi*, "giant snails," are generally stuffed

MACCHERONI: refers to all types of tubular pasta

MALLOREDDUS: resembles small, narrow gnocchi, usually flavored with saffron, giving them a golden hue

MALTAGLIATI: literally, "poorly cut"—essentially scraps from making pasta, usually small, irregularly shaped pieces

ORECCHIETTE: "little ears," tiny ridged pinched pasta disks

PENNE: short tubes, cut on the diagonal; may be ridged or smooth

RADIATORE: look like little radiators

RAVIOLI: stuffed pasta squares

RIGATONI: large, fat ridged macaroni

ROTINI: "spirals" or "twists," best served with chunky sauces or in baked pasta dishes

STROZZAPRETI: "priest stranglers," looking like a rolled towel or rolled pieces of paper, with one long irregular lengthwise crease

ZITI: "bridegrooms," small, thin pasta tubes that are about 2 inches long (there's also a long version)

For more information, see
www.foodsubs.com/Pasta.html.

SPAGHETTI
WITH MUSSELS
Spaghetti con le Cozze

MAKES 4 SERVINGS

½ cup EXTRA-VIRGIN OLIVE OIL

4 cloves GARLIC, thinly sliced

1 cup DRY WHITE WINE

2 pounds small MUSSELS, scrubbed and debearded

1 pound SPAGHETTI

¼ cup finely chopped ITALIAN PARSLEY

SALT and freshly ground BLACK PEPPER

1 tablespoon HOT RED PEPPER FLAKES

1. Bring 6 quarts of water to a boil in a large pot, and add 2 tablespoons salt.
2. In a 12-inch sauté pan, heat the olive oil over medium-high heat. Add the garlic and cook until light golden brown, about a minute. Add the wine, raise the heat, and bring to a boil, then add the mussels. Cook, stirring and tossing, until all of the mussels have opened, about 4 minutes.
3. Meanwhile, drop the pasta into the boiling water and cook until al dente; drain well.
4. Add the pasta to the pan with the mussels and cook over high heat for 1 minute. Add the parsley and season with salt and pepper to taste. Sprinkle with red pepper flakes and serve immediately.

Clockwise from top: Spaghetti with Bottarga (page 174), Spaghetti with Green Tomatoes , Spaghetti with Mussels, Spaghetti alla Carbonara (page 184).

SPAGHETTI
WITH GREEN TOMATOES
Spaghetti con Pomodori Verdi

The divine sensibility of Sicilian cooking is very evident in this simple Palermo variation on pesto genovese. The use of the raw green tomatoes creates a sparkling tanginess in the final dish that is redolent of the Sicilian garden circa early summer.

MAKES 4 SERVINGS

¼ cup fresh MINT LEAVES

¼ cup fresh BASIL LEAVES

¼ cup ITALIAN PARSLEY LEAVES

¼ cup ARUGULA, washed and spun dry

5 GREEN TOMATOES, coarsely chopped

1 clove GARLIC, chopped

¼ cup EXTRA-VIRGIN OLIVE OIL

SALT and freshly ground BLACK PEPPER

1 pound SPAGHETTI

¼ cup freshly grated PARMIGIANO-REGGIANO

1. Bring 6 quarts of water to a boil in a large pot, and add 2 tablespoons salt.
2. Meanwhile, in a food processor, combine the mint, basil, parsley, arugula, tomatoes, garlic, and olive oil and pulse to form a chunky puree. Season aggressively with salt and pepper, and set aside.
3. Cook the pasta in the boiling water until just al dente. Drain the pasta and return it to the hot pot. Stir in the sauce, sprinkle with the Parmigiano, and serve immediately.

SPAGHETTI *with* GREEN OLIVE SAUCE

Spaghetti al Pesto d'Olive

This is a great example of a dish that can be made in ten minutes with absolutely no shopping—all of these ingredients ought to be permanent members of your pantry.

MAKES 4 SERVINGS

¼ cup EXTRA-VIRGIN OLIVE OIL

¾ cup FRESH BREAD CRUMBS

3 cloves GARLIC, thinly sliced

3 salt-packed ANCHOVIES, filleted, rinsed, and chopped, or 6 oil-packed ANCHOVY FILLETS, rinsed, drained, and chopped

1 teaspoon HOT RED PEPPER FLAKES

1 cup GREEN OLIVES, preferably Ascolana, pitted and chopped

SALT and freshly ground BLACK PEPPER

1 pound SPAGHETTI

1. Bring 6 quarts of water to a boil in a large pot, and add 2 tablespoons salt.

2. Meanwhile, in a small saucepan, heat 1 tablespoon of the olive oil over medium heat until almost smoking. Add the bread crumbs and toss for a few minutes, until toasted golden brown, then transfer to a plate and set aside.

3. In a 10- to 12-inch sauté pan, heat the remaining 3 tablespoons olive oil over medium-high heat until almost smoking. Add the garlic and cook until golden brown, about 2 minutes. Add the anchovies and red pepper flakes and cook, stirring to dissolve the anchovies, for 3 minutes. Stir in the olives and cook for 3 minutes, then add the toasted bread crumbs, stir well, and season with salt and pepper. Remove from the heat and set the pan aside.

4. Cook the spaghetti in the boiling water until just al dente.

5. Drain the pasta and add to the pan with the olive mixture. Place the pan over medium heat and toss to mix well, about 1 minute. Serve immediately.

TRENETTE *with* PESTO, BEANS *and* POTATOES

Trenette Genovese

This is the true pasta with pesto from the stunningly beautiful Ligurian coast in the northwestern corner of Italy, on the border of France. The potatoes serve to soak up the driblets of oil from the pesto and the beans add a delightful crunch and a counterpoint of sweetness.

MAKES 6 SERVINGS

6 NEW POTATOES or small RED POTATOES

1 cup trimmed young GREEN BEANS or HARICOTS VERTS

1 pound TRENETTE or LINGUINE FINI

PESTO

Freshly grated PARMIGIANO-REGGIANO, for serving

1. Place the potatoes in a medium saucepan, add salted water to cover generously, and bring to a boil. Boil gently until the potatoes are tender; drain. Cut the potatoes in half, and set aside.

2. Meanwhile, cook the beans in a large saucepan of boiling salted water until tender, 4 minutes. Have an ice bath ready. Drain the beans, plunge into the ice bath just to cool, and drain again. Set aside.

3. Bring 6 quarts of water to a boil in a large pot, and add 2 tablespoons salt. Cook the pasta until al dente; drain.

4. Pour the pasta into a warmed bowl, add the beans, potatoes, and pesto, and toss to coat the pasta and to warm the beans and potatoes; do not return to the heat. Serve with grated Parmigiano on the side.

PESTO
MAKES 1 CUP

3 tablespoons PINE NUTS

2 cups fresh BASIL LEAVES

1 clove GARLIC, peeled

Pinch of SALT

½ cup EXTRA-VIRGIN OLIVE OIL

¼ cup freshly grated PARMIGIANO-REGGIANO

Combine the pine nuts, basil, garlic, and salt in a large stone mortar and grind with the pestle until the mixture forms a paste. Slowly drizzle in the olive oil, beating all the while with a wooden spoon. Add the Parmigiano 1 tablespoon at a time, beating until the mixture forms a thick paste. The pesto can also be made in a food processor. The pesto can be stored in a jar, topped with a thin layer of extra-virgin olive oil, for several weeks in the refrigerator.

PENNE *with* CAULIFLOWER

Penne con Cavolfiore

Sometimes a recipe can be so simple that it seems, well, almost pathetic, like this one. But eating something that's all about one simple, amazing flavor is what good food is all about.

MAKES 6 SERVINGS

½ cup EXTRA-VIRGIN OLIVE OIL

4 cloves GARLIC, crushed

1 head CAULIFLOWER, cored and broken into florets

SALT and freshly ground BLACK PEPPER

1 pound PENNE

½ cup finely chopped ITALIAN PARSLEY

½ cup freshly grated PARMIGIANO-REGGIANO

1. In a 10- to 12-inch sauté pan, heat the olive oil over medium heat until hot. Add the garlic and cook gently until softened and very light golden brown, about 2 minutes. Add the cauliflower. Season with salt and pepper, stir well, and cook until softened, 12 to 14 minutes.

2. Lower the heat and simmer until the cauliflower is very tender, about 10 minutes more.

3. Meanwhile, bring 6 quarts of water to a boil in a large pot, and add 2 tablespoons salt. Add the penne and cook until just al dente.

4. Drain the pasta and add to the cauliflower. Stir in the parsley and toss for 1 minute over high heat. Divide among six warmed pasta bowls, top with the Parmigiano, and serve immediately.

BAKED ZITI

Ziti al Telefono

Baked pasta is classic comfort food and easy to make, as long as you follow two basic rules: The pasta should not be cooked more than an hour before baking and serving, or it will lose its toothsome bite. And it is *importantissimo* to undercook the pasta in the boiling water so that the finished dish still has real texture.

MAKES 4 SERVINGS

1 pound ZITI

2 cups BASIC TOMATO SAUCE (page 71)

2 cups BESCIAMELLA (page 65)

1 pound fresh BUFFALO MOZZARELLA, cut into ½-inch cubes

½ cup freshly grated PARMIGIANO-REGGIANO

½ cup FRESH BREAD CRUMBS

1. Preheat the oven to 425°F.

2. Bring 6 quarts of water to a boil in a large pot, and add 2 tablespoons salt. Cook the ziti for 2 minutes short of the package instructions; it should be too al dente to eat. Drain and rinse under cold water until cool. Drain a second time and place in a large bowl.

3. Add the tomato sauce, besciamella, mozzarella, and Parmigiano to the ziti and stir to mix well. Divide the pasta and sauce mixture among four individual gratin dishes. Sprinkle with the bread crumbs.

4. Bake for about 20 minutes, until bubbling and crusty on top. Serve immediately.

BAKED PENNE *with* EGGPLANT
Pasta alla Norma

The success of this dish relies on the quality of the eggplant. Older, larger eggplant tend to hold bigger seed pockets and can be bitter, so look for small- to medium-sized eggplants, of any variety. If you cannot find ricotta salata, try a young pecorino or provolone.

MAKES 6 SERVINGS

2 pounds small to medium EGGPLANT, cut into ¼-inch-thick slices

SALT and freshly ground BLACK PEPPER

6 tablespoons EXTRA-VIRGIN OLIVE OIL

1 pound PENNE

2 cups BASIC TOMATO SAUCE (page 71)

1 cup TOASTED BREAD CRUMBS

½ cup freshly grated PECORINO ROMANO

10 fresh BASIL LEAVES, roughly torn

An 8-ounce piece of RICOTTA SALATA, for grating

1. Bring 6 quarts of water to a boil in a large pot, and add 2 tablespoons salt.

2. Meanwhile, in a 10- to 12-inch sauté pan, heat 3 tablespoons of the olive oil over medium-high heat until almost smoking. Working in batches, sauté the eggplant slices, seasoning them with salt and pepper, turning once, until golden brown on both sides. Transfer to a plate lined with paper towels to drain.

3. Preheat the oven to 375°F. Grease a 9-by-12-inch baking dish with 1 tablespoon of the olive oil.

4. Cook the penne in the boiling water for 2 minutes short of the package instructions; it should still be quite firm. Drain and rinse under cold water until cool. Drain very well, place in a large bowl, and toss with 1 cup of the tomato sauce.

5. Cover the bottom of the baking dish with ¼ cup of the tomato sauce. Top with half the bread crumbs, then add half the pasta. Arrange half of the eggplant slices, overlapping them slightly, on top of the pasta. Dot about ¼ cup of tomato sauce over the eggplant, and top with half of the pecorino and half of the basil. Top with the remaining pasta, arrange the remaining eggplant over the pasta, and dot with the remaining tomato sauce. Sprinkle with the remaining pecorino and basil, and then the remaining bread crumbs, and drizzle with the remaining 2 tablespoons olive oil.

6. Bake for 45 minutes. Let rest for 10 minutes before serving. Place a generous portion of pasta on each plate, grate ricotta salata over, and serve.

SPAGHETTI *with* CLAMS, MUSSELS *and* PEPPERS

Spaghetti con Cozze e Vongole

In Puglia, there are so many peppers—both sweet and hot—that virtually every table has peppers on it from June to October. The bruschetta at this time of year are covered with peppers, the classic *zuppa di pesce* is filled with peppers, and this classic clam pasta is sweetened by them.

MAKES 4 SERVINGS

¼ cup EXTRA-VIRGIN OLIVE OIL

4 cloves GARLIC, thinly sliced

1 teaspoon HOT RED PEPPER FLAKES

2 RED BELL PEPPERS, cored, seeded, and cut into ½-inch dice

2 YELLOW BELL PEPPERS, cored, seeded, and cut into ½-inch dice

1 cup BASIC TOMATO SAUCE (page 71)

1 cup DRY WHITE WINE

1 pound SPAGHETTI

1 pound MANILA CLAMS, scrubbed

1 pound small MUSSELS, preferably Prince Edward Island, scrubbed and debearded

¼ cup finely chopped ITALIAN PARSLEY

SALT and freshly ground BLACK PEPPER

1. Bring 6 quarts of water to a boil in a large pot, and add 2 tablespoons salt.

2. Meanwhile, in a 10- to 12-inch sauté pan, heat the olive oil over medium-high heat until hot. Add the garlic, red pepper flakes, and bell peppers and cook, stirring, until the peppers are light golden brown, about 6 minutes. Add the tomato sauce and wine, raise the heat to high, and bring to a boil.

3. Drop the pasta into the boiling water and cook until just al dente.

4. Meanwhile, add the clams to the sauce, cover, and cook until the clams are just opening, 4 to 5 minutes. Add the mussels, cover again, and cook until all the clams and mussels have opened, about 4 more minutes.

5. When the pasta is cooked, drain well and toss into the pan with the sauce. Cook over high heat for 1 minute, stirring to mix well. Add the parsley and season with salt and pepper to taste. Serve immediately.

SPAGHETTI *with* CARAMELIZED ONIONS,
ANCHOVIES AND TOASTED BREAD CRUMBS

Spaghetti con Salsa

The trick here is to buy the best anchovies you can find. The brand for me is Recca, for their dependable quality. But I have been known to use a can of sardines in a pinch, or even a tablespoon of oil-packed Italian tuna. Hey, life is short!

MAKES 4 SERVINGS

¼ cup plus 3 tablespoons EXTRA-VIRGIN OLIVE OIL

2 large SPANISH ONIONS, cut lengthwise in half and then into ¼-inch-thick half-moons

5 salt-packed ANCHOVIES, filleted and rinsed

½ cup MILK

4 cloves GARLIC, thinly sliced

1 tablespoon HOT RED PEPPER FLAKES

1 pound SPAGHETTI

½ cup roughly chopped ITALIAN PARSLEY

1 cup TOASTED BREAD CRUMBS

1. In a 10- to 12-inch sauté pan, combine 3 tablespoons of the olive oil and the onions and cook over medium heat, stirring occasionally, until the onions are very soft and golden brown, 20 to 25 minutes. Set aside.

2. Meanwhile, bring 6 quarts of water to boil in a large pot, and add 2 tablespoons salt. Soak the anchovies in the milk for 10 minutes.

3. In another 10- to 12-inch sauté pan, heat the remaining ¼ cup olive oil over medium-high heat until smoking. Add the garlic and red pepper flakes and cook until the red pepper flakes are lightly toasted, about 30 seconds. Drain the anchovies, toss them into the pan, and cook, stirring, until they have broken down, 4 to 5 minutes. Add the cooked onions and lower the heat to a simmer.

4. Drop the spaghetti into the boiling water and cook until just al dente.

5. Drain the pasta and toss into the pan with the anchovy mixture. Add the parsley and stir to coat. Pour into a warmed serving bowl, sprinkle with the bread crumbs, and serve.

SPAGHETTI *with* BOTTARGA
Spaghetti con Bottarga

This simple Sicilian dish is all about the quality of the bottarga. Unfortunately, the bottarga Sicilians eat in Italy is much softer—and tastier!—than the bottarga they ship to America. With increasing demand here, however—and luck —perhaps that will change soon.

MAKES 4 SERVINGS

½ cup EXTRA-VIRGIN OLIVE OIL

1 tablespoon HOT RED PEPPER FLAKES

2 cloves GARLIC, thinly sliced

1 pound SPAGHETTI

½ cup roughly chopped ITALIAN PARSLEY

6 ounces TUNA or MULLET BOTTARGA

Grated zest of 2 LEMONS

1. Bring 6 quarts of water to a boil in a large pot, and add 2 tablespoons salt.

2. In a 10- to 12-inch sauté pan, combine the olive oil, red pepper flakes, and garlic and heat over low heat until just fragrant, about 2 minutes. Remove from the heat.

3. Cook the spaghetti until just al dente. Remove ½ cup of the pasta cooking water and set aside. Drain the pasta well, and add to the oil mixture. Add the reserved pasta water and the parsley and toss to mix well over medium heat.

4. Transfer the pasta to a warmed serving bowl. Using a hand-held mandoline or a vegetable peeler, shave the bottarga over the pasta. Sprinkle with the lemon zest and serve immediately.

Photograph on page 167.

BOTTARGA

The tradition of preserving seafood, and farming the nutrient-rich sea salt of the tidal marshes to that end, is well maintained in Sicily and Sardinia. Once known as the poor man's caviar, bottarga is the salted, pressed, and dried roe of either tuna (*tonno*) or gray mullet (*mugine*). The long, fat roe sacs are salted and massaged by hand over several weeks to cure them. Then the roe is pressed under wooden planks weighted with stones and sun-dried for one to two months. Although both types are salty, tuna bottarga has a lively, sharp flavor, stronger than mullet bottarga.

Bottarga may be shaved, sliced, chopped, or grated, and just a little can add a ton of flavor to a whole host of dishes. One of my all-time favorites is spaghetti con bottarga. I also love a salad of bitter greens dressed with fresh orange, olive oil, and shaved bottarga. We keep our bottarga tightly wrapped in the freezer.

LINGUINE *with* CRABMEAT, RADICCHIO *and* GARLIC

Linguine con Granchio

Growing up in Seattle, I fell in love with crab-meat early on, but I didn't realize the magnificence of the local Dungeness and Alaskan king crab until I moved away. Now I also love Maryland lump crabmeat, in part because it is so easy to find and of consistently excellent quality. Use whichever grows closest to your house.

MAKES 4 SERVINGS

¼ cup EXTRA-VIRGIN OLIVE OIL

3 SHALLOTS, finely chopped

4 cloves GARLIC, thinly sliced

1 teaspoon HOT RED PEPPER FLAKES

1 cup DRY WHITE WINE

2 tablespoons UNSALTED BUTTER

1 pound LINGUINE

8 ounces JUMBO LUMP CRABMEAT, picked over for shells and cartilage

½ head RADICCHIO, finely shredded

2 SCALLIONS, thinly sliced

1. Bring 6 quarts of water to a boil in a large pot, and add 2 tablespoons salt.

2. Meanwhile, in a 10- to 12-inch sauté pan, heat the olive oil over medium-high heat until smoking. Add the shallots, garlic, and red pepper flakes and sauté until golden brown, 4 to 5 minutes. Add the wine and bring to a boil, then stir in the butter and remove from the heat.

3. Cook the pasta in the boiling water until just al dente; drain.

4. Add the pasta to the sauté pan and return the pan to medium heat. Add the crab, radicchio, and scallions and toss until the radicchio is wilted, about 1 minute. Transfer to a warmed serving bowl and serve immediately.

ST. JOHN'S EVE PASTA

Pasta di San Giovanello

There is great controversy in Puglia about the exact ingredients of this pasta, but my fave includes toasted almonds, often scorned by some of the cooks I know, particularly in Lecce, where almonds are not cool. I first had this version in Brindisi on June 24th, St. John's Eve, in a tiny, since-closed osteria near the port, and it is my personal favorite.

MAKES 4 TO 6 SERVINGS

¾ cup SLICED BLANCHED ALMONDS

½ cup EXTRA-VIRGIN OLIVE OIL

2 cups fresh BREAD CRUMBS

4 salt-packed ANCHOVIES, filleted, rinsed, and chopped

Freshly ground BLACK PEPPER

1 ONION, finely chopped

1 clove GARLIC, finely chopped

1½ cups BASIC TOMATO SAUCE (page 71)

6 to 8 fresh BASIL LEAVES, chiffonade

1 pound LASAGNETTE or PAPPARDELLE

1. Bring 6 quarts of water to a boil in a large pot, and add 2 tablespoons salt.

2. Meanwhile, in a 10-inch sauté pan, gently toast the almonds in 1 tablespoon of the olive oil over medium heat until golden brown. Using a slotted spoon, transfer the almonds to a plate. In the oil remaining in the pan, toast the bread crumbs, stirring, until golden brown and crisp. Combine the bread crumbs and almonds in a small bowl.

3. Add 2 tablespoons more olive oil to the pan and reduce the heat to medium-low. Stir in the anchovies and crush them into the oil with a fork. Add the anchovies and oil to the bread crumb mixture and season with lots of black pepper. Set aside.

4. Add the remaining 5 tablespoons olive oil to the pan, add the onion and garlic, and cook gently until softened but not browned. Add the tomato sauce, bring to a brisk simmer, and cook until the sauce has reduced by one-third. Add the basil, remove from the heat, and set aside.

5. Drop the pasta into the boiling water and cook until just al dente. Drain the pasta well, and toss into the pan with the sauce. Add half of the bread crumb mixture and toss to mix well.

6. Transfer the pasta to a warmed serving bowl. Sprinkle the remaining bread crumb mixture over the top, and serve immediately.

LINGUINE *with* MONKFISH, THYME *and* ZUCCHINI

Linguine colla Coda

Monkfish, one of my favorite fish, is not yet hip enough to be on the endangered species list, or even cost too much. It barbecues beautifully and does well in the oven, "roasted" like meat. And it is nearly impossible to overcook, so it stays moist and juicy.

MAKES 4 SERVINGS

¼ cup EXTRA-VIRGIN OLIVE OIL

1 medium RED ONION, finely chopped

1 medium ZUCCHINI, cut lengthwise in half and then into thin half-moons

2 teaspoons fresh THYME LEAVES

8 ounces MONKFISH FILLET, cut into ½-inch cubes

SALT and freshly ground BLACK PEPPER

1½ cups BASIC TOMATO SAUCE (page 71)

1 cup DRY WHITE WINE

1 pound LINGUINE

¼ cup finely chopped ITALIAN PARSLEY

1. Bring 6 quarts of water to a boil in a large pot, and add 2 tablespoons salt.

2. Meanwhile, in a 10- to 12-inch sauté pan, heat the olive oil over medium heat until almost smoking. Add the onion, zucchini, and thyme and sauté until the onion and zucchini are lightly browned and soft, 8 to 10 minutes.

3. Season the monkfish with salt and pepper, add to the pan, and toss until it is starting to whiten, about 1 minute. Add the tomato sauce and wine and bring to a boil. Lower the heat and simmer for 10 minutes.

4. Drop the linguine into the boiling water and cook until just al dente; drain.

5. Toss the pasta into the pan with monkfish, add the parsley, and toss over medium heat until well mixed. Transfer to a warmed serving bowl, and serve immediately.

BUCATINI *with* BABY OCTOPUS, WHITE BEANS *and* BROCCOLI

Bucatini con Polipetti

Most seafood and fish shops can sell you baby octopus. The frozen is actually preferred, as freezing renders it more tender in the final dish. The combination of the rich and creamy octopus with the king of cruciferous vegetables makes for a symphony on the palate.

MAKES 4 SERVINGS

4 cloves GARLIC, thinly sliced

¼ cup EXTRA-VIRGIN OLIVE OIL

1 teaspoon HOT RED PEPPER FLAKES

2 pounds BABY OCTOPUS, cleaned and cooked with a cork in boiling water for 45 minutes (see page 261)

1 cup small BROCCOLI FLORETS

SALT and freshly ground BLACK PEPPER

½ cup cooked CANNELLINI BEANS, rinsed and drained if canned

1 pound BUCATINI

¼ cup chopped ITALIAN PARSLEY

1 cup TOASTED BREAD CRUMBS

1. Bring 6 quarts of water to a boil in a large pot, and add 2 tablespoons salt.

2. Meanwhile, in a 10- to 12-inch sauté pan, combine the garlic and olive oil, set over medium heat, and cook until the garlic is light brown, about 4 minutes. Add the red pepper flakes, octopus, and broccoli and sauté until the broccoli is softened, 3 to 4 minutes. Season with salt and pepper, remove from the heat, and stir in the beans. Set aside.

3. Cook the bucatini in the boiling water until just al dente; drain.

4. Toss the pasta into the pan with the octopus mixture, return the pan to medium heat, and toss to mix for 30 seconds. Add the parsley and toss to mix well. Transfer the pasta to a warmed serving dish and serve immediately, with the bread crumbs on the side.

BUCATINI *with* SKATE SAUCE

Bucatini alla Razza

This is a variation on a traditional Roman dish, where they actually cook the pasta in the sauce. For maximum flavor, the broccoli should *not* be bright green and al dente, but hammered and gray green. Only then is it truly Roman.

MAKES 4 SERVINGS

¼ cup EXTRA-VIRGIN OLIVE OIL

2 cloves GARLIC, thinly sliced

2 tablespoons fresh MARJORAM LEAVES

2 pounds SKATE WING, skinned and removed from the bone (by your fishmonger), cut into 5 or 6 pieces

1 cup small BROCCOLI FLORETS

1 cup BASIC TOMATO SAUCE (page 71)

½ cup HOT WATER

1 pound BUCATINI

2 tablespoons ITALIAN PARSLEY, chiffonade

SALT and freshly ground BLACK PEPPER

1. In a 10- to 12-inch sauté pan, heat the olive oil over medium heat until hot. Add the garlic, marjoram, skate, and broccoli and cook, stirring frequently, until the skate is falling apart, about 10 minutes. Add the tomato sauce and water and bring to a boil, then reduce to a simmer and cook for 10 minutes. Remove from the heat and set aside.

2. Meanwhile, bring 6 quarts of water to a boil in a large pot, and add 2 tablespoons salt.

3. Cook the bucatini in the boiling water until just al dente; drain.

4. Add the pasta to the sauce, along with the parsley and salt and pepper to taste. Toss over high heat for 1 minute, then divide among warmed pasta bowls and serve immediately.

SPAGHETTI *alla* CARBONARA

A true carbonara has no cream, and it can be slightly tricky in its execution. The key is to toss and thoroughly mix the cooked pasta off the heat with the cheese, eggs, pepper, and pasta water, to create a creamy yet not overly thick sauce. I like to separate the eggs and present the individual egg yolks in nests of pasta; then each guest stirs the yolk into the pasta to cook it and form an even creamier sauce. Be sure to use the best-quality eggs you can get.

MAKES 4 SERVINGS

3 tablespoons EXTRA-VIRGIN OLIVE OIL

8 ounces GUANCIALE (page 186), PANCETTA, or good BACON

1 pound SPAGHETTI

1¼ cups freshly grated PARMIGIANO-REGGIANO

4 large EGGS, separated

Freshly ground BLACK PEPPER

1. Bring 6 quarts of water to a boil in a large pot, and add 2 tablespoons salt.

2. Meanwhile, combine the olive oil and guanciale in a 12- to 14-inch sauté pan set over medium heat, and cook until the guanciale has rendered its fat and is crispy and golden. Remove from the heat and set aside (do not drain the fat).

3. Cook the spaghetti in the boiling water until just al dente. Scoop out ¼ cup of the pasta cooking water and set aside. Drain the pasta.

4. Add the reserved pasta water to the pan with the guanciale, then toss in the pasta and heat, shaking the pan, for 1 minute. Remove from the heat, add 1 cup of the Parmigiano, the egg whites, and pepper to taste, and toss until thoroughly mixed.

5. Divide the pasta among four warmed serving bowls. Make a nest in the center of each one, and gently drop an egg yolk into each nest. Season the egg yolks with more pepper and sprinkle the remaining ¼ cup Parmigiano over the top. Serve immediately.

Photograph on page 167.

BUCATINI *with* BACON *and* TOMATO
Bucatini all'Amatriciana

This dish is named for the town of Amatrice, about an hour east of Rome, considered by many Italians to be birthplace of the best cooks on the peninsula. Many dishes at the heart of Roman cooking may indeed have actually started in the region to the east of Lazio, Abruzzo.

MAKES 4 SERVINGS

¼ cup EXTRA-VIRGIN OLIVE OIL

12 ounces thinly sliced GUANCIALE (page 186), PANCETTA, or good BACON

1 RED ONION, cut lengthwise in half and then into ¼-inch-thick half-moons

3 cloves GARLIC, sliced

1½ teaspoons HOT RED PEPPER FLAKES

2 cups BASIC TOMATO SAUCE (page 71)

1 pound BUCATINI

Freshly grated PECORINO ROMANO

1. Bring 6 quarts of water to a boil in a large pot, and add 2 tablespoons salt.

2. Meanwhile, in a 10- to 12-inch sauté pan, combine the olive oil, guanciale, onion, garlic, and red pepper flakes; set over low heat and cook until the onion is softened and the guanciale has rendered much of its fat, about 12 minutes.

3. Drain all but ¼ cup of the fat out of the pan (and set aside to cook your eggs for tomorrow's breakfast). Add the tomato sauce, turn up the heat, and bring to a boil, then lower the heat to a simmer and allow to bubble for 6 to 7 minutes.

4. While the sauce simmers, cook the bucatini in the boiling water for about a minute less than the package directions, until still very firm; drain.

5. Add the pasta to the simmering sauce and toss for about 1 minute to coat. Divide the pasta among four heated bowls and serve immediately, topped with freshly grated pecorino.

GUANCIALE

While bacon and most similar products come from the belly of a pig, guanciale is made by salt-curing and drying the meat from a hog's jowls (see page 186). Although the meat is leaner than traditional pancetta or bacon, it has a richer flavor. Making guanciale may require a little more planning than simply buying good-quality pancetta or bacon, but its richness of flavor, combined with a delicate porkiness, distinguishes guanciale from the others, making every dish that much more succulent. At Babbo, we use our homemade guanciale in various dishes, but nowhere is its fullness of flavor and porky richness more celebrated than in our Bucatini all'Amatriciana.

If you decide not to make your own guanciale, I suggest you order it from my dad at: www.salumicuredmeats.com.

SPAGHETTI *with* GARLIC, ONIONS *and* GUANCIALE

Spaghetti alla Gricia

This dish is similar to Bucatini all'Amatriciana (page 185), but there is no tomato sauce. Italians often feel that eating white food (*in bianco*) serves to settle an upset stomach and gives the internal organs a rest.

MAKES 4 SERVINGS

2 tablespoons EXTRA-VIRGIN OLIVE OIL

1 teaspoon HOT RED PEPPER FLAKES

8 ounces GUANCIALE, PANCETTA, or BACON, diced

1 small RED ONION, cut lengthwise in half and then into ¼-inch-thick half-moons

2 cloves GARLIC, thinly sliced

1 pound SPAGHETTI

½ cup freshly grated PECORINO-ROMANO, plus extra for serving

¼ cup ITALIAN PARSLEY LEAVES, for garnish

1. Bring 6 quarts of water to a boil in a large pot, and add 2 tablespoons salt.

2. Meanwhile, in a 10- to 12-inch sauté pan, heat the olive oil over low heat. Add the red pepper flakes and guanciale and cook slowly until the guanciale has rendered its fat and is crisp and golden brown, about 10 minutes. Add the onion and garlic and cook gently until golden brown, about 5 minutes longer. Remove from the heat.

3. Cook the spaghetti in the boiling water until just al dente; drain.

4. Add the pasta to the pan with the guanciale, add the pecorino, and toss over high heat for 1 minute. Divide among four warmed pasta bowls, garnish with parsley, and serve, with additional pecorino on the side.

GUANCIALE

MAKES 2 POUNDS

½ cup SUGAR

½ cup SALT

15 BLACK PEPPERCORNS

4 sprigs THYME, leaves only

2 pounds HOG JOWLS

1. Combine the sugar, salt, peppercorns, and thyme leaves in a small bowl. Put the hog jowls in a nonreactive casserole and coat with the mixture, rubbing gently. Cover and refrigerate for 5 to 7 days.

2. Remove the cheeks from the casserole and hang them, using butcher's twine, in the refrigerator for at least 3 weeks. The cheeks should be firm and dry, with a slight give. Slice and use like bacon or pancetta; refrigerated, it keeps for weeks.

"WEEDS" with SAUSAGE

Gramigne con Salsiccia

The "weeds" in question are kind of like a slightly unraveled phone cord, with a great texture that the sausage ragu just barely clings to, creating a very full mouthfeel. If you cannot find gramigne, use short fusilli or rotelle.

MAKES 6 SERVINGS

1 tablespoon EXTRA-VIRGIN OLIVE OIL

1 tablespoon UNSALTED BUTTER

1 large ONION, diced

1 pound ITALIAN PORK SAUSAGE, homemade (pages 368 to 370) or store-bought, removed from casings

6 tablespoons TOMATO PASTE

½ cup DRY WHITE WINE

½ cup WHOLE MILK

SALT and freshly ground BLACK PEPPER

1 pound GRAMIGNE, short FUSILLI, or ROTELLE

Freshly grated PARMIGIANO-REGGIANO, for serving

1. In a 12- to 14-inch sauté pan, heat the olive oil and butter over high heat. Add the onion and cook until soft and golden brown, 6 to 8 minutes. Add the sausage and cook, stirring occasionally and draining the excess fat if necessary, until the sausage is very brown and somewhat crisp, about 10 minutes.

2. Add the tomato paste and cook, stirring often, until a deep rust color, about 8 minutes. Add the wine and, cook, stirring frequently, until evaporated. Stir in the milk, season with salt and pepper to taste, and reduce the heat to a simmer. Cook for 15 minutes.

3. Meanwhile, bring 6 quarts of water to a boil in a large pot, and add 2 tablespoons salt. Drop the gramigne into the boiling water and cook until just al dente.

4. Scoop out about ¼ cup of the cooking water, and drain the pasta. Add the pasta to the sauce and toss over high heat for 1 minute to coat, adding a splash or two of the reserved pasta water if necessary to loosen the sauce.

5. Divide the pasta among six warmed pasta bowls, top with Parmigiano, and serve immediately.

BAKED PASTA *with* RICOTTA *and* HAM

Pasticcio di Maccheroni

Pasticcio is a full-on party for Easter—in one beautiful mess (*pasticcio*). No problem serving it *tièpido*, at room temperature.

MAKES 8 SERVINGS

3 tablespoons EXTRA-VIRGIN OLIVE OIL

1 pound ITALIAN COOKED HAM, preferably parmacotto, cut into ½-inch cubes

SALT and freshly ground BLACK PEPPER

1 small CARROT, cut into ¼-inch dice

1 ONION, cut into ¼-inch dice

1 rib CELERY, thinly sliced

1 cup DRY RED WINE

1½ cups BASIC TOMATO SAUCE (page 71)

1½ pounds ZITI

1 pound fresh RICOTTA

8 ounces CACIOTTA or HARD PROVOLONE, cut into small dice

½ cup freshly grated PARMIGIANO-REGGIANO

1. In a Dutch oven, heat the olive oil over high heat until smoking. Add the ham cubes and brown for 5 to 6 minutes. Season with salt and pepper. Add the carrot, onion, and celery and cook until the vegetables are golden brown, about 10 minutes.

2. Add the wine, bring to a boil, and cook until reduced by half, about 5 minutes. Add the tomato sauce and bring to a boil, then reduce the heat to low, cover the pan, and cook until the meat is just about falling apart, about 50 minutes. Transfer the meat to a large bowl. Keep the sauce warm.

3. Meanwhile, preheat the oven to 450°F. Bring 6 quarts of water to a boil in a large pot, and add 2 tablespoons salt.

4. Cook the ziti in the boiling water for 1 minute less than the package directions, until still very al dente. While the pasta is cooking, place the ricotta in a small bowl and stir in a ladle of the pasta cooking water to "melt" it.

5. Drain the pasta and add it to the bowl with the meat. Add the ricotta, caciotta, and tomato sauce and stir to combine.

6. Grease a round 12-inch deep pie dish or a casserole with olive oil. Place a ladleful of the cheese and sauce mixture in the bottom of the dish, followed by a layer of the pasta and meat mixture. Sprinkle 2 to 3 tablespoons of the Parmigiano over, then repeat with another layer of the cheese and sauce mixture, then pasta and meat, and Parmigano. Continue until all the ingredients are used up.

7. Bake for 25 minutes, until bubbling and heated through. Serve in warmed pasta bowls.

FRESH
PASTA

Homemade pasta exemplifies all of the best, the most delicious and emotional qualities of the matriarchal Italian kitchen. It can put a smile on anyone's face the moment it reaches the mouth.

There are countless versions of so-called fresh pasta in the land of the refrigerated cases of the grocery store, not many of them worth more than the water you cook it in. But it is not very difficult to make the real thing, nor does it take much time, and I can guarantee you that it will change the way you think about food, pasta, and life. Whenever I make tagliatelle, or pici, or ravioli at home, I make a double batch and freeze half. I am always building my freezer and pantry for "crisis" management, or maybe just to have a little bit of perfection on a day or night when we might have otherwise ordered in Chinese take-out food.

The unique texture of handmade pasta is the result of three factors: The first is shopping for the ingredients, and there are really only three of these. The first is flour. All-purpose flour works beautifully, and that is what I use, but Italian double zero ("00"), or even cake flour mixed half and half with all-purpose yields excellent results. Number two? Eggs. I always use organic ones, and you should too. The third ingredient is water, and we've all got it on tap back at the house. So the shopping, which is often the most difficult step, is easy.

The second factor is equipment. You can make any pasta dough on a board or a counter using only a fork. Then, to roll out the pasta you need a metal pasta machine, available at any gourmet "tool and trick" store—and at about fifty bucks, some of the best money you'll ever spend. The key is to knead the dough by hand for about 10 minutes and then to let it rest for a half hour before rolling it. This develops the gluten to the maximum and will create a noodle that has an almost al dente and chewy feel to it. Keep in mind that fresh pasta will never be as al dente as dried pasta, but, if made right and kneaded a bit longer, it will have an elusive yet perceptible and delightful feel in your mouth. I have actually modified my traditional egg pasta recipe for this book, adding another egg and omitting the oil. After years of experience, I now prefer a softer and more initially pliable dough that, with extended kneading, will result in the same texture as my original recipe for the purpose of feeding it into the machine, but will yield a livelier chew in the cooked noodle.

The third factor is, of all of these, the most essential and the easiest—the human touch. In an age where time is money, many people have forgotten the beauty of working with your own hands to make a meal. I am not suggesting everyone quit their job and spend the whole day cooking—that's my job. But to take the time every now and then, say once a week, to make some good food with your own hands for your friends and loved ones, that is something that may vastly improve the overall quality of life. And what easier and more satisfying dish to make than pasta? The following recipes are my favorites because they are not too difficult to shop for, not too difficult to make, and extremely easy to eat and enjoy.

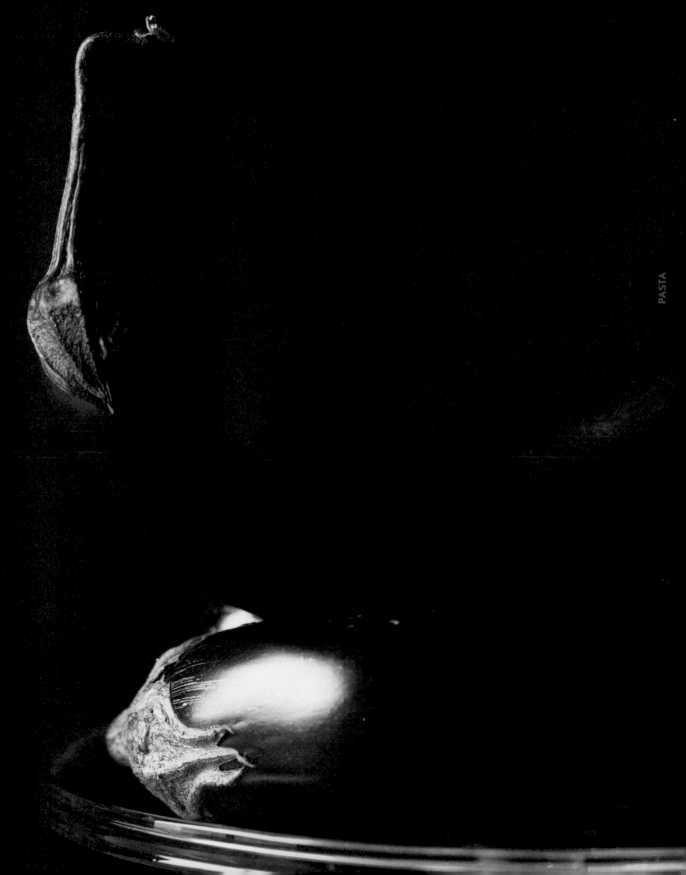

BASIC PASTA DOUGH

Pasta Sfoglia

MAKES ABOUT 1¼ POUNDS

3½ cups ALL-PURPOSE FLOUR, plus extra for kneading

5 large EGGS

1.   Mound the flour in the center of a large wooden board. Make a well in the center of the flour and add the eggs. Using a fork, beat the eggs together and then begin to incorporate the flour, starting with the inner rim of the well. As you expand the well, keep pushing the flour up to retain the well shape (do not worry if it looks messy). When half of the flour is incorporated, the dough will begin to come together. Start kneading the dough, using primarily the palms of your hands. Once the dough is a cohesive mass, set the dough aside and scrape up and discard any dried bits of dough.

2.   Lightly flour the board and continue kneading for 10 minutes, dusting the board with additional flour as necessary. The dough should be elastic and a little sticky. Wrap the dough in plastic wrap and allow to rest for 30 minutes at room temperature before using.

RED PASTA DOUGH

Add 2 tablespoons tomato paste along with the eggs.

BLACK PASTA DOUGH

Add 2 packets (2 tablespoons) squid ink along with the eggs.

BLACK PEPPER PASTA DOUGH

Add 2 tablespoons freshly ground black pepper along with the eggs.

GREEN PASTA DOUGH

Bring 3 quarts of water to a boil in a large pot, and add 1 tablespoon salt. Set up an ice bath next to the stove. Blanch 1 cup packed spinach leaves in the boiling water for 45 seconds, then remove with tongs or a slotted spoon and immediately plunge into the ice bath to cool for 2 minutes. Drain the spinach and squeeze dry in a kitchen towel, removing as much moisture as possible. Chop the spinach very fine and combine with the eggs in a small bowl. Stir well until as smooth as possible, then add to the well in the flour and proceed as directed.

ROLLING AND CUTTING FRESH PASTA

Always knead the dough for 10 full minutes—it may seem like a long time, but it is essential for a silken dough. Then wrap the dough in plastic wrap and allow it to rest. When you unwrap it, the dough will have softened—that is what you want, so do not be tempted to knead it into tension before rolling it out.

Cut the dough into 4 pieces, and wrap 3 of them again in plastic or just cover with a slightly damp kitchen towel. Flatten the piece of dough into a burger shape that is somewhat thicker in the middle and about ¼ inch thick at the edges. Set the rollers of the pasta machine to the widest setting. Dust the rollers with a bit of flour to be sure they are completely dry, and make sure there aren't any bits of dried dough from last time. Using one hand, crank the handle to start the rollers, and feed the dough in with your other hand. As the flattened piece of dough emerges, catch it gently with a flat palm so as not to tear it. Fold the dough in thirds, flatten it slightly with your palms, and roll it out again. Repeat this process 5 times, then set the rollers to the next-thinnest setting and repeat the folding and rolling process 6 times. At the third setting, repeat the process only 3 times, since the dough will be becoming more delicate. If the pasta sheet becomes too long to work with easily, cut it into 2 pieces and continue. As you work, dust the pasta sheet with a tiny pinch of flour only if it seems to be sticking—too much flour will dry out the dough. Roll the dough out through the progressively thinner settings, without folding it again, until you have reached the thinnest or next-to-the-thinnest setting, depending on the specific recipe. Do not pull the sheets of pasta out of the machine; rather, support each one lightly underneath as it emerges from the machine. Cut into strands or shapes and allow the cut pieces to dry for a bit on a board or floured work surface. (We used to hang them over all of the chairs in the kitchen and dining room and occasionally had to use our beds for a large batch.)

FETTUCCINE OR TAGLIATELLE: Use the wider cutter attachment of the pasta machine to cut the sheets into ½-inch-wide strips. Or, to cut the pasta by hand, cut each sheet of pasta into 10-inch lengths. Brush lightly with flour, then roll up the sheet, and, using a sharp knife, cut into ¼-inch-wide strips; unroll.

PAPPARDELLE: Cut the sheets of pasta into 5-inch lengths. Stack several sheets at a time and cut crosswise into ½-inch-wide strips.

TAGLIARINI: Use the narrow cutter on the pasta machine to cut the sheets of pasta into ⅛-inch-wide strips. Or, to cut the pasta by hand, follow the same procedure as for fettuccine, but cut into ⅛-inch-wide strips.

TIPO 00 FLOUR

In Italy, flour is classified as 1, 0, or 00, depending on how fine it is ground and how much of the bran and germ have been removed. *Doppio zero (tipo 00)* is the most highly refined and is talcum-powder soft. But the softness of this wheat flour does not, as is often assumed, indicate a low level of protein—a 00 flour can be either high or low protein, so 00 flour is suitable for making both pasta and bread, depending on the level of protein. High-protein 00 flours are often labeled "*panifiable*," or "bread ready." I use easy-to-find regular all-purpose flour for my egg pasta, because it produces toothsome noodles—noodles with attitude.

EGGLESS PASTA DOUGH FROM PUGLIA

Pasta di Semola

MAKES ABOUT 1¼ POUNDS

2 cups SEMOLINA FLOUR

2 cups ALL-PURPOSE FLOUR, plus extra for kneading

1 to 1¼ cups TEPID WATER

1. Mound the flours in the center of a large wooden board. Make a well in the center of the flour and add the water a little at a time, stirring with your hands until a dough forms. As you incorporate the water, keep pushing the flour up to retain the well shape (do not worry if it looks messy). When about half of the flour is incorporated, the dough will begin to come together in a shaggy mass. Start kneading the dough, using primarily the palms of your hands. You may need more or less water depending on the humidity in your kitchen. Once the dough is a cohesive mass, set the dough aside and scrape up and discard any dried bits.

2. Lightly flour the board and continue kneading for 10 more minutes, dusting the board with more flour when necessary. The dough should be elastic and a little sticky. Wrap the dough in plastic wrap and let rest for 30 minutes at room temperature before using.

MALLOREDDUS FROM SARDINIA

Malloreddus

MAKES ABOUT 1¼ POUNDS

4 cups SEMOLINA FLOUR

1½ cups WARM WATER

½ teaspoon SALT

1 teaspoon ground SAFFRON

1. Mound the semolina in the center of a large wooden board. Make a well in the center of the semolina and add the water, salt, and saffron. Using a fork, beat together the water, salt, and saffron, and then begin to incorporate the semolina, starting with the inner rim of the well. As you expand the well, keep pushing the flour up to retain the well shape. When half of the flour is incorporated, the dough will begin to come together. Start kneading the dough, using primarily the palms of your hands. Once you have a cohesive mass, set the dough aside and scrape up and discard any dried bits of dough.

2. Lightly flour the board and continue kneading for 10 more minutes, dusting the board with more flour when necessary. The dough should be elastic and a little sticky. Wrap the dough in plastic wrap and allow to rest for 30 minutes at room temperature before using.

3. Cut the pasta into 4 pieces. Roll each into a 1-inch cylinder, and cut into ¼-inch-thick pieces. Roll each piece down the back of a fork to give it the characteristic ridges, and set aside on a floured surface until ready to cook.

MALLOREDDUS *with* FENNEL SEEDS *and* TOMATOES

Malloreddus al Pomodoro

The cooking of Sardegna is mysterious and even counterintuitive on many levels for a peninsula-trained cook like myself. The first time I visited, the only dish I remember eating was grilled meat that had been stuffed inside a pig's bladder, and a whole lot of really good bread and cheese. The second time, I was in Olbia at one of the great restaurants of Italy, Ristorante Gallura, which in itself merits a trip, where I had these saffron cavatelli cousins. Malloreddus are classic to the cooking of Sardegna but rarely spotted in American restaurants.

MAKES 4 SERVINGS

¼ cup EXTRA-VIRGIN OLIVE OIL

4 SCALLIONS, thinly sliced

4 cloves GARLIC, thinly sliced

2 pounds TOMATOES, cut into ½-inch dice

1 tablespoon FENNEL SEEDS

1 tablespoon HOT RED PEPPER FLAKES

1 teaspoon SALT

1¼ pounds MALLOREDDUS (opposite)

½ cup freshly grated CROTONESE or other SEMI-AGED SHEEP'S MILK CHEESE

1. Bring 6 quarts of water to a boil in a large pot, and add 2 tablespoons salt.

2. Meanwhile, in a 10- to 12-inch sauté pan, heat the olive oil over medium heat until smoking. Add the scallions and garlic and sauté until light golden brown, about 1 minute. Add the tomatoes, fennel seeds, red pepper flakes, and salt and cook, stirring occasionally, until the tomatoes begin to break down, 7 to 8 minutes.

3. Cook the malloreddus in the boiling water until tender, 6 to 8 minutes; drain.

4. Toss the pasta into the pan with the tomatoes. Toss until well coated, and sprinkle with the cheese. Serve immediately.

TAGLIATELLE *with* SAUSAGE, BASIL *and* SUN-DRIED TOMATOES

Tagliatelle con Salsiccia

Sun-dried tomatoes may have become almost a cliché in the finer kitchens of Italy and America, but I still remember the first ones I tasted, carried back from Italy in 1974 by my dad, along with a couple of boxes of tortellini from Bologna. 'Twas a great, great day.

MAKES 4 SERVINGS

¼ cup EXTRA-VIRGIN OLIVE OIL

6 cloves GARLIC, thinly sliced

6 ounces SWEET ITALIAN SAUSAGE, casings removed and crumbled

6 SUN-DRIED TOMATO HALVES, thinly sliced

5 tablespoons TOMATO PASTE

¼ cup DRY WHITE WINE

1¼ pounds BASIC PASTA DOUGH (page 196), cut into tagliatelle

12 fresh BASIL LEAVES

1. Bring 6 quarts of water to a boil in a large pot, and add 2 tablespoons salt.

2. Meanwhile, in a 10- to 12-inch sauté pan, heat the olive oil over medium heat until hot. Add the garlic and cook until light golden brown, about 2 minutes. Add the sausage and sun-dried tomatoes and cook, stirring, until the sausage is cooked through, 7 to 8 minutes. Drain the fat from the pan, then stir in the tomato paste and wine and cook for 5 minutes. Remove from the heat and set aside.

3. Drop the tagliatelle into the boiling water and cook until tender, 1 to 2 minutes. Drain the pasta and add to the pan with the sun-dried tomatoes. Return to the heat, toss in the basil, and stir gently for about 30 seconds. Serve immediately.

TAGLIATELLE *with* MUSHROOM RAGU
Tagliatelle al Sugo di Funghi

Italians love mushrooms, and you will spot mushroom foragers under every tree and in every field in season. If you cannot find porcini, the crowning glory of all foragers, do try to find other wild mushrooms, which will make for a more interesting and authentic dish. In a pinch, though, you can use portobellos.

MAKES 4 SERVINGS

¼ cup EXTRA-VIRGIN OLIVE OIL

1 medium SPANISH ONION, finely chopped

12 ounces PORCINI or other WILD MUSHROOMS, trimmed if necessary and finely chopped (or substitute PORTOBELLO mushroom caps)

½ cup DRY RED WINE

1 cup BASIC TOMATO SAUCE (page 71)

1 tablespoon UNSALTED BUTTER

SALT and freshly ground BLACK PEPPER

1¼ pounds BASIC PASTA DOUGH (page 196), cut into tagliatelle

PARMIGIANO-REGGIANO, for grating

1. Bring 6 quarts of water to a boil in a large pot, and add 2 tablespoons salt.

2. Meanwhile, in a 10- to 12-inch sauté pan, heat the olive oil over high heat until smoking. Add the onion and cook until light golden brown, about 5 minutes. Add the mushrooms and cook until they have given off most of their water and it has evaporated, 8 to 10 minutes. Add the wine, tomato sauce, butter, and salt and pepper to taste, reduce the heat to medium, and cook until the consistency of a thick sauce, about 5 more minutes.

3. Cook the pasta in the boiling water until tender, 1 to 2 minutes. Drain the pasta, reserving about ¼ cup of the cooking water, and add to the ragu. Toss over high heat for 1 minute to coat the pasta, adding a few tablespoons of the reserved cooking water if necessary to loosen the sauce.

4. Divide the pasta evenly among four warmed pasta bowls, grate Parmigiano over, and serve immediately.

TAGLIATELLE PANCAKES

Pattone

In the unlikely event that there is pasta left over from the preceding recipe, this is the classic dish for the next day—or much, much later in the same Chianti-infused evening. (I suppose you could make a batch just for these pancakes.) This *pattone* was often served by my friend Bruno's mom, Adele, who would happily get up at 4 a.m. to make us breakfast after a night of dancing. She'd even put a bowl of sugar on the side, to make it feel like a breakfast dish.

MAKES 2 SERVINGS

2 servings TAGLIATELLE WITH MUSHROOM RAGU (page 201)

2 large EGGS, beaten

2 tablespoons FRESH BREAD CRUMBS

¼ cup freshly grated PARMIGIANO-REGGIANO

¼ cup EXTRA-VIRGIN OLIVE OIL

SALT and freshly ground BLACK PEPPER

Pinch of SUGAR (optional)

1. Place the pasta in a large bowl, add the eggs, bread crumbs, and Parmigiano, and mix in, by hand or with a wooden spoon. Take small handfuls of the pasta mixture and form it into lightly compressed nests about 4 inches in diameter and 1 inch thick; you should have 2 to 3 nests.

2. In a 10- to 12-inch heavy-bottomed skillet, heat the olive oil over high heat until it is almost smoking. Carefully place the nests in the hot oil and cook, turning once, until they are golden brown and the edges are crispy. Transfer to a plate lined with paper towels to drain and season with salt and pepper. Sprinkle with the sugar, if desired, and serve immediately.

FETTUCCINE *with* OYSTER MUSHROOMS,

SWEET GARLIC AND ARUGULA

Fettuccine Capricciose

The sweet garlic trick here is one worth remembering for other dishes where heightened sweetness from savory beginnings is desirable.

MAKES 4 SERVINGS

¼ cup EXTRA-VIRGIN OLIVE OIL

12 cloves GARLIC

½ cup CINZANO ROSSO or other sweet red vermouth

8 ounces OYSTER MUSHROOMS, trimmed

4 tablespoons UNSALTED BUTTER

SALT and freshly ground BLACK PEPPER

1¼ pounds BASIC PASTA DOUGH (page 196), cut into fettuccine

1 bunch ARUGULA, stemmed, washed, spun dry, and chopped

¼ cup freshly grated PECORINO CHEESE

1. Bring 6 quarts of water to a boil in a large pot, and add 2 tablespoons salt.

2. Meanwhile, in a 10- to 12-inch sauté pan, heat the olive oil over medium heat until almost smoking. Add the garlic and sauté until lightly browned, 6 to 7 minutes. Remove from the heat and add the Cinzano. Replace the pan on the burner, add the oyster mushrooms and butter, and bring to a boil. Boil until reduced by half. Season with salt and pepper. Remove from the heat and keep warm.

3. Drop the pasta into the boiling water and cook until tender, 1 to 2 minutes. Drain.

4. Add the hot pasta to the mushrooms and stir gently over medium heat for 1 minute to coat the noodles. Add the arugula and toss for 30 seconds, or until wilted. Transfer to a warmed serving dish, sprinkle with cheese, and serve immediately.

FETTUCCINE *with* LEMON,
HOT PEPPERS AND PECORINO ROMANO

Fettuccine al Limone

This is a variation on a dish I first tried at the Paradiso Perduto, a "lost paradise" on a back canal in Venice. I have made the very unItalian addition of jalapeños—and feel it works to great success. But then, I am a serious fan of the Mex-Italo cooking so often found at "family meals" in great Italian restaurant kitchens in the United States.

MAKES 4 SERVINGS

2 tablespoons EXTRA-VIRGIN OLIVE OIL

1 medium RED ONION, thinly sliced

1 teaspoon RED PEPPER FLAKES

3 JALAPEÑOS, seeded and cut into thin slivers

Zest and juice of 3 LEMONS

8 tablespoons (1 stick) UNSALTED BUTTER

SALT and freshly ground BLACK PEPPER

1¼ pounds BASIC PASTA DOUGH (page 196), cut into fettuccine

½ cup freshly grated PECORINO ROMANO

1. Bring 6 quarts of water to a boil in a large pot, and add 2 tablespoons salt.

2. Meanwhile, in a 10- to 12-inch skillet, heat the olive oil over medium heat until almost smoking. Add the onion and the red pepper flakes and sauté until softened and translucent, 8 to 10 minutes. Add the jalapeños and sauté for 1 minute. Add the lemon zest and juice, bring to a boil, and boil for 1 minute. Remove from the heat, stir in the butter, and season to taste with salt and pepper. Set aside.

3. Drop the pasta into the boiling water and cook until tender, 1 to 2 minutes. Drain.

4. Toss the hot pasta into the pan with the lemon mixture, return to medium heat, and mix well, stirring gently. Add the pecorino and toss quickly. Transfer to a warmed serving platter, and serve immediately.

FETTUCCINE ALFREDO

The true history of this twentieth-century pasta is uncertain, but it was probably invented during the golden age of the Cinecittà in Rome, specifically for American actors looking for some comfort food. The noodles have outlived most of the actors. To really tune up the presentation, you could buy a wheel of Parmigiano and request that they halve it at the cheese shop. Carefully eat nearly all of the cheese out of one of the halves, and use the resulting "bowl" for the cooked noodles.

MAKES 4 SERVINGS

1¼ pounds BASIC PASTA DOUGH (page 196), cut into fettuccine

8 tablespoons (1 stick) UNSALTED BUTTER, cut into ⅛-inch dice

¼ cup freshly grated PARMIGIANO-REGGIANO

SALT and freshly ground BLACK PEPPER

1. Bring 6 quarts of water to a boil in a large pot, and add 2 tablespoons salt. Cook the fettuccine in the boiling water until tender, 1 to 2 minutes. Drain, reserving about ¼ cup of the pasta water, and place in a large warmed bowl.

2. Add the butter and Parmigiano and toss until the butter and cheese have melted, adding a splash or two of the pasta cooking water if necessary to loosen the sauce. Season with salt and pepper to taste, and serve immediately.

GREEN MALTAGLIATI
WITH OVEN-DRIED TOMATOES, BASIL AND BLACK PEPPER MASCARPONE
Maltagliati con Pomodori Secchi e Mascarpone

Maltagliati, which translates as "poorly made," refers to the irregular shape of this pasta.

MAKES 6 SERVINGS

1¼ pounds GREEN PASTA DOUGH (page 196)

1 cup BASIC TOMATO SAUCE (page 71)

¼ cup OVEN-DRIED TOMATOES

6 ounces MASCARPONE

2 tablespoons freshly ground BLACK PEPPER

1 cup loosely packed fresh BASIL LEAVES

1. Bring 6 quarts of water to a boil in a large pot, and add 2 tablespoons salt.

2. Meanwhile, divide the pasta dough into 4 pieces. Roll each one out through the thinnest setting of a pasta machine and lay the sheets out on a work surface. Cut with a pizza cutter or a sharp knife into similar-sized irregularly shaped 3- to 4-inch pieces. Cover with slightly dampened kitchen towels.

3. Put the tomato sauce in a blender and blend until smooth. Transfer to a 10- to 12-inch sauté pan and bring to a simmer. Add the oven-dried tomatoes and return to a simmer, then remove from the heat and set aside.

4. In a food processor, blend the mascarpone and black pepper until well mixed and smooth, about 1 minute. Transfer to a small bowl and set aside.

5. Drop the pasta into boiling water and cook until tender, 1 to 2 minutes. Drain. Add the pasta to the pan with the tomato mixture, return to medium heat, and toss until hot, about 1 minute. Add the basil and toss for about 30 more seconds. Divide among warm serving dishes, dollop each with a tablespoon of the mascarpone mixture, and serve immediately.

OVEN-DRIED TOMATOES
MAKES 6 CUPS

4 pounds ripe PLUM TOMATOES

3 tablespoons KOSHER SALT

3 tablespoons SUGAR

1. Preheat the oven to 150°F.

2. Slice the tomatoes lengthwise in half and place cut side up on baking sheets. Combine the salt and sugar and sprinkle a little bit, about ½ teaspoon, over each tomato. Place in the oven and cook slowly for 10 hours (it works well to put the tomatoes in right before you go to bed and remove them in the morning). Allow to cool, then refrigerate.

BLACK SPAGHETTI *with* MUSSELS, CHILES *and* MINT

Maccheroni alla Chitarra

Maccheroni alla chitarra is a specialty from the Abruzzo region, made by rolling a sheet of pasta slightly thicker than normal (dime-and-a-half thick) and pressing it through a *chitarra*, a rectangular box strung lengthwise with steel wires, hence the name—they look very much  like the strings of a guitar or a zither. The result is long strands of pasta that are square in cross section. At one time, there wasn't a family in Abruzzo that didn't have a chitarra, but finding one outside Italy can be difficult, to say the least. Without a chitarra, the easiest way to shape up the square strands is to roll out the sheets of dough and let them dry for fifteen minutes on the counter, then roll up each sheet loosely and cut into noodles with a large knife.

MAKES 4 SERVINGS

1¼ pounds BLACK PASTA DOUGH (page 196)

¼ cup EXTRA-VIRGIN OLIVE OIL

1 medium RED ONION, cut into ⅛-inch-wide strips

2 pounds MUSSELS, preferably Prince Edward Island, scrubbed and debearded

¼ cup DRY WHITE WINE

1 tablespoon HOT RED PEPPER FLAKES

1 cup BASIC TOMATO SAUCE (page 71)

½ cup packed fresh MINT LEAVES

1.   Divide the dough into 4 pieces. Roll each one out through the next-to-the-thinnest setting on a pasta machine and lay out on a lightly floured surface. Press the sheets of pasta through a chitarra and set aside. (If you do not have a chitarra, follow the instructions in the headnote.)

2.   Bring 6 quarts of water to a boil in a large pot, and add 2 tablespoons salt.

3.   Meanwhile, in a 10- to 12-inch sauté pan, heat the olive oil over medium-high heat until smoking. Add the onion and cook until softened, about 3 minutes. Add the mussels, wine, and red pepper flakes, cover, and cook until the mussels have just opened, about 2 minutes.

4.   Add the tomato sauce to the mussels and bring to a boil.

5.   Meanwhile, drop the pasta into the boiling water and cook until tender, 1 to 2 minutes. Drain well and toss into the pan of mussels. Add the mint leaves, toss the pasta to coat, and serve immediately.

RED PAPPARDELLE *with* BACCALÀ, POTATOES *and* CHIVES

Pappardelle con Baccalà

The combination of potatoes, garlic, and salt cod is timeless across many cultures in the West. The red dough turns almost the color of saffron when it is cooked and makes this dish even more beautiful than it appears on the page.

MAKES 6 SERVINGS

¼ cup EXTRA-VIRGIN OLIVE OIL

2 cloves GARLIC, thinly sliced

1 large RUSSET POTATO, peeled and cut into ¼-inch cubes

8 ounces BACCALÀ, soaked for 3 days in cold water in the refrigerator (change the water daily), drained, and cut into ½-inch cubes

1 cup BASIC TOMATO SAUCE (page 71)

¼ cup DRY WHITE WINE

1¼ pounds RED PASTA DOUGH (page 196), cut into pappardelle

¼ cup snipped fresh CHIVES

HOT RED PEPPER FLAKES (optional)

1. Bring 6 quarts of water to a boil in a large pot, and add 2 tablespoons salt.

2. Meanwhile, in a 10- to 12-inch sauté pan, heat the olive oil over medium heat until almost smoking. Add the garlic and potato cubes and sauté until the potatoes are golden brown, 4 to 5 minutes. Add the salt cod, tomato sauce, and wine and bring to a boil. Lower the heat and simmer for 20 minutes.

3. Plunge the pasta into the boiling water and cook until tender, 1 to 2 minutes. Drain.

4. Toss the pasta into the pan with the salt cod mixture. Transfer to a heated serving dish, sprinkle with chives, and serve immediately, with hot pepper flakes on the side, if desired.

TAGLIATELLE *with* FRESH TUNA RAGU
Tagliatelle al Ragu di Tonno

Along the Adriatic Coast of Romagna, there is a tradition of soft wheat pasta dressed with seafood. This is an uptown version of an osteria classic, which would impose a canned oil-packed tuna onto a dry pasta such as spaghetti or penne.

MAKES 4 SERVINGS

¼ cup EXTRA-VIRGIN OLIVE OIL

1 large RED ONION, thinly sliced

2 cups BASIC TOMATO SAUCE (page 71)

1 teaspoon HOT RED PEPPER FLAKES

8 ounces SUSHI-GRADE TUNA, cut into ¼-inch cubes

1 teaspoon fresh ROSEMARY LEAVES

SALT

1¼ pounds BASIC PASTA DOUGH (page 196), cut into tagliatelle

¼ cup finely chopped ITALIAN PARSLEY

1. Bring 6 quarts of water to a boil in a large pot, and add 2 tablespoons salt.

2. Meanwhile, in a 10- to 12-inch sauté pan, heat 2 tablespoons of the olive oil over medium heat until almost smoking. Add the onion and cook until softened, 6 to 8 minutes. Add the tomato sauce and red pepper flakes and bring to a boil. Add the tuna and rosemary, return just to a boil, and remove from the heat. Season with salt to taste.

3. Drop the tagliatelle into the boiling water and cook until tender, 1 to 2 minutes. Drain.

4. Toss the pasta into the pan with the tuna sauce, set over medium-high heat, and stir gently to coat the noodles. Add the parsley and cook for 1 minute. Transfer to a warmed serving bowl and serve immediately.

GARGANELLI *with* DUCK RAGU
Garganelli al Ragu d'Anatra

This duck ragu is even good with plain old penne out of a box, but when enrobing the handmade penne variation referred to in hushed tones as *garganelli*, it is elevated to mythic status.

MAKES 4 SERVINGS

¼ cup EXTRA-VIRGIN OLIVE OIL

4 DUCK LEGS, skinned, cut apart at the joint, visible fat removed, rinsed, and patted dry

SALT and freshly ground BLACK PEPPER

1 medium SPANISH ONION, cut into ¼-inch dice

1 medium CARROT, finely chopped

2 cloves GARLIC, thinly sliced

1 rib CELERY, cut into ¼-inch dice

4 fresh SAGE LEAVES

2 cups DRY RED WINE, preferably Sangiovese

1 cup CHICKEN STOCK (page 125)

One 6-ounce can TOMATO PASTE

1¼ pounds BASIC PASTA DOUGH (page 196)

SEMOLINA or CORNMEAL, for dusting

PARMIGIANO-REGGIANO, for grating

1. In a Dutch oven, heat the oil over medium-high heat until almost smoking. Season the duck pieces with salt and pepper and cook, turning occasionally, until browned on all sides, 10 to 12 minutes. Transfer to a plate.

2. Add the onion, carrot, garlic, celery, and sage to the pot, reduce the heat to low, and cook until the vegetables are softened, 7 to 9 minutes. Add the wine, stock, and tomato paste, stir well, and bring to a boil. Add the duck, lower the heat, cover, and simmer for 1 hour.

3. Transfer the duck pieces to a plate (keep the sauce at a simmer). When cool enough to handle, pull all the meat off the bones, return the meat to the pot and simmer, uncovered, for 30 minutes, or until the sauce is quite thick. Season with salt and pepper, remove from the heat, and set aside.

4. Divide the pasta dough into 4 balls. Roll each ball out to the thinnest setting on a pasta machine, and lay out on a lightly floured work surface. Cut the pasta into 2-inch squares. One at a time, lay a thin dowel or a pencil diagonally across a bottom corner of each square, and roll up to form a quill, then slip the garganello off the dowel onto a baking sheet dusted with semolina. Cover with a damp towel.

5. Bring 6 quarts of water to a boil in a large pot, and add 2 tablespoons salt.

6. Meanwhile, transfer the ragu to a 10- to 12-inch sauté pan, and heat through over medium heat, stirring occasionally.

7. Drop the garganelli into the boiling water and cook until tender, 2 minutes. Drain the pasta, reserving ½ cup of the water, and add the pasta to the ragu. Toss over high heat for 2 minutes to coat, adding a splash of the pasta cooking water if necessary to loosen the sauce.

8. Divide the pasta among four bowls, grate Parmigiano over each, and serve immediately.

GREEN FETTUCCINE *with* CHICKEN LIVERS

Fettuccine Verdi ai Fegatini

Chicken livers and gizzards cause no squea-mishness among Italians; indeed, they would be perplexed to find anyone who was willing to eat a roast chicken but not its *regali* —which translates as "gifts." These are very inexpensive, they are an excellent source of protein, and, most important, they have a very rich, distinctive flavor.

MAKES 4 SERVINGS

2 ounces dried PORCINI

2 cups HOT WATER

2 tablespoons EXTRA-VIRGIN OLIVE OIL

2 ounces PANCETTA or 6 slices good BACON, diced

1 CARROT, finely chopped

1 ONION, cut into ¼-inch dice

1 clove GARLIC, crushed

8 ounces CHICKEN GIBLETS, chopped coarsely (ask your butcher to save you the giblets, or substitute additional chicken livers if necessary)

8 ounces CHICKEN LIVERS, coarsely chopped

2 tablespoons TOMATO PASTE

2 CLOVES

1 BAY LEAF

1 cup DRY WHITE WINE

2 SCALLIONS, finely chopped

1½ ounces sliced PROSCIUTTO DI PARMA, cut into ¼-inch dice

SALT and freshly ground BLACK PEPPER

1¼ pounds GREEN PASTA DOUGH (page 196), cut into fettuccine

½ cup freshly grated PECORINO ROMANO

1. In a small bowl, soak the dried mushrooms in the hot water for 10 minutes.

2. Lift out the mushrooms, reserving the liquid, and finely chop; set aside. Strain the liquid through a fine sieve and set aside.

3. In a 10- to 12-inch sauté pan, combine the olive oil and pancetta and cook over medium-low heat until the pancetta has rendered its fat. Add the carrot, onion, and garlic, increase the heat to high, and sauté until softened, about 3 minutes. Add the chicken giblets and livers and cook, stirring occasionally, until they are browned. Stir in the tomato paste, then add the cloves, bay leaf, and wine and bring to a boil. Reduce the heat and simmer for 30 minutes.

4. Remove the cloves and bay leaf. Add the scallions, prosciutto, and reserved porcini liquid and simmer for 10 more minutes. Season to taste with salt and pepper.

5. Meanwhile, bring 6 quarts of water to a boil in a large pot, and add 2 tablespoons salt. Add the pasta and cook until tender, 1 to 2 minutes. Drain.

6. Add the pasta to the pan with the sauce and toss over high heat for 1 minute. Divide evenly among four warmed pasta bowls, top with the pecorino, and serve immediately.

PICI *with* LAMB SAUCE
Pici col Sugo d'Agnello

These noodles have a splendid chew to them, the perfect foil for the lusty lamb ragu. If you do not have time to make the pasta, I recommend orecchiette or big rigatoni.

MAKES 4 SERVINGS

¼ cup EXTRA-VIRGIN OLIVE OIL

1 ONION, cut into ¼-inch dice

1 CARROT, finely chopped

4 ounces thinly sliced PANCETTA, finely diced

1 bunch BASIL, leaves only, finely chopped

1 pound boneless LAMB SHOULDER, cut into ½-inch chunks

SALT and freshly ground BLACK PEPPER

1 cup DRY WHITE WINE

1½ cups BASIC TOMATO SAUCE (page 71)

1¼ pounds EGGLESS PASTA DOUGH (page 198)

SEMOLINA or CORNMEAL, for dusting

1.   In a 10- to 12-inch deep sauté pan, heat the olive oil over high heat until almost smoking. Add the onion, carrot, pancetta, and basil, reduce the heat to medium-high, and cook until the pancetta has rendered its fat. Season the lamb with salt and pepper, add it to the pan, and cook, stirring occasionally, until browned on all sides.

2.   Add the wine and simmer for 5 minutes. Add the tomato sauce and bring to a boil, then lower the heat to a simmer and season with salt and pepper. Cover and simmer gently until the meat is tender, about 1 hour.

3.   Meanwhile, shape the pasta into golf ball–sized balls. One at a time, on a surface very lightly dusted with flour, roll each one into a rope ¼-inch thick and 16 to 18 inches long. Cut the ropes into 5- to 6-inch-long pieces and set aside on a baking sheet dusted with semolina.

4.   Bring 6 quarts of water to boil in a large pot, and add 2 tablespoons salt.

5.   Drop the pasta into the boiling water and cook until tender, 7 to 8 minutes. Drain the pasta, toss into the pan with the sauce, and stir gently over medium-high heat for 1 minute. Divide evenly among four warmed pasta bowls, and serve.

PAPPARDELLE *with* BOAR RAGU
Pappardelle al Ragu di Cinghiale

This is Tuscan through and through. What's important here is to sauce the wide noodles with a pauper's touch. In Toscana they are particularly miserly with their sauce-to-noodle ratio, which is why it tastes better there—austere, in a brilliant sort of way.

MAKES 6 SERVINGS

¼ cup EXTRA-VIRGIN OLIVE OIL

½ medium SPANISH ONION, cut into ⅛-inch dice

½ small CARROT, cut into ⅛-inch dice

½ rib CELERY, cut into ⅛-inch-thick slices

1 teaspoon ANCHOVY PASTE

1 tablespoon HOT RED PEPPER FLAKES

1 teaspoon chopped fresh ROSEMARY

1 cup DRY RED WINE

1 cup BASIC TOMATO SAUCE (page 71)

1 pound BONELESS BOAR, LAMB, or VENISON shoulder, cut into ½-inch cubes

SALT and freshly ground BLACK PEPPER

1¼ pounds BASIC PASTA DOUGH (page 196), cut into pappardelle

1. In a heavy 6- to 8-quart pot, heat the olive oil over high heat until smoking. Add the onion, carrot, and celery and cook until softened and lightly browned, 8 to 10 minutes. Add the anchovy paste, red pepper flakes, rosemary, wine, and tomato sauce and bring to a boil.

2. Season the meat with salt and pepper and drop it into the tomato sauce. Return to a boil, then lower the heat to a simmer and cook until the meat falls apart with the poke of a fork, about 1½ hours. Remove from the heat and allow to cool for 10 minutes.

3. Transfer the stew about ½ cup at a time to a food processor and pulse just until the consistency of a thick sauce. Pour into a saucepan, check for seasoning, and set aside.

4. Bring 6 quarts of water to a boil in a large pot, and add 2 tablespoons salt. Meanwhile, bring the ragu to a gentle boil.

5. Drop the pappardelle into the boiling water and cook until tender, 1 to 2 minutes. Drain.

6. Add the pasta to the ragu and toss gently to coat. Transfer to a warmed serving bowl and serve immediately.

BASIC GNOCCHI
Gnocchi di Patate

4 SERVINGS AS A MAIN COURSE,
8 SERVINGS AS AN APPETIZER

3 pounds RUSSET POTATOES

2 cups ALL-PURPOSE FLOUR

1 extra-large EGG

1 teaspoon KOSHER SALT

½ cup CANOLA OIL

1. Put the potatoes in a large pot, add water to cover, and bring to a boil. Reduce the heat and cook at a low boil until the potatoes are tender, about 45 minutes; drain.

2. While they are still warm, peel the potatoes, then pass them through a vegetable mill onto a clean work surface.

3. Bring 6 quarts of water to a boil in a large pot, and add 1 tablespoon salt. Set up an ice bath nearby. Make a well in the center of the potatoes, and sprinkle them all over with the flour. Break the egg into the center of the well, add the salt, and, using a fork, blend the egg and salt together. Using the fork, begin to incorporate the flour and potatoes as if you were making pasta. Once the dough begins to come together, begin kneading it gently until it forms a ball. Knead gently for another 4 minutes, or until the dough is dry to the touch.

4. Divide the dough into 6 balls. Roll one ball into a rope ¾ inch in diameter, and cut it into 1-inch pieces. Roll each piece down the back of a fork to create the characteristic ridges. Drop the gnocchi into the boiling water and cook until they float to the surface, about 1 minute. Use a slotted spoon to transfer the gnocchi to the ice bath. Repeat with the remaining dough, replenishing the ice as necessary.

5. When all the gnocchi have been cooked and cooled in the ice bath, drain them and transfer to a bowl. Toss with the oil. The gnocchi can be stored, covered, in the refrigerator for up to 48 hours.

ROMAN-STYLE GNOCCHI

Gnocchi alla Romana

These golden coins are one of three variations on gnocchi in my world, the other two being potato, *Gnocchi di Patate* (opposite), and ricotta, *Gnocchi di Ricotta* (page 226). All three are excellent when executed perfectly, heinous any other way.

MAKES 4 SERVINGS

3 cups WHOLE MILK

1 teaspoon SALT

8 tablespoons (1 stick) UNSALTED BUTTER

1 cup SEMOLINA FLOUR

1 cup freshly grated PARMIGIANO-REGGIANO

4 large EGG YOLKS

4 ounces TALEGGIO or other fragrant SOFT CHEESE (even Brie), cut into dice

1. Butter a rimmed baking sheet.
2. In a 3- to 4-quart saucepan, combine the milk, salt, and 6 tablespoons of the butter and bring to just under a boil, stirring to melt the butter. Pour in the semolina in a thin stream, whisking vigorously, and cook for about a minute, switching to a wooden spoon as the semolina begins to thicken. Remove from the heat and stir in ½ cup of the Parmigiano and the egg yolks, mixing well. Pour the semolina onto the buttered baking sheet and spread evenly to a thickness of ½ inch. Allow to cool.
3. Preheat the oven to 425°F.
4. Butter a 9-by-12-inch baking dish with a tablespoon of the remaining butter. Using a cookie cutter or a glass, cut 3-inch rounds out of the semolina. Arrange them in the buttered baking dish, overlapping them slightly. Sprinkle with the remaining ½ cup Parmigiano, scatter the Taleggio over the top, and dot with the remaining tablespoon of butter.
5. Bake for 15 to 20 minutes, until the top is light golden brown. Serve immediately.

GNOCCHI *with* FRESH TOMATOES,
GREEN OLIVES AND SMOKED MOZZARELLA
Gnocchi al Pizzaiolo

These are the gnocchi of my childhood, but we almost always ate them with an oxtail ragu (we lived to chew on the little "hubcap" bones on the sides of the pinwheels of the oxtail bones). This is a much quicker and lighter recipe, one that your friends will want to eat. My friends used to think we were the odd ones on the block, they who ate frozen dinners in front of the TV.

4 SERVINGS AS A MAIN COURSE,

8 SERVINGS AS AN APPETIZER

1 pound PLUM TOMATOES

6 tablespoons EXTRA-VIRGIN OLIVE OIL

2 cloves GARLIC, thinly sliced

½ cup GREEN OLIVES, such as Picholine, pitted

1 BASIC GNOCCHI (page 222)

4 ounces smoked fresh MOZZARELLA, cut into ¼-inch cubes

2 tablespoons fresh MARJORAM LEAVES

SALT and freshly ground BLACK PEPPER

1. Bring 6 quarts of water to a boil in a large pot, and add 2 tablespoons salt.

2. Meanwhile, core the tomatoes and chop them into ¼-inch cubes, reserving all the juices.

3. In a 10- to 12-inch sauté pan, heat the olive oil over medium-high heat until smoking. Add the garlic and cook until light golden brown, about 30 seconds. Add the tomatoes and their juices and cook until softened, about 2 minutes. Add the olives and remove from the heat.

4. Drop the gnocchi into the boiling water and cook until they float to the surface, about 3 minutes. Drain.

5. Carefully add the gnocchi to the pan with the tomato mixture. Return to the heat and toss gently until bubbling. Add the mozzarella and marjoram and season with salt and pepper. Transfer to a warmed serving dish, and serve immediately.

RICOTTA GNOCCHI *with* SAUSAGE *and* FENNEL

Gnocchi di Ricotta con Salsiccia e Finocchi

This is definitely an elaborate recipe, but the payoff is huge when you realize the gnocchi you are serving in your home are the same gnocchi we serve at Lupa Osteria in Greenwich Village. Feel the City of Rome!

MAKES 6 SERVINGS

GNOCCHI

1½ pounds fresh GOAT'S MILK RICOTTA, preferably Coach Farm, or regular ricotta

1 cup UNBLEACHED ALL-PURPOSE FLOUR, plus more as needed

2 large EGGS, beaten

1 tablespoon chopped ITALIAN PARSLEY

1 teaspoon SALT

½ teaspoon freshly ground BLACK PEPPER

¼ teaspoon freshly grated NUTMEG

OLIVE OIL

2 pounds ITALIAN SAUSAGE, homemade (pages 368 to 370) or store-bought, removed from casings and crumbled

1 tablespoon FENNEL SEEDS, toasted and finely ground in a spice grinder or mortar and pestle

1 tablespoon HOT RED PEPPER FLAKES

1 RED ONION, finely chopped

1 FENNEL BULB, trimmed, cored, and finely chopped

1 CARROT, finely diced

1 rib CELERY, finely diced

4 cloves GARLIC, thinly sliced

2 cups BASIC TOMATO SAUCE (page 71)

SALT and freshly ground BLACK PEPPER

Freshly grated PECORINO ROMANO

1. Put the ricotta in a fine sieve set over a bowl, cover with plastic wrap, and refrigerate for at least 8 hours, or overnight, to drain. The cheese will become firmer and drier.

2. To make the gnocchi, in a medium bowl combine the drained ricotta, flour, eggs, parsley, salt, pepper, and nutmeg and stir together gently until a soft dough forms. Add a little more flour if the dough is sticky when poked with a fingertip.

3. Dust your hands with flour and shape the dough into balls, using about 2 tablespoons dough for each one. Place the gnocchi on a baking sheet lined with a lightly floured kitchen towel.

4. Meanwhile, bring 6 quarts of water to a boil in a large pot, and add 2 tablespoons salt. Set up an ice bath next to the stovetop.

5. Gently slip only as many gnocchi at a time as will float freely into the boiling water, stirring gently with a wooden spoon to separate them, and cook until they rise to the surface, about 7 minutes. Test one for doneness by cutting into the center; it should be the same color and consistency all the way through. Scoop them out of the pot with a wire skimmer as soon as they are cooked and transfer to the ice bath.

As soon as the gnocchi are cooled, drain and transfer to an airtight container. Toss with olive oil to coat and refrigerate until ready to cook.

6. In a heavy-bottomed 10- to 12-inch sauté pan, cook the sausage over high heat, stirring occasionally, until it begins to brown, about 15 minutes. Using a slotted spoon, transfer the sausage to a plate. Add the fennel seeds, red pepper flakes, onion, fennel, carrot, celery, and garlic to the pan and cook until the vegetables are well browned, about 10 minutes.

7. Return the sausage to the pan, add the tomato sauce, and bring to a simmer. Simmer until the vegetables are very tender and the sauce has thickened, about 30 minutes. Season well with salt and pepper, and remove from the heat.

8. Meanwhile, bring 6 quarts of water to a boil in a large pot, and add 2 tablespoons salt. Add the gnocchi to the boiling water, and cook until they float to the top. Drain.

9. Add the gnocchi to the pan with the sauce, return to medium-high heat, and toss gently for about 1 minute to coat. Transfer to a warmed serving bowl, top with pecorino, and serve immediately.

SAUSAGE

Italian sausage, usually made of ground pork, is either hot (flavored with chile pepper) or sweet (flavored with fennel seeds and maybe some anise seeds). At its most basic, a sausage is ground meat, fat, salt and other seasonings, and preservatives packed into a casing. A renewed American interest in sausage making has led to a variety of flavor and meat combinations available fresh, partially cooked, or frozen in many markets. But even in grocery stores, large ones at least, there is always a big shiny-clean grinder in the butcher section, and I rarely see them being used. Why not give your butcher the chance to use his equipment? Generally speaking, a butcher is a kindhearted and helpful person who loves the idea that you might be making some personalized meat products and will be happy to grind to your specifications (and would no doubt love a taste of your final results!). By making your own sausage, you will not only gain a basic understanding of meat and salt and spice,

 but in the larger picture, you will increase the quality of your meals, and life in general.

BUTTERNUT SQUASH TORTELLI

Tortelli di Zucca

This pasta is from Mantua, where many of the savory dishes have a sweetish component to them. When we serve the pasta, we grate an amaretti cookie over it instead of cheese—and the crowd goes wild.

MAKES 4 SERVINGS

1 pound BUTTERNUT SQUASH

2 large EGGS

1¼ cups freshly grated PARMIGIANO-REGGIANO

Generous grating of NUTMEG

SALT and freshly ground BLACK PEPPER

1¼ pounds BASIC PASTA DOUGH (page 196)

8 tablespoons (1 stick) UNSALTED BUTTER

8 fresh SAGE LEAVES

4 AMARETTI

1. Preheat the oven to 350°F.
2. Cut the squash in half and remove the seeds. Place cut side down on a baking sheet and bake for 25 to 35 minutes, or until very soft. Let cool, then scoop the flesh from the skin.
3. In a large bowl, combine the squash, eggs, 1 cup of the Parmigiano, the nutmeg, and salt and pepper to taste, and mix well. Set aside.
4. To make the tortelli, divide the dough into 4 pieces. Roll each one out through the thinnest setting on a pasta machine, and lay the sheets on a lightly floured surface. Cut each sheet into 5-inch squares. Place a generous tablespoon of the squash mixture in the center of each square, fold the dough over to form a triangle, and press the edges together to seal. Then bring the two bottom points together, overlapping them slightly, and pinch to seal. Transfer the tortelli to a baking sheet dusted with flour.
5. Bring 6 quarts of water to a boil in a large pot, and add 2 tablespoons salt.
6. Meanwhile, in a 12-inch sauté pan, heat the butter until it foams and then subsides. Keep warm over very low heat.
7. Drop the tortelli into the boiling water and cook until tender, 2 to 3 minutes. Drain the pasta, reserving about ¼ cup of the cooking water, and add the pasta to the pan with the butter. Add a splash of the pasta water and the sage leaves and toss over high heat for 1 minute to coat the pasta and emulsify the sauce.
8. Divide the pasta evenly among four warmed pasta bowls, sprinkle with the remaining ¼ cup Parmigiano, and serve immediately. Grate an amaretti cookie over each plate at the table.

TORTELLONI *with* SAGE BUTTER
Tortelloni con Burro e Salvia

Emilia-Romagna's is the most respected and elaborate cooking in all of Italy, and this dish, along with lasagne bolognese and tortellini in brodo, forms the magnificent triumvirate and crown jewel in Emilia's crown. It may be difficult to believe that such a simple dish could be the calling card for such a complex "cucina," but taste . . . and then believe.

MAKES 6 SERVINGS

1¼ pounds PASTA DOUGH (page 196)

8 ounces fresh SHEEP'S MILK or COW'S MILK RICOTTA

1½ cups freshly grated PARMIGIANO-REGGIANO

2 large EGGS, lightly beaten

½ teaspoon freshly grated NUTMEG

¼ cup finely chopped ITALIAN PARSLEY

SALT and freshly ground BLACK PEPPER

4 tablespoons UNSALTED BUTTER

8 fresh SAGE LEAVES

1. Divide the pasta into 4 pieces. Roll each one out through the thinnest setting of a pasta machine, lay the sheets on a lightly floured work surface, and cover with a damp kitchen towel.

2. To make the filling, in a large bowl, combine the ricotta, 1 cup of the Parmigiano, the eggs, nutmeg, and parsley and mix until thoroughly blended. Season with salt and pepper. Set aside.

3. To make the tortelloni, cut the pasta into 2½- to 3-inch squares, cutting only 4 or so at a time so that the pasta doesn't dry out while you assemble the tortelloni. Place a generous teaspoon of the filling in the center of each square, fold the dough over to form a triangle, and press the edges together to seal. Then bring the two bottom points together, overlapping them slightly, and pinch together to seal. Transfer the tortellini to a baking sheet lined with a kitchen towel.

4. Bring 6 quarts of water to a boil in a large pot, and add 2 tablespoons salt.

5. Meanwhile, in a 12-inch sauté pan, melt the butter with the sage leaves. Set aside.

6. Drop the pasta into the boiling water, lower the heat to a brisk simmer, and cook until tender, 3 to 4 minutes. Turn off the heat and, using a slotted spoon or spider, remove the tortelloni from the water, draining well, and place in the pan with the butter and sage. Toss to coat, then add the remaining ½ cup Parmigiano and toss gently over medium heat until the pasta is well coated. Transfer to a warmed serving bowl, and serve immediately.

RADICCHIO TORTELLONI *with* PARMIGIANO CREAM

Tortelloni di Treviso con Fonduta di Parmigiano

Bitter Treviso radicchio works brilliant magic against the natural sweetness of the Parmigiano and the balsamic vinegar. The addition of fonduta may seem like gilding the lily, but this dish is definitely not for everyday eating.

MAKES 8 SERVINGS

¼ cup EXTRA-VIRGIN OLIVE OIL

1 medium RED ONION, cut into ¼-inch dice

4 heads RADICCHIO DI TREVISO, chopped into ¼-inch pieces, rinsed, and spun dry

1 cup RICOTTA

1 cup freshly grated PARMIGIANO-REGGIANO

½ cup finely chopped ITALIAN PARSLEY

1 tablespoon BALSAMIC VINEGAR

SALT and freshly ground BLACK PEPPER

1¼ pounds BASIC PASTA DOUGH (page 196)

½ cup HEAVY CREAM

2 large EGG YOLKS

¼ teaspoon freshly grated NUTMEG

8 tablespoons (1 stick) UNSALTED BUTTER, cut into 8 pieces

1. To make the filling, in a 10- to 12-inch sauté pan, heat the olive oil over medium-high heat until smoking. Add the onion and cook until softened and lightly browned, 6 to 7 minutes. Add all but ¼ cup of the radicchio and cook, tossing occasionally, until very soft, 6 to 7 more minutes. Transfer to a medium bowl and allow to cool.

2. Add the ricotta, ½ cup of the Parmigiano, the parsley, vinegar, and salt and pepper to taste to the radicchio mixture and mix well.

3. Divide the pasta into 4 pieces. Roll each one out through the thinnest setting on a pasta machine and lay the sheets out on a lightly floured surface.

4. To make the tortelloni, cut the pasta into 4-inch squares, cutting only 4 or so at a time so the pasta doesn't dry out. Place 1 tablespoon of the filling in the center of each pasta square, fold the dough over to form a triangle, and press the edges together to seal. Then fold the two bottom points together, overlapping them slightly, and pinch to seal. Transfer the tortelloni to a baking sheet lined with a kitchen towel.

5. Bring 6 quarts of water to a boil in a large pot, and add 2 tablespoons salt. Drop the tortelloni into the boiling water, lower the heat to a brisk high simmer, and cook until tender, 3 to 4 minutes.

6. Meanwhile, to make the fonduta, bring the cream to a boil in a 1-quart saucepan. Remove from the heat, add the remaining ½ cup Parmigiano, the egg yolks, and nutmeg and stir until thoroughly blended.

7. Drain the tortelloni, transfer to a 10- to 12-inch sauté pan, and add the butter and reserved ¼ cup radicchio. Simmer gently over low heat, tossing gently to coat the pasta. Place 3 tortelloni on each plate, spoon about 2 tablespoons fonduta over the pasta, and serve.

GOAT CHEESE *and* SCALLION RAVIOLI
WITH BLACK OLIVE BUTTER
Ravioli di Caprino con Burro di Oliva

One thing that really makes me happy is a well-stuffed raviolo, one in which the stuffing is soft and runny and can barely contain itself when sliced into, with a sauce that is just sufficient to complement the little package but not overwhelm or challenge it. These are that type of ravioli.

MAKES 6 SERVINGS

1¼ pounds GREEN PASTA DOUGH (page 196)

FILLING

2 cups fresh SOFT GOAT CHEESE (about 1 pound), preferably Coach Farm

¼ cup freshly grated PECORINO ROMANO

½ cup EXTRA-VIRGIN OLIVE OIL

1 extra-large EGG, lightly beaten

6 SCALLIONS, thinly sliced

Pinch of freshly grated NUTMEG

SALT and freshly ground BLACK PEPPER

SAUCE

6 tablespoons UNSALTED BUTTER

2 tablespoons OLIVE PASTE

¼ cup freshly grated PECORINO ROMANO

1. Divide the pasta dough into 4 pieces. Roll each piece through the thinnest setting on a pasta machine and lay the sheets on a lightly floured surface. Cut each sheet into twelve 3-inch squares. Cover with a towel.

2. To make the filling, combine the goat cheese, pecorino, olive oil, egg, scallions, nutmeg, and salt and pepper to taste in a large bowl and mix until well blended.

3. To assemble the ravioli, place 1 scant tablespoon filling in the center of each pasta square. Fold two opposite corners together to form a triangular pillow, gently pressing out any air pockets, then press the edges together to seal; if the pasta is a little dry, moisten the edges with a little water to help them adhere. Transfer to a lightly floured work surface.

4. Bring 6 quarts of water to a boil in a large pot, and add 2 tablespoons salt.

5. Meanwhile, to make the sauce, combine the butter and olive paste in a 12-inch sauté pan and heat over medium heat, stirring, until the butter is just starting to bubble. Remove from the heat.

6. Gently drop the ravioli into the boiling water, reduce the heat to a low boil, and cook until the pasta is tender, 3 to 4 minutes. Remove from the water with a slotted spoon or a skimmer, draining well, and place in the pan with the sauce. Simmer for 1 minute over low heat.

7. Transfer the ravioli to a warmed serving platter, sprinkle with the pecorino, and serve immediately.

TORTELLINI *in* BROTH
Tortellini alla Bolognese

Preparing this dish is truly a labor of love, and one that benefits from a couple of helping hands, to boot. But one bite of these on a special Sunday lunch or dinner, and your privileged guests will call the Pope to have you canonized, or excommunicated, or whatever you want. This is the food that empowers a cook. This is all that is good about the Italian family structure. This is tradition and love in one simple bowl of pasta and broth. Can you tell I have lived near Bologna?

MAKES 6 SERVINGS

BRODO

1 pound BEEF SCRAPS, or 1 pound BEEF CHUCK, cut into chunks

1 pound BEEF or VEAL BONES, cut into ½-inch cubes (have the butcher do this)

One 2½- to 3-pound CHICKEN, cut into 6 pieces

1 ONION, coarsely chopped

1 CARROT, coarsely chopped

1 rib CELERY, coarsely chopped

10 to 12 quarts COLD WATER

FILLING

4 tablespoons UNSALTED BUTTER

6 ounces GROUND TURKEY

6 ounces GROUND VEAL

6 ounces GROUND BONELESS PORK SHOULDER

6 ounces PROSCIUTTO, finely diced

6 ounces MORTADELLA, finely diced

1 large EGG, beaten

2 cups freshly grated PARMIGIANO-REGGIANO

¼ teaspoon freshly grated NUTMEG, or to taste

SALT and freshly ground BLACK PEPPER

1¼ pounds BASIC PASTA DOUGH (page 196)

Freshly grated PARMIGIANO-REGGIANO

1.   To make the broth, combine the beef, bones, chicken, onion, carrot, and celery in a large stockpot, add enough water to cover, and very slowly bring almost to a boil. Reduce the heat to a simmer and simmer gently for 4 hours, skimming off the foam and fat that rises to the surface.

2.   While the broth is simmering, make the filling: In a small Dutch oven or a large heavy-bottomed skillet, heat the butter over medium-high heat until it foams and subsides. Add the turkey, veal, and pork shoulder and cook, stirring occasionally, until the meat is well browned but still juicy, about 20 minutes. Add the prosciutto and mortadella, lower the heat to medium, and cook, stirring occasionally, for 20 minutes longer. Remove from the heat and allow to cool.

3.   Strain the broth through a sieve, then strain through a cheesecloth-lined sieve into a large saucepan, and allow to cool. (The broth

can be made ahead and refrigerated for up to 3 days.)

4. Add the egg and Parmigiano to the filling mixture and mix well. Season with the nutmeg and salt and pepper to taste. Cover and refrigerate until ready to use.

5. To make the tortellini, divide the pasta dough into 4 portions. Roll out each one through the thinnest setting on a pasta machine, and lay the sheets on a lightly floured surface. Working with 1 sheet at a time, cut into 2-inch squares. Place 1 teaspoon of the tortellini filling in the center of each square, fold two opposite corners together to form a triangle, and press the edges together firmly to seal. Bring the two bottom points of the triangle together, overlapping then slightly, and press to seal. Transfer the tortellini to a baking sheet dusted with flour and cover with a damp towel.

6. In a large pot, bring the brodo to a boil, and season with salt and pepper. Drop the tortellini into the broth and cook until tender, 3 to 4 minutes.

7. With a slotted spoon, transfer the tortellini to heated pasta bowls. Ladle some of the broth into each bowl and serve immediately, topped with Parmigiano.

TWO TOWERS IN BOLOGNA

The most instantly recognizable symbols of Bologna, the Due Torri, Asinelli and Garisenda, were built in the center city during the Middle Ages as a sign of wealth and prestige. At one time, there were more than two hundred towers marking the skyline of Bologna, all built by individual aristocratic families as a way of flaunting their wealth. Today, only the two remain and only the taller one, Asinelli, can be climbed. The thirteenth-century tower is 318 feet high, and the climb provides a spectacular view of the city's terra-cotta–tiled rooftops. The early proliferation of the Bolognese towers prompted a classic fourteenth-century toast, "You can build it as tall as you'd like, but you build it from our ground," a precursor of the leftist tendencies for which Bologna continues to be famous.

PANSOTTI *with* WALNUT SAUCE

Pansotti con Salsa di Noci

The simple and clean taste of zucchini is elevated to supreme heights in this filling dish—especially when mixed with the crazy walnut and bread crumb *condimento*.

MAKES 4 SERVINGS

¼ cup plus 3 tablespoons EXTRA-VIRGIN OLIVE OIL

½ medium RED ONION, finely chopped

4 cloves GARLIC, thinly sliced

1 medium ZUCCHINI, sliced into ⅟₁₆-inch-thick rounds

1 bunch OREGANO, leaves only

½ cup TOASTED BREAD CRUMBS

1 cup roughly chopped WALNUTS

1 tablespoon HOT RED PEPPER FLAKES

1 large EGG

½ cup RICOTTA

¾ cup freshly grated PECORINO ROMANO

½ teaspoon freshly grated NUTMEG

¼ cup finely chopped ITALIAN PARSLEY

SALT and freshly ground BLACK PEPPER

1¼ pounds BASIC PASTA DOUGH (page 196)

1. In a 10- to 12-inch sauté pan, heat 3 tablespoons of the olive oil over medium heat until smoking. Add the onion and half the garlic and cook until softened and lightly browned, 8 to 10 minutes. Add the zucchini and oregano and cook until the zucchini is very soft, 3 to 4 minutes. Remove from the heat and allow to cool.

2. In another large sauté pan, heat the remaining ¼ cup olive oil over medium heat until smoking. Add the remaining garlic and cook until light golden brown, 2 to 3 minutes. Add half of the bread crumbs, the walnuts, and red pepper flakes and cook, stirring to mix well, for 2 to 3 minutes. Remove from the heat and set aside.

3. In a medium bowl, stir together the zucchini mixture, egg, ricotta, ½ cup of the pecorino, the nutmeg, and parsley until well mixed. Season the filling lightly with salt and pepper. Set aside ¼ cup to finish the dish.

4. To make the pansotti, divide the dough into 4 pieces. Roll each one through the second-thinnest setting of a pasta machine and lay the sheets on a lightly floured work surface. Cut the pasta into 3-inch rounds. Place 1½ teaspoons of filling in the center of each round and fold over to make a half-moon, pressing to seal the edges. Transfer to a baking sheet dusted with flour.

5. Bring 6 quarts of water to a boil in a large pot, and add 2 tablespoons salt. Drop the pansotti into the water and cook until the pasta is tender, 3 to 4 minutes.

6. Drain the pasta, reserving ½ cup of the cooking water, and add the pasta to the pan with the walnut mixture.

7. Place the pan over medium heat, add ¼ cup of the cooking water and the reserved filling mix, and toss to lightly coat. Add the parsley and the remaining pecorino and toss well, adding more pasta water if necessary. Transfer to a heated bowl, sprinkle with the remaining bread crumbs, and serve immediately.

ORATA *and* POTATO RAVIOLI *with* MARJORAM *and* GREEN OLIVES

Ravioli di Orata

The idea for these ravioli developed after we'd tasted more than a dozen whole fish one day to see which should go on the menu. Each was so delicious it would have been criminal to throw any of it away, so I added some potato to the leftover orata to soften it for a ravioli filling and made this sauce, and they are delicious.

MAKES 8 SERVINGS

FILLING

¾ cup plus 2 tablespoons EXTRA-VIRGIN OLIVE OIL

2 cloves GARLIC, thinly sliced

1 pound ORATA FILLETS (or any other firm white fish, such as sole, halibut, or grouper), skin removed, cut into ½-inch cubes

3 tablespoons chopped fresh MARJORAM plus 1 tablespoon whole leaves

1 RUSSET POTATO, cooked in boiling salted water until tender, peeled, and mashed

SALT and freshly ground BLACK PEPPER

1¼ pounds BASIC PASTA DOUGH (page 196)

1 cup BASIC TOMATO SAUCE (page 71)

¼ cup SICILIAN GREEN OLIVES, pitted, coarsely chopped

1. In a 10- to 12-inch sauté pan, heat ¼ cup of the olive oil over medium heat until smoking. Add the garlic and cook until light golden brown, about 1 minute. Add the fish and cook, stirring frequently, until the fish is just cooked through, 8 to 9 minutes. Transfer to a large bowl, add the chopped marjoram, mashed potato, and 6 tablespoons oil, and stir well to break up all of the fish. Season to taste with salt and pepper and let cool.

2. To make the ravioli, divide the pasta into 4 pieces. Roll out each piece through the thinnest setting on a pasta machine and place on a lightly floured surface. Cut 1 sheet of pasta into 2 by 1-inch rectangles. Place a teaspoon of the fish mixture in the center of each rectangle, fold the pasta over to enclose the filling, and press to seal the edges. Transfer to a lightly floured surface, and repeat with the remaining pasta and filling.

3. Bring 6 quarts of water to a boil in a large pot, and add 2 tablespoons salt. Drop the ravioli into the boiling water and cook until the pasta is tender, 6 to 7 minutes.

4. Meanwhile, in a 10- to 12-inch sauté pan, combine the tomato sauce, remaining olive oil, whole marjoram leaves, and olives and warm over medium heat, stirring occasionally.

5. Scoop out ½ cup of the cooking water and drain the ravioli. Add the ravioli to the tomato sauce and toss to coat it, adding a little of the pasta water if necessary to loosen the sauce. Transfer to a warmed serving platter and serve immediately.

AGNOLOTTI

These are luxurious and sometimes decadent Piemontese ravioli that are often filled with a combination of rabbit, sausage, veal, and pork. They can be served sauced with mushrooms and butter, per this recipe, or in a broth.

MAKES 6 SERVINGS

8 tablespoons (1 stick) UNSALTED BUTTER

1 medium SPANISH ONION, cut into ⅛-inch dice

6 ounces skinless, boneless CHICKEN BREAST, cut into 2-inch pieces

4 ounces SWEET ITALIAN SAUSAGE, removed from casings and cut into 2-inch lengths

¼ cup RICOTTA

¼ cup grated ITALIAN FONTINA

3 tablespoons fresh GOAT CHEESE

2 tablespoons fresh MARJORAM LEAVES

¼ cup finely chopped ITALIAN PARSLEY, plus 1 tablespoon, chiffonade

¼ teaspoon freshly grated NUTMEG

SALT and freshly ground BLACK PEPPER

1¼ pounds BASIC PASTA DOUGH (page 196)

4 ounces PORCINI or CREMINI, sliced paper-thin

¼ cup freshly grated PARMIGIANO-REGGIANO

1. To make the filling, in a 10- to 12-inch sauté pan, heat 4 tablespoons of the butter over medium heat until it foams and subsides. Add the onion and cook until soft and golden brown, 7 to 8 minutes. Add the chicken and sausage and cook until cooked through, about 10 minutes. Remove from the heat and allow to cool.

2. Transfer the chicken mixture to a food processor and pulse until finely chopped. Transfer to a medium bowl, add the ricotta, Fontina, goat cheese, marjoram, parsley, nutmeg, and salt and pepper to taste, and mix well. Set aside.

3. To make the agnolotti, divide the pasta into 4 pieces. Roll out each one through the thinnest setting on a pasta machine and lay on a lightly floured work surface. Cut each sheet lengthwise in half to form strips 2 inches wide and 24 inches long. Starting 1 inch from one end, spoon tablespoons of the filling 2 inches apart along the bottom of each strip. Fold the top half of the pasta over the bottom and press the edges together to seal, gently pressing out any air pockets. Using a fluted round pastry cutter, cut out the agnolotti. Transfer to a baking sheet dusted with flour.

4. Bring 6 quarts of water to a boil in a large pot, and add 2 tablespoons salt. Drop the agnolotti carefully into the boiling water, lower the heat, and cook at a brisk simmer until tender, 3 to 4 minutes.

5. Meanwhile, in a 10- to 12-inch sauté pan, melt the butter over medium heat. Add the mushrooms, season with salt and pepper, and sauté until tender.

6. Drain the agnolotti, add to the mushrooms, and sprinkle with the remaining parsley and the Parmigiano. Toss for about 1 minute to coat with sauce. Transfer to a platter, and serve.

POTATO "CANDIES" *with* RAGU BOLOGNESE

Caramelle Ripiene di Patate al Ragu

This is an excellent example of the magnificent cooking of Bologna, referred to as Bologna the Fat throughout Italy because of the many luxury food items found in and around the "red" city (from the color of its stone buildings), including prosciutto di Parma, Parmigiano-Reggiano, and true aceto balsamico.

MAKES 6 SERVINGS

2½ pounds RUSSET POTATOES, peeled and cut into chunks

4 tablespoons UNSALTED BUTTER

1 tablespoon finely chopped ONION

1 clove GARLIC, finely chopped

1½ cups freshly grated PARMIGIANO-REGGIANO, plus more for serving

4 ounces STRACCHINO CHEESE or TALEGGIO

½ cup finely diced MORTADELLA

1½ teaspoons finely chopped fresh THYME

1½ teaspoons finely chopped fresh OREGANO

SALT and freshly ground BLACK PEPPER

1 large EGG, beaten (optional)

1¼ pounds BASIC PASTA DOUGH (page 196)

2 cups RAGU BOLOGNESE (opposite)

1. Cook the potatoes in a large pot of boiling salted water until tender, about 20 minutes.

2. Meanwhile, melt 1 tablespoon of the butter in a small skillet, add the onion and garlic, and cook over low heat until soft and translucent, about 10 minutes. Set aside.

3. Drain the potatoes and allow to cool and dry for a few minutes, then pass through a food mill or ricer into a large bowl. Add the onion mixture, Parmigiano, stracchino, mortadella, thyme, oregano, and salt and pepper to taste. If it seems dry, add some or all of the egg to moisten the mixture. Set aside.

4. To make the caramelle, divide the pasta into 4 portions. Roll each one out through the thinnest setting on a pasta machine and lay the sheets on a lightly floured surface. Cut the sheets into 3-by-1-inch rectangles. Place a scant tablespoon of the potato mixture in the center of half the rectangles. Top with the remaining rectangles and press the edges to seal. Twist the rectangles to create the look of hard candies wrapped in cellophane twists.

5. Bring 6 quarts of water to a boil in a large pot, and add 2 tablespoons salt. Meanwhile, heat the ragu in a 10- to 12-inch sauté pan over medium-high heat.

6. Drop the pasta into the boiling water and cook until tender, about 3 minutes. Drain and add to the ragu. Add the remaining 3 table-spoons butter and toss over high heat for about 1 minute to coat the pasta.

7. Divide the pasta evenly among six warmed pasta bowls, top with Parmigiano, and serve immediately.

RAGU BOLOGNESE

MAKES ABOUT 5 CUPS

¼ cup EXTRA-VIRGIN OLIVE OIL

2 medium ONIONS, finely chopped

4 ribs CELERY, finely chopped

2 CARROTS, finely chopped

5 cloves GARLIC, sliced

1 pound ground VEAL

1 pound ground PORK

4 ounces PANCETTA or SLAB BACON, run through
 the medium holes of the butcher's grinder

One 6-ounce can TOMATO PASTE

1 cup WHOLE MILK

1 cup DRY WHITE WINE

1 teaspoon fresh THYME LEAVES

SALT and freshly ground BLACK PEPPER

In a 6- to 8-quart heavy-bottomed pot, heat the olive oil over medium heat until hot. Add the onions, celery, carrots, and garlic and cook until the vegetables are translucent but not browned, about 5 minutes. Add the veal, pork, and pancetta, increase the heat to high, and brown the meat, stirring frequently. Add the tomato paste, milk, wine, and thyme and bring just to a boil, then reduce the heat to medium-low and simmer for 1 to 1½ hours.

Season the ragu with salt and pepper, remove from the heat, and let cool. (The ragu can be refrigerated for up to 2 days; it can also be frozen for up to 1 month.)

RAGU BOLOGNESE

Ragu bolognese is perhaps one of the most common recipes in the cucina of Emilia-Romagna and is an excellent example of the individual cook's mark on a true regional classic. Everyone agrees that in a real ragu there is more than one kind of meat, and everyone agrees that there needs to be some tomato "stuff" in the ragu. But whether it is equal parts veal, pork, and beef, or whether or not there is pancetta or prosciutto, or whether it is tomato paste or *doppio concentrato* are issues and differences that will be hotly contested by cooks forever—all of whom learned the "real recipe" from the relevant mother, aunt, or *nonna*. Often, two sisters who learned from the same mom may have entirely different ragu recipes, each based on the different perception of the same base *condimento*. Other possible variations could be the addition of chicken livers, porcini mushrooms, or anchovies or even leaving out tomato altogether, because a ragu is by no Italian's definition a "tomato" sauce—in my world, there should be just a trace of pale pinkish brown. Suffice it to say that my recipe was learned from Mara Giacometti, the chef at La Volta, who was born twenty-five minutes south of Bologna proper. In my opinion, this ragu is just perfect.

PASTA

CANNELLONI
Cannelloni al Forno

I have eaten these made with crepes and I have eaten them made with pasta. My preference is pasta, because of the toothsome bite it brings to the table.

MAKES 4 SERVINGS

7 tablespoons UNSALTED BUTTER

8 ounces GROUND PORK

8 ounces GROUND VEAL

¾ cup freshly grated PARMIGIANO-REGGIANO

1 tablespoon ALL-PURPOSE FLOUR

1 cup WHOLE MILK

1 large EGG, beaten

Pinch of freshly grated NUTMEG

SALT and freshly ground BLACK PEPPER

1¼ pounds BASIC PASTA DOUGH (page 196)

1 cup BASIC TOMATO SAUCE (page 71)

1 cup BESCIAMELLA (page 65)

1. In a 10- to 12-inch sauté pan, heat 1 tablespoon of the butter over high heat until it foams and subsides. Add the ground pork and veal and cook, stirring occasionally and breaking up any lumps of meat, until browned. Drain off the excess fat, then add ½ cup of the Parmigiano, the flour, and milk and bring to just under a boil. Reduce the heat to a simmer and cook for 10 minutes, stirring frequently. Remove from the heat and allow the filling to cool. Stir in the egg and season with the nutmeg, salt, and pepper. Set aside.

2. Bring 6 quarts of water to a boil in a large pot, and add 2 tablespoons salt. Set up an ice bath next to the stove.

3. Divide the pasta dough into 4 pieces. Roll each one through the thinnest setting on a pasta machine and lay the sheets on a lightly floured work surface. Cut the pasta into 4 by 6-inch rectangles. Drop the pasta rectangles into the boiling water, 5 or 6 at a time, and cook until tender, about 1 minute. Transfer to the ice bath to cool for 1 minute, then drain on kitchen towels, laying the rectangles flat.

4. Preheat the oven to 350°F.

5. Spoon about 3 tablespoons of the meat filling just above one long edge of each rectangle, and roll the pasta up around the filling to form a cylinder.

6. Spoon half the tomato sauce across the bottom of a large baking dish in an even layer. Arrange the cannelloni seam side down in the dish in a single layer. Top with the remaining tomato sauce, then the besciamella. Sprinkle with the remaining ¼ cup Parmigiano.

7. Bake for 20 to 25 minutes, until the sauces and cheese are bubbling and the edges of the pasta are crisp and browned. Serve immediately, from the baking dish.

LASAGNE

Lasagne alla Bolognese al Forno

When I first arrived in Emilia-Romagna, I was shocked to see lasagne made so simply. Then I tried the dish and was surprised at how truly delicious it tasted. It is almost a miracle how a few such simple ingredients can create such a complex symphony of flavors.

MAKES 8 SERVINGS

2½ pounds GREEN PASTA DOUGH (page 196)

2 tablespoons EXTRA-VIRGIN OLIVE OIL

RAGU BOLOGNESE (page 245)

8 ounces PARMIGIANO-REGGIANO, grated

3½ cups BESCIAMELLA (page 65)

1. Divide the pasta dough into 8 portions. Roll each one out through the thinnest setting on a pasta machine and lay the sheets on a lightly floured surface to dry for 10 minutes. Cut the pasta into 5-inch squares and cover with a damp kitchen towel.

2. Bring 6 quarts of water to a boil in a large pot, and add 2 tablespoons salt. Set up an ice bath next to the stovetop, and add the oil. Drop the pasta into the boiling water, 6 or 7 pieces at a time, and cook until tender, about 1 minute. Transfer to the ice bath to cool, then drain on kitchen towels, laying the pasta flat.

3. Preheat the oven to 375°F.

4. Assemble the lasagne in a 10-by-20-inch lasagne pan (or use two 9-by-12-inch pans): Spread a layer of ragu over the bottom and top with a sprinkling of Parmigiano, a layer of pasta, a layer of besciamella, another layer of ragu, a sprinkling of Parmigiano, and pasta. Repeat until all the ingredients are used up, finishing with a layer of pasta topped with besciamella and a sprinkling of Parmigiano.

5. Bake for 45 minutes, or until the edges are browned and the sauces are bubbling. Let stand for 10 minutes before serving.

NEAPOLITAN LASAGNE
Lasagne alla Napoletana

The Neapolitans are much more dramatic than the Bolognese, a characteristic that is evident right down to their lasagne. The ragu napoletano takes some time, but you can easily squeeze at least two meals out it, since you use just the sauce and sausage for the lasagne.

MAKES 10 SERVINGS

2½ pounds BASIC PASTA DOUGH (page 196)

2 tablespoons EXTRA-VIRGIN OLIVE OIL

RAGU NAPOLETANO (page 251), sausages thinly sliced, meats reserved for another use

3 cups RICOTTA

POLPETTE (page 251), cut in half

1 cup freshly grated PARMIGIANO-REGGIANO

1 pound fresh MOZZARELLA, shredded

1. Divide the pasta dough into 8 portions. Roll each one out through the thinnest setting on a pasta machine and lay the sheets on a lightly floured work surface to dry for 10 minutes. Cut the pasta into 10-by-5-inch strips and cover with a damp kitchen towel.

2. Bring 6 quarts of water to a boil in a large pot, and add 2 tablespoons salt. Set up an ice bath next to the stovetop, and add the oil. Cook the noodles, 6 to 7 at a time, in the boiling water until tender, about 1 minute. Transfer to the ice bath to cool, then lay out on clean kitchen towels to drain.

3. Preheat the oven to 350°F.

4. Assemble the lasagne in a 10-by-20-inch lasagne pan (or use two 9-by-12-inch pans): Spread ½ cup ragu over the bottom of the dish, then top with a layer of pasta, a layer of ricotta, a layer of polpette and sausage, and a layer of Parmigiano and mozzarella. Continue until you have at least 3 layers, finishing with cheese.

5. Bake for 1 hour and 15 minutes, or until the edges are bubbling. Let rest for 15 minutes before serving.

RAGU NAPOLETANO

MAKES 3 QUARTS

¼ cup EXTRA-VIRGIN OLIVE OIL

8 ounces boneless VEAL SHOULDER, cut into chunks

8 ounces boneless BEEF CHUCK, cut into chunks

SALT and freshly ground BLACK PEPPER

1 ONION, finely chopped

¾ cup DRY RED WINE

Two 28-ounce cans PLUM TOMATOES with their juice, passed through a food mill

8 ounces SWEET ITALIAN SAUSAGES

Pinch of HOT RED PEPPER FLAKES

1. In a large Dutch oven, heat the olive oil over medium heat until smoking. Season the veal and beef with salt and pepper to taste, and sear, in batches to avoid overcrowding the pot, until dark golden brown. Transfer to a plate.

2. Add the onion to the pot and sauté, scraping the bottom of the pot with a wooden spoon to loosen any brown bits, until golden brown and very soft, about 10 minutes. Add the wine, browned meat chunks, tomatoes, sausages, and red pepper flakes and bring just to a boil. Reduce the heat to a simmer and cook, stirring occasionally and skimming off the fat as necessary, for 2½ to 3 hours.

3. Remove from the heat, remove the meat and sausages, and set aside. Adjust the seasoning with salt and pepper and allow the sauce to cool.

NEAPOLITAN MEATBALLS

Polpette alla Napoletana

MAKES 12 TO 15 MEATBALLS

3 cups 1-inch cubes of DAY-OLD BREAD

1¼ pounds GROUND BEEF

3 large EGGS, lightly beaten

3 cloves GARLIC, minced

¾ cup freshly grated PECORINO ROMANO

¼ cup finely chopped ITALIAN PARSLEY

¼ cup PINE NUTS, toasted

½ teaspoon SALT

½ teaspoon freshly ground BLACK PEPPER

¼ cup EXTRA-VIRGIN OLIVE OIL

1. In a shallow bowl, soak the bread cubes in water to cover for 20 minutes. Drain the bread cubes and squeeze out the excess moisture.

2. In a large bowl, combine the bread, beef, eggs, garlic, pecorino, parsley, pine nuts, salt, and pepper and mix with your hands just until blended. With wet hands, form the mixture into 12 to 15 large meatballs.

3. In a large heavy-bottomed skillet, heat the olive oil over high heat until almost smoking. Add the meatballs, working in batches if necessary to avoid overcrowding the pan, and cook, turning occasionally, until deep golden brown on all sides, about 10 minutes per batch. Remove from the heat.

FISH

There are three words that sum up the philosophy of Italian fish cookery: *Leave it alone!* The Italians are so proud of the micro-regionality of fish varieties from their waters —even specific spots within a three-hundred-yard stretch of water, or the back side of a favorite rock—that the last thing they want to do is mask their delicate, unique, and elusive flavors with such frippery as heavy sauces, or culinary showmanship.

The only acceptable condiment for local fish or seafood in Italy is local extra-virgin olive oil—that's it. This is based on every Italian's belief that the taste of the wind, or the rain, or the stream, or the clam or fish, from the particular place where they grew up is precious and superior to anything from any other place. Italians' pride and faith in their local products (*nostrano*, "ours," is always the most prized produce, or meat, or fish) is transcendental—it is high religion, it is life. And with seafood, it is all that and even more.

The concept of *terroir* in French winemaking is that the specific mineral conditions of the soil, the location of the plot of soil with respect to the sun's rays, the water that rains on that soil, and so on result in a very specific taste and feel particular to that soil. The same goes for Italian piscatorial delights. Little red mullets caught in the bay of Naples have a different flavor from those caught twenty kilometers north in Pozzuoli. And the tiny little sole caught in the lagoon of Venice taste different from the ones caught in Chioggia, forty kilometers to the south.

The same is true in the United States, at least in terms of wild fish, which always taste better than farmed fish. We have some of the most delicious local fish in the world in our waters. Pacific salmon, Dungeness crab, Gulf shrimp, and Chatham cod are internationally recognized as gold standards in the denizens of the deep department. And when things are really running in season, like Alaskan king salmon in the late spring, they are obviously fresher and more abundant, and thus less expensive. There is also the possibility that too many fish that happen to be "in style" are being taken out of the sea by seagoing profitmongers with no regard for the potential for extinction of a species. The Monterey Bay Aquarium's website (www.montereybayaquarium.com) posts an up-to-date list of the species that are being overfished both in the United States and in the rest of the world. I use that as a shopping guide, both at my restaurants and at home, and I urge you to use it too. Thinking globally while buying locally is more than a slogan for fish, it is a mantra.

CALAMARI NEAPOLITAN-STYLE

Calamari alla Luciana

This simple classic is often interpreted to include anything from bacon to zucchini, all of which may be good but are not traditional. The hero in this game is the brief cooking time, which results in calamari with a silken, tender texture, complemented but not overpowered by the slightly spicy tomato sauce.

MAKES 6 SERVINGS

½ cup EXTRA-VIRGIN OLIVE OIL

4 cloves GARLIC, thinly sliced

1 tablespoon HOT RED PEPPER FLAKES

1 cup BASIC TOMATO SAUCE (page 71)

½ cup DRY WHITE WINE

2½ pounds CALAMARI, cleaned, bodies cut into ¼-inch-wide rings, tentacles left whole

1 tablespoon RED WINE VINEGAR

¼ cup ITALIAN PARSLEY, chiffonade

SALT

1. In a 6-quart pot, combine ¼ cup of the olive oil, the garlic, and red pepper flakes and cook over medium heat until the garlic is light golden brown, about 2 minutes. Add the tomato sauce and wine and bring to a boil.

2. Add the calamari and stir to mix well, then reduce the heat and simmer until tender, 2 to 3 minutes. Stir in the vinegar, parsley, and the remaining ¼ cup olive oil, adjust the seasoning if necessary, and serve, or allow to cool and serve at room temperature.

CALAMARI *and* RAZOR CLAMS "IN CACCIUCCO"

Cacciucco

The name of this dish is allegedly derived from the five c's in its title and implies the presence of five different kinds of fish to correspond with the c's. I have taken a little poetic liberty, but the flavors of its birthplace of Livorno on the Tuscan coast are still quite evident.

MAKES 4 SERVINGS

¼ cup EXTRA-VIRGIN OLIVE OIL

1 medium RED ONION, thinly sliced

1 small CARROT, finely chopped

1 rib CELERY, thinly sliced

2 cloves GARLIC, thinly sliced

1 teaspoon HOT RED PEPPER FLAKES

1 cup DRY WHITE WINE

1 cup BASIC TOMATO SAUCE (page 71)

1 pound CALAMARI, cleaned and tubes cut into ½-inch rings

2 dozen RAZOR CLAMS, scrubbed

SALT and freshly ground BLACK PEPPER

4 thick slices ITALIAN PEASANT BREAD

¼ cup ITALIAN PARSLEY, chiffonade

1. Preheat the grill or broiler.

2. In a 10- to 12-inch sauté pan, heat the olive oil over medium heat until almost smoking. Add the onion, carrot, celery, garlic, and red pepper flakes and sauté until the vegetables are lightly browned and very soft, 10 to 12 minutes. Add the wine and tomato sauce and bring to a boil.

3. Add the calamari and clams to the sauce, season with salt and pepper, and bring the sauce to a low boil. Cook for 1 minute.

4. Meanwhile, toast the bread on the grill or under the broiler, turning once, until golden brown on both sides. Place in four shallow serving bowls.

5. Add the parsley to the seafood and stir well. Divide the seafood and sauce among the bowls, and serve immediately.

CALAMARI STEW *with* PEAS

Calamari in Zimino con Piselli

This dish is ubiquitous on the Adriatic Coast south of Venice, all the way down to Puglia. Calamari or cuttlefish can be cooked one of two ways: briefly or long-simmered. In this recipe, the calamari is simmered for an hour, which gives the dish a rich, deep, bottom-of-the-sea flavor, which Italians love. The other way to prepare the dish is to make a twenty-minute stew of all of the ingredients except for the calamari, then add it at the last minute for a lighter flavor, reminiscent of the foam on top of the sea.

MAKES 6 SERVINGS

6 tablespoons EXTRA-VIRGIN OLIVE OIL

1 medium SPANISH ONION, sliced into ¼-inch-thick rounds

3 ribs CELERY, cut into ¼-inch-thick slices

4 cloves GARLIC, peeled

4 ANCHOVY FILLETS, rinsed and patted dry

2 DRIED HOT CHILE PEPPERS

1 cup BASIC TOMATO SAUCE (page 71)

3 pounds CALAMARI, cleaned, bodies cut into ½-inch-wide rings, tentacles cut lengthwise in half

½ cup DRY WHITE WINE

2 tablespoons WHITE VINEGAR

SALT and freshly ground BLACK PEPPER

1½ pounds fresh PEAS, shucked (approximately 1 cup)

LEMON WEDGES

1. In a 10- to 12-inch deep sauté pan, heat the olive oil over medium heat until almost smoking. Add the onion, celery, garlic, anchovies, and chile peppers and cook until the vegetables are softened and light golden brown, about 10 minutes.

2. Add the tomato sauce, calamari, wine, and vinegar and bring to a boil. Season with salt and pepper, lower the heat, cover, and simmer until the calamari is tender, about 1 hour.

3. Check for seasoning, add the peas, and simmer for 10 minutes. Remove the dried chiles, and serve with lemon wedges.

CEPHALOPODS

OCTOPUS

A member of the cephalopod class of the mollusk family, the octopus s a close cousin of squid and cuttlefish. Octopi can grow to as long as 50 feet, but the majority in the market are from 2 to 3 feet in size. As with most species, the smaller octopus is usually the most tender.

Octopi feast on a diet of clams and mussels, which enriches the flavor of their own meat. Each octopus has eight tentacles (if one is cut off in the wild, it will regrow), and both the body and tentacles are edible. Like squid, octopus has an ink sac, which, in the wild, can be used to create a veritable liquid smoke screen that hides the octopus from his foe and allows the octopus to escape safely. The black ink can be used in cooking to color risotto, pasta, or soups.

Many fish markets sell octopus already cleaned; or ask the fishmonger to do it for you. Frozen octopus is fine—in fact, freezing helps tenderize it.

COOKING AND TENDERIZING OCTOPUS

Many cooks disdain octopus as rubbery, an unfortunate reputation it gained from tourist images of fishermen squatting on the rocks by the sea, flailing away at some poor octopus. I've tried beating them with a mallet, puncturing them with tiny fork holes, and marinating them in an acid base, but the only thing that really makes octopus tender is a cork. Cooking the octopus at a low boil with an ordinary wine cork in the water results in edible flesh in as much as twenty minutes less than the standard cooking time and with far less of the toughness associated with OPC (other people's cephalopods). I've heard that the effect is the result of an enzymatic reaction between something in the cork and the protein in the octopus flesh, but beyond that I cannot say. Just add a cork to your cooking water, and enjoy.

SQUID

A squid, *calamari* in Italian, has ten tentacles. Squid can grow to eighty or ninety feet long, but those found in the marketplace, of course, are much smaller. Always look for squid with a fresh, clean sea smell; cleaned squid are sold in most fish markets.

Squid can be either quickly cooked or long-cooked—nothing in between, or it will be tough. Braise or stew it for 45 minutes or so, or cook for just a few minutes. As with octopus, squid also have an ink sac that can be used to color pastas, risottos, and soups.

CUTTLEFISH

Cuttlefish is related to squid, but its body is more oval and flatter. Usually six to ten inches long, it has ten tentacles and a light, chalky bone that runs through the center of its body. Birds often use this bone, rounded on one end and pointed on the other, as a beak sharpener.

Found in most European coastal regions, cuttlefish are yellow or beige striped with black, and they can adapt to their surroundings by means of camouflage. Much like their squid cousins, cuttlefish have a sac of ink. It is dark brown in color, rather than black; it, too, may be used in cooking. At the fish market, look for cuttlefish with moist, firm flesh that smells faintly of the ocean. Cuttlefish must be tenderized like octopus (see above).

BARBECUED OCTOPUS *with* GRILLED ESCAROLE *and* MINT

Polpo colla Scarola

For whatever scientific reason, adding a cork to the cooking water works to make this cephalopod tender. The blanched octopus can sit for an hour in the marinade—but no longer, or the acidity may cause it to toughen.

MAKES 4 SERVINGS

One 3-pound OCTOPUS, sac, beak, and eyes removed (have the fishmonger do this)

½ cup EXTRA-VIRGIN OLIVE OIL

Grated zest and juice of 1 LEMON

1 tablespoon HOT RED PEPPER FLAKES

1 bunch OREGANO, leaves only, roughly chopped

1 tablespoon freshly ground BLACK PEPPER

2 heads ESCAROLE

½ cup fresh MINT LEAVES

1. Place the octopus a large pot, add cold water to cover and a cork, and bring to a boil. Reduce the heat to a low boil and cook until tender, 35 to 40 minutes. Drain, rinse under cold water, and drain again. Cut lengthwise into 8 pieces. (The octopus can be prepared up to 1 day in advance; cover and refrigerate.)

2. Preheat the grill.

3. In a large bowl, stir together the olive oil, lemon zest and juice, red pepper flakes, oregano, and black pepper. Add the octopus pieces and marinate for at least 10 minutes, or up to 1 hour.

4. Remove the octopus from the marinade, reserving the marinade, and place on the grill. Cook, turning once, until crisp and slightly charred, 5 to 7 minutes per side.

5. Meanwhile, trim any flimsy outer leaves from the escarole and cut lengthwise in half. Rinse well to remove any grit, and pat dry. Place cut side down on the grill and cook until lightly charred, 7 to 8 minutes. Turn and cook until lightly charred on the second side, about 5 more minutes. Transfer to a platter and set aside.

6. When the octopus is cooked, return it the marinade. Allow to cool slightly, then using scissors, cut the octopus into bite-sized pieces, letting them drop back into the marinade. Spoon the octopus and marinade over the escarole, sprinkle with the mint, and serve.

FISH

BIG SEAFOOD SOUP *from* AMALFI
Zuppa di Pesce

Fish soups vary from region to region and even from port to port, each variation celebrating the local varieties of fish and the bounty of the coastal land. Amalfitani are particularly proud of their tomatoes and simple white wine, so those are the main ingredients in this bare-bones ode to the piscatorial supremacy of their particular part of the Campania coastline. If you can't get crayfish, you could add scallops or even small lobsters to the soup instead.

MAKES 4 SERVINGS

¼ cup EXTRA-VIRGIN OLIVE OIL

1 medium RED ONION, finely chopped

1 rib CELERY, finely chopped

5 cloves GARLIC, 4 thinly sliced, 1 left whole

1 tablespoon HOT RED PEPPER FLAKES

2 cups BASIC TOMATO SAUCE (page 71)

2 cups DRY WHITE WINE

1 cup chopped TOMATOES

8 giant CRAYFISH

12 MANILA CLAMS, scrubbed

8 MUSSELS, scrubbed, debearded, and rinsed

8 ounces SHRIMP, peeled and deveined

4 young RED MULLET, cleaned and scaled

Four 1-inch-thick slices ITALIAN PEASANT BREAD

½ cup finely chopped ITALIAN PARSLEY

2 teaspoons fresh MARJORAM leaves

1. Preheat the grill or broiler.

2. In a large Dutch oven, heat the olive oil over medium heat until almost smoking. Add the onion, celery, sliced garlic, and red pepper flakes and cook until the onion is translucent, 6 to 8 minutes. Add the tomato sauce, wine, and tomatoes and bring to a boil. Add the shellfish and fish, cover, and bring back to a boil. Uncover, reduce the heat to a simmer, and cook, stirring once or twice, until the shellfish have opened, 5 to 6 minutes.

3. Meanwhile, toast the bread on the grill or under the broiler. While it is still hot, rub on both sides with the whole garlic clove. Lay 1 slice in each of four warmed bowls.

4. Divide the seafood among the bowls, then divide the broth among the bowls, and sprinkle with the parsley and marjoram. Serve immediately.

JUMBO SHRIMP MARSALA HOUSEWIFE-STYLE

Gamberoni alla Casalinga Siciliana

The tradition of Sicilian cooking is well documented in Anna Tasca Lanza's works, and she is the zen mistress of all of the island's fascinating food lore. Her school at Regaleali Winery is one of the best I have visited, and it was an experience to cook shoulder to shoulder with a modern national treasure. This is a variation on a dish from her first book, *Flavors of Sicily*.

MAKES 4 SERVINGS

¼ cup EXTRA-VIRGIN OLIVE OIL

1 medium RED ONION, cut into ¼-inch dice

1 rib CELERY with leaves, cut into ½-inch pieces

4 medium PLUM TOMATOES, roughly chopped

1 tablespoon PINE NUTS

1 tablespoon CURRANTS

2 tablespoons small CAPERS, rinsed and drained

1 cup DRY MARSALA

½ teaspoon FENNEL SEEDS

½ teaspoon HOT RED PEPPER FLAKES

1 BAY LEAF, preferably fresh

2 pounds JUMBO SHRIMP (U-12), peeled and deveined

SALT and freshly ground BLACK PEPPER

FENNEL FRONDS for garnish, optional

1. In a 10- to 12-inch sauté pan, heat the olive oil over medium-high heat until almost smoking. Add the onion and celery and cook until softened. Add the tomatoes, pine nuts, currants, capers, marsala, fennel seeds, red pepper flakes, and bay leaf and bring to a boil.

2. Remove the pan from the heat and lay the shrimp in one layer in the tomato mixture. Cover, set over low heat, and simmer for 4 minutes. Remove from the heat, season with salt and pepper to taste, and allow to stand for 5 minutes, covered.

3. Serve warm, or allow to cool to room temperature. Garnish with fennel fronds, if using.

GRILLED JUMBO SHRIMP *with* WHITE BEANS, ROSEMARY *and* MINT OIL

Gamberoni alla Toscana

This is a classic combination throughout Italy, truly emblematic of the general style of all seafood cooking—less is more! The shrimp are cooked quite simply and left alone to dance with sensual rosemary and the emerald-green mint oil, all at the white beans' party.

MAKES 4 SERVINGS

1½ cups cooked WHITE BEANS (great northern or cannellini), rinsed and drained if canned

½ medium RED ONION, sliced paper-thin

2 tablespoons finely chopped fresh MARJORAM

1 tablespoon chopped fresh ROSEMARY

¾ cup plus 2 tablespoons EXTRA-VIRGIN OLIVE OIL, plus extra for brushing

Grated zest and juice of 1 LEMON

SALT and freshly ground BLACK PEPPER

½ cup packed fresh MINT LEAVES

12 SUPER-COLOSSAL SHRIMP (about 1¼ pounds), heads on, body peeled, leaving the tail segments intact

2 cups ARUGULA, washed and spun dry

1. Preheat the grill or broiler.

2. In a medium bowl, stir together the beans, onion, marjoram, rosemary, 2 tablespoons of the olive oil, and the lemon zest and juice. Season to taste with salt and pepper and set aside.

3. Bring 3 cups of water to a boil in a small saucepan. Set up an ice bath next to the stove. Plunge the mint leaves into the boiling water for 30 seconds, then drain and add to the ice bath. Once the mint is cool, drain, squeeze any excess liquid from the leaves, and transfer to a food processor. Add the remaining ¾ cup olive oil and process for 1 minute. Set aside.

4. Season the shrimp with salt and pepper. Brush with oil and grill or broil, turning once, until cooked through.

5. Meanwhile, mix the arugula with the beans, and arrange in the center of four plates. Arrange 3 shrimp on each plate, leaning them against the arugula and beans in lounge-chair fashion. Drizzle with the mint oil, and serve.

SHRIMP *from the* DEVIL PRIEST
Gamberoni fra Diavolo

This "guido" red sauce restaurant dish has probably never been served anywhere in Italy, but I have tasted thousands of versions in Little Italys all across the United States. Usually it is served with the option of "linguine, fettuccine, bucatini, or capellini," but I like it as a main course, after a light antipasto and a plate of spaghetti with bottarga (page 174). Italians serve most of their shellfish head and shell on, but you could use peeled shrimp here as well.

MAKES 4 SERVINGS

½ cup EXTRA-VIRGIN OLIVE OIL

6 cloves GARLIC, thinly sliced

4 JALAPEÑOS, seeded and thinly sliced

1 tablespoon HOT RED PEPPER FLAKES

2 cups BASIC TOMATO SAUCE (page 71)

1 cup DRY WHITE WINE

20 large SHRIMP, head on, split down the back and deveined

Four 1-inch-thick slices RUSTIC PEASANT BREAD

2 tablespoons fresh MARJORAM LEAVES

¼ cup toasted BREAD CRUMBS

1. Preheat the broiler. In a 12-inch sauté pan, heat ¼ cup of the oil over medium heat. Add the garlic and jalapeños and cook until softened, about 3 minutes. Add the red pepper flakes, tomato sauce, and wine and bring to a boil. Lower the heat and simmer for 4 minutes.

2. Lay the shrimp in the sauce and simmer until just cooked through, 4 to 6 minutes.

3. Meanwhile, toast the bread on a baking sheet under the broiler, turning once. Place a slice of toasted bread in the center of each of four plates.

4. Place 5 shrimp on each piece of toast, and spoon the sauce over them. Sprinkle with the marjoram leaves and bread crumbs, drizzle with the remaining ¼ cup oil, and serve.

FISH

SHRIMP SKEWERS

Spiedini di Gamberoni

Rosemary can overpower seafood if used to excess, but in this dish it is merely the perfume of the stems that flavors the interior of the shrimp, and the delicate smokiness of the burning leaves that scents the outside.

MAKES 6 SERVINGS

3 pounds LARGE SHRIMP (about 30), peeled and deveined

6 long branches ROSEMARY, leaves removed to make skewers, and leaves reserved if grilling the shrimp, or wooden skewers

Grated zest and juice of 2 LEMONS

¼ cup LIMONCELLO

2 bunches OREGANO, leaves only, cut into chiffonade

¼ cup EXTRA-VIRGIN OLIVE OIL

1. Divide the shrimp into six equal portions, and skewer them on the rosemary branches.

2. In a baking dish or casserole large enough to hold the skewers in a single layer, combine the lemon zest and juice, limoncello, oregano, and olive oil. Place the shrimp in the marinade, turning the skewers so the shrimp are well coated. Cover and place in the refrigerator to marinate for 3 hours.

3. Preheat the grill or broiler.

4. If using a charcoal grill, just before cooking the shrimp, scatter the rosemary leaves over the coals. Remove the shrimp from the marinade, reserving the marinade, and grill or broil for 3 minutes. Turn, baste with the marinade, and cook for 1 minute more, or until just cooked through. Serve hot, or allow to cool to room temperature.

SHRIMP SIZES

There are hundreds of shrimp species, most of which can be categorized as warm-water (or tropical) or cold-water shrimp. Generally, the colder the water, the smaller and more tender the shrimp. Shrimp fall into a variety of size categories, listed below. Be aware, though, that labels such as "large" and "medium" may vary from store to store—but the "count," or number per pound, is always marked on the boxes the market receives, so that will be consistent.

SUPER-COLOSSAL (U-12): 12 or fewer per pound

COLOSSAL (U-15): 11 to 15 per pound

EXTRA-LARGE: 16 to 20 per pound

LARGE: 21 to 30 per pound

MEDIUM: 31 to 35 per pound

SMALL: 36 to 40 per pound

COCKTAIL OR SALAD: 41 or more per pound

SOFT-SHELL CRABS
WITH BROCCOLI RABE AND SUN-DRIED TOMATO PESTO
Molecche con Rapini

Soft-shell crabs, along with fava beans, ramps, and asparagus, are the true harbingers of spring in all of my restaurants. I prefer to cook soft-shell crabs simply and with no adornment —no batter, no flour, no dusting, nothing that might obscure the natural briny crabbiness of these jewels from the sea. I like the smaller sizes, called "prime" or "hotel," just because they look cooler. Here they are grilled, but you could just as easily sauté them in a hot pan—no flour or batter, of course.

MAKES 4 SERVINGS

1 pound BROCCOLI RABE, trimmed

¼ cup SUN-DRIED TOMATOES (not oil-packed)

½ cup BOILING WATER

¼ cup plus 3 tablespoons EXTRA-VIRGIN OLIVE OIL

8 SCALLIONS or SMALL SPRING ONIONS, root ends trimmed and sliced

½ cup SWEET RED VERMOUTH

SALT and freshly ground BLACK PEPPER

2 tablespoons BALSAMIC VINEGAR

1 tablespoon CAPERS

12 small ("prime") SOFT-SHELL CRABS

1. Preheat the grill.

2. Bring a large pot of salted water to a boil. Prepare an ice bath. Trim away the bottom inch of the broccoli rabe stems. Blanch the broccoli rabe in the boiling water for 1 minute, then drain and plunge into the ice bath to cool. Drain again, pat dry, and cut into 1-inch pieces.

3. Meanwhile, in a small bowl, soak the sun-dried tomatoes in the boiling water for 10 minutes.

4. In a 10- to 12-inch sauté pan, heat 3 tablespoons of the olive oil over medium-high heat until just smoking. Toss in the scallions and cook, stirring often, until just wilted, about 2 minutes. Add the broccoli rabe and vermouth and cook until the scallions are quite soft, 2 to 3 minutes. Season with salt and pepper. Set aside to cool to room temperature.

5. In a blender, combine the sun-dried tomatoes, with their soaking water, the vinegar, capers, and the remaining ¼ cup olive oil and blend until smooth, about 1 minute. Set aside.

6. To clean the soft-shell crabs, cut off the eyes and mouth. Season with black pepper. Grill, turning once, until crisp and red, about 5 minutes on each side.

7. Divide the broccoli rabe mixture among four plates. Place 3 crabs on each plate, drip 2 tablespoons of the sun-dried tomato pesto around the crabs, and serve immediately.

SNAILS
LE MARCHE–STYLE
Lumache alla Marchigiana

If you have trouble finding fresh snails, other sea critters such as whelks or even conch would work well in this recipe (as do canned snails). If you cook the stew for another twenty minutes, you have an excellent sauce for a chewy, rustic dry pasta like rigatoni.

MAKES 4 SERVINGS

5 pounds fresh SNAILS, purged overnight in 2 gallons water with 2 cups cornmeal, or two 18-ounce cans ESCARGOTS

6 tablespoons EXTRA-VIRGIN OLIVE OIL

2 medium ONIONS, thinly sliced

6 cloves GARLIC, thinly sliced

2 tablespoons chopped fresh THYME

1 cup DRY WHITE WINE

1 cup BASIC TOMATO SAUCE (page 71)

1 cup BLACK OLIVES

SALT and freshly ground BLACK PEPPER

1. If using live snails, steam them over boiling water for 1 hour, or until they leave their shells. Rinse well.

2. In a 10- to 12-inch sauté pan, heat the olive oil over medium heat until smoking. Add the onions and garlic and cook until softened and lightly browned, 8 to 10 minutes. Add the thyme, snails, wine, tomato sauce, and olives and bring to a boil. Lower the heat and simmer for 30 minutes. Season with salt and pepper and serve.

SCAMPI *with*
GARLIC, CHILES AND FENNEL
Scampi con Aglio e Finocchio

Scampi, or *langostinos*, are one of the most prized delicacies in the Italian kitchen, often purchased still alive and then eaten raw. You could successfully substitute other shellfish, from shrimp to soft-shell crabs to crayfish, the best being the one most recently at home in the water.

MAKES 4 SERVINGS

2 pounds JUMBO SCAMPI (langostinos; about 12)

¼ cup EXTRA-VIRGIN OLIVE OIL

4 cloves GARLIC, thinly sliced

4 RED JALAPEÑOS, seeded and thinly sliced

½ cup DRY WHITE WINE

¼ cup fresh MINT LEAVES

¼ cup chopped FENNEL FRONDS

1. Split the scampi (still in the shell) lengthwise in half, and devein.

2. In a 10- to 12-inch sauté pan, heat the olive oil over medium-high heat until smoking. Add the scampi, garlic, and jalapeños and cook until the scampi have turned red on the first side but the garlic is just lightly browned, about 4 minutes. Add the wine, turn the scampi over, and cook until just cooked through, about 2 more minutes.

3. Add the mint and fennel and toss well. Transfer to a warmed serving dish, and serve immediately.

GRILLED SARDINES *with* PEPERONATA

Sarde Con Peperonata

These sardines can also be served at room temperature and be just as delicious. I often make a double recipe of the peperonata—it is a good thing to have in the fridge for sammies and snacks.

MAKES 4 SERVINGS

PEPERONATA

⅓ cup EXTRA-VIRGIN OLIVE OIL

1 large RED ONION, cut into ½-inch-thick slices

2 cloves GARLIC, thinly sliced

6 large BELL PEPPERS—2 each red, yellow, and green, cored, ribs and seeds removed, and cut into ½-inch-wide strips

1 DRIED HOT CHILE, crushed

1 tablespoon SUGAR

1 teaspoon fresh THYME LEAVES

1 cup BASIC TOMATO SAUCE (page 71)

SALT and freshly ground BLACK PEPPER

8 fresh SARDINES, cleaned, scaled, rinsed, and dried

SALT and freshly ground BLACK PEPPER

1. To make the peperonata, in a 10- to 12-inch sauté pan, heat the olive oil over medium heat until almost smoking. Add the onion and garlic and cook until softened and translucent, 8 to 10 minutes. Add the peppers and cook until softened, about 5 minutes.

2. Add the crushed chile, sugar, thyme, and tomato sauce and bring to a boil, then lower the heat and simmer for 15 minutes. Season to taste with salt and pepper. Transfer the peperonata to a plate or platter.

3. Meanwhile, preheat the grill or broiler.

4. Season the sardines on both sides with salt and pepper. Grill or broil, turning once, until the skin is crisp and slightly charred, about 2 minutes per side.

5. Divide the peperonata evenly among four serving plates. Arrange 2 sardines on top of the peperonata on each plate, and serve.

FISH

CITRUS-CURED SARDINES
with CRACKED WHEAT
Sarde alla Lupa

MAKES 6 SERVINGS

1 cup SUGAR

1 cup KOSHER SALT

15 fresh SARDINES, cleaned, scaled, and filleted

Grated zest of 1 ORANGE

Grated zest of 1 LIME

Grated zest of ½ GRAPEFRUIT

½ cup fresh ORANGE JUICE

¼ cup fresh LIME JUICE

¼ cup fresh GRAPEFRUIT JUICE

1 cup plus 1½ tablespoons EXTRA-VIRGIN OLIVE OIL

½ cup BULGUR WHEAT

1½ cups BOILING WATER

2½ tablespoons fresh LEMON JUICE

SALT and freshly ground BLACK PEPPER

¼ cup CELERY LEAVES

¼ cup ITALIAN PARSLEY LEAVES

¼ cup ½-inch lengths fresh CHIVES

¼ cup roughly chopped FENNEL FRONDS

1. Put the sugar in a small bowl and put the kosher salt in another small bowl. Toss each sardine fillet in the sugar to coat lightly, and pat off the excess, then toss in the salt and pat off the excess. Arrange the fillets in one layer in a shallow casserole or baking dish. Cover tightly and refrigerate until chilled, at least 2 hours.

2. Rinse the sugar and salt from the sardines and drain on a plate lined with paper towels. Wash and dry the casserole or baking dish.

3. Combine the orange, lime, and grapefruit zest and juices in the casserole. Place the sardine fillets in the casserole, making sure that each one is covered with juice. Cover and refrigerate for 2 days, stirring occasionally.

4. Remove the fillets from the citrus marinade and discard it. In a bowl, toss the fillets with ¼ cup of the olive oil. Set aside. (The sardines can be refrigerated for up to 1 week.)

5. Place the bulgur in a small saucepan with a lid. Pour the boiling water over the bulgur, immediately cover with the lid, and let stand for 5 minutes. Remove the lid and fluff the bulgur with a fork, to make sure it is tender; if necessary, cover again and let stand for a few minutes longer. Transfer the bulgur to a tray and spread it out in a thin layer to cool quickly.

6. Put the bulgur in a medium bowl and toss with 2 tablespoons of the lemon juice, ¾ cup of the olive oil, and salt and pepper to taste. Combine the celery leaves, parsley, chives, and fennel fronds in a small bowl and toss with the remaining 1½ tablespoons olive oil, 1½ teaspoons lemon juice, and salt and pepper to taste.

7. To serve, place a mound of the bulgur in the middle of each of six chilled plates. Crisscross 5 sardine fillets over each mound of bulgur, and top with a small handful of the herb salad. Serve immediately.

FISH

STUFFED SARDINES *with* SWEET-AND-SOUR PEPPERS

Sarde in Agrodolce

The rich, oily flavor of sardines meets its perfect foil in this slightly spicy and acidic pepper stew, while the bread crumb stuffing results in a moist and crunchy mouthfeel that makes the world a sunny place.

MAKES 4 SERVINGS

20 fresh SARDINES, cleaned and scaled

6 tablespoons EXTRA-VIRGIN OLIVE OIL

2 ANCHOVY FILLETS, rinsed

2 cloves GARLIC, thinly sliced

1 cup FRESH BREAD CRUMBS

2 tablespoons dried CURRANTS

2 tablespoons SLICED ALMONDS

½ cup finely chopped ITALIAN PARSLEY

Grated zest and juice of 2 ORANGES

1 RED ONION, thinly sliced

2 RED BELL PEPPERS, cored, seeded, and thinly sliced

1 GREEN BELL PEPPER, cored, seeded, and thinly sliced

1 teaspoon HOT RED PEPPER FLAKES

¼ cup RED WINE VINEGAR

2 tablespoons SUGAR

10 LEMON SLICES

1. Using your thumbnail, remove the spine from each sardine, being careful to leave the head and tail intact. Rinse the fish to remove any small bones, and set aside.

2. In a 10- to 12-inch sauté pan, heat ¼ cup of the olive oil over medium-high heat until almost smoking. Add the anchovies and garlic and cook until the garlic starts to brown lightly, about 2 minutes. Add the bread crumbs and toast, stirring, until golden, 3 to 4 minutes. Transfer to a medium bowl, add the currants, almonds, parsley, orange zest, and half of the orange juice, and mix well. Set aside.

3. Lay the sardines on their backs on a work surface. Open each one, place a heaping tablespoon of the stuffing inside, and pinch closed. Set on a plate and refrigerate for 20 minutes.

4. Preheat the oven to 350°F.

5. In a 10- to 12-inch sauté pan, heat the remaining 2 tablespoons olive oil over medium-high heat until almost smoking. Add the onion, bell peppers, and red pepper flakes and sauté just until the vegetables are softened, 3 to 4 minutes. Add the remaining orange juice, the vinegar, and sugar, stir well, and remove from the heat.

6. Spread the pepper stew over the bottom of a 12-inch ovenproof casserole. Scatter the lemon slices over the peppers, and place the sardines on top.

7. Bake, uncovered, for 25 minutes. Serve hot or at room temperature.

BLACK BASS *with* TOMATOES
Spigole in Guazzetto

MAKES 4 SERVINGS

¼ cup EXTRA-VIRGIN OLIVE OIL

1 medium SPANISH ONION, thinly sliced

1 clove GARLIC, roughly chopped

3 tablespoons chopped fresh MINT

3 tablespoons chopped FENNEL FRONDS

1½ teaspoons HOT RED PEPPER FLAKES

One 15-ounce can WHOLE TOMATOES, preferably San Marzano, drained

1 cup DRY WHITE WINE

SALT and freshly ground BLACK PEPPER

4 small BLACK BASS or small ROCKFISH (3 to 4 pounds total), cleaned and scaled

¼ cup finely chopped ITALIAN PARSLEY

1.   In a 10- to 12-inch sauté pan, heat the olive oil over medium-high heat until almost smoking. Add the onion, garlic, 2 tablespoons of the mint, 2 tablespoons of the fennel fronds, and the red pepper flakes and cook until the onion is softened and lightly browned, 8 to 10 minutes.

2.   Add the tomatoes, crushing them between your fingers as you do so, and the wine, season with salt and pepper to taste, and cook for 15 minutes. Remove from the heat.

3.   Lay the fish in a deep skillet just big enough to hold them. Pour the sauce over the fish, cover, and set the pan over low heat. Cook until the fish is just cooked through, 10 to 12 minutes. Sprinkle with the parsley and the remaining 1 tablespoon each mint and fennel, and serve immediately.

TOMATOES

A perfectly ripe tomato is a beautiful thing. Unfortunately, tomatoes, which need to ripen slowly under a hot sun, have a short season. So, while a fresh tomato sauce made with ripe tomatoes may be perfect in summertime, it is always better to use high-quality canned tomatoes during the off-season. I like two types: the canned San Marzano tomatoes, and Pomi, packaged in plasticized square pints.

Pear-shaped San Marzano tomatoes are of the plum variety, and the real thing is only grown in San Marzano, near Mount Vesuvius outside of Naples. They can be ordered through www.sanmarzanoimports.com. I recommend buying canned whole tomatoes and crushing them by hand for sauces. If you can't find plain San Marzano tomatoes (and it can be difficult), buy the cans that include a basil leaf and simply remove the basil. Pomi tomatoes are easy to find in most grocery stores and are simply delicious. You can buy them whole, crushed, or pureed; as with the San Marzano, I prefer to buy them whole.

MARINATED FISH *with* VINEGAR *and* MINT

Pesciolini in Scapece

This dish is typical of Roman home cooking, but it may seem a little strange to the American cook because it's cooked first, then marinated. Stick with it—the marinade changes the texture of the fish and the flavors literally meld together, forming poetry in your mind as you snack on these, a chilled glass of Frascati in your other hand, on a warm afternoon in the shade.

MAKES 4 SERVINGS

4 to 5 cloves GARLIC, crushed

1 tablespoon chopped fresh MINT

1 cup WHITE WINE VINEGAR

¼ cup ALL-PURPOSE FLOUR

2 to 2½ pounds small fish such as SARDINES or SMELTS, cleaned, scaled, and heads removed

1 cup EXTRA-VIRGIN OLIVE OIL

1. In a small saucepan, combine the garlic, mint, and vinegar and bring just to a boil over medium-low heat. Reduce the heat to below a simmer and leave the aromatics to steep in the vinegar.

2. Spread the flour on a plate and dredge the fish lightly in it. In a 10- to 12-inch sauté pan, heat ½ cup of the olive oil over medium-high heat until smoking. Add the fish, in batches, and cook, turning once, until golden brown and just cooked through. Transfer to paper towels to drain.

3. Discard the oil and wipe out the pan. Add the remaining ½ cup oil to the pan and set over very low heat to warm.

4. Strain the vinegar into a small bowl, reserving the garlic and mint. Layer the fish in a glass or ceramic dish just large enough to hold them, distributing the reserved garlic and mint over them. Combine the warm vinegar and the warmed oil, and pour over the fish.

5. Cover the dish and refrigerate for 2 to 3 days. Serve slightly chilled or at room temperature.

MARINATED SOLE VENETIAN-STYLE
Sogliola in Saor

The delicate flavor of sole is beautifully accentuated with the sweet and tart marinade so traditional to Venetian cooking. This dish is typically served as part of a buffet in the little bars called *bacari* in the city of Venice, where there is a culture of stand-up snacking at lunch, and then throughout the afternoon. The glass of wine served in a *bacaro* is called *l'ombra*, which translates to "a little shade"—a respite from an overly sunny day.

MAKES 4 SERVINGS

1¼ cups EXTRA-VIRGIN OLIVE OIL

½ cup ALL-PURPOSE FLOUR

SALT and freshly ground BLACK PEPPER

2 pounds SOLE FILLETS

1 SPANISH ONION, cut into ½-inch dice

½ cup dried CURRANTS

¼ cup PINE NUTS

2 tablespoons SUGAR

1½ cups RED WINE VINEGAR

1. In a 10- to 12-inch sauté pan, heat 1 cup of the olive oil to 375°F. Meanwhile, season the flour with salt and pepper and spread on a plate.

2. Working in batches to avoid overcrowding the pan, dredge the fillets in the seasoned flour and fry in the hot oil until golden brown on one side, then turn and cook until golden brown on the other. Transfer to paper towels to drain.

3. In another 10- to 12-inch sauté pan, heat the remaining ¼ cup olive oil over medium heat until almost smoking. Add the onion and cook until softened and golden brown, 8 to 10 minutes. Add the currants, pine nuts, sugar, and vinegar and bring to a boil. Cook until the currants are soft, 5 to 6 minutes. Remove from the heat and let cool.

4. Choose an earthenware or other baking dish that just holds the fried fillets, slightly overlapping. Arrange them in the dish and top with the onion mixture. Cover and refrigerate for 24 hours. Serve at room temperature.

SAUTÉED SOLE MILLER'S-STYLE

Sogliola alla Mugnaia

There is probably nothing as simple and delicate as this sautéed fish with just flour and butter and lemon. And for that reason, the fish must be an exquisite piece of piscatorial perfection.

MAKES 4 SERVINGS

FLOUR for dredging

SALT and freshly ground BLACK PEPPER

2 pounds SOLE FILLETS

4 tablespoons UNSALTED BUTTER

1 tablespoon EXTRA-VIRGIN OLIVE OIL

Juice of 1 LEMON

2 tablespoons finely chopped ITALIAN PARSLEY

LEMON WEDGES

1. Season the flour with salt and pepper and spread on a plate. Dredge the fish in the flour and shake off the excess.

2. In a large nonstick skillet, heat 2 tablespoons of the butter with the olive oil over medium heat until the butter foams and subsides. Add the fish and cook, turning once, until nicely golden brown, about 5 minutes per side. Transfer the fish to a serving platter and cover loosely to keep warm.

3. Discard the cooking fat and wipe the skillet clean. Return the skillet to medium heat and melt the remaining 2 tablespoons butter. Stir in the lemon juice and parsley, and pour over the fish. Arrange lemon wedges around the fish, and serve immediately.

WHOLE FISH BAKED *in a* SALT CRUST

Pesce al Sale

Cooking a whole fish in a salt crust changes the texture of the flesh, making it more succulent, more elastic, almost in a lip-smacking way similar to a good cotechino. The only sauce you will need for this fish is a bit of lemon and a splash of the best extra-virgin olive oil you can find.

MAKES 6 SERVINGS

4 pounds COARSE SEA SALT or KOSHER SALT

2 large EGG WHITES

One 4- to 5-pound SNAPPER or SALMON, cleaned and scaled

LEMON WEDGES

EXTRA-VIRGIN OLIVE OIL, for drizzling

1. Preheat the oven to 475°F.

2. Pour the salt into a large bowl, add the egg whites, and mix vigorously until the salt is evenly moistened. Spread one-third of the salt mixture over the bottom of a large rectangular or oval baking dish big enough to hold the fish. Place the fish on top, then cover it with the rest of the salt mixture, making sure it is completely covered.

3. Place the baking dish in the oven and reduce the heat to 400°F. Bake for 20 to 30 minutes, depending on the thickness of the fish—the rule of thumb is 10 minutes for every inch of thickness at the fish's widest part. Remove from the oven.

4. Crack the crust open at the table with the handle of a knife or a small hammer, and lift it off. Fillet the fish, and serve with lemon wedges, drizzling the olive oil over the flesh.

SNAPPER *with* OLIVES
Cernia alle Olive

A magnificent American delicacy, a real red snapper from the Gulf is one of the few American fish, along with wild striped bass and king salmon, that incite Italians to crazy jealousy when they eat here. The simplest method of cooking is always preferable with a fish as delicate as a snapper.

MAKES 4 SERVINGS

One 3- to 4-pound RED SNAPPER, cleaned and scaled

FLOUR for dredging

6 tablespoons EXTRA-VIRGIN OLIVE OIL

1 cup GAETA OLIVES, pitted and coarsely chopped

3 tablespoons salt-packed CAPERS, rinsed

5 LEMONS, zested and segmented (see page 55)

Juice of 3 LEMONS

1 cup DRY WHITE WINE

About ¼ cup best-quality EXTRA-VIRGIN OLIVE OIL

¼ cup finely chopped ITALIAN PARSLEY

COARSE SEA SALT

1. Preheat the oven to 450°F.
2. With a sharp knife, score the snapper twice on each side. Dredge the fish in the flour. In a 14-inch ovenproof sauté pan or a flameproof roasting pan, heat the 6 tablespoons olive oil over medium-high heat until just smoking. Place the fish in the pan and cook until golden brown on the first side. Carefully turn the fish and add the olives, capers, lemon zest, segments, and juice, and wine.
3. Place the pan in the oven and roast for 14 to 15 minutes, until the fish is just cooked through. Allow the fish to rest for 5 minutes.
4. To serve, fillet the fish, cut each fillet in half, and arrange on four plates. Drizzle with the pan juices and the ¼ cup best-quality olive oil, sprinkle with the parsley and salt, and serve.

BREAM *in a* PACKAGE
Orata al Cartoccio

Cooking fish in a simple package is one of the purest expressions of Italian fish ideology. As I've tried to make abundantly clear, any kind of manipulation of fish with culinary tricks or complicated techniques or sauces is viewed as heresy in the Italian kitchen, where the sanctity of gifts from the sea is never questioned or toyed with.

MAKES 4 SERVINGS

Two 2-pound ORATA, SEA BREAM, or PORGY, cleaned and scaled

SALT and freshly ground BLACK PEPPER

4 cloves GARLIC, thinly sliced

1 teaspoon HOT RED PEPPER FLAKES

½ bunch THYME, leaves only

¼ cup EXTRA-VIRGIN OLIVE OIL

¼ cup DRY WHITE WINE

2 tablespoons fresh LEMON JUICE

1 EGG WHITE, beaten

½ cup best-quality EXTRA-VIRGIN OLIVE OIL

LEMON WEDGES

1. Preheat the oven to 500°F.

2. Cut two 18-by-14-inch pieces of parchment paper (or large enough to hold each fish with a few inches margin when folded in half), fold each one crosswise in half to mark the center, and then unfold. Aggressively season the fish inside and out with salt and pepper. Place 1 fish on one side of each piece of parchment. Sprinkle with the garlic, red pepper flakes, and thyme leaves and drizzle with the ¼ cup olive oil, the wine, and lemon juice.

3. Brush the edges of each sheet of parchment with the egg white. Fold the paper over to enclose the fish and then fold the edges over all around, making a double or triple fold to seal. Place the packages on a baking sheet and bake for 16 minutes, or until puffed. Transfer each package to a serving platter.

4. To serve, quickly but carefully slash the packages open with a knife. Fillet the fish, and place 1 fillet on each serving plate. Drizzle with the remaining ¼ cup olive oil and serve with lemon wedges.

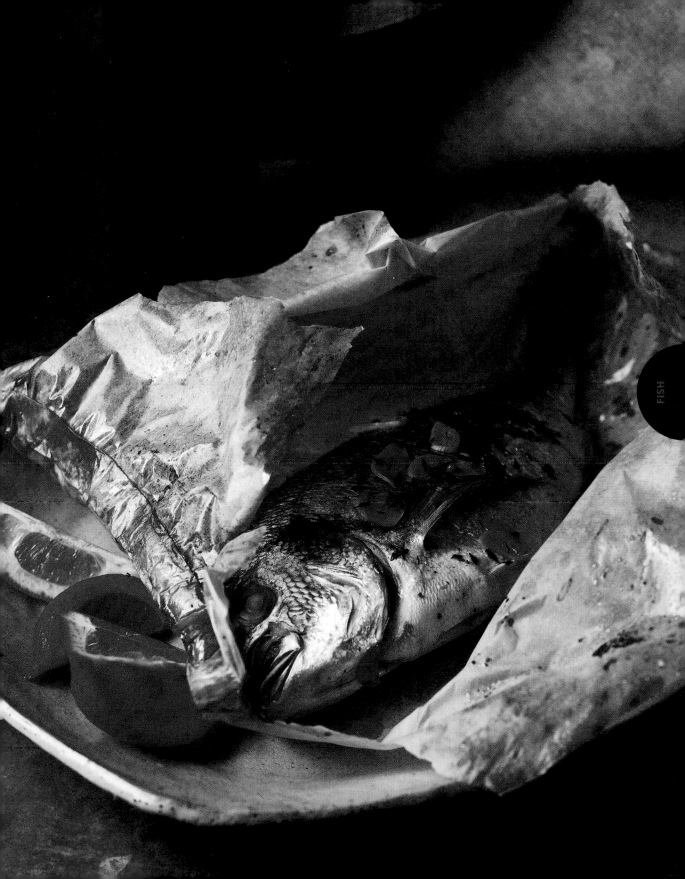

RED MULLET WRAPPED *in* PAPER

Triglie al Cartoccio

Try to find the small mullets called rouget. Usually from Spain, Portugal, or France, they have the most delicate flavor. Fish cooked in a package like this retains all of its delicious juices and tastes more like the sea itself—for Italians, the ultimate objective.

MAKES 4 SERVINGS

Four 8-ounce RED MULLET, cleaned and scaled

Juice of 1 LEMON

2 cloves GARLIC, crushed

½ cup EXTRA-VIRGIN OLIVE OIL

3 BAY LEAVES, crushed

1 teaspoon freshly ground BLACK PEPPER, plus more to taste

SALT

½ cup small BLACK OLIVES, pitted and finely chopped

LEMON WEDGES

1. Place the fish in a single layer in a baking dish or a nonreactive casserole. In a small bowl, combine the lemon juice, garlic, ¼ cup of the olive oil, the bay leaves, and pepper and whisk to emulsify. Pour the marinade over the fish. Cover and refrigerate for 2 hours, turning the fish once.

2. Preheat the oven to 400°F.

3. Cut 4 sheets of parchment paper that are large enough to hold a single fish with a few inches margin when folded in half. Fold each one crosswise in half to mark the center, and then unfold. Brush each one with 1 tablespoon of the remaining olive oil. Remove the fish from the marinade and place 1 on one side of each piece of paper. Season with salt and pepper and sprinkle with the olives. Fold the paper over to enclose the fish and then fold the edges over all around, making a double or triple fold to seal.

4. Place the packages on one or two baking sheets and bake for 10 minutes, or until puffed. Transfer to serving plates. Slash the top of each package open with a sharp knife and serve immediately, with lemon wedges.

MARINATED TUNA SICILIAN-STYLE
with SCALLION FRITTATA

Tonno in Scapece con Frocia

This dish seems simultaneously exotic and familiar. The marinated tuna cubes, somewhat like a kind of ceviche, work beautifully with the firm, piquant frittata. It's perfect for brunch or as a casual lunch because you can make everything a couple of hours ahead and serve it at room temperature.

MAKES 4 SERVINGS

1 pound SUSHI-GRADE TUNA, cut into ¾-inch cubes

¼ cup plus 3 tablespoons EXTRA-VIRGIN OLIVE OIL

¼ cup RED WINE VINEGAR

1 clove GARLIC, thinly sliced

2 PLUM TOMATOES, finely chopped

¼ cup fresh MINT LEAVES

1 teaspoon dried OREGANO FLOWERS or regular dried OREGANO

1 teaspoon HOT RED PEPPER FLAKES

6 large EGGS

SALT and freshly ground BLACK PEPPER

½ cup thinly sliced SCALLIONS

½ cup freshly grated PECORINO ROMANO

1. Bring 2 quarts of water to a boil in a medium saucepan. Drop the tuna into the boiling water, lower the heat to a simmer, and cook for 2 minutes. Drain carefully and place in one layer on a platter to cool.

2. In a small bowl, stir together ¼ cup of the olive oil, the vinegar, garlic, tomatoes, mint, oregano, and red pepper flakes. Pour over the cooled tuna and set aside.

3. In a 6- to 8-inch nonstick sauté pan, heat the remaining 3 tablespoons olive oil over medium heat until smoking. Meanwhile, in a medium bowl, beat the eggs and salt and pepper to taste, then stir in the scallions and pecorino. Pour into the hot pan and cook until the frittata is set on the bottom. Invert the frittata onto a plate, then slide it back into the pan and cook until completely set. Transfer to a plate and let cool.

4. Cut the frittata into 4 wedges. Place on serving plates, arrange the tuna on top, and serve.

SALT COD ROMAN-STYLE

Baccalà alla Romana

The success of the dish depends on the quality of the baccalà. Buy the thickest, whitest pieces you can find, with the bones already removed. Do note that you will need to start soaking the baccalà two days ahead.

MAKES 4 SERVINGS

2 pounds BACCALÀ, soaked in cold water in the refrigerator for 2 days (change the water daily)

¾ cup ALL-PURPOSE FLOUR

¼ cup SELTZER

¼ cup WHOLE MILK

1 large EGG

1 cup EXTRA-VIRGIN OLIVE OIL

SALT and freshly ground BLACK PEPPER

¼ cup finely chopped ITALIAN PARSLEY

2 LEMONS, cut into wedges

1. Drain the baccalà, rinse, and pat dry. Cut it into 2-inch pieces and set aside.
2. Place the flour in a medium bowl and whisk in first the seltzer, then the milk, and then the egg, whisking until the batter is smooth.
3. In a 10- to 12-inch sauté pan, heat the olive oil over medium-high heat until it reaches 375°F. Working in batches to avoid crowding the pan, dip the baccalà pieces into the batter, tap gently against the side of the bowl to remove the excess, and place in the hot oil. Cook until deep golden brown on the first side, then turn over and cook until golden on the second side. Transfer to a plate lined with paper towels to drain.
4. Transfer the baccalà to a warmed platter, season with salt and pepper, and sprinkle with the parsley. Serve with the lemon wedges.

BACCALÀ AND STOCCAFISSO

Baccalà and stoccafisso are both names for preserved cod, differentiated by the way in which it is preserved. Stoccafisso is preserved by air-drying, the most ancient method of preserving cod, dating to the fifteenth century. (The name *stoccafisso* comes from the Dutch word *stokvish*, which means, literally, fish stick, or fish dried on a stick.) The cod was in fact dried on sticks in the open air on the fishing boats or fixed on sticks embedded into the beach. Before being eaten, stoccafisso must be beaten to break up its fibers and soaked in several changes of cold water for two days.

Baccalà is cod that has been decapitated, split open, and preserved covered with salt in special small casks. The technique was developed in northern Spain by Basque fishermen in the fifteenth century. This method became widely used in North Europe, especially among the Norwegians who, by the seventeenth century, had become the greatest exporters of baccalà. As with stoccafisso, baccalà must be soaked for at least two days in cold water to remove the excess salt.

GRILLED WHOLE BLACK BASS *with* ONIONS, OLIVES *and* RED CHARD

Branzino alla Griglia

Whole fish cooked on the bone retain a special juiciness and an almost gelatinous texture because of the gelatin-rich bones. This dish was inspired by a visit to an amazing place called Ca Peo, just outside of Genoa.

MAKES 4 SERVINGS

6 tablespoons EXTRA-VIRGIN OLIVE OIL

1 large RED ONION, thinly sliced

1 cup LIGURIAN BLACK OLIVES

2 pounds RED SWISS CHARD, trimmed and cut into 1-inch-wide ribbons, including stalks (about 8 cups)

Grated zest and juice of 1 LEMON

SALT and freshly ground BLACK PEPPER

Two 2-pound BLACK BASS, cleaned and scaled

½ cup OLIVE PASTE

2 LEMONS, cut into 6 wedges each

1. Preheat the grill or barbecue.

2. Heat a 12-inch sauté pan over medium heat, and add ¼ cup of the olive oil. Add the onion and cook until wilted, 1 to 2 minutes. Add the olives, chard, and lemon zest and juice and toss until the chard is wilted, 2 to 3 minutes. Season to taste with salt and pepper, remove from the heat, and cover to keep warm.

3. Season the fish inside and out with salt and pepper and brush with the remaining 2 table-spoons olive oil. Place on the grill or on a baking sheet under the broiler and cook, turning every 3 to 4 minutes, for 12 to 15 minutes, until cooked through yet still moist.

4. Just before serving, reheat the chard if necessary.

5. Place the fish on a large serving platter, arrange the chard around the border, and serve immediately, with the olive paste and lemon wedges alongside.

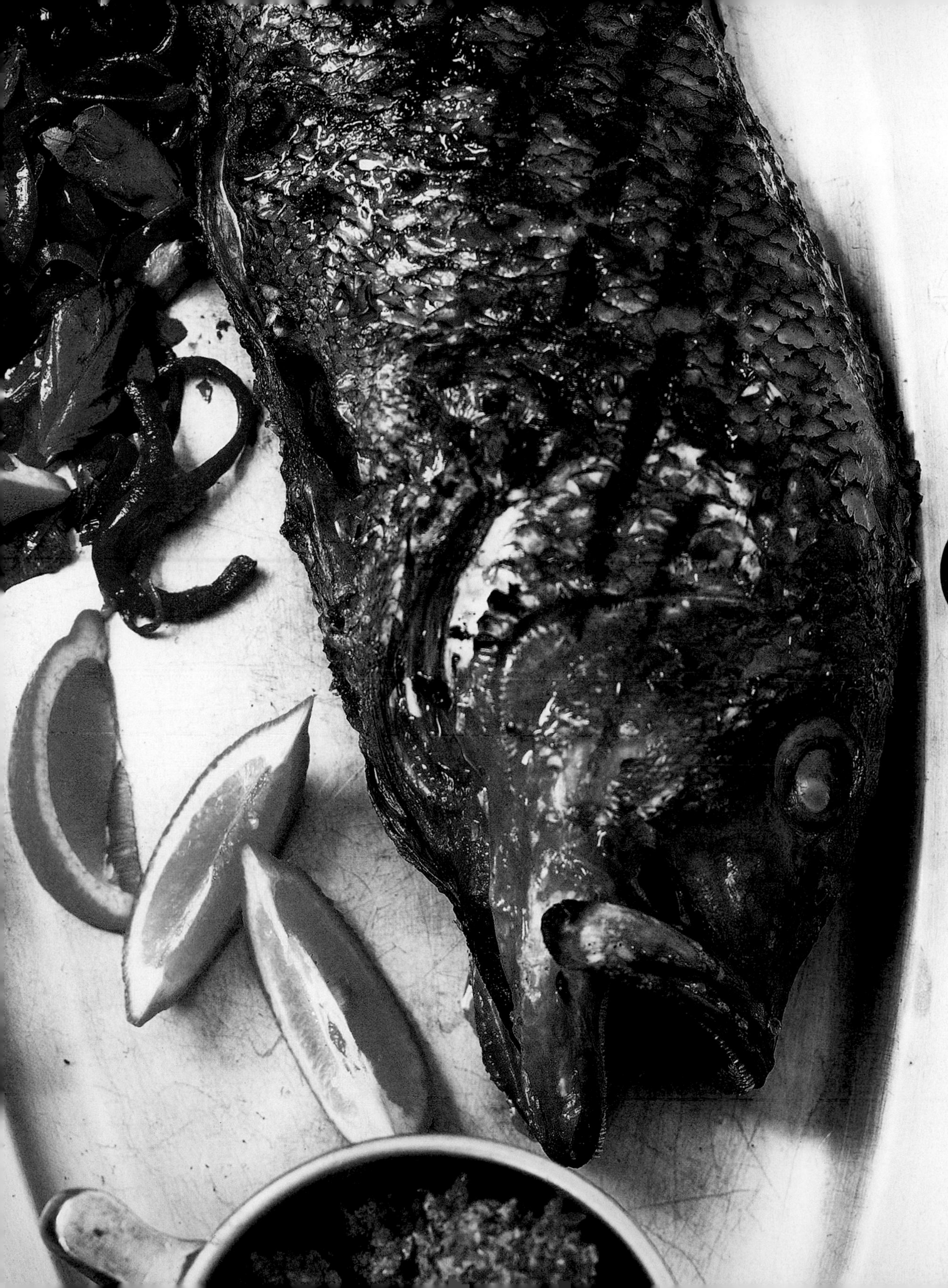

MONKFISH SCALOPPINE *with* CHIANTI *and* SAGE

Coda al Chianti

Although red wine with fish is still a novelty in Rome, a variation on this dish, with the monkfish roasted in a wood-burning oven, was part of an exceptional lunch at a simple yet great restaurant frequented by journalists just off the Po River. We drank cellar-temperature Chianti Classico and argued art and politics well into the afternoon.

MAKES 4 SERVINGS

1 pound MONKFISH FILLET, cut into eight ½-inch-thick slices

¼ cup EXTRA-VIRGIN OLIVE OIL

¼ cup ALL-PURPOSE FLOUR

SALT and freshly ground BLACK PEPPER

4 SCALLIONS, white part only, sliced paper-thin

8 fresh SAGE LEAVES

1 cup DRY RED WINE, preferably Chianti

8 JUMBO OLIVES, pitted and halved

½ cup BASIC TOMATO SAUCE (page 71)

2 tablespoons cold UNSALTED BUTTER

2 tablespoons finely chopped ITALIAN PARSLEY

1. With a meat mallet, gently pound each slice of monkfish between sheets of wax paper to flatten it to ¼-inch thick.

2. In a 10- to 12-inch nonstick sauté pan, heat the olive oil over medium-high heat until almost smoking. Meanwhile, season the flour with salt and pepper and spread on a plate. Dredge the fish in the flour, add to the hot oil, and cook, turning once, until golden brown on both sides, about 5 to 6 minutes in all. Transfer the fish to a platter and place in a warm place.

3. Add the scallions and sage to the pan and stir until the scallions are softened and starting to brown, about 1 minute. Add the wine, olives, and tomato sauce, stir well, and bring to a boil.

4. Place the fish in the sauce and add the cold butter, then lower the heat and simmer for 5 minutes; the sauce will thicken slightly to coat the fish. Add the parsley and swirl to mix.

5. Transfer to a warmed platter, and serve.

EEL *with* OLIVES, CHILES *and* CAPER BERRIES

Anguilla Messinese

Eel can be a tough sell, until you have tried it. In Italy, however, it appears in a magnificent and succulent dish on almost every table during Christmas week, particularly on La Vigilia, Christmas Eve, when it is perhaps the most traditional dish of all the many fish dishes served that night.

MAKES 4 SERVINGS

2 cups BASIC TOMATO SAUCE (page 71)

1 cup DRY RED WINE

12 CAPER BERRIES

12 GAETA OLIVES

2 tablespoons DRIED CURRANTS

2 tablespoons PINE NUTS

1 teaspoon HOT RED PEPPER FLAKES

2 pounds EEL (from the sea or river), skinned and gutted by your fishmonger, rinsed, patted dry, and cut into 4-inch-long pieces

SALT and freshly ground BLACK PEPPER

2 tablespoons chopped FENNEL FRONDS

1. Preheat the oven to 450°F.

2. In a large saucepan, combine the tomato sauce, wine, caper berries, olives, currants, pine nuts, and red pepper flakes and bring to a boil over medium heat.

3. Meanwhile, season the eel with salt and pepper and arrange in a single layer in a baking dish.

4. Pour the sauce over the eel, put the dish in the oven, and bake for about 20 minutes, until the eel is cooked through. Transfer to a warmed platter, sprinkle with the fennel fronds, and serve immediately.

TUNA ROLLS MESSINA-STYLE

Involtini Messinese

While rare and raw tuna has become a cliché in American restaurants, Italians still prefer their cooked fish cooked through. Wrapped around a simple stuffing and cooked in a spicy tomato sauce in the oven, the tuna stays moist and juicy, and it is easy to cook just right.

MAKES 4 SERVINGS

¼ cup EXTRA-VIRGIN OLIVE OIL

1 medium SPANISH ONION, cut into ⅛-inch dice

2 salt-packed ANCHOVIES, filleted and rinsed

6 tablespoons PINE NUTS

6 tablespoons DRIED CURRANTS

Grated zest of 2 ORANGES

1 cup FRESH BREAD CRUMBS

2 pounds TUNA, cut into eight ¼-inch-thick slices (ask the fishmonger to cut the slices from a "loin" cut)

½ cup ITALIAN PARSLEY LEAVES

2 cups BASIC TOMATO SAUCE (page 71)

¼ cup SICILIAN OLIVES

2 teaspoons HOT RED PEPPER FLAKES

½ cup DRY WHITE WINE

1. In a 10- to 12-inch sauté pan, heat the olive oil over medium-high heat until smoking. Add the onion, anchovies, 2 tablespoons of the pine nuts, and 2 tablespoons of the currants and cook until the anchovies have begun to dissolve and the onion has softened and is lightly browned, about 5 minutes. Add the orange zest and bread crumbs and cook until the bread crumbs are browned and toasted, about 5 minutes more. Remove from the heat and let cool.

2. Using a meat mallet, gently flatten each slice of tuna between sheets of oiled wax paper or aluminum foil to ⅛-inch thick. Lay out on a work surface in a cool spot.

3. Preheat the oven to 450°F.

4. Add the parsley to the bread crumb mixture and stir well. Divide the bread crumb mixture among the tuna slices. Roll up each one like a jelly roll, starting from a long side, and secure with a toothpick.

5. In a 2-quart saucepan, stir together the tomato sauce, the remaining ¼ cup each pine nuts and currants, the olives, red pepper flakes, and wine and bring to a boil. Pour the sauce into an small earthenware or other baking dish and arrange the involtini in the sauce. Bake for about 25 minutes, until the fish is cooked through and the stuffing is hot. Allow to rest for 10 minutes before serving.

SWORDFISH PAILLARDS *with* LEEKS *and* GRAPEFRUIT

Paillard di Spada

This dish was inspired by the cooking of Sicily, yet Sicilians would not use a mustard vinaigrette on fish. I love the texture of the barely cooked paillards, as well as the flavor of the tangy mustard and the sweet grapefruit in the sauce working with the natural sweetness of the leeks.

MAKES 4 SERVINGS

12 ounces boneless center-cut SWORDFISH, sliced horizontally into 4 thin slices by the fishmonger

2 PINK GRAPEFRUITS

2 large LEEKS, white and light green parts only, cut into 4-inch-long julienne and rinsed well

1 teaspoon DIJON MUSTARD

2 teaspoons BLACK MUSTARD SEEDS

6 tablespoons EXTRA-VIRGIN OLIVE OIL

1 tablespoon fresh LEMON JUICE

1. Preheat the oven to 450°F.

2. Place the swordfish paillards on four ovenproof serving plates, cover with plastic wrap, and place in the refrigerator.

3. Grate the zest from both grapefruits; reserve. Squeeze the juice from 1 grapefruit and set aside. Segment the remaining grapefruit (see page 55).

4. Bring 2 quarts of water to a boil in a medium saucepan, and add 1 tablespoon salt. Set up an ice bath near the stovetop. Drop the leeks into the boiling water and cook until tender, about 2 minutes. Drain the leeks and plunge into the ice bath to cool, about 1 minute. Drain well and set aside.

5. In a small bowl, whisk together half the grapefruit zest, the grapefruit juice, mustard, mustard seeds, and ¼ cup of the olive oil until lightly emulsified; set aside.

6. Uncover the swordfish plates, place in the oven, and cook until the fish is just opaque, 35 to 45 seconds. Remove from the oven and set aside.

7. Dress the leeks with the remaining 2 tablespoons olive oil and the lemon juice, and divide among the swordfish plates, making a pile in the center of each. Place 3 grapefruit segments on each plate and sprinkle with the remaining zest. Drizzle with the sauce, and serve warm.

GRILLED MACKEREL *and* EGGPLANT *with* SALSA VERDE

Sgombro con Melanzane

Mackerel is not the most popular fish in most homes, probably because of the fact that its high oil content makes it an almost too-fragrant fish when not absolutely fresh. Just out of the sea, though, it is delicious, and it works incredibly well with this tangy green sauce and almost any of the vegetables I associate with summer—eggplant and cucumber in particular.

MAKES 4 SERVINGS

4 long, thin EGGPLANT, preferably Asian, cut lengthwise in half

6 tablespoons EXTRA-VIRGIN OLIVE OIL

3 tablespoons RED WINE VINEGAR

1 tablespoon HOT RED PEPPER FLAKES

1 tablespoon dried OREGANO

4 MACKEREL FILLETS (about 2 pounds total), any bones removed

SALSA VERDE

1½ cups ITALIAN PARSLEY LEAVES

½ cup fresh MINT LEAVES

2 salt-packed ANCHOVIES, filleted and rinsed

1 cup EXTRA-VIRGIN OLIVE OIL

1 HARD-BOILED EGG, finely chopped

2 tablespoons CAPERS, finely chopped

Grated zest and juice of 1 LEMON

SALT, if necessary

1. Preheat the grill.

2. Place the eggplant in a large bowl, add 3 tablespoons of the olive oil, the vinegar, red pepper flakes, and oregano, and toss to coat. Place the eggplant cut side down on the grill (reserve the marinade) and cook, turning once, until dark golden brown and lightly charred, about 6 minutes per side. Return to the marinade, turning to coat.

3. Brush the mackerel skin with the remaining 3 tablespoons olive oil and place skin side down onto the grill. Cook for 5 to 6 minutes, until the skin is nicely charred, then turn carefully and cook for 1 minute longer. Arrange in the center of a round platter.

4. To make the salsa, combine the parsley, mint, anchovies, and olive oil in a blender and pulse until smooth. Transfer to a serving bowl, add the chopped egg, capers, and lemon zest and juice and mix well. Season to taste with salt if necessary.

5. Arrange the eggplant around the mackerel, drizzle the dish with the sauce, and serve.

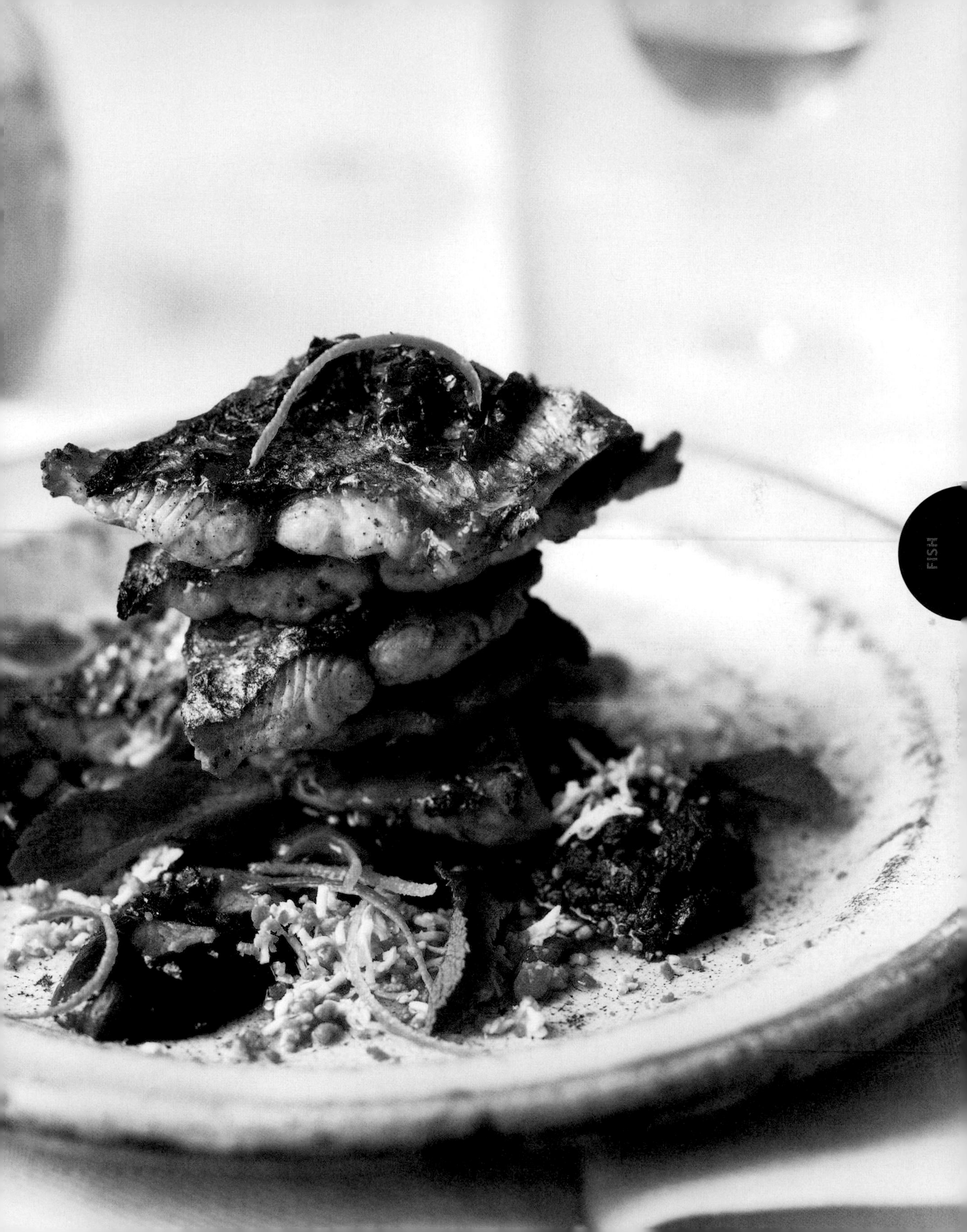

FOWL

Cooking birds in the United States is a lot easier than cooking birds in Italy. We have an excellent supply of delicious farm-raised organic and free-range poultry, unlike any other place on the planet—unless you have your own coop and pen.

And not only do organic and free-range birds taste better, treating animals in a safe and smart way also avoids a lot of the health-related risks associated with commercial animal production. So, let it be said that we should support and buy from our true organic and free-range farmers, and even if the price is a bit higher, it is worth it for us, our children, and theirs.

Italians love their courtyard animals, both to raise and to eat. Chickens, turkeys, squab, quail, and guinea fowl are running all over the yards of rural Italian farm houses, and for one main reason: because they are delicious. And what Italians can not raise successfully, they hunt. Duck, pheasant, thrush, hare, boar, and deer are all part of the European culture of the hunt and the feast, a centuries-old way of life that started as a way of survival. Fortunately for us, here we have a well-developed trade in all game, all of it inspected by the USDA. For that reason, it is quite simple to find a source for excellent-quality and very safe game birds of all types.

Smaller birds like quail and squab are traditionally roasted or grilled over coals quite simply in the Italian kitchen—unless they have a tendency to dry out, as partridge or pheasant can, in which case they are braised slowly to retain their moisture. Medium-sized birds such as chickens and guinea fowl are typically roasted or braised in a light stew with vegetables. Larger birds like capon or turkey are often boiled or poached whole and then carved, or cut up raw into thin slices or cutlets and treated like scaloppine.

One of the best things about all of the recipes in this chapter is that none of them takes much preparation or cooking time. Once you have done the shopping, most of these can be prepared in under an hour, with the bulk of the time being unmonitored cooking in the oven or in the pot. And that frees you up for the rest of life, like opening a bottle of wine or napping on the porch.

CHICKEN THIGHS *with* SAFFRON, GREEN OLIVES *and* MINT

Pollo allo Zafferano

Thighs are the best part of all birds. And now that chicken thighs can be bought already separated from the rest of the bird, we can avoid the expense of feeding the breasts to the dog.

MAKES 4 SERVINGS

FLOUR for dredging

12 CHICKEN THIGHS (2½ to 3 pounds), rinsed and patted dry

SALT and freshly ground BLACK PEPPER

¼ cup EXTRA-VIRGIN OLIVE OIL

2 large RED ONIONS, thinly sliced

½ teaspoon SAFFRON THREADS

1 cup small GREEN OLIVES

1 medium CARROT, finely chopped

3 cups CHICKEN STOCK (page 125)

½ cup fresh MINT LEAVES

1. Spread the flour on a plate. Season the chicken thighs liberally with salt and pepper and dredge in the flour. In a Dutch oven, heat the olive oil over high heat until smoking. Add 6 thighs at a time and brown well on all sides. Transfer to a plate.

2. Add the onions and saffron to the pot and cook until the onions are softened, 8 to 10 minutes. Add the olives, carrot, and stock and bring to a boil. Return the chicken thighs to the pot, arranging them in a single layer, and bring to a boil. Lower the heat to a simmer, cover the pot tightly, and simmer for 15 minutes.

3. Remove the lid and cook, uncovered, until the chicken is just cooked through, about 10 minutes. Transfer the chicken to a platter. Season the sauce with salt and pepper to taste and add the mint leaves. Pour the sauce over the chicken thighs, and serve.

STUFFED CHICKEN LEGS
Braciole di Pollo

Braised or roasted chicken legs are perhaps the number one favorite meal of the staffs of my restaurants because they are quick to make, they never dry out, and they are easy to eat with only one hand while standing. These drummies need no sauce and are excellent cold as well.

MAKES 6 SERVINGS

4 ounces thinly sliced PROSCIUTTO DI PARMA, cut into ¼-inch-wide strips

1½ cups FRESH BREAD CRUMBS

1½ cups freshly grated PARMIGIANO-REGGIANO

½ cup grated PROVOLONE

2 large EGGS, lightly beaten

¼ cup finely chopped ITALIAN PARSLEY

1 bunch BASIL, leaves only

1 tablespoon chopped fresh ROSEMARY

Grated zest of 4 LEMONS

12 whole CHICKEN LEGS, including thighs, bones removed by your butcher (each leg left in one piece), rinsed, and patted dry

SALT and freshly ground BLACK PEPPER

1. Preheat the oven to 450°F.

2. In a medium bowl, gently stir together the prosciutto, bread crumbs, Parmigiano, provolone, eggs, parsley, basil, rosemary, and lemon zest until mixed.

3. Lay the chicken legs skin side down on a cutting board and season all over with salt and pepper. Place 2 tablespoons of the filling into the cavity of each leg, spreading it into the thigh and the upper part of the leg. Roll each leg up, starting from a long side, and tie tightly twice with butcher's twine. Season the thighs with salt and pepper and place on a roasting rack in a roasting pan.

4. Roast the chicken for 35 to 40 minutes, until it is crisp and golden and the internal temperature registers 160°F on an instant-read thermometer. Remove from the oven and allow to rest for 10 minutes.

5. Slice each leg into ¾-inch-thick medallions, and serve.

FOWL

CHICKEN STEW *with* POLENTA, CELERY ROOT *and* SAGE

Pollo all'Americano

This stew is easy to make and reheats well. The trick is to use leftover polenta from another dish to stretch out the stew for more guests, which is no doubt how this dish came into being. I love the sweet "corn dumpling" flavor and the way it works with the celery root.

MAKES 4 SERVINGS

5 cups WATER

1 cup quick-cooking POLENTA or fine CORNMEAL

½ cup ALL-PURPOSE FLOUR

SALT and freshly ground BLACK PEPPER

One 3½- to 4-pound CHICKEN, cut into 8 serving pieces, rinsed, and patted dry

4 ounces CHICKEN LIVERS

6 tablespoons EXTRA-VIRGIN OLIVE OIL

1 large SPANISH ONION, cut into ½-inch dice

1 large CELERY ROOT, peeled and cut into ¼-inch dice

2 cups BARBARESCO or other fruity red wine

1 cup BASIC TOMATO SAUCE (page 71)

8 fresh SAGE LEAVES

1 tablespoon PARSLEY, chiffonade

1 tablespoon LEMON ZEST

1. In a 4-quart saucepan, bring the water to a boil. Add the polenta in a steady stream, whisking constantly. Pull the pan off the heat and stir with a wooden spoon until the polenta is as thick as molten lava. Pour into an 8-by-10-inch baking pan and allow to cool.

2. Season the flour with salt and pepper and spread on a plate. Dredge the chicken pieces in the flour, then dredge the chicken livers in the flour. In a large Dutch oven, heat the olive oil over medium-high heat until smoking. Brown the chicken pieces in two batches, then transfer to a plate. Add the livers, onion, and celery root to the pot and cook until the vegetables are golden brown, 10 to 12 minutes.

3. Add the wine, tomato sauce, and sage and return the chicken pieces to the pot. Bring to a boil, then lower the heat to a simmer and cook until the thighs are nearly cooked through, about 20 minutes.

4. Meanwhile, cut the polenta into ½-inch cubes. Add the polenta to the pot and cook for another 10 minutes. Season with salt and pepper, place on platter, sprinkle with parsley and zest, and serve immediately.

CHICKEN *with* "COOKED WINE"
Pollo al Vin Cotto

You can buy bottles of vin cotto, which translates as "cooked wine," in fancy specialty shops, but it is quite easy to make a version of it at home. And it is a great way to use up those less-than-acceptable wine gifts from your enologically challenged friends.

MAKES 4 SERVINGS

VIN COTTO

4½ cups RED WINE

½ cup HONEY

2 CINNAMON STICKS

3 CLOVES

¼ cup EXTRA-VIRGIN OLIVE OIL, plus more for drizzling

One 3-pound CHICKEN, cut into 8 serving pieces, rinsed, and patted dry

SALT

1 large ONION, cut into large dice

2 CARROTS, diced

½ cup GREEN OLIVES, such as Sicilian, pitted and chopped

3 tablespoons RAISINS

1 tablespoon CAPERS, rinsed and drained

1 tablespoon PINE NUTS, toasted

3 tablespoons BLANCHED ALMONDS, toasted

1 cup RED WINE VINEGAR

½ cup SUGAR

Freshly ground BLACK PEPPER

Cracked BLACK PEPPER

1 tablespoon HOT RED PEPPER FLAKES

¼ cup finely chopped ITALIAN PARSLEY

1. To make the vin cotto, combine all the ingredients in a heavy-bottomed saucepan and bring to a boil over high heat. Reduce the heat and simmer, stirring occasionally, until reduced to 1 cup, about 20 minutes. Remove from the heat and let cool; remove the cinnamon sticks and cloves before using.

2. In a 10- to 12-inch sauté pan, heat the olive oil over high heat until very hot but not smoking. Season the chicken with salt, add skin side down to the pan, and brown on both sides, about 4 minutes per side. Reduce the heat to medium, add the onion and carrots, and cook, stirring, until deep golden brown. Add the olives, raisins, capers, pine nuts, and almonds to the pan, stirring well. Add ½ cup of the vin cotto to deglaze the pan, stirring up the browned bits on the bottom, then boil until reduced by half. Add the remaining ½ cup vin cotto, and bring to a boil.

3. Meanwhile, in a small bowl, combine the vinegar and sugar. Add to the pan and cook, stirring, until the liquid has reduced to a glaze. Season to taste with salt and pepper.

4. Transfer the chicken to a warmed platter and drizzle with olive oil. Sprinkle with cracked black pepper, the red pepper flakes, and parsley, and serve.

FOWL

SPICY SICILIAN CHICKEN

Pollo in Stemperata

This is my bird take on a traditional Sicilian rabbit dish that is perfect for spice lovers. The dried hot chile can come from your Bobby Flay shelf of Mexican and Southwestern turn-and-burners, or you can use the fiery Asian or Thai chiles. Whatever you decide, this dish must be hot!

MAKES 4 SERVINGS

One 3½-pound CHICKEN, cut into 8 serving pieces, rinsed, and patted dry

SALT and freshly ground BLACK PEPPER

3 tablespoons EXTRA-VIRGIN OLIVE OIL, plus extra for drizzling

2 medium RUSSET POTATOES, peeled and cut into large cubes

2 RED, YELLOW, GREEN, or ORANGE BELL PEPPERS, cored, seeded, and cut into ½-inch-wide strips

1 rib CELERY, cut into 1-inch-long pieces

2 small EGGPLANT, cut into large cubes

2 medium CARROTS, sliced into ½-inch-thick rounds

4 PLUM TOMATOES, cut into chunks

½ cup SICILIAN OLIVES, pitted

2 tablespoons salt-packed CAPERS, rinsed and drained

5 DRIED HOT CHILES

1½ cups DRY RED WINE

2 tablespoons chopped fresh MINT

2 tablespoons chopped ITALIAN PARSLEY

Pinch of HOT RED PEPPER FLAKES

1. Season the chicken pieces with salt and pepper. In a 10- to 12-inch sauté pan, heat 3 tablespoons of the olive oil over medium-high heat until hot but not smoking. Add the chicken pieces skin side down, and brown on both sides, about 5 minutes per side. Transfer to a plate and set aside.

2. Add the potatoes, peppers, celery, eggplant, carrots, tomatoes, olives, capers, and chiles to the pan, tossing them together. Season with salt and pepper, then add the wine, return the chicken to the pan, and bring to a boil. Cover, lower the heat to a simmer, and cook until the chicken is cooked through, about 15 minutes.

3. Stir in the mint, parsley, and red pepper flakes, and transfer the stew to a serving dish. Allow to cool to room temperature.

4. Drizzle the stew with olive oil and serve.

THE DEVIL'S CHICKEN
Pollo al Diavolo

MAKES 4 SERVINGS

One 2½- to 3-pound CHICKEN, rinsed and patted dry

SALT

¼ cup freshly ground BLACK PEPPER, plus more to taste

6 tablespoons EXTRA-VIRGIN OLIVE OIL

2 tablespoons DIJON MUSTARD

1 cup roughly chopped ITALIAN PARSLEY

1 RED ONION, thinly sliced

12 CHERRY TOMATOES, cut in half

1 tablespoon SHERRY VINEGAR

SPICY OIL for drizzling

1. Preheat the oven to 400°F.

2. Season the chicken inside and out with salt and pepper. Truss it and brush with 2 tablespoons of the olive oil. Place on a rack in a roasting pan and roast until browned but only about half-cooked, about 40 minutes.

3. Meanwhile, in a small bowl, combine the ¼ cup black pepper, a pinch of salt, and the mustard and stir well. Drizzle in 1 tablespoon of the olive oil, whisking until blended.

4. Remove the browned chicken from the oven and brush with the black pepper and mustard mixture. Return to the oven and continue roasting until the juices run clear when a thigh is pricked, about another 30 minutes. Let rest for 10 minutes.

5. While the chicken rests, in a medium bowl, combine the parsley, onion, tomatoes, the remaining 3 tablespoons olive oil, the vinegar, and salt and pepper to taste and toss well.

6. Carve the chicken and arrange on serving plates. Drizzle with the pan juices and the spicy oil, top with the parsley salad, and serve immediately.

SPICY OIL
Olio Piccante

2 cups EXTRA-VIRGIN OLIVE OIL

8 JALAPEÑOS, seeded and cut into ⅛- inch dice

2 tablespoons HOT RED PEPPER FLAKES

1 tablespoon SWEET *PIMENTÓN* (Spanish smoked paprika)

1. In a medium saucepan, combine the oil, jalapeños, red pepper flakes, and pimentón and heat over medium heat until the oil reaches 175°F. Remove from the heat, and allow to stand overnight.

2. Strain out the solids from the oil. The oil will keep for 3 weeks in a cool, dark place.

FOWL

CHICKEN *in the* STYLE OF CANZANO
Pollo Canzanese

This Canzanese recipe is anything but a peasant dish, with the prosciutto and wine—it probably descended from Spanish royalty, long-time tenants in and around Napoli.

MAKES 4 SERVINGS

Two 3-pound CHICKENS, cut into 8 serving pieces each

1 tablespoon SALT

2 sprigs ROSEMARY

2 fresh SAGE LEAVES

4 BAY LEAVES

3 cloves GARLIC, sliced

12 CLOVES

A small handful of BLACK PEPPERCORNS, crushed

1 small DRIED HOT CHILE

Two ¼-inch-thick slices PROSCIUTTO DI PARMA, finely chopped

¾ cup DRY RED WINE

2 tablespoons finely chopped ITALIAN PARSLEY

1. Place the chicken in a large bowl and season with the salt. Add cold water to cover, and set aside for 30 minutes (see Brining, page 376).

2. Drain the chicken, rinse, and pat dry with paper towels. Place in a large Dutch oven and add the rosemary, sage, bay leaves, garlic, cloves, peppercorns, chile, prosciutto, and wine. Cover, bring to a simmer, and cook, stirring occasionally, until the chicken is almost tender, about 35 minutes.

3. Remove the lid and simmer to reduce the sauce by half, about 15 minutes longer. Remove the chile, if desired.

4. Transfer the chicken to a warmed serving platter, garnish with the parsley, and serve.

GRILLED BABY CHICKEN *in* OLIVE PASTE *with* BROCCOLI RABE

Galletto con Rapini

Baby chickens, often called poussins in the marketplace, are juicier when butterflied and cooked skin side down on the grill. The real game is to marinate them overnight, because their tender and delicate flesh makes them sponges for flavor. They love salty stuff like olives and capers.

MAKES 4 SERVINGS

¾ cup OLIVE PASTE

1 cup EXTRA-VIRGIN OLIVE OIL

2 teaspoons chopped fresh THYME or 1 teaspoon dried THYME

2 teaspoons freshly ground BLACK PEPPER, plus more to taste

1 teaspoon HOT RED PEPPER FLAKES

Four 1-pound BABY CHICKENS, backbones removed, flattened (have the butcher do this), rinsed, and patted dry

2 cloves GARLIC, thinly sliced

2 bunches BROCCOLI RABE, stems trimmed, blanched in boiling salted water until tender, cooled in an ice water bath, and drained

SALT

1. In a large bowl, combine ½ cup of the olive paste, ¾ cup of the olive oil, the thyme, black pepper, and red pepper flakes and mix until well blended. Add the chicken to the bowl and toss and turn to coat. Cover and marinate in the refrigerator for at least an hour, or, preferably, overnight.

2. Preheat the grill or broiler.

3. Place the chickens skin side down on the grill, 8 to 10 inches from the coals, or place skin side up on a baking sheet under the broiler, 5 to 6 inches from the heat source. Cook, turning once, until the skin is crisp and brown and the juices run clear when the thickest part of a thigh is pierced with a knife, 10 to 15 minutes per side.

4. While the birds are cooking, in a 10- to 12-inch sauté pan, combine the remaining ¼ cup olive oil and the garlic and cook over medium heat until the garlic is lightly browned. Add the broccoli rabe and toss until heated through. Season to taste with salt and pepper.

5. Arrange the broccoli rabe in the center of four plates. Place the chickens on the broccoli rabe, spoon 1 tablespoon of the remaining olive paste over each bird, and serve immediately.

FOWL

CHICKEN HUNTER'S-STYLE

Pollo alla Cacciatora

Chicken "catchatori" seemed to be a subset for every mediocre chicken dish ever served to me at restaurants in the '70s and '80s: anything with a mushroom or an onion in it qualified for the title. In my world, chicken cacciatora is a simple braise that depends a lot on the quality of the bird itself. I recommend an organic, free-range chicken, terms that have been bandied around the restaurant business for twenty years, but in fact mean more now than ever. Find a good organic poultry supplier and support them—or raise your own.

MAKES 4 SERVINGS

2 cloves GARLIC, minced

1 branch ROSEMARY, leaves only, minced

SALT and freshly ground BLACK PEPPER

About ½ cup EXTRA-VIRGIN OLIVE OIL

One 3-pound CHICKEN, cut into 8 serving pieces, rinsed, and patted dry

2 large YELLOW ONIONS, coarsely chopped

1 pound PORTOBELLO MUSHROOMS, stems removed, cut into 1-inch cubes

4 ounces PANCETTA, cut into ½-inch dice

4 ribs CELERY, cut into 1-inch pieces

2 cups BASIC TOMATO SAUCE (page 71)

1 cup DRY WHITE WINE

1 cup CHICKEN STOCK (page 125)

Pinch of SUGAR

Pinch of HOT RED PEPPER FLAKES

1. In a large bowl, combine the garlic, rosemary, and salt and pepper to taste and add enough olive oil (3 to 4 tablespoons) to make a somewhat dry paste. Add the chicken and rub the paste evenly over the pieces of chicken. Cover and refrigerate for 2 hours.

2. In a Dutch oven, heat the remaining ¼ cup olive oil over high heat until smoking. Brush the excess rub from the bird, and sear the chicken, in batches if necessary, until browned on all sides. Transfer to a plate lined with paper towels.

3. Add the onions, mushrooms, pancetta, and celery to the pot and cook until the onions are golden brown and the pancetta has rendered its fat, about 8 minutes. Drain off the excess oil, then add the tomato sauce and wine, stirring with a wooden spoon to dislodge the browned bits from the bottom of the pot. Add the stock, sugar, and red pepper flakes and bring to a boil.

4. Return the chicken to the pot, cover, and cook for 20 minutes. Uncover and cook until cooked through, 15 to 20 minutes more. Transfer the chicken to a festive platter, top with the sauce, and serve.

CHICKEN *from the* TOWN *of* AVELLINO
Pollo Avellino

Campania is the next hot region in Italy for American tourists, especially the gourmet type, if only for the city of Napoli and the Amalfi Coast. But dreamy cuisine spots like Avellino and Benevento also have an abundance of riches to deliver at the table, as well as in the culture department. And the whole region is just dying to talk to you about their mozzarella.

MAKES 4 SERVINGS

6 tablespoons EXTRA-VIRGIN OLIVE OIL

One 3-pound CHICKEN, quartered, rinsed, and patted dry

1 medium RED ONION, cut into ½-inch dice

10 cloves GARLIC

4 RED BELL PEPPERS, cored, seeded, and cut into ½-inch dice

8 small HOT PEPPERS, such as cayenne or jalapeño

1 pound CREMINI MUSHROOMS, trimmed and halved

1 cup DRY WHITE WINE, or as needed

1 cup HOT WATER

1 bunch BASIL, leaves only, chopped

¼ cup finely chopped ITALIAN PARSLEY

1. In a 10- to 12-inch heavy-bottomed sauté pan, heat the olive oil over high heat until smoking. Add the chicken pieces skin side down, working in batches if necessary to avoid crowding the pan, and brown them on both sides, turning once. Transfer to a plate and set aside.

2. Add the onion, garlic, bell peppers, 4 of the hot peppers, and the mushrooms to the pan and sauté until golden brown, about 10 minutes. Add the wine and water and bring to a boil. Return the chicken to the pan, reduce the heat, and cook at a bubbling simmer until cooked through, 25 to 30 minutes; add more wine or water if necessary to keep the pan from getting dry.

3. Transfer the chicken to serving plates. Stir the basil and parsley into the sauce, and spoon over the chicken. Serve with 1 hot pepper atop each portion.

GRILLED SQUAB *with* POMEGRANATE MOLASSES

Piccione alla Melagrana

Squab is, in my humble opinion, the most sophisticated of all game birds—and a true test for chefs and cooks. It is not that it is so difficult to cook or prepare, but I can judge the commitment and skill level of any kitchen by the way they treat this delicate meat. I order squab at a restaurant whenever I am confident I will eat well, and I always order a killer wine to go with it—they deserve each other, and I deserve them!

MAKES 4 SERVINGS

½ cup plus 3 tablespoons EXTRA-VIRGIN OLIVE OIL

2 tablespoons HONEY

2 tablespoons RED WINE VINEGAR

2 tablespoons PAPRIKA

4 SQUABS, backbones removed, flattened (have the butcher do this), rinsed, and patted dry

SALT and freshly ground BLACK PEPPER

1 medium RED ONION, thinly sliced

Grated zest and juice of 1 LEMON

1 large bunch KALE, trimmed and cut crosswise into ¼-inch-wide ribbons (about 4 cups)

¾ cup POMEGRANATE MOLASSES (available in Indian and other specialty shops)

1. In a large shallow baking dish, combine ½ cup of the olive oil, the honey, vinegar, and paprika. Add the squab, turning to coat, cover, and marinate, preferably overnight in the refrigerator, or for 3 hours at room temperature.

2. Preheat the grill.

3. Remove the squab from the marinade (discard the marinade), sprinkle with salt and pepper, and place skin side down on grill. Squab should be served medium to medium-rare at the breast bone: Grill for 8 to 10 minutes, then turn over and grill for 4 to 5 minutes, or until the breasts are cooked medium-rare to medium.

4. Meanwhile, in a 10- to 12-inch sauté pan, heat the remaining 3 tablespoons olive oil over high heat until almost smoking. Add the onion and sauté until softened, 8 to 10 minutes. Add the lemon zest and juice and kale and toss until the kale is wilted, 3 to 4 minutes. Season with salt and pepper, and pile in the center of four serving plates.

5. Arrange the cooked squab over the greens. Drizzle 3 tablespoons of the pomegranate molasses over each bird and serve immediately.

FOWL

GAME HENS *with* POMEGRANATE

Beccazini alla Melagrana

In this recipe from Sardegna, the natural sweetness of the tasty bird is accentuated by the pomegranate seeds and the orange peel, so there is no need for a gravy or elaborate sauce.

MAKES 6 SERVINGS

Seeds of 1 large POMEGRANATE

About 1 cup sweet MARSALA

1 tablespoon chopped fresh MINT

6 CORNISH GAME HENS, rinsed and patted dry

SALT and freshly ground BLACK PEPPER

10 tablespoons (1¼ sticks) UNSALTED BUTTER

2 tablespoons EXTRA-VIRGIN OLIVE OIL

12 fresh SAGE LEAVES

Zest of 2 ORANGES, cut into ¼-inch-wide strips

1. In a small bowl, just cover the pomegranate seeds with the Marsala. Gently mix in the mint and set aside, covered, for 1 hour.

2. Preheat the oven to 375°F.

3. Season the birds inside and out with salt and pepper. Drain the pomegranate seeds, reserving the liquid. Stuff the birds with half of the seeds, reserving the remainder for later. Using a kitchen twine, tie together the legs of each bird.

4. In a large ovenproof sauté pan, heat 2 tablespoons of the butter with the olive oil over high heat (if necessary, use two pans). Add 3 of the sage leaves and cook for 1 minute. Add the hens and brown well on all sides, about 5 minutes. Lower the heat to medium and add the remaining 9 sage leaves and reserved pomegranate seeds.

5. Transfer the pan to the oven and roast for 7 minutes. Remove the pan from the oven, drizzle 3 tablespoons of the reserved Marsala over the hens, and dot with 4 tablespoons of the remaining butter. Baste the hens with the pan juices and roast for 10 more minutes, or until the juices run clear when a thigh is pierced.

6. Meanwhile, in a small saucepan, melt the remaining 4 tablespoons butter over low heat. Add the orange zest and cook for 5 minutes, stirring gently so that the zest absorbs the butter. Remove from the heat.

7. Transfer the hens to a serving dish. Sprinkle with the orange zest and drizzle the pan juices, with the pomegranate seeds, over them. Serve immediately.

DUCK SCALOPPINE *with* DRIED CHERRIES *and* GRAPPA

Scaloppine d'Anatra alle Ciliegie e Grappa

Duck breast is not typically served this way in Italy, but I find the deep red meat with the fat still attached delicious, as well as easy to prepare. Cold duck fat gets ugly, so serve this immediately, with Braised Red Cabbage (page 424).

MAKES 4 SERVINGS

1 whole MAGRET DUCK BREAST (about 1½ pounds), split

½ cup ALL-PURPOSE FLOUR

SALT and freshly ground BLACK PEPPER

¼ cup EXTRA-VIRGIN OLIVE OIL

¼ cup DRIED CHERRIES

½ cup GRAPPA

½ cup DRY RED WINE

½ cup CHICKEN STOCK (page 125)

2 tablespoons UNSALTED BUTTER

1 bunch SCALLIONS, thinly sliced on the diagonal

1. Leaving the fat on, slice each duck breast across the grain into 6 equal pieces. Using a meat mallet, pound the pieces into "scaloppine" ⅛-inch thick and about 4 inches long. Season the flour with salt and pepper, and dredge the scaloppine in the seasoned flour.

2. In a 10- to 12-inch sauté pan, heat the olive oil over high heat until smoking. Add the duck pieces and cook, *without* turning, until deep golden brown on the first side. Add the cherries, grappa, wine, stock, and butter and bring to a boil. Cook until the liquid is reduced by half, 6 to 7 minutes, then turn the duck pieces over. Cook for 30 more seconds.

3. Transfer the duck to warmed serving plates, sprinkle with scallions, and serve immediately.

DUCKS

We tend to eat the avian species who sing less well. No one to my mind has produced a CD called "Summer Duck Songs," and the wild forms of these species, the mallards, pintails, ringbills, bluebills, wood ducks, and teal I shot for the table long ago were equally unmelodious. In ancient times, among many primitive peoples ducks were sacred creatures—albeit readily eaten, which makes them even more sacred. Doubtless part of our current crisis of values in America is that so few of us raise any of a dozen types of delicious ducks for the table. This is not a fashionable time to compare us unfavorably with the French, but driving through the Burgundy countryside I've counted tens of thousands of ducks. Perhaps they should be raised on the wide-open spaces surrounding monuments in Washington, D.C.?

My friend Mario Batali is a high priest of ducks, an intercessor for the less gifted. I will cook everything he writes down, because it makes life far less brutal.

—Jim Harrison

FOWL

DUCK SCALOPPINE *with* GREEN APPLES *and* MALVASIA

Scaloppine d'Anatra alle Mele

This is another way of cooking duck scaloppine, which takes a little more time, but delivers firmer, drier meat. The technique still uses only one pan, but there is more dancing at the ball than with the previous dish. Serve with Marinated Eggplant (page 429) as accompaniment.

MAKES 4 SERVINGS

1 whole MAGRET DUCK BREAST (about 1½ pounds), split

FLOUR for dusting

SALT and freshly ground BLACK PEPPER

¼ cup EXTRA-VIRGIN OLIVE OIL

2 GREEN APPLES, such as Granny Smith, peeled, halved, cored, and sliced into ½-inch-thick half-rounds

1 cup MALVASIA WINE

1 cup CHICKEN STOCK (page 125)

2 tablespoons cold UNSALTED BUTTER

1 bunch CHIVES, cut into 2-inch pieces

1. Leaving the fat on, slice each duck breast across the grain into 6 equal pieces. Using a meat mallet, pound the pieces into "scaloppine" ⅛-inch thick and about 4 inches long. Season the flour with salt and pepper, and dust the scallopine with the flour.

2. In a 10- to 12-inch sauté pan, heat the olive oil over high heat until smoking. Place 6 pieces of duck in the pan and cook until dark golden brown, about 2 minutes. Turn over and cook until browned on the second side, about 1 minute. Transfer to a plate. Repeat with the remaining 6 pieces, and transfer to the same plate.

3. Drain the oil from the pan and add the apple slices. Cook until softened and light brown, about 3 minutes. Add the wine and stock and bring to boil. Return the duck to the pan, add the cold butter, and simmer until the duck is heated through, about 5 minutes.

4. Transfer the duck to warmed serving plates, sprinkle with the chives, and serve.

DUCK *in a* SALT CRUST

Anatra al Sale

Roasting a bird in a salt crust will not result in the crisp skin Chinese-style duck *appassionati* crave, but the method creates such moist and tender flesh it will change your mind about the importance of skin—duck skin, anyway.

MAKES 4 SERVINGS

One 3- to 4-pound DUCK, rinsed and patted dry

¼ cup GRAPPA

SALT and freshly ground BLACK PEPPER

6 fresh SAGE LEAVES

1 branch ROSEMARY

2 pounds KOSHER SALT

4 EGG WHITES

¼ cup SABA

1. Preheat the oven to 425°F.
2. Rinse the duck cavity with the grappa. Season the cavity with salt and pepper, place the herbs inside, and truss the duck with butcher's twine.
3. Cover the bottom of a roasting pan just large enough to hold the duck with a ½-inch-thick layer of kosher salt. Place the duck atop the salt. In a large bowl, beat the egg whites to a light froth. Mix in enough of the remaining salt to form a moist paste. Cover the duck completely with the salt mixture.
4. Roast the duck for 1½ hours. Remove and allow to rest for 10 minutes.
5. Carefully remove the salt crust from the bird and brush off any remaining salt with a pastry brush. Remove the skin and then carve the bird. Transfer to warmed plates, drizzle with the saba, and serve with wilted greens (page 443).

SABA

Saba is the unfermented must (juices and pulp) of Trebbiano grapes that has been cooked down to a nearly syrupy texture. It is the first stage of what could eventually become balsamic vinegar if treated in the traditional aging methods approved by the consortium of vinegar makers in Modena and Reggio Emilia. Significantly lighter in color and consistency than balsamic vinegar, saba adds a grapey sweetness and slight bite to roasted or grilled meats, and it is also quite at home in the simple, fruit-based desserts so beloved by Italians. We get our saba from Manicaretti; see Sources, page 504.

BRAISED DUCK LEGS *with* DRIED ORANGES *and* ALMONDS

Coscie d'Anatra con Mandorle

When it comes to eating birds, I have always been a thigh guy. Although often scorned by the breast eaters, they are doubtless the richest part of the bird this side of the gizzards. This braising method incorporates the classic orange flavor from Tuscany but whacks it a bit with dried orange and almonds, for a kind of Renaissance feel.

MAKES 4 SERVINGS

4 large whole DUCK LEGS (2 to 3 pounds)

SALT and freshly ground BLACK PEPPER

6 tablespoons EXTRA-VIRGIN OLIVE OIL

FLOUR for dredging

2 medium SPANISH ONIONS, sliced into ¼-inch-thick rounds

1 medium LEEK, white and light green parts only, cut into ½-inch rounds and rinsed well

1 medium CARROT, sliced into ¼-inch-thick rounds

2 cups CHICKEN STOCK (page 125)

1 cup DRY WHITE WINE

½ cup GRAND MARNIER

6 tablespoons DRIED ORANGE PEEL (available at ethnic food stores and some supermarkets)

¾ cup BLANCHED ALMONDS

1. Preheat the oven to 375°F.

2. Trim the duck legs of any excess fat along the inner thighs, and season well with salt and pepper.

3. In a 6- to 8-quart Dutch oven, heat the olive oil over medium-high heat until smoking. Dredge the duck legs in flour, carefully place in the hot oil, and brown well on both sides, 8 to 10 minutes. Transfer to a plate.

4. Add the onions, leek, and carrot to the pot and cook until lightly browned and softened, 8 to 10 minutes. Add the stock, wine, Grand Marnier, ¼ cup of the dried orange peel, and ½ cup of the almonds and bring to a boil.

5. Place the duck legs in the pot, submerging them in the liquid, and cover the pot tightly. Place the pot in the oven and cook for about 1½ hours, until the duck is tender.

6. Transfer the duck legs to warmed plates. Season the braising liquid with salt and pepper, and spoon over the duck. Sprinkle with the remaining 2 tablespoons dried orange peel and ¼ cup almonds, and serve.

DUCK SAUSAGE *with* ONIONS
Salsiccia d'Anatra

There are two types of people in the world, those who make their own sausage and those who merely eat sausage. This duck sausage is so delicious that there may be some converts from the second group. Have your butcher help in home sausage-making—let her grind the meats you buy. A commercial machine takes all the hard work out of this.

MAKES 8 SERVINGS

4 pounds DUCK MEAT (from 3 to 4 ducks), run through the largest holes of the butcher's grinder

2 pounds PANCETTA, run through the same grinder

¼ cup COARSE SEA SALT

2 tablespoons freshly ground BLACK PEPPER

½ cup DRY WHITE WINE

8 feet SAUSAGE CASING (about 8 ounces) (optional)

2 tablespoons EXTRA-VIRGIN OLIVE OIL

1 RED ONION, cut into ½-inch dice

2 cloves GARLIC, minced

1 tablespoon TOMATO PASTE

1 cup DRY RED WINE

½ cup CHICKEN STOCK (page 125)

¼ cup finely chopped ITALIAN PARSLEY

1. In a large bowl, mix the duck and pancetta with your hands just until well blended. Add the salt, pepper, and white wine and mix just until well blended. (You must work quickly here so the warmth of your hands doesn't start to melt the fat, or the texture of the sausages could be affected.)

2. Set up a sausage stuffer and attach the casing to the funnel feeder. (If you do not have a sausage stuffer, you can form the sausage into 4-ounce patties by hand, working quickly to avoid overhandling the mixture.) Stuff the sausage into the casing, then twist it every 3½ to 4 inches to form about 24 sausages. Prick the sausages all over with a pin, and refrigerate until ready to cook. (The sausages can be made up to 2 days ahead.)

3. Pour 1 tablespoon of the olive oil in a 10- to 12-inch sauté pan, add half the sausages, and cook over low heat, turning frequently, until light brown on all sides. Transfer to a plate and brown the remaining sausages in the remaining oil, then add them to the plate.

4. Add the onion and garlic to the pan and cook until soft and golden, 8 to 9 minutes. Add the tomato paste and cook for 5 minutes. Add the red wine and stock, scrape the browned bits from the bottom of the pan, increase the heat to medium, and bring to a simmer.

5. Return the sausages to the pan, cover, and cook, turning occasionally, until cooked through, about 15 minutes. Stir in the parsley, and serve immediately.

FOWL

PHEASANT FARMER-STYLE
Fagiano alla Contadina

I always found pheasant to be dry, bland, and a little grainy, until I tried brining (see page 376). Wild birds have a lot more flavor than farmed ones and tell a much more interesting story when properly cooked.

MAKES 4 SERVINGS

BRINE

1 cup KOSHER SALT

1 cup SUGAR

2 SCALLIONS, roughly chopped

2 cloves GARLIC

1 CINNAMON STICK

3½ quarts WATER

2 small PHEASANTS (2 to 2½ pounds), quartered and rinsed

Freshly ground BLACK PEPPER

8 slices PANCETTA

2 tablespoons EXTRA-VIRGIN OLIVE OIL

1 ONION, cut into ¼-inch dice

3 cloves GARLIC, thinly sliced

3 large CARROTS, cut into 1-inch lengths

4 fresh SAGE LEAVES

2 BAY LEAVES

2 sprigs ROSEMARY

1 cup DRY WHITE WINE

One 15-ounce can WHOLE TOMATOES

¼ cup finely chopped ITALIAN PARSLEY

1. Combine the kosher salt, sugar, scallions, garlic, and cinnamon in a small saucepan, add 2 cups of the water, and bring to a boil, stirring to dissolve the salt and sugar. Remove from the heat and allow to cool.

2. Combine the cooled liquid and the remaining 3 quarts water in a pot or bucket large enough to hold the birds and stir well. Add the pheasant, cover, and refrigerate overnight.

3. Remove the pheasant from the brine and pat dry with towels. Season aggressively with pepper. Wrap each piece in a slice of pancetta and secure with a toothpick.

4. In a 12-inch skillet, heat the olive oil over high heat. Add the pheasant, in batches if necessary, and sear, turning occasionally, until dark golden brown on all sides. Transfer to a plate.

5. Add the onion, garlic, carrots, sage, bay leaves, and rosemary to the pan and cook until the vegetables are golden, about 5 minutes. Add the wine and tomatoes, crushing them between your fingers into the pan, and bring to a boil. Add the pheasant pieces, reduce the heat to a simmer, and cook, uncovered, until the juices run clear when a leg is pierced with a sharp knife, about 20 minutes. Transfer the pheasant pieces to a serving platter.

6. Check for seasoning and stir in the parsley. Spoon the sauce over the meat, and serve.

GUINEA HEN *with* VINEGAR
Faraona al Aceto

I love the flavor and texture of guinea hens. There is a certain tanginess to the leg meat and the breast meat always seems a little more moist and juicy than chicken, particularly when braised, as in this recipe.

MAKES 4 SERVINGS

2 GUINEA HENS, quartered, rinsed, and patted dry

SALT and freshly ground BLACK PEPPER

6 tablespoons EXTRA-VIRGIN OLIVE OIL

1 cup DRY WHITE WINE

1 cup BALSAMIC VINEGAR

2 tablespoons CAPERS, rinsed and drained

¾ cup BLACK PITTED OLIVES

4 ounces PROSCIUTTO COTTO (Italian cooked ham), cut into ½-inch dice

3 salt-packed ANCHOVIES, rinsed and filleted

2 tablespoons TOMATO PASTE

2 cups CHICKEN STOCK (page 125)

2 tablespoons roughly chopped PARSLEY

¼ cup AGED BALSAMIC VINEGAR

1. Season the hen pieces aggressively with salt and pepper. In a large Dutch oven, heat the olive oil over high heat until smoking. Add the hen pieces and sear, turning occasionally, until browned on all sides. Add the wine and the 1 cup vinegar, bring to a boil, and boil until reduced to a glaze, turning the meat occasionally to coat.

2. Add the capers, olives, prosciutto, anchovies, and tomato paste to the pot and cook, stirring, for 5 minutes. Add the stock and bring to a boil. Lower the heat and simmer until the hen is just cooked through, about 20 minutes.

3. Season with salt and pepper, sprinkle with parsley, and transfer to serving plates. Drizzle the aged balsamic vinegar over each portion, and serve.

QUAIL *with* ARTICHOKES
Quaglie con Carciofi

Quail can very easily dry out if overcooked, but wrapping the birds in prosciutto makes that almost impossible. Serving them with these artichokes makes the wine pairing difficult—but is there anything wrong with a delicious dark ale on occasion?

MAKES 4 SERVINGS

8 semiboneless QUAIL

SALT and freshly ground BLACK PEPPER

8 slices PROSCIUTTO DI PARMA

¼ cup EXTRA-VIRGIN OLIVE OIL

8 medium ARTICHOKES, trimmed, choke removed, cut into wedges, and held in a bowl of lemon water

8 cloves GARLIC, lightly crushed

2 tablespoons TOMATO PASTE

1 cup DRY WHITE WINE

¼ cup PARSLEY LEAVES

1. Season each quail inside and out with salt and pepper. Wrap each one in a slice of prosciutto, securing it with toothpicks.

2. In a 10- to 12-inch sauté pan, heat the olive oil over high heat until almost smoking. Add the quail, a few at a time, and brown on all sides. Transfer to a large plate and set aside in a warm spot.

3. Add the artichokes, garlic, and tomato paste to the pan and cook, stirring occasionally, until the tomato paste turns a deep rust color, about 8 minutes. Add the wine, cover, and cook until the artichokes are tender, about 6 minutes. Add parsley and set aside.

4. Add the quail, cover, and cook until the meat is just pink at the leg bone, 5 to 7 minutes. Transfer to a festive platter, and serve.

TRIMMING ARTICHOKES

Remove the tough outer layers of leaves by snapping them off until you reach the inner leaves that are pale yellow in color. (The larger the artichoke, the more layers you will have to remove.) Cut off the top third of the artichoke leaves with a knife. As you work, rub the cut surfaces of the artichoke with a lemon half to prevent oxidation, or discoloring. Using a vegetable peeler or paring knife, trim the outer layer of the artichoke stem. Pull away the inedible purple leaves that sometimes surround the choke. Using a small sharp spoon—a serrated grapefruit spoon works best—scoop out the fuzzy choke. Place in a bowl of lemon water until ready to use.

When serving artichokes whole, cut the stem of each artichoke so it will stand upright on the plate. Using a paring knife, cut off the smaller leaves around the base of the artichoke. Cut off the top third of the artichoke. Rub all the cut surfaces with a lemon half to prevent oxidation, or place in a bowl of lemon water until ready to cook.

FOWL

QUAIL *with* PANCETTA
Quaglie con Pancetta

This recipe reflects the reliance of Emilia-Romagna on its spectacular pantry to create dishes that are haunting and memorable. The pancetta and coppa create such an evocative flavor with the beans and balsamic vinegar that even a boneless chicken breast would look good with this. (I did not say that.)

MAKES 4 SERVINGS

8 ounces PANCETTA in one piece, cut into 1-inch cubes

¼ cup BALSAMIC VINEGAR

¾ cup EXTRA-VIRGIN OLIVE OIL

2 tablespoons HONEY

1 tablespoon freshly ground BLACK PEPPER

8 semiboneless QUAIL

1 medium RED ONION, cut into ¼-inch dice

8 ounces thinly sliced COPPA or CAPPOCOLLO, cut into julienne

6 fresh SAGE LEAVES

2 cups cooked BORLOTTI BEANS or KIDNEY BEANS, rinsed and drained if canned

SALT

1 large bunch CHIVES, cut into 1-inch lengths

1. In a large bowl, combine the pancetta, vinegar, ¼ cup of the olive oil, the honey, and pepper. Add the quail and toss to coat. Set aside.
2. Preheat the grill.
3. Meanwhile, in a 10- to 12-inch sauté pan, heat ¼ cup of the olive oil over high heat until smoking. Add the onion and cook until softened and light golden brown, 4 to 5 minutes. Add the coppa, sage leaves, and beans, lower the heat to medium, and cook until the beans are soft and fragrant, 7 to 8 minutes. Season with salt and pepper, and keep warm on the back of the stove.
4. Remove the quail from the marinade and pat dry. Remove the pancetta from the marinade, drain well, and place in a small nonstick pan (discard the marinade). Place the pan over medium heat and cook the pancetta, turning occasionally, until crisp and golden brown, 8 to 10 minutes.
5. Meanwhile, place the quail breast side down on the hottest part of the grill and cook for about 4 minutes on the first side. Turn over and cook until the breast is medium-rare, about 2 minutes longer.
6. Reheat the beans if necessary, and arrange in the center of four plates. Place the quail on the beans, arrange the pancetta around the beans, and drizzle with the remaining ¼ cup olive oil. Sprinkle with the chives, and serve.

TURKEY MEATBALLS

Polpettine di Tacchino

The fortune and success found by immigrant Italians in America had a great effect on their cooking. The reason a meatball tastes so good and is so tender in Italy is the reliance on day-old bread, soaked in milk or water, to bring lightness to a firm mixture of pure protein. Newly wealthy Italian Americans saw such frugality as a sign of weakness and started to make their meatballs without the bread, losing a whole world of texture.

MAKES 4 SERVINGS

MEATBALLS

1 pound GROUND TURKEY

1 pound GROUND BONELESS PORK SHOULDER (or use all turkey)

2½ cups FRESH BREAD CRUMBS

½ cup MILK

2 large EGGS, lightly beaten

4 cloves GARLIC, finely chopped

1 tablespoon chopped fresh ROSEMARY

1 tablespoon HOT RED PEPPER FLAKES

2 tablespoons SALT

2 tablespoons freshly ground BLACK PEPPER

SAUCE

¼ cup EXTRA-VIRGIN OLIVE OIL

3 RED ONIONS, thinly sliced

6 cloves GARLIC, thinly sliced

1 tablespoon HOT RED PEPPER FLAKES

1 cup DRY RED WINE

1 sprig ROSEMARY

2 cups BASIC TOMATO SAUCE (page 71)

SALT and freshly ground BLACK PEPPER

2 tablespoons roughly chopped ITALIAN PARSLEY

1. Preheat the oven to 475°F.

2. To make the meatballs, in a large bowl combine the turkey, pork, bread crumbs, milk, eggs, garlic, rosemary, red pepper flakes, salt, and pepper, and mix lightly with your hands until just combined. Form into golf ball–sized meatballs and place in a shallow casserole.

3. Roast the meatballs until dark golden brown, about 15 minutes. Remove from the oven, and reduce the oven temperature to 350°F.

4. Meanwhile, to make the sauce, in a large ovenproof skillet heat the olive oil over high heat until smoking. Add the onions and garlic, reduce the heat to medium, and cook until well browned, about 5 minutes. Add the red pepper flakes, then add the wine and rosemary, bring to a boil, and cook until the wine is reduced by half. Add the tomato sauce and bring to a boil, then lower the heat and simmer for 15 minutes.

5. Add the meatballs to the sauce, place the pan in the oven, and cook for 1 hour.

6. Season the meatballs with salt and pepper to taste. Serve in shallow bowls with the sauce, topped with the parsley.

FOWL

BIG TURKEY MEATBALLS
Polpette di Tacchino

These tender puppies make a great main course served just warm with a simple salad on a cool spring evening. They also do well in a great sub roll with some melted provolone over the top and a pile of hot chiles over that. The combo of turkey and sausage makes for a particularly piquant and satisfying flavor and texture in these odes to *la mamma*.

MAKES 6 SERVINGS

8 to 10 thick slices DAY-OLD BREAD, cut into 1-inch cubes (4 cups)

2 pounds GROUND TURKEY

4 ounces PROSCIUTTO DI PARMA, cut into ⅛-inch dice

8 ounces SWEET ITALIAN SAUSAGE, casings removed

3 large EGGS, lightly beaten

½ cup freshly grated PECORINO ROMANO

¼ cup freshly grated PARMIGIANO-REGGIANO

¾ cup finely chopped ITALIAN PARSLEY

Several gratings of NUTMEG

½ cup EXTRA-VIRGIN OLIVE OIL

SALT and freshly ground BLACK PEPPER

2 cups BASIC TOMATO SAUCE (page 71)

½ cup DRY WHITE WINE

1. Soak the bread in water to cover for 5 minutes. Squeeze out the excess water.

2. In a large bowl, combine the turkey, prosciutto, sausage, bread, eggs, ¼ cup of the pecorino, the Parmigiano, ½ cup of the parsley, the nutmeg, and ¼ cup of the olive oil and mix very gently with your hands. Season with salt and pepper. Form the mixture into 3-inch balls. Place the balls on a baking sheet, cover, and refrigerate for 1 hour to allow the flavors to blend.

3. In a 10- to 12-inch heavy-bottomed sauté pan, heat the remaining ¼ cup olive oil over high heat until almost smoking. Add the meatballs and brown on all sides. Transfer the meatballs to a plate and drain off the oil.

4. Add the tomato sauce and wine to the pan and bring to a boil. Place the meatballs in the sauce and return to a boil, then lower the heat and simmer for 30 minutes.

5. Transfer to a platter and serve with the remaining ¼ cup each pecorino and parsley sprinkled over the top.

STUFFED TURKEY *with* PRUNES
Tacchino Ripieno con Prugne

The stuffing in this dish is a song of love in the key of pork—with pancetta, prunes, and pork shoulder as the Pips and the turkey breast the Gladys Knight on that Midnight Train . . .

MAKES 10 TO 12 SERVINGS

1 whole boneless free-range organic TURKEY BREAST, split and butterflied (have the butcher do this)

SALT and freshly ground BLACK PEPPER

¼ cup plus 3 tablespoons EXTRA-VIRGIN OLIVE OIL

8 ounces PANCETTA, cut into ½-inch dice

1½ pounds GROUND BONELESS PORK SHOULDER

10 PRUNES, preferably Italian, pitted and cut into quarters

2 cups FRESH BREAD CRUMBS

1 cup freshly grated PARMIGIANO-REGGIANO

2 large EGGS, lightly beaten

Pinch of freshly grated NUTMEG

1 tablespoon chopped fresh ROSEMARY

1 tablespoon chopped fresh SAGE

3 cups DRY WHITE WINE

1. Season the turkey breast with salt and pepper, and refrigerate.
2. In a 10- to 12-inch sauté pan, heat 3 tablespoons of the olive oil over medium-high heat until smoking. Add the pancetta and cook until golden brown, 7 to 9 minutes. Add the ground pork and cook, stirring frequently, until start-ing to brown, 12 to 15 minutes.
3. Drain all but ¼ cup of the fat from the pan. Add the prunes and cook until the prunes start to really soften, about 8 minutes. Transfer to a large bowl and allow to cool.
4. Preheat the oven to 400°F.
5. Add the bread crumbs, Parmigiano, eggs, 2 tablespoons pepper, the nutmeg, rosemary, and sage to the pork mixture and mix gently. Lay the two turkey pieces skin side down on a cutting board and divide the stuffing between them. Roll up each of the breasts, starting from a long side, like a jelly roll and tie them firmly in several places with butcher's twine. Season with salt and pepper and place seam side down on a rack in a roasting pan. Pour 2 cups of the wine around them.
6. Roast for 50 to 70 minutes, or until the turkey is dark golden brown and a meat ther-mometer inserted into the thickest part of a roll reads 165°F. Transfer to a carving board and allow to rest for 15 minutes.
7. Meanwhile, add the remaining 1 cup wine to the roasting pan and deglaze over high heat, scraping up the browned bits with a wooden spoon. Add the remaining ¼ cup olive oil and season with salt and pepper.
8. Carve the turkey into 1-inch-thick slices and serve with the pan sauce.

FOWL

STUFFED TURKEY LOMBARDY-STYLE

Tacchino Ripieno alla Lombarda

I love serving turkey year-round because it is easy and delicious. (It is also very economical.) This is the way I do my Thanksgiving turkey, which makes it a lot easier than a whole bird when it comes down to carving. When it's not Thanksgiving, you might serve this with the sautéed apples—which work well with any poultry, as well as with pork dishes.

MAKES 4 SERVINGS

8 ounces LUGANEGA or SWEET ITALIAN SAUSAGE

6 tablespoons UNSALTED BUTTER

2 ounces thinly sliced PROSCIUTTO DI PARMA, cut into ¼-inch cubes

1 cup ROASTED CHESTNUT PIECES

4 ounces TURKEY GIBLETS, cut into ¼-inch dice (or substitute chicken giblets or livers)

1 medium SPANISH ONION, diced

½ cup freshly grated PARMIGIANO-REGGIANO

2 large EGGS, lightly beaten

1 tablespoon chopped fresh ROSEMARY

1 tablespoon chopped fresh SAGE

½ boneless TURKEY BREAST with skin, from a free-range organic turkey, butterflied so it is evenly ½ inch thick (have the butcher do this)

4 ounces thinly sliced PROSCIUTTO COTTO (Italian cooked ham)

1 cup CHICKEN STOCK (page 125)

1 cup DRY WHITE WINE

2 tablespoons ALL-PURPOSE FLOUR

SAUTÉED APPLES (recipe follows; optional)

1. Preheat the oven to 350°F.

2. Prick the sausage in a few places, put it in a small baking dish, and bake for 15 minutes. Let cool, then thinly slice. Increase the oven temperature to 450°F.

3. Meanwhile, in a 10- to 12-inch sauté pan, heat 4 tablespoons of the butter over medium heat until it melts and the foam subsides. Add the prosciutto, chestnuts, turkey giblets, and onion and cook until the onion is golden brown, 8 to 10 minutes. Remove from the heat, transfer to a large bowl, and allow to cool.

4. Add the luganega, Parmigiano, eggs, rosemary, and sage to the chestnut mixture and mix lightly, almost as if you were tossing a salad. Lay the turkey breast skin side down on a work surface and spread the filling over the flesh, then roll up, starting from a long side, like a jelly roll. Carefully insert the prosciutto under the skin on the top of the roll, and tie the roast in several places with butcher's twine. Place the turkey in a roasting pan just large enough to hold it. Season with salt and pepper. Pour the stock and wine into the pan.

5. Roast for 50 to 70 minutes, or until the internal temperature is 165°F. Transfer the turkey to a carving board and allow to rest for 10 minutes.

6. Meanwhile, degrease the cooking liquid in the pan, and pour it into a small saucepan. Scrape up all of the brown chunky bits left stuck to the pan, add them to the saucepan, and bring to a boil. Knead the remaining 2 tablespoons butter with the flour to form a smooth paste, and whisk it into the sauce, bit by bit, until it is slightly thickened. Cook for 5 minutes at a brisk simmer. Season with salt and pepper.

7. Carve the turkey into ¾-inch-thick slices and serve with the sauce, and the sautéed apples, if desired.

SAUTÉED APPLES
Mele in Padella

MAKES 4 SERVINGS

6 tart GREEN APPLES, such as Granny Smith

¼ cup EXTRA-VIRGIN OLIVE OIL

3 cloves GARLIC, thinly sliced

2 CLOVES

½ teaspoon chopped fresh ROSEMARY

1. Peel and core the apples, then slice into ¼-inch-thick pieces. Divide into 4 equal piles.

2. Heat a 10- to 12-inch sauté pan over high heat, then add 1 tablespoon of the olive oil. When it is smoking, add one of the piles of apples, spreading the slices over the bottom of the pan. Cook undisturbed—Do not stir!!! Resist!!!—for 4 minutes, then toss for another minute. (This will allow the apples to get great color and develop depth of flavor.) Transfer to a deep platter and cover to keep warm. Repeat the process with 2 more piles of apples, adding another tablespoon of the oil to the pan and allowing it to get hot each time. Add the last tablespoon of oil to the pan, and when it is smoking, add the garlic, cloves, and rosemary. Cook for 1 minute, add the last pile of apples, and toss quickly to mix. Cook for 3 minutes undisturbed, then toss and add to the other cooked apples. Gently stir together to distribute the seasonings well, and serve warm.

STUFFED TURKEY NECK

Collo di Tacchino Ripieno

In this case the turkey neck serves as a delicious and convenient sausage casing with just the right amount of fat and collagen to make the boneless chicken breast taste really good. You could also prepare this using boned large capon legs instead of turkey neck.

MAKES 4 SERVINGS

2 tablespoons EXTRA-VIRGIN OLIVE OIL, plus 1 to 2 tablespoons if necessary

1 pound CHICKEN LIVERS and GIZZARDS, diced

Pinch of freshly grated NUTMEG

Pinch of ground CINNAMON

SALT and freshly ground BLACK PEPPER

1 pound boneless, skinless CHICKEN BREAST, diced

2 HARD-BOILED EGGS, whites cut into strips, yolks crumbled

1 CARROT, finely chopped

1 TURKEY NECK, bone removed by the butcher

8 cups CHICKEN STOCK (page 125)

BALSAMIC VINEGAR, for drizzling

1. In a 10- to 12-inch sauté pan, heat the olive oil over high heat until almost smoking. Add the chicken livers and gizzards and cook until just cooked through, 7 to 8 minutes. Season with the nutmeg, cinnamon, and salt and pepper to taste, and allow to cool.

2. Combine the cooked livers and the chicken in a food processor, and process to a fine paste, adding a tablespoon or two of olive oil if necessary to puree the mixture. Transfer to a small bowl and add the egg whites, yolks, and carrot. Add a generous pinch each of salt and pepper and mix well.

3. Using a spoon or a pastry bag fitted with a large plain tip, stuff the chicken mixture into the turkey neck. Sew the ends of the neck shut with a trussing needle and butcher's twine. Prick the neck in 10 to 12 places and set aside.

4. In a large deep skillet, bring the stock to a boil. Add the turkey neck, reduce the heat to a simmer, and cook, uncovered, for 1 hour, turning the turkey every 15 minutes. Remove the turkey neck from the stock and allow to cool for a few minutes.

5. Slice the turkey neck into ½-inch-thick slices, arrange on plates, and serve with a drizzle of vinegar.

TURKEY CUTLETS BOLOGNA-STYLE

Tacchino alla Bolognese

I first had this dish at one of my favorite places in all of Bologna, a restaurant on Via Indipendenza called Diana. They serve classic Bolognese cooking without apologies to the modern, and it rocks me every time. The dish is easy to make and can be prepared up to an hour in advance of the oven phase without any problem. If you cannot find a fresh truffle, do not substitute a canned one; they are as unacceptable as truffle oil.

MAKES 6 SERVINGS

1 cup ALL-PURPOSE FLOUR

SALT and freshly ground BLACK PEPPER

3 extra-large EGGS

2 cups FRESH BREAD CRUMBS

Six 4-ounce TURKEY CUTLETS, pounded to ¼ inch thick

4 tablespoons UNSALTED BUTTER

PARMIGIANO-REGGIANO, for shaving

1 fresh WHITE or BLACK TRUFFLE

6 slices PROSCIUTTO DI PARMA

½ cup freshly grated young PECORINO TOSCANO

1. Preheat the oven to 475°F.

2. Season the flour with salt and pepper and spread on a plate. Crack the eggs into a shallow bowl and whisk until smooth. Spread the bread crumbs on a plate. Bread the cutlets one by one, dredging each one first in the seasoned flour, then dipping it into the eggs, letting the excess drip off, and finally dredging it in the bread crumbs, and place on a piece of parchment paper or wax paper.

3. In a 10- to 12-inch sauté pan, heat the butter over medium-high heat until it melts and the foam subsides. Place 3 of the turkey cutlets in the pan and cook, turning once, until the flesh begins to turn white and the crumbs are a delicious golden brown, about 2 minutes per side. Transfer to a baking sheet and repeat with the remaining cutlets.

4. Using a vegetable peeler, shave several curls of Parmigiano over each cutlet. Top each one with a few truffle shavings, followed by a slice of prosciutto laid over the top. Sprinkle a generous tablespoon of pecorino over the top of each. Bake for about 6 minutes, until the cheese is slightly bubbly. Shave the remaining truffle over the cutlets, and serve immediately.

MEAT

The butcher, *il macellaio*, is one of the most important people in any neighborhood or small town in Italy.

I do not know a single person in all of Italy who buys meat prepackaged from a giant grocery store, with a little expiration date stamped on the plastic. And I have traveled all over America and found excellent butchers in almost every nook and cranny of the country. So why buy from the huge grocery store? The only compelling reason I can think of, besides the obvious one of convenience, is the presence of a great butcher within a giant store. There he is, in the back, behind the refrigerated gondola of packaged meat, extolling the virtue of this cut or that recipe, all the while cutting fresh meat for his or her valued customers, making sure they get exactly what they need and want and helping them with his vast experience. But I have not met that many butchers, or even seen that many people, in the back of the giant grocery stores. I have seen a heck of a lot of great butchers in their shops, though, helping their customers, one at a time, understand what they are buying and how to make it into something absolutely delicious. The purchase of meat should be a win-win situation for everyone involved, especially the eaters. Our mass-produced commercial-quality beef, pork, and lamb is of a higher standard than anywhere else in the world, yet we are capable of better—and we have it. There are more opportunities to buy high-quality organic and environmentally responsible meat here now than ever before. This allows us the potential to avoid the presence of pesticides and poisons in the feed of our meat, as well as growth hormones and antibiotics whose effects on the animals, let alone ourselves, we still do not understand. It behooves you to find out about these issues and buy accordingly—and there is no one better informed about these matters than a serious butcher.

Once you have found a good butcher shop, give them all of your business, and then ask more of them. They are the people who know the difference between lamb sweetbreads and veal sweetbreads, who know how long an osso buco should cook, who can special-order caul fat so you can wrap the calf's liver they got for you in a little nest with dried orange and fresh bay leaves. They can describe the difference in cooking time for flank steak and skirt steak, and tell you why true prime grade meat is even harder to get now than it was ten years ago.

They might even have some ideas on how to use meat more economically. The dishes I most like to make and eat are made from what are often considered secondary cuts. You will never find a recipe for filet mignon or prime rib in my books. What you will find are recipes for oxtails, kidneys, skirt steak, liver, and lamb shanks and shoulders. I prefer ground chuck for my meatballs over lean and expensive eye of round, and I prefer pork shoulder to pork loin.

We need to find the good butchers and make them our teammates. They are not hiding—they are busy!

GRILLED VEAL ROLLS SICILIAN-STYLE

Involtini alla Siciliana

These involtini are prepared exactly the same way if you are going to braise them in a tomato sauce, fry them, or grill them, as here. Any way you cook them, they are simple and to the point. As I get older, I am liking simpler things—based on the best ingredients. This is an excellent example of such a dish. Garnish with greens, if you're in the mood.

MAKES 4 SERVINGS

8 slices VEAL TOP ROUND (about 4 ounces each)

1 cup freshly grated PECORINO ROMANO

¼ cup FRESH BREAD CRUMBS

½ cup finely chopped ITALIAN PARSLEY

¼ cup PINE NUTS

¼ cup dried CURRANTS or small RAISINS, soaked in warm water for 1 hour and drained

SALT and freshly ground BLACK PEPPER

8 sprigs ROSEMARY, about 5 inches long

2 tablespoons EXTRA-VIRGIN OLIVE OIL

1. Preheat the grill.

2. Using a meat mallet, pound each slice of veal between two oiled pieces of foil to about ¹⁄₁₆-inch thick, being careful not to tear the meat. Lay each piece out on a work surface.

3. In a medium bowl, stir together the pecorino, bread crumbs, parsley, pine nuts, and drained currants until well mixed. Season the veal slices with salt and pepper. Divide the pecorino mixture among the veal, spreading it out thinly. Roll each piece up tightly, starting from a short side, and secure with toothpicks.

4. Lay 2 veal rolls side by side, about ½ inch apart, and skewer them with 2 rosemary sprigs. Repeat to make 3 more sets of rolls. Season with salt and pepper and brush with the olive oil.

5. Grill, turning once, for 3 to 4 minutes per side, until nicely charred but still medium. Serve immediately, with a garnish of salad greens if you wish.

MEAT TEMPERATURE CHART

When you press rare meat with your fingertip, it will feel soft and wobbly, like your palm when your fist is closed. Medium meat will spring back a little; it feels like your palm with your fingers lightly curled in. Well-done meat is firm and unyielding, like your palm when your fingers are fully extended. Meat will always cook for a few minutes after being removed from the heat, so remember to take it off from the heat just before it reaches desired doneness. And always allow meat to rest for ten minutes before carving.

RED MEAT

Rare	*115° to 120°F*
Medium rare	*125° to 130°F*
Medium	*140°F*
Well-done	*inedible*

PORK

Medium rare	*125°F*
Medium	*135°F*

VEAL ROLLS *with* LEMON *and* MUSHROOMS

Involtini di Vitello al Limone

The quality of this dish depends on that of the veal and the mushrooms, so go ahead and splurge. In simple dishes, nothing will disguise the less-than-stellar ingredients.

MAKES 4 SERVINGS

1 pound VEAL LOIN, cut into 4 slices

SALT and freshly ground BLACK PEPPER

½ cup EXTRA-VIRGIN OLIVE OIL

½ RED ONION, cut into ¼-inch dice

4 cloves GARLIC, thinly sliced

1 tablespoon fresh THYME LEAVES

8 ounces WILD MUSHROOMS, such as chanterelles, morels, or cremini, thinly sliced

1 cup DRY WHITE WINE

½ cup BASIC TOMATO SAUCE (page 71)

Grated zest and juice of 2 LEMONS

¼ cup PINE NUTS

½ cup finely chopped ITALIAN PARSLEY

¼ cup chopped fresh MARJORAM

¼ cup freshly grated PECORINO ROMANO

1. Using a meat mallet, gently pound the veal pieces to ⅛-inch thick. Set aside.

2. In a 10- to 12-inch sauté pan, heat ¼ cup of the olive oil over medium heat until just smoking. Add the onion, garlic, and thyme and cook until the onion is light golden brown. Add the mushrooms and cook until they are soft and their liquid has evaporated, about 10 minutes. Transfer to a bowl to cool.

3. Add the wine, tomato sauce, and lemon zest and juice to the pan, stir, and set aside.

4. Add the pine nuts, half of the parsley, the marjoram, and pecorino to the mushroom mixture and stir to mix well. Lay the 4 veal pieces out and season well with salt and pepper. Divide the pine nut mixture among them. Roll each one up, starting from a short side, and tie with butcher's twine. Season aggressively with salt and pepper and set aside.

5. Heat a clean 10- to 12-inch sauté pan over medium heat until hot. Add the remaining ¼ cup olive oil and heat until smoking. Place the veal rolls in the pan and brown on all sides, rolling or turning with tongs or a fork, 8 to 10 minutes. Pour the wine and tomato sauce mixture into the pan and bring to a boil. Lower the heat and simmer for 15 minutes.

6. Remove the veal rolls, snip off the strings, and place in the center of a platter. Add the remaining parsley to the pan, spoon the sauce over the meat, and serve.

BRAISED VEAL ROLLS *in* TOMATO SAUCE

Braciole di Vitello

These are the dreams of all Italian street fairs that occur throughout America from spring to fall. But they are delicate and must be treated right. They will not hold up to hours of sustained heat—and thus would fare poorly at San Gennaro.

MAKES 6 SERVINGS

12 thin slices VEAL SHOULDER or LEG

½ cup PINE NUTS, toasted

¼ cup dried CURRANTS

½ cup freshly grated PECORINO ROMANO

3 ounces sliced PROSCIUTTO DI PARMA, cut into ⅛-inch dice

1 cup coarsely chopped ITALIAN PARSLEY

4 cloves GARLIC, finely chopped

3 large EGGS

SALT and freshly ground BLACK PEPPER

¼ cup EXTRA-VIRGIN OLIVE OIL

2 ounces sliced PANCETTA, cut into ⅛-inch dice

1 large SPANISH ONION, thinly sliced

2 cups BASIC TOMATO SAUCE (page 71)

2 cups DRY RED WINE

1. Using a meat mallet, gently pound each veal slice to ¼ inch thick. Set aside.

2. In a medium bowl, combine the pine nuts, currants, pecorino, prosciutto, parsley, and garlic. Add the eggs and mix well to blend. Season the veal slices on both sides with salt and pepper and lay out on the work surface. Divide the pine nut mixture among the veal slices, leaving a ½-inch-wide border uncovered on each. Roll up each piece tightly, starting from a short side, and tie with butcher's twine.

3. In a large Dutch oven, heat the olive oil over high heat until almost smoking. Add the pancetta and sauté for 2 minutes. Add the onion and sauté for 2 minutes. With a slotted spoon, transfer the pancetta and onion to a plate. Add the veal rolls, working in batches if necessary, and brown on all sides. Transfer to a plate.

4. Add the tomato sauce and wine to the pot and bring to a boil, scraping the bottom of the pot to loosen the browned bits. Reduce to a simmer and add the veal and onions and pancetta. Cover tightly and simmer for 1 hour. Remove from the heat and allow to rest for 10 minutes before serving.

ROMAN-STYLE VEAL CUTLETS *with* SAGE

Saltimbocca alla Romana

There are a lot of recipes that subject this dish to sauces made with sweet wines and all kinds of cheeses; my favorite is this very simple, pared-down classic version from a trattoria in the Trastevere, in Rome.

MAKES 4 SERVINGS

8 VEAL CUTLETS (about 2 ounces each)

8 fresh SAGE LEAVES

8 slices PROSCIUTTO DI PARMA

FLOUR for dusting

SALT and freshly ground BLACK PEPPER

4 tablespoons UNSALTED BUTTER

½ cup DRY WHITE WINE

LEMON WEDGES

1. Using a meat mallet, pound each veal slice to about ⅛-inch thick. Place 1 sage leaf and 1 slice of prosciutto on each veal cutlet and fold over to form a sandwich, with the meat inside the prosciutto. Pound lightly with the meat mallet, then secure with toothpicks.

2. In a 10- to 12-inch sauté pan, heat 2 tablespoons of the butter over high heat until it foams and subsides. Season the flour with salt and pepper, and dredge the cutlets lightly in the flour. Add to the pan and cook for 2 minutes on each side. Transfer to a platter and keep warm.

3. Pour the wine into the pan and bring to a boil, stirring with a wooden spoon to dislodge the browned bits on the bottom of the pan. Whisk in the remaining 2 tablespoons butter and season the sauce with salt and pepper.

4. Return the cutlets to the pan just to reheat, then transfer to plates, pour the sauce over, and serve immediately, with lemon wedges.

VEAL SCALOPPINE *with* MUSHROOMS, MARSALA *and* THYME

Scaloppine alla Marsala

This basic recipe employs mushrooms and Marsala, but below you'll see variations on the scaloppine theme, based on a well-stocked pantry and some savvy shopping. Good veal is the cornerstone of the dish, but you could substitute boneless chicken thighs without a serious loss of face.

MAKES 4 SERVINGS

¼ cup EXTRA-VIRGIN OLIVE OIL

¼ cup ALL-PURPOSE FLOUR

SALT and freshly ground BLACK PEPPER

Eight 2-ounce VEAL MEDALLIONS from the rack or loin

8 ounces OYSTER MUSHROOMS, quartered

1 cup SWEET MARSALA WINE (or slightly sweet sherry)

2 tablespoons cold UNSALTED BUTTER

2 tablespoons fresh THYME LEAVES or ½ teaspoon dried THYME

1. In a 10- to 12-inch sauté pan, heat the olive oil over medium heat until almost smoking. Meanwhile, season the flour with salt and pepper. Dredge the veal medallions in the seasoned flour. Add to the pan and sauté, turning once, until golden brown on both sides, about 2 minutes per side. Transfer the veal to a platter and keep warm.

2. Add the mushrooms to the pan and sauté until they are lightly browned and the juices have evaporated. Add the Marsala, bring to a boil, and reduce by one third. Add the cold butter and replace the veal medallions in the pan. Bring just to a boil, reduce the heat, and simmer for 5 to 6 minutes.

3. Stir in the thyme leaves and season the sauce with salt and pepper to taste. Transfer the veal to a large platter, pour the mushroom sauce over the meat, and serve.

SCALOPPINE VARIATIONS

Omit the mushrooms and substitute the wine for the Marsala.

FOR PICCATA: add 3 tablespoons capers and use 1 cup dry white wine.

FOR PIZZAIOLA: add 2 tablespoons tomato paste and 2 tablespoons fresh oregano leaves, and use 1 cup dry white wine.

FOR SORRENTINA: add ¼ cup Gaeta olives, pitted, and ¼ cup Basic Tomato Sauce (page 71), and use ½ cup dry white wine. Stir in ¼ cup fresh mozzarella cubes at the last minute.

FOR BARESE: add 1 cup Peperonata (page 275) and use ½ cup dry red wine.

FOR SICILIANA: add ½ cup Basic Tomato Sauce (page 71), 1 tablespoon pine nuts, 1 tablespoon dried currants, 1 tablespoon capers, and 1½ teaspoons hot red pepper flakes, and use ½ cup dry white wine. Top with freshly grated pecorino sardo.

WHOLE VEAL SHANK *with* MARJORAM
Stinco di Vitello alla Maggiorana

You will not find an entire veal shank wrapped in plastic at your local grocery store, so you will need to speak a butcher, and you may have to wait a few days for one to come in. But there is no more impressive or tasty cut of braising meat on the planet, and you and your guests will feel the love when you taste it. Sautéed spinach is a good accompaniment to this dish.

MAKES 4 SERVINGS

6 tablespoons EXTRA-VIRGIN OLIVE OIL

1 large whole VEAL SHANK (4 to 4½ pounds), rinsed and patted dry

SALT and freshly ground BLACK PEPPER

1 medium RED ONION, cut into ½-inch dice

1 CARROT, cut into ¼-inch-thick rounds

1 rib CELERY, cut into ½-inch-thick slices

1 bunch MARJORAM, leaves only, with 1 tablespoon reserved

1½ cups DRY WHITE WINE

1 cup BASIC TOMATO SAUCE (page 71)

4 ANCHOVY FILLETS, rinsed and drained

2 tablesoons LEMON ZEST

1 tablespoon PARSLEY, chiffonade

1. In a Dutch oven just large enough to hold the whole shank, heat the olive oil over medium heat until just smoking. Season the veal shank liberally with salt and pepper. Place the shank in the pot and brown well on all sides, 20 to 25 minutes. Transfer the shank to a plate.

2. Add the onion, carrot, celery, and marjoram to the pot and cook until the vegetables are softened, about 10 minutes. Add the wine, tomato sauce, and anchovies and bring to a boil. Add the shank and return to a boil, then lower the heat to a simmer, cover tightly, and simmer until fork-tender, about 2 hours.

3. Carefully remove the shank, place in the center of a serving platter, and pour the sauce and vegetables over. Sprinkle with lemon zest, parsley, and the reserved marjoram.

Note: You can also braise the veal in a 350°F oven; the timing will be about the same.

VEAL CHOPS *with* PORCINI
Costolette di Vitello con Porcini

These chops are considered by many to be the pinnacle of fine dining in Bologna, especially in the spring and fall, when fresh porcini are available. Dried porcini have their own following, however, and deliver a much more earthy and intense flavor to the delicate but regal chops. You could substitute a good pork chop for the veal here without disastrous results.

MAKES 4 SERVINGS

3 tablespoons dried PORCINI

⅔ cup hot WATER

3 tablespoons EXTRA-VIRGIN OLIVE OIL

Four 2-inch-thick VEAL LOIN CHOPS

SALT and freshly ground BLACK PEPPER

1 medium RED ONION, finely chopped

1 clove GARLIC, thinly sliced

1 cup DRY WHITE WINE

½ cup CHICKEN STOCK (page 125)

Juice of ½ LEMON

1 tablespoon UNSALTED BUTTER, at room temperature

1. Rinse the mushrooms under cold running water to rid them of sand; if the pieces are small, drop them into a small bowl of water, swish them around, and let the particles settle, then scoop up the pieces. In another small bowl, soak the mushrooms in the hot water for 30 minutes, or until softened.

2. Remove the mushrooms and coarsely chop. Strain the liquid through a sieve lined with a paper towel, and reserve ½ cup for the sauce.

3. Put a serving platter in a low oven to warm. In a 12-inch sauté pan, heat the olive oil over medium-high heat until almost smoking. Season the veal chops with salt and pepper, add to the pan, and cook, turning once, until deep golden brown, about 5 minutes on each side. Periodically slip a wooden spatula under each chop to keep it from sticking. Lower the heat to medium-low and cook, turning once, until the chops are just cooked to medium. Take care not to overcook them, or the veal will dry out; the interior should be blushed with pink, and they should give a little when pressed with your finger. Transfer to the heated platter to keep warm.

4. Spoon off all but 2 tablespoons of fat from the pan. Turn the heat to medium-high, add the onion and garlic, and cook until softened, 3 to 4 minutes. Add the mushrooms and sauté for 1 minute. Add the reserved mushroom liquid and reduce to ¼ cup. Turn the heat to high, add the wine, and bring to a boil, scraping up the browned bits from the bottom of the pan. Once the wine has reduced by half, about 1 minute, stir in the stock and boil for 1 more minute. Remove from the heat, add the lemon juice and butter, and swirl the pan to make the sauce.

5. Spoon the sauce over the chops, and serve.

OSSO BUCO *with* TOASTED PINE NUT GREMOLATA

Osso Buco con Gremolata di Pignoli

Thick, juicy, meaty osso buco like these are a celebratory tour de force that tastes and seems a lot more difficult to make than it is. For a truly spectacular presentation, you could have your butcher get a whole uncut shank (see the recipe headnote on page 361), and ask her to trim the bottom of the shin bone for access to the marrow. Serve with Risotto Milanese (page 144), the classic accompaniment.

MAKES 4 SERVINGS

Four 3-inch-thick OSSO BUCO (3½ to 4 pounds)

SALT and freshly ground BLACK PEPPER

6 tablespoons EXTRA-VIRGIN OLIVE OIL

1 medium CARROT, cut into ¼-inch-thick rounds

1 small SPANISH ONION, cut into ½-inch dice

1 rib CELERY, cut into ¼-inch dice

2 tablespoons chopped fresh THYME

2 cups BASIC TOMATO SAUCE (page 71)

2 cups CHICKEN STOCK (page 125), plus more if needed

2 cups DRY WHITE WINE

GREMOLATA

½ cup finely chopped ITALIAN PARSLEY

¼ cup PINE NUTS, toasted

Grated zest of 1 LEMON

1. Preheat the oven to 375°F.

2. Season the occo buco all over with salt and pepper. In a large Dutch oven, heat the olive oil over medium-high heat until smoking. Place the osso buco in the pot and brown on all sides, rolling them on their sides to get all the edges, 12 to 15 minutes. Transfer to a plate and set aside.

3. Add the carrot, onion, celery, and thyme to the pot and cook, stirring often, until the vegetables are golden brown and slightly softened, 8 to 10 minutes. Add the tomato sauce, stock, and wine and bring to a boil. Place the osso buco back in the pot, making sure they are submerged at least halfway; if necessary, add additional stock.

4. Tightly cover the pot, place in the oven, and cook for 2 to 2½ hours, until the meat is falling off the bone.

5. Meanwhile, make the gremolata: In a small bowl, gently mix the parsley, pine nuts, and lemon zest.

6. Remove the osso buco from the oven and let stand for 10 minutes. Sprinkle with the gremolata before serving.

COTECHINO "IN JAIL"

Cotechino in Galera

Spiced cotechino sausage is a perfect foil for the delicate, nearly bland veal in this dish. The key is to brown the whole roll very evenly and then roast it gently. Use a serrated knife to slice this, or the thin veal jacket may tear.

MAKES 4 SERVINGS

1 small (12 to 14 ounces) cooked COTECHINO SAUSAGE

One 18-ounce piece LEAN VEAL from the leg, loin, breast, or shoulder, pounded to about ½-inch thick (ask your butcher for a large thin piece of veal, and have him pound it)

2 tablespoons EXTRA-VIRGIN OLIVE OIL

SALT and freshly ground BLACK PEPPER

1 large ONION, finely chopped

1 rib CELERY, finely chopped

1 cup DRY WHITE WINE, or as needed

1 BAY LEAF

1 tablespoon finely chopped ITALIAN PARSLEY

8 small BULB ONIONS or SCALLIONS, trimmed

4 CARROTS, thinly sliced

1. Prick the sausage in several places with a fork. Place in a large deep skillet, add cold water to cover, and bring to a boil. Lower the heat to a simmer and cook for 10 minutes; drain the sausage and allow to cool. (Wipe the pan dry and set aside.)

2. Remove the casing from the sausage and crumble the sausage. Lay the veal out flat on a cutting board. Cover with the sausage in an even layer. Roll the veal up and tie in several places with butcher's twine.

3. Heat the olive oil in the same large pan over medium-high heat until almost smoking. Season the veal roll with salt and pepper and sear on all sides until evenly golden brown. Add the onion and celery and cook until soft, 8 to 10 minutes. Add the wine, bay leaf, and parsley and bring to a boil. Lower the heat to a simmer and cook for 15 minutes, adding more wine or water if necessary to keep the liquid level about ¼-inch deep.

4. Add the bulb onions and carrots and adjust the liquid level if necessary. Cover tightly and simmer for 15 minutes. Transfer the roll to a cutting board and let rest for 10 minutes. Keep the vegetables warm.

5. Remove the string and cut the sausage roll into 1-inch-thick slices. Serve with the pan juices and the carrots and onions.

FRIED COTECHINO *with* CUSTARD SAUCE

Cotechino Fritto con Zabaglione

This is a monumental dish of proportions only the Emiliani can ascend to. I first tried it at perhaps the best restaurant in all of Emilia-Romagna, Hosteria Giusti, in the city of Modena, capital of balsamic vinegar production. The owner, Nano Morandi, is a gifted deli man, a poetic restaurateur, a respected balsamic vinegar expert and *négociant*, and my go-to man for any and all truths about pork. He is also a sick and wacky wine collector, capable of dropping cork on all manner of wine, Italian and otherwise, at a moment's notice. He is a true Italian hero, worthy of the presidency and a lifetime achievement award in gastronomy and PR for all things Modenese.

MAKES 6 SERVINGS

2 raw or precooked COTECHINO SAUSAGES

6 large EGG YOLKS

½ cup SWEET MARSALA

1 tablespoon regular BALSAMIC VINEGAR

3 tablespoons EXTRA-VIRGIN OLIVE OIL

½ cup freshly grated PARMIGIANO-REGGIANO, plus 2 tablespoons

Freshly ground BLACK PEPPER

2 tablespoons traditional BALSAMIC VINEGAR (optional garnish)

1. If the sausages you have purchased are not precooked, place in a large pan, add cold water to cover, and bring to a low boil. Lower the heat to a simmer and cook until cooked through, 1½ to 2 hours, or according to the package instructions. Drain and allow to cool.

2. In a large heatproof bowl, whisk the egg yolks, Marsala, and regular balsamic vinegar until foamy. Place the bowl over a saucepan of aggressively simmering water (the bottom of the bowl should not touch the water) and continue whisking with a passion until the custard is thick and "ribboning," like zabaglione. Remove from the heat and continue whisking until cool.

3. Slice the sausage into ¾-inch-thick pieces. In a 10- to 12-inch nonstick sauté pan, heat the olive oil until just smoking. Working in batches, dredge the sausage slices in the grated Parmigiano, carefully place in the pan, and cook until lightly crusty and golden brown on the bottom. Turn and repeat on the second side, then drain on paper towels.

4. Arrange the sausage on plates, spoon about 2 tablespoons of the custard sauce over each serving. Sprinkle with reserved Parmigiano-Reggiano and freshly ground pepper.

COTECHINO
with LENTILS
Cotechino con Lenticchie

This is the most traditional dish of all for New Year's Eve supper. The lentils represent the coins soon to befall all who consume the dish within an hour of midnight.

MAKES 4 SERVINGS

8 ounces dried LENTILS

2 cloves GARLIC, peeled

12 fresh SAGE LEAVES

¼ cup EXTRA-VIRGIN OLIVE OIL

¼ cup RED WINE VINEGAR

SALT and freshly ground BLACK PEPPER

1 large (about 2 pounds) COTECHINO SAUSAGE

1. In a medium saucepan, bring 6 cups of water to a boil, and add 1 tablespoon salt. Add the lentils, garlic, and sage. Cook the lentils at a gentle boil until tender yet still firm, about 20 minutes. Drain and place in a medium bowl.

2. Add the olive oil and vinegar to the lentils and season with salt and pepper. Set aside.

3. Prick the sausage several times with a pin. Place in a large pot of cold water and bring to a boil over medium heat. Reduce the heat to a very low boil, cover the pot, and cook for 1½ hours. Drain.

4. Spread the marinated lentils on a large serving platter to form a bed for the cotechino. Slice the cotechino into ¼-inch-thick rounds, arrange over the lentils, and serve.

PORK SAUSAGE
from LUCANIA
Salsiccie di Lucania

It's worth the trouble to make sausages at home because you can personalize the spice blend to create something unique to your kitchen.

MAKES 6 SERVINGS

6 cloves GARLIC, crushed and finely chopped

1 ounce GINGER, peeled and finely chopped

3 ounces sliced PANCETTA, finely chopped

2½ pounds PORK SHOULDER, run through the medium holes of the butcher's grinder

8 ounces PORK FATBACK, run through the same grinder

½ cup light-bodied RED WINE

2 teaspoons HOT RED PEPPER FLAKES

2½ teaspoons COARSE SEA SALT

½ cup EXTRA-VIRGIN OLIVE OIL

1. In a large bowl, combine the garlic, ginger, pancetta, pork, fatback, wine, red pepper flakes, and salt and mix well. Cover the bowl and refrigerate for several hours to allow the flavors to develop.

2. Shape the sausage mixture into large egg shapes about 3 inches by 2 inches.

3. In a 10- to 12-inch heavy-bottomed sauté pan, heat the olive oil over medium-high heat until almost smoking. Sauté the sausages until dark golden brown on all sides, about 5 minutes per side. Serve immediately, with braised bitter greens, such as escarole or broccoli rabe, if desired.

FRESH OREGANO SAUSAGE and **BROCCOLI RABE**

Salsiccie e Friarelli

This dish represents the entire region of Puglia, all on one plate. In the heel of Italy, there is an appreciation of bitter and minerally herbs and wild greens that borders on the obsessive. You can buy an incredible variety of local greens here with the same type of range of flavors, such as collards, mustard greens, and kale, and substitute them for the broccoli rabe.

MAKES 8 SERVINGS

4 pounds boneless PORK SHOULDER, run through the largest holes of the butcher's grinder

2 pounds PANCETTA, run through the same grinder

¼ cup KOSHER SALT

2 tablespoons freshly ground BLACK PEPPER

3 tablespoons dried OREGANO

2 tablespoons HOT RED PEPPER FLAKES

½ cup DRY WHITE WINE

8 feet SAUSAGE CASINGS (about 8 ounces; optional)

2 bunches BROCCOLI RABE, trimmed

4 cloves GARLIC, thinly sliced

½ cup FRESH BREAD CRUMBS

¼ cup EXTRA-VIRGIN OLIVE OIL

1. In a large bowl, mix the pork shoulder and pancetta with your hands just until well blended. Add the salt, pepper, oregano, red pepper flakes, and wine and mix just until well blended. (Work quickly here so that the warmth of your hands does not start to melt the fat, or the texture of the sausages could be affected.)

2. Set up a sausage stuffer and attach the casing to the funnel feeder. (If you do not have a sausage stuffer, form the sausage into 4-ounce patties by hand, working quickly to avoid over-handling the mixture.) Stuff the sausage into the casing, then twist it every 3½ to 4 inches to form about 24 sausages. Prick the sausages all over with a pin, and refrigerate until ready to cook.

3. Bring 6 quarts of water to a boil in a large pot, and add 2 tablespoons salt. Set up an ice bath next to the stovetop. Blanch the broccoli rabe for 2 minutes. Refresh in the ice bath and drain.

4. Preheat the broiler. Place the sausages in a large ovenproof sauté pan (use two pans and broil them in batches if necessary, then combine them in one pan) and broil, turning once, until halfway cooked, 5 minutes per side. Place the pan over medium heat (leave the broiler on) and cook, turning once or twice, until the sausages are deep golden brown, 6 to 8 minutes. Add the garlic and broccoli rabe and cook, stirring, until the broccoli rabe is hot, 5 to 7 minutes.

5. Meanwhile, toast the bread crumbs on a small baking sheet under the broiler until golden brown. Transfer to a small bowl, add the olive oil, and mix well.

6. Pile the broccoli rabe on a platter and sprinkle with the bread crumbs. Place the sausages next to the broccoli rabe and serve.

HOMEMADE SAUSAGE *with* PEPPERS
Salsiccie Fresche con Peperoni

If you must, skip the sausage making part and just buy your sausages for this dish.

MAKES 8 SERVINGS

4 pounds boneless PORK SHOULDER, run through the largest holes of the butcher's grinder

2 pounds PANCETTA, run through the same grinder

¼ cup KOSHER SALT

2 tablespoons freshly ground BLACK PEPPER

2 tablespoons FENNEL SEEDS

2 tablespoons HOT RED PEPPER FLAKES

½ cup DRY WHITE WINE

8 feet SAUSAGE CASINGS (about 8 ounces; optional)

6 tablespoons EXTRA-VIRGIN OLIVE OIL

1 medium RED ONION, thinly sliced

5 RED BELL PEPPERS, cored, seeded, and cut into ½-inch-wide strips

5 YELLOW BELL PEPPERS, cored, seeded, and cut into ½-inch-wide strips

2 tablespoons dried OREGANO

One 6-ounce can TOMATO PASTE

1 cup DRY RED WINE

1. In a large bowl, mix the pork shoulder and pancetta with your hands just until well blended. Add the salt, pepper, fennel seeds, 1 table-spoon of the red pepper flakes, and the white wine and mix just until well blended. (Work quickly here so the warmth of your hands does not start to melt the fat, or the texture of the sausage could be affected.)

2. Set up a sausage stuffer and attach the casing to the funnel feeder. (If you do not have a sausage stuffer, form the sausage into 4-ounce patties by hand, working quickly to avoid overhandling the mixture.) Stuff the sausage into the casings, and twist it every 3½ to 4 inches to form about 24 sausages. Prick the sausages all over with a pin, and refrigerate until ready to cook.

3. In a 10- to 12-inch sauté pan, heat the olive oil over medium heat until smoking. Add the onion, bell peppers, the remaining 1 tablespoon red pepper flakes, and oregano, and cook until the vegetables are softened, 8 to 10 minutes. Add the tomato paste and cook, stirring, until the paste turns a darker color, about 10 minutes. Add the red wine and simmer for 10 minutes. Remove from the heat and allow to cool.

4. Place a very large skillet over medium heat (use two pans to brown the sausages if necessary, then combine in one pan), add the sausages, and cook, turning often, until dark golden brown, 7 to 9 minutes. Add the pepper mixture and bring to a boil. Lower the heat and simmer for 15 minutes, adding water, about ¼ cup at a time, to keep the consistency near that of a ragu.

5. Divide the sausage and peppers among six warmed dinner plates, and serve immediately.

SAUSAGES *with* POLENTA
Salsiccie con Polenta

MAKES 4 SERVINGS

3 tablespoons EXTRA-VIRGIN OLIVE OIL

6 ITALIAN SAUSAGES, homemade (see pages 368 to 370) or store-bought

3 cups BASIC TOMATO SAUCE (page 71)

SALT and freshly ground BLACK PEPPER

10 cups COLD WATER

2 tablespoons COARSE SEA SALT

2 cups quick-cooking POLENTA or fine CORNMEAL

1 cup freshly grated CACIOCAVALLO or PECORINO ROMANO

4 ounces smoked MOZZARELLA, thinly sliced

1. In a 10- to 12-inch sauté pan, heat 2 tablespoons of the olive oil over medium-high heat. Prick the sausages all over with a pin, add to the pan, and cook, turning occasionally, until browned on all sides.

2. Pour off the excess fat, then add the tomato sauce to the pan, scraping the bottom of the pan to release any browned bits, and bring just to a boil. Season with salt and pepper to taste, reduce the heat to a low simmer, cover, and cook, stirring occasionally, for 1½ hours. Remove from the heat.

3. Meanwhile, bring the water to a boil in a medium pot and add the sea salt and the remaining 1 tablespoon olive oil. Add the polenta, a little at a time, whisking constantly to prevent lumps. Cook, whisking constantly, until the polenta comes away from the sides of the pot, about 5 minutes. Turn the polenta out onto a clean wooden board or cutting board and allow to cool.

4. Remove the sausages from the sauce, let cool slightly, and slice them. Set aside, along with the sauce.

5. Once the polenta is cool, cut it into strips about 2 inches wide using butcher's twine or a very sharp knife, and set aside.

6. Preheat the oven to 400°F.

7. Cover the bottom of a 9-by-13-inch baking dish with a layer of sauce. Add a layer of polenta slices, then a layer of caciocavallo, a layer of mozzarella, and a layer of sliced sausage. Repeat the process until all the ingredients have been used, ending with a layer of the cheeses.

8. Bake for 25 minutes. Let sit for 5 minutes before serving.

MEAT

PORK LOIN *in the* STYLE *of* PORCHETTA
Arista alla Porchetta

Arista is the traditional pork roast from Tuscany, studded with garlic and rosemary and spit-roasted over hot coals. Porchetta is a nearly boneless whole suckling pig, rubbed with rosemary and stuffed with its own highly seasoned innards. This hybrid is a lot easier than either, with all of the tasty flavors from both.

MAKES 6 TO 8 SERVINGS

One 4-pound boneless PORK LOIN ROAST, butterflied (have the butcher do this)

SALT and freshly ground BLACK PEPPER

½ cup EXTRA-VIRGIN OLIVE OIL

1 medium ONION, thinly sliced

1 FENNEL BULB, trimmed, fronds reserved and chopped, bulb thinly sliced

2 pounds ground PORK SHOULDER

2 tablespoons FENNEL SEEDS

2 tablespoons chopped fresh ROSEMARY

6 cloves GARLIC, thinly sliced

1 cup FRESH BREAD CRUMBS

2 large EGGS, lightly beaten

4 RED ONIONS, cut in half

1 LEMON, halved

1. Lay the pork loin out flat and sprinkle with salt and pepper. Set aside.

2. In a 10- to 12-inch sauté pan, heat ¼ cup of the olive oil over medium-high heat until smoking. Add the sliced onion and fennel and sauté until softened and lightly browned, about 10 minutes. Add the ground pork, fennel seeds, rosemary, garlic, and 2 tablespoons pepper, and cook, stirring occasionally, until the pork is no longer pink, about 10 minutes. Transfer to a bowl and allow to cool.

3. Preheat the oven to 425°F.

4. Add all but 1 tablespoon of the fennel fronds, the bread crumbs, and eggs to the pork mixture and mix gently. Spread the mixture over the pork loin. Roll it up, starting from a long side, like a jelly roll, and tie with butcher's twine. Place the red onions in a roasting pan and set the pork on top. Roast for 1 hour and 15 minutes, or until the internal temperature is 135°F. Remove and let rest for 10 minutes.

5. Slice the pork into 1-inch-thick pieces. Serve drizzled with the remaining ¼ cup olive oil and a good squeeze of lemon, garnished with the reserved fennel fronds, and with the onions on the side. (Or chill overnight in the fridge and slice it thin for the king of sandwiches, for a lot of uninvited guests.)

MEAT

PORK CHOPS *with* PEPPERS *and* CAPERS
Cotolette alla Zingara

Zingara translates as "gypsy," and here the name must be because of the lusty, colorful components of this fiery, festive dish.

MAKES 6 SERVINGS

4½ quarts WATER

1 cup KOSHER SALT

1 cup packed BROWN SUGAR

12 BLACK PEPPERCORNS

4 BAY LEAVES

6 PORK RIB CHOPS

SALT and freshly ground BLACK PEPPER

1 cup ALL-PURPOSE FLOUR

3 tablespoons EXTRA-VIRGIN OLIVE OIL

3 BELL PEPPERS—1 each red, green, and yellow—cored, seeded, and cut into thin strips

5 BULB ONIONS, green tops reserved and sliced, bulbs cut into rings

¼ cup BLACK OLIVES, pitted and chopped

1 tablespoon HOT RED PEPPER FLAKES

1 tablespoon CAPERS, with their brine

1 cup DRY WHITE WINE

1. In a small saucepan, combine 2 cups of the water, the kosher salt, brown sugar, peppercorns, and bay leaves and bring to a boil over high heat, stirring to dissolve the salt and sugar. Pour into a large pot or other container and add the remaining 4 quarts cool water. Stir to mix well, add the pork chops, cover, and refrigerate overnight (see page 376).

2. Drain the chops and pat dry with paper towels. Season the pork on both sides with salt and pepper, then dredge in the flour.

3. In a 12-inch sauté pan, heat the olive oil over high heat until smoking. Add 3 chops to the pan and cook until dark golden brown on the first side, about 7 minutes. Turn over and cook until browned on on the second side, about 4 minutes, then transfer to a plate and repeat with the other 3 chops.

4. Add the peppers, onions, olives, red pepper flakes, and capers and stir with a wooden spoon to loosen the brown bits from the bottom of the pan. Add the wine and bring to a boil. Lower the heat, place the pork chops in the pepper mixture, and simmer for 10 minutes (the pork should be cooked to 135°F).

5. Season the sauce with salt and pepper to taste. Stir in the reserved onion tops, and serve.

PORK SPARERIBS *with* RED WINE

Costine al Vino Rosso

Spareribs cooked like this have a nearly Memphis barbecue–like texture, with all the wine-friendly flavor of a fancy braised dish like osso buco. And these reheat brilliantly on the grill, with or without that sweet gloppy mystery we call barbecue sauce. Serve these with soft polenta (see the recipe on page 159).

MAKES 4 SERVINGS

5 pounds PORK SPARERIBS, cut into 2-inch pieces

6 tablespoons EXTRA-VIRGIN OLIVE OIL

2 medium RED ONIONS, cut into ½-inch dice

2 CARROTS, cut into ½-inch-thick rounds

2 ribs CELERY, cut into 1-inch pieces

2 cups medium-bodied DRY RED WINE, such as Chianti

2 cups CHICKEN STOCK (page 125)

2 cups BASIC TOMATO SAUCE (page 71)

2 ANCHOVY FILLETS, rinsed and patted dry

1 bunch ROSEMARY

1. Place the spareribs in a large pot, add cold water to cover, and bring to a boil. Lower the heat and simmer for 30 minutes. Drain and let cool.

2. In a large Dutch oven, heat the olive oil over high heat until smoking. Add the onions, carrots, and celery and cook until golden brown, 10 to 12 minutes.

3. Add the wine, stock, tomato sauce, anchovies, and rosemary and bring to a boil. Add the spareribs, cover, and bring back to a boil. Lower the heat to a simmer and cook until the ribs are fork-tender, about 1½ hours. Transfer to shallow bowls and serve.

BRINING

Brining was originally used as a means of preserving meats and other foods. Since the advent of refrigeration, such preserving techniques have become unnecessary. But brining has become popular again as a means of increasing the succulence of meat or bird cuts that lack fat or great flavor. Just enough salt is used to help the food retain its moisture content, and other flavors may be added with cider, beer, wine, various vinegars, or other liquids and, sometimes, spices.

For a basic brine recipe, use 1 cup salt for each gallon of liquid. For each cup of salt used, boil 2 cups of water. Add the salt, and any spices and/or sugar, to the boiling water and stir to dissolve. Then add the remaining cold liquid to chill the brine and pour the liquid into a container deep enough to submerge the meat or poultry entirely. Place the meat or bird in the *cool* brine and, if necessary, weight down with a plate to keep it submerged. Refrigerate or place in a suitably cool place. Generally I like to keep it there overnight, but not a full 24 hours. Rinse the meat or fowl twice before cooking, and discard the brine.

BRAISED PORK
in the "BLACK ROOSTER"
Brasato di Maiale Nero

The shoulder roast is essential for this austere and simple braise—any other cut of meat would be too lean and lack the gelatinous fibers essential to creating the succulent texture and lip-smacking flavor.

MAKES 6 TO 8 SERVINGS

One 4-pound BONELESS PORK SHOULDER ROAST, rolled and tied

2 teaspoons KOSHER SALT

8 fresh SAGE LEAVES

2½ ounces PANCETTA

3 cloves GARLIC, crushed

¼ cup ITALIAN PARSLEY LEAVES

¼ cup EXTRA-VIRGIN OLIVE OIL

2 cups DRY RED WINE, such as Chianti Classico

3 cups BASIC TOMATO SAUCE (page 71)

Freshly ground BLACK PEPPER

1. Season the pork with the salt, rubbing it into the meat. Arrange the sage leaves around the meat, tucking them under the twine. Let stand for 30 minutes.

2. Mince together the pancetta, garlic, and parsley to form a smooth paste.

3. In a large Dutch oven, heat the olive oil over medium-high heat until almost smoking. Add the garlic paste and cook until it has melted into the oil. Add the pork and brown on all sides, turning occasionally. Add 1 cup of the wine, bring to a boil, and reduce by three quarters. Add the remaining 1 cup wine and the tomato sauce and bring to a boil.

4. Cover the pot, lower the heat to a simmer, and cook until the meat is fork-tender, about 2 hours. Season with pepper, then transfer the meat to a carving board and allow to rest for 10 minutes.

5. Remove the string and sage leaves and cut the pork into ⅓-inch-thick slices. Arrange the pork on serving plates, spoon the sauce over, and serve.

MEAT

BRAISED RABBIT *with* RED *and* GREEN PEPPERS

Coniglio ai Peperoni

This recipe is prepared all over Italy now, but it probably came from Rome or Sicily, the origin of many sweet-and-sour dishes. The original citizens in the dish may have been wild hare, which still have a big following in Europe. Americans seem to prefer the more delicate flavor of rabbit—which is a lot easier to find.

MAKES 6 SERVINGS

Two 2½-pound FRYER RABBITS, cut into 6 pieces each

1 cup WHITE WINE VINEGAR, mixed with 1 cup water

6 tablespoons EXTRA-VIRGIN OLIVE OIL

2 large ONIONS, halved and thinly sliced

¼ cup DRY WHITE WINE, or as needed

4 to 6 BELL PEPPERS, a mixture of green and red, cored, seeded, ribs removed, and cut into eighths

SALT and freshly ground BLACK PEPPER

1. Place the rabbit pieces in a bowl, add the vinegar-water mixture, and marinate for 1 hour, turning occasionally. Drain and dry thoroughly with paper towels.

2. In a 10- to 12-inch sauté pan, heat 3 tablespoons of the olive oil over medium-high heat until almost smoking. Add the rabbit pieces, in batches to avoid crowding, and brown, turning once, on both sides, 5 to 7 minutes per side. Transfer to a plate and set aside.

3. Reduce the heat to medium-low, add the onions, and cook, stirring, until limp and light golden. Add the wine and bring to a simmer, then add the rabbit pieces, nestling them among the onions. Cover and cook for 30 minutes.

4. While the rabbit is cooking, heat the remaining 3 tablespoons olive oil in another large sauté pan over medium-low heat. Add the peppers and cook for 15 minutes. Cover and continue to gently stew until thoroughly wilted and starting to brown, about 15 minutes longer.

5. Stir the peppers and their juices into the pan with the rabbit. Add salt and pepper to taste and cook until the rabbit is very tender, about 30 minutes longer. Check the amount of liquid in the pan after 15 minutes—there should be a small amount of rather syrupy oil in the bottom of the pan, just enough to keep the meat and vegetables from burning; add a little more wine, or water or stock if necessary to prevent sticking. Serve immediately.

BRAISED RABBIT *with* LEEKS, TURNIPS *and* VIN SANTO

Coniglio al Vin Santo

Italians view courtyard animals like rabbits and pigeons in the same manner they view chickens and turkeys. There is never any squeamishness around the table, and there is certainly no lack of favorite pieces for the kids either. The hind legs are always the most requested, just like chicken drumsticks in America.

MAKES 6 SERVINGS

Two 2½-pound FRYER RABBITS, cut into 6 pieces each

SALT and freshly ground BLACK PEPPER

FLOUR for dusting

6 tablespoons EXTRA-VIRGIN OLIVE OIL

2 medium LEEKS, white and light green parts only, cut into ½-inch-thick rounds and rinsed well

4 large TURNIPS, peeled and cut into ½-inch cubes

1 cup VIN SANTO or DRY SHERRY

2 cups CHICKEN STOCK (page 125)

1 cup BASIC TOMATO SAUCE (page 71)

1. Preheat the oven to 375°F.

2. Season the rabbit liberally with salt and pepper and dredge in the flour. In a large Dutch oven, heat the olive oil over high heat until smoking. Add 4 pieces of rabbit and cook, turning once, until golden brown, 8 to 10 minutes. Transfer to a plate and cook the remaining rabbit in two batches. Set aside.

3. Add the leeks and turnips to the pot and cook until lightly browned, 5 to 7 minutes. Add the vin santo, tomato sauce, and stock and bring to boil. Submerge the rabbit pieces in the liquid and bring to a boil. Tightly cover the pot, place in the oven, and cook for 30 minutes, or until the meat is almost falling off the bone.

4. Carefully transfer the rabbit pieces to the center of a serving dish. Pour the sauce over, and serve immediately.

RABBIT SAUSAGE *with* VINEGAR
Salsiccia di Coniglio al Aceto

Making sausages from meat other than pork is just as simple—and the results are often more delicate in flavor. This recipe also works for any wild or domesticated game birds, as well as for chicken and turkey.

MAKES 6 SERVINGS

2 pounds RABBIT MEAT (from about 8 legs), run through the largest holes of the butcher's grinder

8 ounces PANCETTA, run through the same grinder

2 tablespoons KOSHER SALT

1 tablespoon freshly ground BLACK PEPPER

¼ cup DRY WHITE WINE

4 feet SAUSAGE CASING (about 4 ounces; optional)

5 tablespoons EXTRA-VIRGIN OLIVE OIL

4 tablespoons UNSALTED BUTTER

6 small BULB ONIONS, sliced lengthwise into ¼-inch-thick slices

6 tablespoons BALSAMIC VINEGAR

1 tablespoon TOMATO PASTE

1. In a medium bowl, mix the rabbit and pancetta with your hands just until well blended. Add the salt, pepper, and wine and mix just until well blended, again with your hands. (Work quickly here so the warmth of your hands does not start to melt the fat, or the texture of the sausages could be affected.)

2. Set up a sausage stuffer and attach the casing to the funnel feeder. (If you do not have a sausage stuffer, form the sausage into 4-ounce patties by hand, working quickly to avoid overhandling the mixture.) Stuff the sausage into the casing, and twist it every 3½ to 4 inches to form 10 to 12 sausages. Prick the sausages all over with a pin, and refrigerate until ready to cook.

3. Preheat the grill or broiler.

4. In a Dutch oven, heat the olive oil and butter over medium heat until hot. Add the onions, reduce the heat to low, cover, and cook until the onions are very soft and browned, 8 to 10 minutes.

5. Meanwhile, grill or broil the sausages, turning once, until just cooked through, about 6 minutes per side. Transfer to a plate.

6. Stir the vinegar and tomato paste into the caramelized onions and cook for 5 minutes. Add the sausages and simmer, covered, for 10 minutes. Serve immediately.

MEAT

LAMB SHANKS *with* ORANGES *and* OLIVES

Stinco di Agnello con Aranci e Olive

I am certain that the combination of oranges and olives must be part of my primordial stew. I never tire of the combination—in fact, I am forever thinking of new variations on their life together.

MAKES 4 SERVINGS

4 large meaty LAMB SHANKS, rinsed and patted dry

SALT and freshly ground BLACK PEPPER

6 tablespoons EXTRA-VIRGIN OLIVE OIL

2 RED ONIONS, cut into ¼-inch dice

12 cloves GARLIC

1 NAVEL ORANGE, cut into 8 wedges

2 tablespoons chopped fresh ROSEMARY

½ cup GAETA OLIVES

1 cup DRY WHITE WINE

1 cup BASIC TOMATO SAUCE (page 71)

1 cup CHICKEN STOCK (page 125)

Zest of one NAVAL ORANGE

1. Preheat the oven to 375°F.

2. Season the shanks liberally with salt and pepper. In a large Dutch oven, heat the olive oil over high heat until smoking. Reduce the heat and sear the shanks, turning occasionally, until dark golden brown, 15 to 18 minutes. Transfer to a plate and set aside.

3. Add the onions, garlic, and orange wedges to the pot and cook until the garlic is softened, 8 to 10 minutes. Add the rosemary, olives, wine, tomato sauce, and stock and bring to a boil.

4. Replace the lamb shanks in the pot and return to a boil. Cover tightly, place in the oven, and cook for 1 to 1½ hours, until the meat is fork-tender.

5. Allow the shanks to rest for 10 minutes in the sauce, then transfer to warmed plates, sprinkle with zest, and serve.

LEG *of* LAMB *with* GREEN OLIVES, PRUNES *and* ROASTED SHALLOTS

Coscia d'Agnello alle Prugne

A whole roast like this evokes a party for me—a couple more dishes such as eggplant involtini and a frittata with herbs, and you have a springtime feast. I like lamb medium-rare, not bloody, but if you want it rare, cook it for about 15 minutes less at 375°F, to an internal temperature of 115°F.

MAKES 4 TO 6 SERVINGS

1 cup EXTRA-VIRGIN OLIVE OIL

1 medium RED ONION, cut into ⅛-inch dice

12 cloves GARLIC

1 LEMON, roughly chopped

1 sprig ROSEMARY, roughly chopped

One 5-pound LEG OF LAMB, boned and butterflied (have the butcher do this)

SALT and freshly ground BLACK PEPPER

2 cups DRY WHITE WINE

1 cup GREEN SICILIAN OLIVES

12 SHALLOTS

1 cup PITTED PRUNES

1. In a large bowl, combine the olive oil, onion, garlic, lemon, and rosemary. Add the lamb, turning to coat. Cover and let marinate overnight in the refrigerator, turning occasionally.

2. Preheat the oven to 450°F.

3. Remove the lamb from the marinade and season liberally with salt and pepper (discard the marinade). Place the lamb fat side down on a rack in a roasting pan. Pour 1 cup of the wine into the pan and scatter the olives, shallots, and prunes around the lamb.

4. Place in the oven and roast for 45 minutes. Lower the heat to 375°F, turn the lamb over, and cook for about 30 minutes more, or until a thermometer inserted in the thickest part of the leg reads 135°F. Transfer the lamb to a cutting board and allow to rest for 10 minutes before slicing.

5. Meanwhile, pour the contents of the roasting pan into a 4-quart saucepan. Deglaze the roasting pan with the remaining 1 cup wine, scraping up the browned bits in the bottom of the pan, and add to the saucepan. Bring to a boil and boil for 3 minutes to thicken slightly.

6. Slice the lamb and arrange on warmed plates. Spoon some sauce over each portion, and serve the remainder on the side.

MEAT

GRILLED LAMB CHOPS *with* GARLIC CONFIT *and* MINT

Scottaditi

Scottaditi are little Roman-style lamb chops that are impossible to stop eating once they have landed on the table. Both American and New Zealand lamb are delicious, with the American chops being larger than their Kiwi cousins and the down-under lamb being substantially less expensive. For this dish, I prefer smaller chops and buy the New Zealand stuff. Were I preparing a rack of lamb cooked whole, I would buy American.

MAKES 4 SERVINGS

½ cup EXTRA-VIRGIN OLIVE OIL

30 cloves GARLIC, peeled

2 cups DRY WHITE WINE

1 cup SWEET WINE, such as Malvasia

One 8-rib RACK OF LAMB, trimmed and cut into chops

SALT and freshly ground BLACK PEPPER

4 sprigs MINT, leaves only

1. Preheat the grill or broiler.

2. In an 8- to 10-inch sauté pan, heat the olive oil over medium heat. Add the garlic cloves and sauté slowly, shaking the pan frequently to keep the garlic moving, until browned on all sides, about 10 minutes. Add the wines, bring to a slow boil, and cook until the liquid is reduced to ¼ cup; the garlic should be very soft. Remove from the heat and set aside.

3. Season the lamb chops with salt and pepper. Grill or broil, turning once, until medium-rare, 4 to 5 minutes per side. Transfer to a platter.

4. Season the garlic mixture with salt and pepper and add the mint leaves. Spoon into the center of four warmed plates, lean the chops against the garlic, and serve immediately.

SUCKLING LAMB BRAISED *in* MILK
Abbacchio al Latte

The delicate flavor imparted by braising in milk is absolute poetry when the meat is a true suckling lamb, with a scattering of fennel seeds. This is the flavor of the markets in Lazio in the spring, this is what the Roman Empire must have tasted like—supreme!

MAKES 6 SERVINGS

1½ teaspoons FENNEL SEEDS, crushed

2 cloves GARLIC, crushed

⅔ cup ITALIAN PARSLEY LEAVES

½ cup EXTRA-VIRGIN OLIVE OIL

4 pounds BONE-IN LEG or SHOULDER of SUCKLING LAMB or KID, cut into 2-inch pieces (have the butcher do this)

COARSE SEA SALT

3 cups WHOLE MILK

1 cup HEAVY CREAM

Several sprigs fresh ROSEMARY

Freshly ground WHITE PEPPER

1. With a sharp heavy knife, finely chop the fennel seeds, garlic, and parsley together to form a paste.

2. In a large Dutch oven, warm the olive oil over medium heat. Add the fennel, garlic, and parsley paste and sauté until softened, taking care not to let it brown. Add the lamb, working in batches to avoid overcrowding the pot, and brown well on all sides. Transfer to a plate, season well with coarse salt, and set aside.

3. Pour ½ cup milk into the pot and stir over high heat for 2 minutes to deglaze the pot. Add the remaining 2½ cups milk, the heavy cream, rosemary, and lamb and bring to a low simmer. Cover and cook until the meat is very tender, about 1 hour.

4. With a slotted spoon, transfer the meat to a deep bowl, and cover loosely. Strain the cooking juices and return to the pot. Reduce over high heat for 3 minutes, and season with salt and white pepper. Return the meat to the sauce to warm through, then serve.

MEAT

ROMAN-STYLE BABY LAMB
Abbacchio alla Romana

This deceptively simple dish delivers the full frontal lamb attack with all the flavor of meat cooked on the bone, yet it is cooked on the stovetop. It behooves you to buy a spring lamb shoulder—lamb is so tender and sweet in April and May.

MAKES 4 SERVINGS

5 tablespoons EXTRA-VIRGIN OLIVE OIL

5 cloves GARLIC, 1 finely chopped, 4 left whole

4 pounds bone-in YOUNG LAMB SHOULDER, cut into 2-inch pieces (have the butcher do this)

2 sprigs ROSEMARY, leaves only

4 salt-packed ANCHOVIES, filleted, rinsed, and drained

½ cup WHITE WINE VINEGAR

1 tablespoon SALT, plus more to taste

2 cups DRY WHITE WINE

1 tablespoon PARSLEY, chiffonade

12 fresh MINT leaves

1. In a large deep heavy-bottomed skillet, combine the olive oil and whole garlic cloves and sauté over medium heat until the garlic begins to brown, about 5 minutes. Remove the garlic and set aside. Increase the heat to medium-high, add the lamb, working in batches to avoid overcrowding the pan, and brown well on all sides. Transfer to a shallow bowl.

2. Meanwhile, in a small bowl, combine the rosemary, anchovies, vinegar, salt, and chopped garlic and mix well.

3. Add the vinegar mixture to the meat, tossing to coat, and return to the pan. Reduce the heat to medium-low and cook slowly until the vinegar evaporates, about 10 minutes. Add half of the wine and the reserved whole garlic cloves and cook until the meat is tender, about 1 hour. As the wine evaporates, add the remaining wine as needed.

4. Transfer the lamb to warmed plates, sprinkle with parsley and mint, and serve immediately.

BARBECUED GOAT *with* LEMON SALAD *and* ALMOND PESTO

Capretto con Pesto di Mandorle

If you cannot find goat, this dish would still be excellent made with lamb. Because the leg likes to sit near the heat but not over it, or it would burn, build a charcoal or wood fire under half of the grill rack and then just move the leg around frequently until it is cooked. The extra work will be well worth it.

MAKES 6 SERVINGS

4 cloves GARLIC

1 cup fresh MINT LEAVES

2 tablespoons freshly ground BLACK PEPPER

½ cup EXTRA-VIRGIN OLIVE OIL

One 5-pound bone-in LEG OF GOAT, rinsed and patted dry

COARSE SEA SALT

LEMON SALAD

4 LEMONS, peeled and sliced very thin, seeds removed

6 tablespoons EXTRA-VIRGIN OLIVE OIL

2 tablespoons SALT

1 tablespoon freshly ground BLACK PEPPER

2 bunches ARUGULA, washed and spun dry, chiffonade

ALMOND PESTO

1 cup blanched ALMONDS

½ cup OLIVE PASTE

1 tablespoon HOT RED PEPPER FLAKES

¼ cup fresh ORANGE JUICE

¼ cup EXTRA-VIRGIN OLIVE OIL

1. In a blender, combine the garlic, mint leaves, pepper, and olive oil and blend until a smooth paste is formed. Rub the paste all over the leg of goat and season with coarse salt. Place in a large baking dish, cover, and refrigerate for at least 2 hours, or overnight.

2. Preheat a grill, building the fire in one side of the grill.

3. Place the goat on the grill, away from the direct heat, and cook, turning and moving it frequently, until the meat is pink at the bone and the internal temperature at the thickest part of the leg is 135°F, 45 to 55 minutes.

4. Meanwhile, to prepare the lemon salad, mix together the lemons, olive oil, salt, and pepper in a large bowl. Set aside at room temperature.

5. To prepare the pesto, combine the almonds, olive paste, red pepper flakes, orange juice, and olive oil in a blender, and blend until smooth and thick. Set aside.

6. When the goat is cooked, transfer to a cutting board and allow to rest for 10 minutes.

7. Toss the arugula with the lemon salad and arrange on a platter. Carve the goat into ¼-inch-thick slices and arrange on the salad. Drizzle with the almond pesto, and serve.

MEAT

SWEET-AND-SOUR BOAR
Cinghiale in Agrodolce

The brining step that used to be essential to tenderize the muscular wild animals is now employed to add flavor to domesticated game (for more on brining, see page 376).

MAKES 8 SERVINGS

1 cup DRY WHITE WINE

⅔ cup WHITE WINE VINEGAR

3 SCALLIONS, thinly sliced

8 cloves GARLIC, 2 thinly sliced, 6 left whole

4 CARROTS, 2 thinly sliced, 2 cut into 1-inch-long pieces

2 CLOVES

1 small BAY LEAF

1 sprig THYME

One 3- to 4-pound boneless BOAR, PORK, or VENISON SHOULDER ROAST, string removed if tied

SALT and freshly ground BLACK PEPPER

¼ cup EXTRA-VIRGIN OLIVE OIL

1 rib CELERY, sliced

4 ounces PROSCIUTTO DI PARMA, finely diced

2 tablespoons SUGAR

1 tablespoon grated UNSWEETENED CHOCOLATE

¼ cup RAISINS, soaked in warm water for 30 minutes and drained

¼ cup PINE NUTS

1.   In a small saucepan, combine ⅔ cup of the wine, ⅓ cup of the vinegar, half the scallions, the sliced garlic, sliced carrots, cloves, bay leaf, and thyme, bring to a boil over high heat, and boil for 5 minutes. Remove from the heat and let cool completely.

2.   Put the boar meat in a nonreactive casserole and pour the cooled marinade over, turning to coat. Cover and let marinate in the refrigerator for 2 days, turning often.

3.   Remove the meat and pat dry; reserve the marinade. Roll the meat up into a compact roast and tie it with butcher's twine. Season aggressively with salt and pepper.

4.   In a Dutch oven, heat the olive oil over high heat until almost smoking. Brown the meat on all sides, turning it frequently, about 15 minutes. Add the remaining scallions, garlic, and carrots, the celery, and prosciutto and cook for 5 minutes.

5.   Add the remaining ⅓ cup wine and the reserved marinade; if necessary, add just enough water to cover the meat. Bring to a boil, then reduce the heat to a gentle simmer and cook until the meat is fork-tender, about 1 hour. Transfer the meat to a cutting board and cover loosely to keep warm.

6.   Transfer the pan juices to a blender or food processor and puree until smooth. Return to the pot and stir in the sugar, chocolate, and the remaining ⅓ cup vinegar. Simmer for 3 minutes over medium-high heat, then add the raisins and pine nuts and remove from the heat.

7.   Slice the meat and serve with the sauce.

VENISON GOULASH

Gulyas di Capriolo

A great rib-sticker for the winter, this recipe feels more a part of the Austro-Hungarian Empire than the Roman, but it is very much a part of the regional cooking of Trentino, in the northeastern part of Italy.

MAKES 6 SERVINGS

2 SPANISH ONIONS, cut into ½-inch dice

2 ribs CELERY, cut into ½-inch dice

1 CARROT, cut into ½-inch dice

1 sprig ROSEMARY

1 sprig THYME

6 fresh SAGE LEAVES

6 cloves GARLIC

6 BLACK PEPPERCORNS

6 JUNIPER BERRIES

1 bottle DRY RED WINE

4 pounds bone-in VENISON SHOULDER, cut into 2-inch chunks (have the butcher do this)

¼ cup EXTRA-VIRGIN OLIVE OIL

SALT and freshly ground BLACK PEPPER

3 tablespoons ALL-PURPOSE FLOUR

4 ounces SPECK (smoked prosciutto) or smoked ham, cut into ½-inch dice

1½ teaspoons ground CINNAMON

4 CLOVES

1 cup MASCARPONE

2 tablespoons roughly chopped ITALIAN PARSLEY

Grated MONTASIO CHEESE

1. In a 6-quart nonreactive pot, combine the onions, celery, carrot, rosemary, thyme, sage, garlic, peppercorns, juniper berries, and wine and bring to a boil. Remove from the heat and allow the marinade to cool completely.

2. Submerge the venison in the marinade, cover, and refrigerate overnight.

3. Remove the meat from the marinade and pat dry; reserve the marinade. In a large Dutch oven, heat the olive oil over medium-high heat until smoking. Season the venison with salt and pepper. Add the venison to the pot, working in batches to avoid overcrowding, and sear, turning occasionally, until deep golden brown all over. Transfer to a plate.

4. Add the flour and speck to the pot and cook, stirring, until the flour turns golden brown, about 10 minutes. Meanwhile, strain the marinade.

5. Add the cinnamon, cloves, and marinade to the pot and bring to a boil, stirring vigorously to prevent lumps. Add the browned meat, including the juices on the plate, and bring to a boil. Lower the heat to a simmer and cook until the meat is very tender, about 1¼ hours.

6. Remove from the heat, stir in the mascarpone, and sprinkle with the parsley and Montasio. Check for seasoning, and serve.

BEEF BIRDS

Uccelletti Scappati

Skirt steak is the meat of choice among my Latin cooks, and they know their food. Most grew up in a house without any McDonald's near it, so every meal they ate as kids was handmade by the matriarch. Never having partaken of fast food, they are as averse to shortcuts and wimpy undeveloped flavors as I am. This is a cut of steak considered not quite "fancy enough" by many chefs, but it is the only cut of beef I offer from the grill. Well, besides T-bones.

MAKES 6 SERVINGS

2 pounds SKIRT STEAK, about ½-inch thick, cut into twelve 4-inch-long pieces

12 thin slices PROSCIUTTO DI PARMA

12 fresh SAGE LEAVES

1 pound PANCETTA, cut into 1-inch cubes (you will need 18 cubes)

6 WOODEN SKEWERS

EXTRA-VIRGIN OLIVE OIL, for brushing, plus 1 tablespoon for salad

SALT and freshly ground BLACK PEPPER

1 cup roughly cut ESCAROLE

½ RED ONION, sliced

1. Preheat the grill or broiler.

2. Lay the beef out on a work surface. Cover each slice with a slice of prosciutto, place a sage leaf in the middle of each slice of prosciutto, and roll up, starting from a short side. Thread the pancetta and beef rolls alternately on wooden skewers, using 2 rolls and 3 cubes of pancetta per skewer. Brush the meat with olive oil and season with salt and pepper.

3. Grill or broil, turning once, until the beef is cooked medium-rare, about 3 minutes per side. Meanwhile, toss the escarole and onions with remaining olive oil and salt to taste. Place on platter. Place the skewers on the salad and season again with salt. Serve.

STUFFED MEAT LOAF

Polpettona Ripieno

This is a very luxurious take on classic meat loaf, but it does not take much more effort and really pays off in the fancy presentation department. The vegetables in the center can be leftovers, as long as they were cooked long enough to become very soft.

MAKES 6 SERVINGS

1 pound ground lean PORK

1 pound ground lean BEEF

2 cups plus 3 tablespoons FRESH BREAD CRUMBS

1 cup freshly grated PECORINO ROMANO

3 large EGGS, lightly beaten

SALT and freshly ground BLACK PEPPER

8 ounces BABY SPINACH LEAVES, stems removed, washed, and spun dry

2 CARROTS, cut lengthwise into 6 slices each

3 tablespoons ALL-PURPOSE FLOUR

6 slices PROSCIUTTO DI PARMA

6 slices CACIOCAVALLO or other semi-soft cheese

2 sprigs ROSEMARY

1 cup WATER

½ cup EXTRA-VIRGIN OLIVE OIL

1. In a large bowl, combine the pork, beef, 2 cups of the bread crumbs, the pecorino, eggs, and salt and pepper to taste. Mix gently but thoroughly with your hands. Cover and refrigerate.

2. Preheat the oven to 400°F.

3. Bring 6 quarts of water to a boil in a large pot, and add 1 tablespoon salt. Dip the spinach leaves in the water just to wilt them; immediately remove. Add the carrots to the boiling water and cook for 10 minutes, then drain and set aside.

4. Combine the flour with the remaining 3 tablespoons bread crumbs and heavily dust a wooden board or other work surface with the mixture. Pat the meat mixture into a ½-inch-thick rectangle about 16 inches by 6 inches on the dusted board. Lay the spinach leaves over the meat, leaving a 1-inch border on the short sides. Lay the carrot slices over the spinach, lengthwise down the rectangle, then layer the prosciutto and caciocavallo over the carrots. Starting from a long side, roll the meat up into a jelly roll, making it as compact as possible; it should be about 16 inches long. Dust the outside with flour.

5. Place the loaf on a rack in a broiler pan. Put the rosemary under the rack and pour the water into the pan. Pour the olive oil down the length of the loaf. Bake for 1 hour, or until the loaf reaches an internal temperature of 165°F.

6. Transfer the loaf to a cutting board. Pour the pan juices into a saucepan and bring to a boil. Season with salt and pepper to taste.

7. Slice the meat loaf into 1-inch-thick slices and arrange on warmed plates. Drizzle with the sauce, and serve.

MEATBALLS *with* RICOTTA *in* MILK
Polpette con la Ricotta

Serving meatballs in a "broken" white sauce may seem strange to American sensibilities, but these lactic love bombs will quickly change your mind. The Renaissance touch of the sour pickles might seem a little weird, but trust me on this—they work as an excellent foil to an otherwise acid-free dish.

MAKES 4 SERVINGS

8 ounces ground PORK

8 ounces ground VEAL

8 ounces RICOTTA, preferably fresh

2 large EGGS, lightly beaten

¼ cup freshly grated PARMIGIANO-REGGIANO

¼ cup FRESH BREAD CRUMBS

6 CORNICHONS, chopped

3 PISTACHIO NUTS, chopped

3 tablespoons UNSALTED BUTTER

1 cup CHICKEN STOCK (page 125), or more if necessary

½ cup WHOLE MILK

SALT and freshly ground BLACK PEPPER

1. In a large bowl, combine the ground meats, ricotta, eggs, Parmigiano, bread crumbs, cornichons, and pistachios and mix with your hands just until blended. Form into balls 1 inch in diameter.

2. In a large heavy-bottomed skillet, heat the butter over medium heat until it foams and subsides. Place the meatballs in the pan and brown on all sides. Add the stock and milk; the liquid should come halfway up the sides of the meatballs. Bring the liquid to a boil, then reduce to a simmer and cook until the meatballs are cooked through, about 15 minutes. Season the broth with salt and pepper.

3. Serve in warmed shallow bowls, with the broth poured over the meatballs.

MIXED MEATS *in* BROTH *with* GREEN SAUCE

Bollito Misto con Salsa Verde

If you are a lover of all things delicious, with no fear or squeamishness, then this map will get you where you want to be.

MAKES 10 SERVINGS

1 CALF'S TONGUE

5 quarts WATER

¼ cup RED WINE VINEGAR

2 CARROTS, quartered

2 ribs CELERY, cut into 1-inch pieces

1 SPANISH ONION, stuck with 2 CLOVES

One 3- to 4-pound VEAL SHANK

1 pound BEEF BRISKET

2 BEEF CHEEKS

1 COTECHINO SAUSAGE

1 small CAPON, quartered

½ boneless TURKEY BREAST (about 2 pounds)

SALSA VERDE

1 bunch ITALIAN PARSLEY, leaves only

4 salt-packed ANCHOVIES, filleted and rinsed

1 bunch MINT, leaves only

Fronds from 1 FENNEL BULB

2 tablespoon CAPERS, preferably salt-packed, rinsed and drained

1 HARD-BOILED EGG, roughly chopped

4 CORNICHONS

2 tablespoons WHITE WINE VINEGAR

1 cup EXTRA-VIRGIN OLIVE OIL

Freshly ground BLACK PEPPER

1. Put the calf's tongue in a pot, cover with warm water, and bring to a boil. Boil for 40 minutes. Drain and let cool, then peel off the outer skin and membrane.

2. In a large pot, combine the 5 quarts water, vinegar, carrots, celery, onion, and veal shank and bring to a boil over high heat. Cover and boil for 45 minutes.

3. Add the brisket, beef cheeks, and sausage and bring to a boil. Lower the heat to a brisk simmer, cover, and cook for 30 minutes.

4. Add the capon and turkey breast and bring to a boil, then lower the heat to a brisk simmer and cook, uncovered, for 45 minutes, adding water as necessary to keep the ingredients covered. Add the tongue to the pot during the last 5 to 10 minutes to heat through.

5. Meanwhile, to make the salsa verde, combine the parsley, anchovies, mint, fennel fronds, capers, egg, cornichons, vinegar, olive oil, and pepper to taste in a food processor and blend until smooth.

6. Transfer the cooked meats to a platter. Bring the broth to a boil and reduce to 2 quarts. Season with salt and pepper.

7. Carve the meats and place in large soup bowls. Pour a good ladleful of broth over each bowl, and serve with the salsa verde on the side.

T-BONE FIORENTINA *with* SAUTÉED SPINACH

Bistecca alla Fiorentina

The quality of the steak is the quality of the whole dish in something as simple as this classic Florentine carnivore's fantasy. I had never realized this dish was the true pinnacle of Tuscan cooking until I got there and tasted it—simple, sublime, and all about the shopping, not the cook. Da Vero is my favorite olive oil, with all of the peppery palate ticklers and olfactory love juice of any great Tuscan oil, yet it is created by my good friends Colleen McGlynn and Ridgely Evers in the Dry Creek Valley in Sonoma, California.

MAKES 4 SERVINGS

1 tablespoon chopped fresh ROSEMARY

1 tablespoon chopped fresh SAGE

1 tablespoon fresh THYME LEAVES

2 tablespoons KOSHER SALT, plus more to taste

2 tablespoons freshly ground BLACK PEPPER, plus more to taste

1 T-BONE STEAK, at least 3 inches thick, 3 to 3½ pounds

2 tablespoons PURE OLIVE OIL

¾ cup EXTRA-VIRGIN OLIVE OIL, preferably Da Vero

6 cloves GARLIC, thinly sliced

4 pounds BABY SPINACH, stems removed, washed, and spun dry

Juice of 1 LEMON

1 tablespoon COARSE SALT

1. Preheat the grill.

2. In a small bowl, mix together the rosemary, sage, thyme, salt, and pepper until well blended. Pat the steak dry and coat the entire steak with the herb mix. Brush gently with the pure olive oil. Place on the grill and cook until well charred, about 12 minutes on the first side, then cook about 9 minutes on the second side; this is traditionally served rare. Transfer to a platter and let stand for 8 minutes.

3. Meanwhile, in a 10- to 12-inch sauté pan, heat ¼ cup of the extra-virgin olive oil over high heat until smoking. Add the garlic and cook just until light brown. Add the spinach and stir until just wilted. Remove from the heat and add the lemon juice and salt and pepper to taste. Set aside.

4. Carve the fillet and the strip steak from the bone and slice. Divide the steak among four plates, arrange the spinach next to it, and drizzle with the remaining ½ cup extra-virgin olive oil. Season with coarse salt. Serve immediately.

SHORT RIBS *in* BAROLO
Brasato al Barolo

This is the daddy of all great braises from the Piemonte, and it is consistently a huge seller in the restaurants there because it offers big beef flavor, super-tender "fork-cutting" meat, and the opportunity to drop big ducats on the delicious Barolos and Barbarescos that match it perfectly. I like that.

MAKES 4 SERVINGS

6 tablespoons EXTRA-VIRGIN OLIVE OIL

2 pounds boneless BEEF SHORT RIBS, cut into 3-inch cubes

SALT and freshly ground BLACK PEPPER

2 large SPANISH ONIONS, cut into ½-inch dice

1 medium CARROT, sliced into ½-inch-thick rounds

2 ribs CELERY, cut into ½-inch-thick slices

4 ounces PANCETTA, cut into ¼-inch dice

2 cups BAROLO or other hearty red wine

2 cups BASIC TOMATO SAUCE (page 71)

1. In a large Dutch oven, heat the olive oil over high heat until smoking. Season the meat liberally with salt and pepper. Working in batches to avoid overcrowding the pot, brown the meat all over, turning frequently, until dark golden brown, 10 to 12 minutes per batch. Transfer to a platter and set aside.

2. Pour the excess oil out of the pot. Add the onions, carrot, celery, and pancetta and cook until the vegetables are light brown and starting to soften, about 8 minutes. Add the wine and tomato sauce and bring to a boil.

3. Add the meat and bring back to a boil, then lower the heat to a gentle simmer. Cook until the meat is very tender, 1½ to 2 hours. Transfer the meat to a festive platter.

4. Bring the cooking liquid to a boil and reduce to 2½ cups. Season with salt and pepper, pour over the meat, and serve immediately.

FRIED LAMB SWEETBREADS ROMAN-STYLE

Animelle Fritte alla Romana

If it proves to be difficult to find the elusive lamb sweetbreads, go ahead and substitute veal sweetbreads, which are bigger and clunkier but equally delicious. The trickiest part of this recipe is the first blanch of the sweetbreads: if you overcook them, they are forever lost, so be careful.

MAKES 4 SERVINGS

1½ pounds LAMB SWEETBREADS

1½ FENNEL BULBS, trimmed, whole bulb coarsely chopped, ½ bulb thinly sliced

2 CARROTS, coarsely chopped

2 ribs CELERY, coarsely chopped

10 cloves GARLIC

2 ONIONS, 1 coarsely chopped, 1 thinly sliced

1 teaspoon MUSTARD SEEDS

Pinch of HOT RED PEPPER FLAKES

1 tablespoon SALT, plus more to taste

1 teaspoon BLACK PEPPERCORNS

4 cups DRY WHITE WINE

2 tablespoons WHITE WINE VINEGAR

8 cups WATER

4 cups EXTRA-VIRGIN OLIVE OIL, for deep-frying

1 cup SEMOLINA FLOUR

1 cup WONDRA

3 LEMONS, cut into quarters

Freshly ground BLACK PEPPER

1. In a large bowl, soak the sweetbreads in several changes of ice water for 2 hours. Drain and place on a plate. Set another heavy plate on top to flatten the sweetbreads.

2. In a large pot, combine the chopped fennel, carrots, celery, garlic, chopped onion, mustard seeds, red pepper flakes, salt, peppercorns, wine, vinegar, and water and bring to a boil. Immediately reduce to a simmer and cook for 20 minutes. Add the sweetbreads, return to a simmer, and cook until creamy white (and about as firm as a hard-boiled egg), about 10 minutes. Drain (discard the liquid) and set aside.

3. In a large deep pot, heat the olive oil to 375°F. Combine the flours in a shallow bowl or on a plate. Working in batches to avoid over-crowding the pot, dredge the sweetbreads, sliced onion, sliced fennel, and 8 of the lemon quarters in the flour mixture and fry until golden brown. With a spider or slotted spoon, remove the fried foods and drain on paper towels. Season with salt and pepper and serve with the remaining 4 lemon wedges on the side.

CALF'S LIVER
WITH ORANGE
Fegato di Vitello all'Arancia

This is an easy way to coax the non–liver lovers in the family to try it. The charred crust and orange fragrance make it very hard to turn down.

MAKES 4 SERVINGS

Grated zest and juice of ½ ORANGE

1 clove GARLIC, finely chopped

1 sprig ROSEMARY, leaves only, finely chopped

5 BAY LEAVES, 1 crushed, 4 broken into pieces

Pinch of HOT RED PEPPER FLAKES

SALT

1½ pounds CALF'S LIVER, cut into pieces about 2 inches square

About 1 pound CAUL FAT

Freshly ground BLACK PEPPER

1 tablespoon ORANGE ZEST

4 whole SCALLIONS, grilled, set aside

1. Preheat the grill or broiler.
2. In a small bowl, combine the orange zest, garlic, rosemary, crushed bay leaf, red pepper flakes, and 1 tablespoon salt. Rub each piece of liver all over with the mixture. Wrap each piece in a square of caul fat, tucking a bay leaf into each package.
3. Grill or broil the packages, turning often and basting with the orange juice, for about 5 minutes per side for medium-rare. Season with salt and pepper. Serve immediately, with the zest and scallions.

CALF'S LIVER
VENETIAN-STYLE
Fegato alla Veneziana

MAKES 4 SERVINGS

1 cup ALL-PURPOSE FLOUR

SALT and freshly ground BLACK PEPPER

3 tablespoons EXTRA-VIRGIN OLIVE OIL

2 tablespoons UNSALTED BUTTER

1 pound CALF'S LIVER, cut into ¼-inch-thick slices

1 SPANISH ONION, halved and sliced into ¼-inch-thick half-moons

¼ cup BALSAMIC VINEGAR

2 tablespoons finely chopped ITALIAN PARSLEY

1. Season the flour with salt and pepper and spread on a plate.
2. In a 10- to 12-inch sauté pan, heat the olive oil over medium-high heat until hot but not smoking. Add the butter and allow it to foam and then subside. Working in batches to avoid overcrowding the pan, dredge the liver slices in the seasoned flour and cook until browned just on the first side, about 4 minutes. Transfer the liver to a warm plate.
3. Add the onion to the pan and cook until golden and very soft, about 10 minutes. Add the vinegar and season with salt and pepper. Place the liver on top of the onions, uncooked side down, reduce the heat to medium, and cook until just cooked through, about 5 minutes.
4. Divide the liver and onions among four warmed plates, sprinkle with the parsley, and serve.

MEAT

OXTAIL BUTCHER'S-STYLE

Coda alla Vaccinara

Oxtails were always present on the table when grandma came over for Sunday supper, and we never thought anything of it other than how much we loved it. Now it has become the chic meat in fancy restaurants, probably due in part to reverse snob appeal.

MAKE 6 SERVINGS

5 pounds OXTAILS, cut into ½-pound chunks (by the butcher) and rinsed

3 tablespoons TOMATO PASTE

3 tablespoons EXTRA-VIRGIN OLIVE OIL

4 ounces PANCETTA, cut into ½-inch cubes

1 large ONION, finely chopped

2 cloves GARLIC, finely chopped

2 CARROTS, finely chopped

½ cup finely chopped ITALIAN PARSLEY

1 cup DRY WHITE WINE

5 ribs CELERY, leaves reserved, stalks finely chopped

¼ cup RED BELL PEPPER, julienne

¼ cup RED ONION, sliced thin

Pinch of HOT RED PEPPER FLAKES

Pinch of ground CINNAMON

Juice of ½ LEMON

SALT and freshly ground BLACK PEPPER

1. Bring 6 quarts of water to a boil in a large pot. Add the oxtails, reduce the heat to a simmer, and cook for 10 minutes. Drain the oxtails, reserving the broth, and set aside. Measure out 2 cups of the broth and discard the rest. Dissolve the tomato paste in the reserved broth and set aside.

2. In a large Dutch oven, heat 2 tablespoons of the olive oil over high heat until smoking. Add the pancetta and sauté until golden brown. Add the oxtails, a few pieces at a time, and brown on all sides, then transfer to a plate.

3. Add the onion, garlic, carrots, and half the parsley to the pot and sauté until the vegetables are browned. Return the oxtails to the pot, add the wine, and bring to a boil. Reduce the heat to a simmer and cook, uncovered, until the wine is reduced by half.

4. Pour the tomato paste–broth mixture over the meat. Cover and simmer for 2 hours. Add the chopped celery, cover, and cook for 15 minutes. Remove from the heat and transfer the oxtails to a platter to cool. Set the pot aside.

5. Carefully and thoroughly remove the meat from the bones; this will take time, but it is worth it. Stir the meat into the sauce and bring to a boil, stirring occasionally.

6. Meanwhile in a small bowl, mix the celery leaves, the remaining parsley, the red pepper, red onion, red pepper flakes, and cinnamon together. Toss with the remaining 1 tablespoon olive oil and the lemon juice, and season with salt and pepper.

7. Arrange the meat in nice mounds on six warmed plates. Divide the celery mixture evenly over the meat and serve immediately.

MEAT

VEGETABLES

Italians view vegetables with a passion that finally seems to be catching on here in the United States, with greenmarkets and farmers' stands now approaching (deservedly) cult status.

The most important step in cooking any vegetable, whether for antipasto or a pasta sauce, or for the following *contorni*, is the very first one: the shopping. Look for produce that was picked ripe and shipped carefully to the market. Try to find vegetables grown as organically as possible, for both nutritional and health benefits—not to mention the environment—and, as much as possible, select truly seasonal, local produce grown near your own home. That can create a problem for those of us with a hankering for a strawberry in December, but in Italy it is part of the very backbone of the edible culture to understand seasonality and to live with it happily. Americans of my generation have always found strawberries in the winter, right next to the asparagus. Growing up, it was not part of our lives to realize how criminal that could be. But if you buy your produce following the premises listed above, I can personally guarantee greater success and flavor in everything you cook.

Whether the dishes in this chapter are served as a side dish or an antipasto, that is a debate for your house.

ROMAN-STYLE ARTICHOKES

Carciofi alla Romana

Artichokes and asparagus are both difficult to pair with wine because of the presence of certain compounds that turn the wine bitter in the mouth. Braising the chokes in wine makes them easier to eat with wine.

MAKES 6 SERVINGS

6 large ARTICHOKES with long stems, trimmed, halved, choke removed, and held in lemon water (see page 339)

3 cloves GARLIC, thinly sliced

1 LEMON, thinly sliced and seeds removed

1 bunch fresh MINT, leaves only, roughly chopped, 1 tablespoon reserved

1 teaspoon HOT RED PEPPER FLAKES

½ cup EXTRA-VIRGIN OLIVE OIL, plus extra for drizzling

½ cup DRY WHITE WINE

½ cup WATER

COARSE SEA SALT

¼ cup thinly sliced RED ONIONS

Juice of half a LEMON

2 tablespoons ORANGE ZEST

1. Place the artichokes end side up in the smallest pot that holds them. Scatter the garlic and lemon slices around them, pushing them down around the artichokes, then do the same with the mint. Sprinkle the red pepper flakes over the top. Add the olive oil, wine, and water.

2. Cover the pan tightly and bring to a boil over medium-high heat, then lower the heat to a simmer and cook until the artichokes are just tender, about 30 minutes. Remove from the heat and allow to stand, covered, for 10 minutes.

3. Place the onions and the lemon juice in a bowl and let stand 5 minutes. Strain out the lemon juice, add the zest and the reserved mint, and sprinkle over the artichokes.

4. Serve warm or at room temperature, with a sprinkling of coarse sea salt and a drizzle of olive oil.

FIRE-ROASTED ARTICHOKES
Carciofi al Carbone

Wrapping these thistles in foil and roasting them in a really hot oven also works, if the grill is put away for the winter.

MAKES 4 SERVINGS

8 jumbo ARTICHOKES

12 cloves GARLIC, thinly sliced

1 cup sliced ALMONDS

3 tablespoons SALT

3 tablespoons freshly ground BLACK PEPPER

2 LEMONS, peeled, seeded, and finely chopped

1½ cups fresh OREGANO LEAVES

2 to 2½ cups EXTRA-VIRGIN OLIVE OIL

1. Preheat the grill.
2. Cut off the top 1½ inches of each artichoke. Trim the bottoms if necessary so they will stand upright. In a small bowl, mix the garlic, almonds, salt, pepper, lemons, and oregano well. Using your fingers, spread the artichokes open like flowers. Divide the oregano mixture among the artichokes, stuffing it down between the leaves. Drizzle 4 to 5 tablespoons olive oil over each artichoke.
3. Set the artichokes directly on the coals if using hardwood charcoal, or on the grill grate. Cook, turning occasionally, for 1 hour. The outer base will char and become inedible, but the inside will be fully cooked and amazing.

ARTICHOKES
IN THE STYLE OF THE ITALIAN JEWS
Carciofi alla Giudia

Slow-frying these babies in extra-virgin olive oil is the whole game here. It makes them sing like Pavarotti in the Eternal City.

MAKES 6 SERVINGS

4 cups EXTRA-VIRGIN OLIVE OIL, for deep-frying

6 medium round ARTICHOKES, trimmed, chokes removed, stalks peeled, and held in lemon water (see page 339)

SALT and freshly ground BLACK PEPPER

1. In a large deep pot, heat the olive oil to 300°F. Meanwhile, drain the artichokes and pat dry. Press them firmly, face down, against a hard surface so that they open like flowers. Season the inside of each choke with salt and pepper.
2. Working in batches to avoid crowding the pot, add the artichokes to the hot oil and cook for 10 minutes, using a slotted spoon or a spider to keep them submerged. Increase the heat to 350°F and cook until tender. Remove from the oil and drain on paper towels; if necessary, season with salt and pepper again. (Reduce the heat and allow the oil to cool to 300°F between batches.)

TUSCAN-STYLE ARTICHOKES

Carciofi alla Toscana

Tuscans sauté every vegetable from green beans to cauliflower in this style. Although they will turn a little gray, you will never taste anything that expresses its intense flavor so clearly as these little chokes. I love baby artichokes for this dish, as you do not need to remove the undeveloped fuzzy centers, but larger ones will work fine, provided you remove the choke. This can also be served as an antipasto.

MAKES 4 SERVINGS

1 LEMON, halved

16 BABY ARTICHOKES

¼ cup EXTRA-VIRGIN OLIVE OIL

4 cloves GARLIC, thinly sliced

4 fresh SAGE LEAVES

10 fresh BASIL LEAVES

1 teaspoon freshly ground BLACK PEPPER

SALT

1. Pour 8 cups of cold water into a large bowl and squeeze the juice of the lemon into it. Remove the tougher outer leaves from each artichoke and trim about ½ inch off the top of each one. Cut each lengthwise in half, and drop into the lemon water.

2. Heat a 10- to 12-inch sauté pan over medium-high heat, then add the olive oil and heat until smoking. Meanwhile, drain the artichokes well and press between two kitchen towels to remove almost all of the water (not all of it!).

3. Add the artichokes to the smoking oil and toss quickly to sear. Add the garlic, sage, basil, and pepper and cook, stirring frequently, until the artichokes are tender and slightly crisp at the edges. Season with salt, and serve warm or at room temperature.

ROOT VEGETABLE MASH
WITH ORANGE ZEST
Puree all'Arancia

This is what I like to serve instead of mashed potatoes. The complexity of the sweet potato and parsnip combo might seem as if it would be too sweet, but this really works well under any rich braised meat or bird.

MAKES 4 SERVINGS

1 large CARROT, cut into ½-inch-thick rounds

1 RUSSET POTATO, peeled and cut into ½-inch cubes

1 medium TURNIP, cut into ½-inch cubes

1 medium ONION, cut into ¼-inch dice

1 medium PARSNIP, cut into ¼-inch-thick rounds

1 medium SWEET POTATO, cut into ½-inch cubes

Pinch of ground CINNAMON

2 tablespoons EXTRA-VIRGIN OLIVE OIL

Grated zest of 1 ORANGE

SALT and freshly ground BLACK PEPPER

1 bunch CHIVES, finely chopped

1. Combine the carrot, potato, turnip, onion, parsnip, and sweet potato in a 4-quart saucepan and add water to cover. Bring to a boil, then lower to a simmer and cook until all the vegetables are soft, about 15 minutes.

2. Drain the vegetables and pass through a food mill into a large bowl. Stir in the cinnamon, olive oil, and orange zest and season with salt and pepper. Stir in the chives, and serve.

ASPARAGUS *with* CITRUS, PARSLEY *and* GARLIC

Asparagi alla Gremolata

I love the way jumbo asparagus trumpet the arrival of spring. There are restaurants in Italy, particularly Rome, where they devise whole menus of asparagus to celebrate this king of vegetables. This can be served as a side dish or an antipasto.

MAKES 4 TO 6 SERVINGS

1½ pounds jumbo ASPARAGUS

Zest and juice of 2 large LEMONS

Zest of 1 large ORANGE

2 cloves GARLIC, roughly chopped

2 tablespoons finely chopped ITALIAN PARSLEY

2 tablespoons fresh MINT cut into chiffonade

¼ cup EXTRA-VIRGIN OLIVE OIL

1 tablespoon COARSE SEA SALT

1. Snap off the fibrous bottom part of each stalk of asparagus (it will break off naturally where it becomes tough, provided that you grasp the very bottom of the woody stalk with your fingertips).

2. Bring 4 quarts of water to a boil in a large pot, and add 3 tablespoons salt. Set up an ice bath next to the stovetop. Drop the asparagus into the boiling water and cook until crisp-tender, about 1½ minutes. Remove and immediately submerge in the ice bath to cool for 5 minutes, moving the stalks frequently to be sure no hot spots remain; add more ice if it all melts.

3. Remove the asparagus and drain on a kitchen towel, then transfer to a large bowl. Add the lemon zest and juice, orange zest, the garlic, parsley, mint, and olive oil and toss gently to mix well. Arrange the spears on a platter and pour the mixture remaining in the bowl over them. Sprinkle with the sea salt, and serve with a flourish.

ROASTED ASPARAGUS *with* CAPERS *and* EGGS

Asparagi al Forno

Roasting asparagus in the oven or on a hot grill adds another world of intensity to its sweetness and brings out its woodsy, meaty component. The dressing may be optional for some, but it is essential for me and the several hundred thousand citizens of the Veneto region of northern Italy.

MAKES 4 TO 6 SERVINGS

1½ pounds jumbo ASPARAGUS

½ cup plus 2 tablespoons EXTRA-VIRGIN OLIVE OIL

1 tablespoon COARSE SEA SALT

2 tablespoons RED WINE VINEGAR

2 tablespoons tiniest CAPERS

1 HARD-COOKED EGG, white and yolk separated and chopped separately

1 SCALLION, thinly sliced

SALT and freshly ground BLACK PEPPER

1. Preheat the oven to 500°F or preheat the grill.

2. Snap off the fibrous bottom part of each stalk of asparagus (it will break off naturally where it becomes tough, provided that you grasp the very bottom of the woody stalk with your fingertips). Place the asparagus in a large bowl. Drizzle with ¼ cup of the olive oil, sprinkle with the sea salt, and toss to coat.

3. Spread on a baking sheet or arrange on the grill rack and cook, turning occasionally, until tender and golden brown in some spots, about 8 minutes in the oven or 6 to 7 minutes on the grill. Transfer to a platter.

4. In a small bowl, stir together the vinegar, capers, chopped egg white, scallion, and the remaining 6 tablespoons olive oil. Season with salt and pepper. Pour the sauce over the asparagus, sprinkle with the chopped egg yolk, and serve.

BAKED CARDOONS ROMAN-STYLE

Cardi Gratinati alla Romana

Even shoes would taste great if baked submerged in besciamella with cheese and bread crumbs, so using my favorite vegetable of all time makes this gratin a real home run. If you cannot find cardoons, you can use celery or fennel in exactly the same way. For a light, elegant lunch, serve with grilled bread.

MAKES 4 SERVINGS

5 pounds CARDOONS

½ cup ALL-PURPOSE FLOUR

2 LEMONS, halved

2 cups BESCIAMELLA (page 65)

1 cup freshly grated PARMIGIANO-REGGIANO

1 cup FRESH BREAD CRUMBS

HOT RED PEPPER FLAKES

1. Trim the cardoons so they are about 14 to 16 inches long, and separate the stalks. Using a paring knife, peel off the fibrous outer ribs and hard green skin.

2. Fill a large pot with water (about 10 cups) and add the flour. Squeeze the lemons into the water, and add the lemon halves. Cut each cardoon into 3 pieces, adding them to the water as you work.

3. Place the pot over medium-high heat and bring to a boil. Lower the heat and cook at just below a boil for 15 minutes. Drain the cardoons, rinse, and allow to cool.

4. Preheat the oven to 400°F.

5. Lay the cardoons in an ovenproof casserole and cover with the besciamella. Sprinkle with the Parmigiano and bread crumbs and bake for 30 to 35 minutes, until dark golden brown on top and very bubbly. Serve hot with red pepper flakes for sprinkling.

BROCCOLI
SAUTÉED IN WINE AND GARLIC
Broccoli al Frascati

Cooking cruciferous vegetables without boiling them, as in this recipe, seems to make them more fragrant and heady—just the way the robust Romans like their food.

MAKES 6 SERVINGS

6 tablespoons EXTRA-VIRGIN OLIVE OIL

4 cloves GARLIC, sliced

3 pounds BROCCOLI, cut into spears

1 cup FRASCATI or other dry white wine

1 tablespoon HOT RED PEPPER FLAKES

Zest of 1 LEMON

Zest of 1 ORANGE

In a 10- to 12-inch sauté pan, heat the olive oil with the garlic over medium-high heat until just sizzling. Add the broccoli and cook, tossing frequently and gradually adding the wine to keep the garlic from browning, until the stalks are tender, 8 to 10 minutes. Add the red pepper flakes and zests, tossing well, and serve immediately.

BROCCOLI RABE
BRAISED IN THE STYLE OF PUGLIA
Broccoli Rabe alla Pugliese

This slowly simmered dish delivers incredible impact—it always seems as if I am tasting rabe for the first time. The olives are truly all the seasoning it needs.

MAKES 4 SERVINGS

¼ cup EXTRA-VIRGIN OLIVE OIL

1 clove GARLIC, crushed and coarsely chopped

1 teaspoon HOT RED PEPPER FLAKES

3 bunches BROCCOLI RABE, trimmed and washed well

¼ cup small BLACK OLIVES, pitted and coarsely chopped

1. In a deep pot large enough to hold all of the broccoli rabe, heat the olive oil over medium heat. Add the garlic and red pepper flakes and cook until the garlic begins to soften, 3 to 5 minutes.

2. While the garlic is cooking, wash the broccoli rabe thoroughly. Add it to the pot with the water still clinging to its leaves, cover tightly, and cook until the rabe is very tender and just a few spoonfuls of liquid remain, 20 to 30 minutes.

3. When the broccoli rabe is tender, stir it well to mix with the sauce, then stir in the olives. Serve hot.

RED CABBAGE
BRAISED IN VINEGAR
Cavolo al Aceto

I love the sweet-and-sour aspect of this dish. Good both hot and cold, it is particularly tasty on a sandwich with mortadella and horse-radish.

MAKES 6 SERVINGS

1 medium head (about 2 pounds) RED CABBAGE

¼ cup EXTRA-VIRGIN OLIVE OIL

1 medium RED ONION, thinly sliced

2 tablespoons CARAWAY SEEDS

2 tablespoons SUGAR

½ cup RED WINE VINEGAR

SALT and freshly ground BLACK PEPPER

1. Remove the tough outer leaves of the cabbage. Cut the cabbage into quarters, remove the core, and cut into ½-inch-wide strips.

2. Heat a large heavy-bottomed pot over medium-high heat, then add the olive oil and heat until smoking. Add the onion and caraway seeds and cook, stirring, until the onion is soft, 3 to 5 minutes. Add the cabbage, sugar, and vinegar and stir well. Cover and cook until the cabbage is quite tender, about 20 minutes. Season with salt and pepper.

3. Serve warm, or allow to cool and serve with sammies.

SPICED CABBAGE
FROM LAKE GARDA
Cavolo alla Lombarda

If you cannot find speck, smoked prosciutto from northern Italy, you can substitute a smoky Black Forest ham, or even smoky bacon. This is good with roast goose or duck.

MAKES 6 SERVINGS

1 medium head (about 2 pounds) WHITE CABBAGE

¼ cup EXTRA-VIRGIN OLIVE OIL, preferably from Garda

1 teaspoon CUMIN SEEDS

2 tablespoons grated fresh HORSERADISH

1 tablespoon freshly ground BLACK PEPPER

1 ounce SPECK, cut into julienne

Juice of 1 LEMON

1. Remove the tough outer leaves of the cabbage. Cut the cabbage into quarters, remove the core, and cut into ½-inch-wide ribbons.

2. Bring a large pot of lightly salted water to a boil. Add the cabbage and cook for 20 minutes. Drain and cool.

3. In a 10- to 12-inch sauté pan, heat the olive oil over medium-high heat until smoking. Add the cumin, horseradish, pepper, and speck and toss to mix. Add the cabbage and toss again. Cook, stirring occasionally, until the cabbage is soft, 8 to 10 minutes. Sprinkle with the lemon juice, and serve.

STUFFED CABBAGE
Cavolo Ripieno

This is an elaborate side dish that makes any meal fit for a king, but it could also serve as a main course.

MAKES 4 SERVINGS

1 large head GREEN CABBAGE

1½ pounds ground TURKEY

½ cup FRESH BREAD CRUMBS

½ cup finely chopped ITALIAN PARSLEY

10 fresh SAGE LEAVES, finely chopped

½ medium RED ONION, finely chopped

3 large EGGS

1 teaspoon SALT

2 teaspoons freshly ground BLACK PEPPER

2 cups BASIC TOMATO SAUCE (page 71)

½ cup DRY WHITE WINE

½ cup TOASTED BREAD CRUMBS

1 bunch MINT, leaves only

1. Bring 6 quarts of water to a boil in a large pot, and add 2 tablespoons salt. Meanwhile, remove and discard any tough outer leaves from the cabbage. Carefully remove 14 whole leaves from the cabbage (reserve the remainder for another use).

2. Plunge the leaves into the boiling water and cook until soft and pliable, 4 to 5 minutes. Drain and rinse under cold water, then lay out on kitchen towels to cool.

3. Preheat the oven to 375°F.

4. In a large bowl, combine the ground turkey, fresh bread crumbs, ¼ cup of the parsley, the sage, onion, eggs, salt, and pepper and mix well with your hands. Lay out 12 of the cabbage leaves on a cutting board (the 2 extra leaves are for backup in case any of the leaves tear) and place a medium-sized handful of the turkey mixture in the center of the bottom of each leaf. Fold the sides over and roll up from the bottom to make a neat package.

5. Pour half the tomato sauce and all the wine into a baking dish large enough to hold the cabbage rolls. Lay the cabbage rolls seam side down atop the sauce. Spoon the remaining sauce over and bake 1 hour. Sprinkle with the toasted bread crumbs, the remaining ¼ cup parsley, and the mint, and serve immediately.

EGGPLANT CAPONATA

Caponata di Melanzane

This is my take on the Sicilian eggplant classic. I like it pretty zippy, but you can tone down the hot pepper flakes to your taste. It can be a *contorno*, an antipasto, or a pasta sauce. It is also excellent served *tiépido* (at room temperature) on a hot day as the main event at a light lunch.

MAKES 8 SERVINGS

½ cup EXTRA-VIRGIN OLIVE OIL

1 large SPANISH ONION, cut into ½-inch dice

2 cloves GARLIC, thinly sliced

3 tablespoons PINE NUTS

3 tablespoons dried CURRANTS

1 tablespoon HOT RED PEPPER FLAKES

2 medium EGGPLANT, cut into ½-inch cubes (about 4 cups)

1 tablespoon SUGAR

1 teaspoon ground CINNAMON

½ teaspoon unsweetened COCOA POWDER

2 teaspoons fresh THYME LEAVES or ½ teaspoon dried THYME

¾ cup BASIC TOMATO SAUCE (page 71)

⅓ cup BALSAMIC VINEGAR

SALT and freshly ground BLACK PEPPER

1 BAGUETTE, cut into ¾-inch rounds and toasted

1.   In a 10- to 12-inch sauté pan, heat the olive oil over medium-high heat until almost smoking. Add the onion, garlic, pine nuts, currants, and red pepper flakes and cook until the onion is softened, 4 to 5 minutes. Add the eggplant, sugar, cinnamon, and cocoa and cook for 5 minutes.

2.   Add the thyme, tomato sauce, and vinegar and bring to a boil. Lower the heat and simmer for 5 minutes. Remove from the heat and let cool to room temperature. (The caponata can be covered and refrigerated for up to 2 days. Bring to room temperature before serving.)

3.   To serve, spoon the caponata onto the crostini and arrange on a platter, or put it into a bowl with the crostini on the side so your guests can help themselves.

CACAO

The tree that yields cacao is named *Theobroma cacao*, literally, "food of the gods," and is native to Latin America. Cocoa was introduced to Europe via the conquistadors. Once brought back to Spain, cacao was kept a secret from the rest of Europe for more than a hundred years, while the Spanish nobles treated cocoa like liquid gold. (The Church, ever suspicious of anything the public found desirable, declared cocoa off-limits during Lent and on holy days.) Cocoa eventually found its way; Italian chocolate was first manufactured in Florence. Italians have their own, very rich version of hot cocoa, but they also use powdered cocoa to give depth to both sweet and savory dishes. It adds a richness to meat dishes, such as braised fowl or roast pork, as well as to sweeter vegetables, such as eggplant.

SAUTÉED EGGPLANT

Melanzane in Padella

The simplest dishes are often the most tasty. Here the vinegar (though it's Italian balsamic) and scallion combination almost gives the dish an Asian flair.

MAKES 6 SERVINGS

6 medium JAPANESE EGGPLANT

¼ cup EXTRA-VIRGIN OLIVE OIL

2 SCALLIONS, thinly sliced

2 tablespoons chopped fresh THYME

2 tablespoons BALSAMIC VINEGAR

SALT and freshly ground BLACK PEPPER

1. Trim the stem ends from the eggplant and cut each one lengthwise in half.

2. In a large skillet (use two pans if necessary), heat the olive oil over medium heat until smoking. Add the eggplant and cook, stirring occasionally, until softened, 6 to 8 minutes. Add the scallions, thyme, and vinegar and cook until the vinegar evaporates. Remove from the heat and season with salt and pepper. Serve hot or at room temperature.

EGGPLANT

The eggplant (*Solanum melongena*) a member of the nightshade family, which also includes the potato, is native to India and what is now Pakistan, where it has been cultivated for more than four thousand years. The first varieties known to the English bore egg-shaped fruit, thus the name. The Spaniards of the sixteenth century called the eggplant *berengena*, "apple of love," but northern Europeans at first called it *mala insana*, or "mad apple," because they thought it could cause insanity. The Italians, however, were almost instant converts (and the Italian name, *melanzane*, means "love apple"). It plays a starring role in many of the regional cuisines of Italy, particularly in the south, where the vegetable grows in abundance under the hot sun.

Italian eggplants tend to be smaller, with a more delicate skin and flesh, than the large purple globes more common in American markets. Your best bet is to look for baby eggplant, or use the slim Asian varieties that are increasingly available. Choose plump, unwrinkled specimens that are firm to the touch and heavy for their size. Avoid any with blemishes or bruises.

Always use stainless steel knives when prepping eggplant, as carbon steel knives can cause discoloration and a bitter aftertaste. Some cooks recommend lightly salting cut-up eggplant and letting it stand for 15 minutes before cooking to reduce bitterness, but I find that this is usually unnecessary, and results in a leathery texture.

MARINATED EGGPLANT

Melanzane in Scapece

Salting eggplant causes a collapse of the cell walls and reduces its ability to absorb both fat and other liquids. I do not salt eggplant unless I am preserving it by canning or pickling. These can be served as a side dish or, with a salad of bitter lettuce, such as chicory or radicchio, as an antipasto.

MAKES 8 SIDE-DISH SERVINGS OR 4 ANTIPASTO SERVINGS

8 small perfect JAPANESE EGGPLANT (3 to 4 inches long, about 2 pounds total)

¾ cup EXTRA-VIRGIN OLIVE OIL

¼ cup RED WINE VINEGAR

3 cloves GARLIC, finely minced

20 fresh MINT LEAVES, roughly chopped

Grated zest of 1 medium ORANGE

2 tablespoons freshly ground BLACK PEPPER

1. Preheat the grill or broiler.
2. Slice the eggplants lengthwise in half. Brush the cut sides with ¼ cup of the olive oil. Grill or broil the eggplant for about 5 minutes, turning once or twice, until deep golden brown. Transfer to a serving bowl.
3. In a small bowl, stir together the vinegar, garlic, mint, orange zest, and the remaining ½ cup olive oil. Pour over the eggplant, and season with the pepper. Allow to sit for 30 minutes before serving.

SAUTÉED FENNEL

WITH ANCHOVIES, GARLIC AND SAMBUCA

Finocchio alla Sambuca

MAKES 4 SERVINGS

4 FENNEL BULBS, trimmed, fronds reserved and finely chopped

¼ cup EXTRA-VIRGIN OLIVE OIL

4 cloves GARLIC, thinly sliced

1 medium RED ONION, thinly sliced

3 salt-packed ANCHOVIES, filleted, rinsed, and patted dry

¼ cup SAMBUCA or other anise-flavored liqueur

1. Bring 6 quarts of water to a boil in a large pot, and add 2 tablespoons salt. Set up an ice bath next to the stovetop. Add the whole fennel bulbs to the boiling water and cook until fork-tender, 10 to 12 minutes. Drain and transfer to the ice bath to cool, then drain again and cut each bulb lengthwise in half.
2. In a 10- to 12-inch nonstick sauté pan, heat the olive oil over medium-low heat until hot. Add the fennel bulbs cut side down and cook slowly until golden brown on the first side. Add the garlic and onion to the pan and turn the fennel over.
3. Mash the anchovies to a paste and add to the pan, stirring well. Add the sambuca and swirl the pan, then cook until the alcohol evaporates, about 1 minute. Transfer the fennel bulbs to a decorative platter. Stir the fronds into the sauce, pour over the fennel, and serve.

BRAISED BABY FENNEL

Finocchi Brasati

This is a case when soft, fully cooked vegetables have much fuller flavor than al dente ones. Most of the recipes inspired by Puglia produce very well done vegetables, and the flavor is quite distinctive.

MAKES 6 SERVINGS

12 very small FENNEL BULBS, trimmed, or 4 to 6 larger bulbs, trimmed and quartered

¼ cup EXTRA-VIRGIN OLIVE OIL

3 cloves GARLIC, finely chopped

3 salt-packed ANCHOVIES, filleted, rinsed, and chopped

½ teaspoon HOT RED PEPPER FLAKES

Grated zest of 1 ORANGE

SALT and freshly ground BLACK PEPPER

1. Bring a large pot of water to a boil, and add 2 tablespoons salt. Drop in the fennel, return to a boil, and cook until tender, about 10 minutes. Drain and set aside.

2. In a skillet large enough to hold the fennel in one layer, heat the olive oil over medium-low heat until very hot. Add the garlic, anchovies, and red pepper flakes and cook, stirring, until the garlic has softened and the anchovies are beginning to dissolve. Add the fennel and cook, stirring to coat the fennel with the oil, for 5 minutes. Add orange zest and season with salt and pepper. Serve hot or at room temperature.

FENNEL GRATIN *with* ROBIOLA

Finocchi al Forno

Pungent robiola is a magnificent foil for the sweetness of the fennel in this autumnal heart warmer.

MAKES 4 SERVINGS

2 FENNEL BULBS, trimmed, halved lengthwise, and cut into ½-inch-thick slices

1 cup BESCIAMELLA (page 65)

4 ounces ITALIAN FONTINA, grated

8 ounces ROBIOLA CHEESE

About ¼ cup lightly TOASTED BREAD CRUMBS

1. Preheat the oven to 450°F. Butter four 4-inch round gratin dishes.

2. Bring 4 quarts of water to a boil in a large pot, and add 2 tablespoons salt. Add the fennel and blanch until tender, 8 to 10 minutes. Drain thoroughly.

3. In a medium bowl, mix the fennel with the besciamella and Fontina. Divide among the gratin dishes, and pat down with the back of a spoon. Bake in the upper third of the oven for 25 minutes, or until bubbling and hot.

4. Place a 2-ounce dollop or square of robiola in the center of each gratin, and sprinkle the bread crumbs over the robiola. Bake for 5 to 6 more minutes, until the robiola is hot and soft and the crumbs have melted into it. Allow to stand for 3 minutes before serving.

DRIED FAVAS *with* CHICORY
Fave e Cicoria

This is a great example of a dish that was created out of pure poverty and then became such a sentimental favorite that today it is served in fancy restaurants, at fancy prices.

MAKES 6 SERVINGS

8 ounces dried peeled FAVA BEANS, soaked overnight in cold water

1 pound CHICORY or other bitter greens, trimmed

½ cup EXTRA-VIRGIN OLIVE OIL

SALT and freshly ground BLACK PEPPER

1. Drain the favas, place in a saucepan, and cover with water. Cover the pan and bring to a boil over medium-high heat. Add a pinch of salt and cook, stirring occasionally, for about an hour, or until the beans have dissolved and taken on the consistency of clotted cream; add boiling water as necessary to keep the beans from scorching.

2. While the beans cook, rinse the greens, then place them in a saucepan over high heat, cover, and cook them in the water that clings to their leaves until tender, adding a little more water if necessary to prevent scorching. Drain the greens, squeeze out the excess water, and transfer to a medium bowl. Toss with ¼ cup of the olive oil and salt and pepper to taste.

3. When the favas are cooked, remove from the heat and beat in the remaining ¼ cup olive oil. Season with salt and pepper. Stir in the greens, and serve.

FAVA *and* ARTICHOKE STEW
Fave e Carciofi al Tegame

This is the traditional first taste of spring in Rome, where favas and artichokes rule the markets for a couple of weeks in March.

MAKES 4 SERVINGS

⅓ cup EXTRA-VIRGIN OLIVE OIL

1 medium ONION, coarsely chopped

1 clove GARLIC, coarsely chopped

2 pounds fresh young FAVA BEANS, shelled and peeled

4 small to medium ARTICHOKES, trimmed, chokes removed, cut into ¼-inch-thick slices, and held in lemon water (see page 339)

SALT and freshly ground BLACK PEPPER

1. In a 10- to 12-inch sauté pan, heat the olive oil over medium-low heat until hot. Add the onion and garlic and sweat the vegetables until they are soft and just golden brown, 8 to 10 minutes.

2. Add the fava beans and stir well.

3. Drain the artichoke slices and add to the pan. Add ½ cup water, increase the heat, and bring to a boil. Cook until the vegetables are tender, about 15 minutes. Season with salt and pepper, and serve immediately.

GRILLED MARINATED CHANTERELLES

Funghi Marinati

If you can't find chanterelles, shiitake work really well as a substitute for the exotic yeasty flavor I love.

MAKES 4 SERVINGS

¼ cup plus 3 tablespoons EXTRA-VIRGIN OLIVE OIL

Grated zest and juice of 1 LEMON

½ medium RED ONION, thinly sliced

5 large YELLOW or GREEN ANAHEIM CHILES, stems, seeds, and ribs removed, cut into ⅛-inch-wide julienne

4 cups WILD GREENS, such as mizuna or field cress, washed and spun dry (or substitute baby spinach)

1 pound CHANTERELLES, brushed clean

1 tablespoon freshly ground BLACK PEPPER

SALT

1. Preheat the grill or broiler.
2. In a 10- to 12-inch sauté pan, heat ¼ cup of the olive oil over medium heat until hot. Add the lemon zest and onion and cook until the onion is soft and translucent. Add the chiles and sauté for 1 minute. Toss in the wild greens and lemon juice and remove from the heat.
3. In a large bowl, toss the chanterelles with the remaining 3 tablespoons olive oil and the black pepper to thoroughly coat. Spread out on the grill rack (use a wire mesh rack if necessary so the mushrooms don't fall through the grill grate) or on a baking sheet and grill or broil, turning often, for 8 to 10 minutes, until softened and lightly browned.
4. Add the chanterelles to the greens, place over high heat, and stir gently with tongs to wilt the greens. Season with salt, transfer to a serving bowl, and serve.

ONIONS
WITH BALSAMIC GLAZE
Cipolle al Aceto

Redolent of the sweet, syrupy true balsamic vinegar, onions cooked like this are ubiquitous in the great delis of Modena and Bologna.

MAKES 4 SERVINGS

¼ cup EXTRA-VIRGIN OLIVE OIL

3 tablespoons UNSALTED BUTTER

2 pounds medium SPANISH ONIONS, halved

2 tablespoons SUGAR

1 cup regular BALSAMIC VINEGAR

1 cup WATER

1 teaspoon chopped fresh ROSEMARY

1. In a 10- to 12-inch sauté pan, heat the olive oil over medium-high heat until just smoking. Add the butter and cook until the foam subsides. Add the onions cut side down and sauté until light golden brown, 8 to 10 minutes.
2. Add the sugar, vinegar, water, and rosemary and bring to a boil, stirring occasionally. Cook the onions, uncovered, until they are just al dente and the liquid has reduced to a glaze and the onions are tender all the way through, about 20 minutes. If the liquid evaporates too quickly, add more water, ¼ cup at a time. Serve warm or at room temperature.

SPICY PEPPER STEW
Peperoni Piccanti

This zippy variation on peperonata is perfect with anything off the grill in the summer. You can up or down the heat by leaving in the jalapeño seeds and ribs or not.

MAKES 4 SERVINGS

½ cup plus 2 tablespoons EXTRA-VIRGIN OLIVE OIL

1 medium RED ONION, thinly sliced

1 clove GARLIC

4 ITALIAN FRYING PEPPERS

2 RED BELL PEPPERS, cored, seeded, and cut into ½-inch-wide strips

2 YELLOW BELL PEPPERS, cored, seeded, and cut into ½-inch-wide strips

2 large JALAPEÑOS, stemmed, seeded if desired, and julienned

3 tablespoons RED WINE VINEGAR

2 tablespoons chopped fresh MARJORAM

SALT and freshly ground BLACK PEPPER

1. In a 10- to 12-inch sauté pan, heat ¼ cup of the olive oil over medium-high heat until smoking. Add the onion and garlic and cook until softened, 4 to 5 minutes. Add the peppers and cook, stirring, until quite soft but not falling apart, 10 to 12 minutes. Transfer to a large bowl to cool.
2. In a small bowl, whisk together the vinegar, marjoram, and remaining 6 tablespoons olive oil. Season with salt and pepper. Pour over the peppers, toss gently, and serve.

STUFFED PEPPERS, ONIONS
and **TOMATOES**
Gratin di Verdura

These are classics from the kitchens of Emilia-Romagna, birthplace of Parmigiano-Reggiano. If it seems as if you might want to add some more ingredients to kick it up... resist!

MAKES 4 SERVINGS

2 medium RED ONIONS

2 large TOMATOES

2 large RED BELL PEPPERS, halved lengthwise, seeds and ribs removed

1 cup lightly TOASTED BREAD CRUMBS

½ cup freshly grated PARMIGIANO-REGGIANO

½ cup finely chopped ITALIAN PARSLEY

¼ cup EXTRA-VIRGIN OLIVE OIL, plus extra for drizzling

SALT and freshly ground BLACK PEPPER

1. Preheat the oven to 450°F.

2. Peel the onions, leaving the root and stem ends intact, and halve lengthwise; set aside. Cut the tomatoes in half and squeeze the seeds and juices into a small bowl; set the tomatoes and juices aside.

3. Bring a large saucepan of water to a boil. Drop the onion halves into the boiling water and blanch for 2 minutes; drain. When cool enough to handle, using a paring knife, remove the centers of the onions, leaving the outer three or four layers intact.

4. Chop the onion centers and transfer to a large bowl. Add the tomato seeds and juices, bread crumbs, Parmigiano, parsley, and olive oil and mix well. Season with salt and pepper.

5. Arrange the peppers, onion cups, and tomatoes cut side up in a shallow baking dish. Stuff the vegetables with the bread crumb mixture, filling them just to the top. Drizzle a thin stream of olive oil over each vegetable. Bake, uncovered, for about 30 minutes, or until the bread crumbs on top are dark brown and crisp. Serve hot or at room temperature.

PUNTARELLE
IN ANCHOVY SAUCE
Puntarelle alla Romana

Along with *carciofi alla giudia*, this is perhaps the dish I associate most with sitting in the shadow of the Colosseum and eating in the Roman way. The dressing is probably the predecessor to a Caesar dressing, but it is much more aggressive.

MAKES 4 SERVINGS

1 pound PUNTARELLE, washed and trimmed

1 clove GARLIC, chopped

4 ANCHOVY FILLETS, rinsed and chopped

2 tablespoons WHITE WINE VINEGAR

¼ cup EXTRA-VIRGIN OLIVE OIL

SALT and freshly ground BLACK PEPPER

1. Cut the puntarelle lengthwise into thin strips. Put them into a bowl of cold water and let stand until they curl up.

2. In a food processor, combine the garlic, anchovies, and vinegar. With the machine running, slowly drizzle in the olive oil. Season with salt, if necessary, and pepper.

3. Drain the puntarelle, pat dry with paper towels, and place in a large bowl. Add the sauce and toss well to coat. Serve.

RADICCHIO
WITH GUANCIALE AND ROSEMARY
Radicchio al Rosmarino

I love the way bitter greens behave when under the spell of a great salted pork. If you cannot find guanciale (or make it!—see page 186), substitute good pancetta or an artisanal American bacon (see Sources, page 504).

MAKES 4 SERVINGS

4 ounces GUANCIALE, cut into 1-inch-long batons

4 long heads RADICCHIO DI TREVISO

2 tablespoons chopped fresh ROSEMARY

¼ cup WHITE WINE VINEGAR

SALT and freshly ground BLACK PEPPER

1. Place the guanciale in a 10- to 12-inch sauté pan, set over medium heat, and cook until the fat is rendered, 5 to 6 minutes. Add the radicchio, increase the heat to high, and sauté until wilted. Add the rosemary and vinegar, season with salt and pepper, and toss to coat. Serve hot or at room temperature.

POTATO TORTA

Tortiera di Patate

This is the Italian version of spuds au gratin. There is no cream or milk, but with the creamy texture of the pecorino and the pleasing crunch of the bread crumbs, it is definitely comfort food.

MAKES 8 SERVINGS

6 tablespoons EXTRA-VIRGIN OLIVE OIL

4 pounds WAXY POTATOES, peeled

2 cups FRESH BREAD CRUMBS

SALT and freshly ground BLACK PEPPER

½ cup finely chopped ITALIAN PARSLEY

1 cup freshly grated PECORINO ROMANO

1. Preheat the oven to 350°F. Grease a 2- to 3-quart, 2- to 3-inch-deep earthenware casserole or baking dish with 2 tablespoons of the olive oil.
2. Slice the potatoes ¼-inch thick and place in a large bowl. Toss with ½ cup of the bread crumbs and season well with salt and pepper. In a small bowl, mix the remaining 1½ cups bread crumbs with the parsley, the remaining ¼ cup olive oil, and the pecorino.
3. Spread a layer of potatoes in the bottom of the casserole and sprinkle with 3 to 4 tablespoons of the bread crumb and cheese mixture. Continue layering, finishing with the bread crumb cheese mixture.
4. Bake for 1 hour, or until the potatoes are tender and the top is golden brown. Serve hot.

POTATOES
ROASTED WITH GARLIC CLOVES

Patate al Forno

The blanching step helps develop the crusty, crunchy texture that makes these irresistible. (No one ever had to tell you to finish your potatoes, did they?)

MAKES 4 SERVINGS

6 large WAXY POTATOES, such as Yukon Gold

1 head GARLIC, separated into cloves but not peeled

1 bunch ROSEMARY, leaves finely chopped

¼ cup EXTRA-VIRGIN OLIVE OIL

SALT and freshly ground BLACK PEPPER

1. Preheat the oven to 425°F.
2. Bring 4 quarts of water to a boil in a large pot. Cut the potatoes into 1-inch cubes. Blanch in the boiling water for 2 minutes; drain.
3. Put the potatoes on a baking sheet and toss with the garlic, rosemary, and olive oil. Season with salt and pepper and spread out on the baking sheet. Bake for about 30 minutes, until golden brown. Serve hot.

SWEET-AND-SOUR PUMPKIN

Zucca in Agrodolce

This can be a side dish, a pasta sauce, and even a dessert in my world, with a little sour cream or yogurt. I love my first taste of the pungent chile-flecked sweet squash in the autumn; it means that summer is just about gone and that the really intense cooking is headed my way.

MAKES 4 SERVINGS

¼ cup EXTRA-VIRGIN OLIVE OIL

1 pound SUGAR PUMPKIN or ACORN SQUASH, peeled, seeded, and cut into 1-inch cubes

4 cloves GARLIC, thinly sliced

1 teaspoon HOT RED PEPPER FLAKES

3 tablespoons RED WINE VINEGAR

3 tablespoons HONEY

3 tablespoons roughly chopped fresh MINT

1. In a 10- to 12-inch sauté pan, heat the olive oil over medium-high heat until smoking. Add the pumpkin and garlic and cook until the pumpkin is light golden brown, 4 to 5 minutes. Add the red pepper flakes, vinegar, and honey and bring to a boil. Reduce the heat and simmer until the liquid is reduced to a syrupy glaze and the pumpkin is tender, 10 to 12 minutes.
2. Remove from the heat, add the mint, and serve.

WILTED GREENS
WITH GARLIC AND ANCHOVIES

Scarola alle Acciughe

There are basically two ways of cooking greens: the long, slow method, and this one, where much of their water content is still present, leaving the leaves with a definite chew.

MAKES 6 TO 8 SERVINGS

¼ cup EXTRA-VIRGIN OLIVE OIL

3 ANCHOVY FILLETS, rinsed

4 cloves GARLIC, thinly sliced

1 head ESCAROLE or 1 head or bunch other sturdy leafy green, such as dandelions or turnip greens, cut crosswise into ½-inch-wide ribbons, washed, and spun dry

SALT and freshly ground BLACK PEPPER

½ LEMON

Heat a 10- to 12-inch sauté pan over medium-high heat until hot. Add the olive oil, anchovies, and garlic and cook just until the garlic is light golden brown, about 30 seconds. Add the greens and cook, stirring constantly, until wilted, about 5 minutes. Season with salt and pepper, squeeze the lemon juice over, and serve.

RADICCHIO PANCAKES

Fritelle di Radicchio

This is so eggy as to actually feel kind of frittata-esque. The little pancakes can be made with any salad green or lettuce. In Treviso they are even made with leftover cooked vegetables from dinner the night before and served as a light lunch.

MAKES 4 SERVINGS

2 medium heads RADICCHIO

9 large EGGS, beaten

½ cup FRESH BREAD CRUMBS

¼ cup ALL-PURPOSE FLOUR

2 tablespoons freshly grated PARMIGIANO-REGGIANO

¼ cup EXTRA-VIRGIN OLIVE OIL

4 tablespoons UNSALTED BUTTER

4 ounces RICOTTA SALATA, coarsely grated

1. Core the radicchio, cut lengthwise in half, and slice into ⅛-inch-wide strips. Place in a large bowl, add the eggs, bread crumbs, flour, and Parmigiano, and stir to mix.

2. In a 10- to 12-inch nonstick sauté pan, heat the olive oil over medium heat. Add 1 tablespoon batter for each pancake, working in batches to avoid crowding, and cook, turning once, until the pancakes are golden brown on both sides. Transfer to a serving platter.

3. Sprinkle the pancakes with the ricotta salata, and serve.

PAN-ROASTED TURNIPS

Rape al Forno

This is a dish from Friuli, with clear Mittel Europe inspiration and flavor, and it is one of the few occasions where butter is actually better than olive oil. (Did I actually write that?)

MAKES 4 SERVINGS

4 tablespoons UNSALTED BUTTER

2 pounds TURNIPS, scrubbed and quartered

SALT and freshly ground BLACK PEPPER

2 tablespoons POPPY SEEDS

1 tablespoon PAPRIKA

¼ cup RED WINE VINEGAR

1. In a 10- to 12-inch sauté pan, heat the butter over medium-high heat until it melts and begins to brown. Add the turnips, season with salt and pepper, and toss to coat well. Add the poppy seeds and sauté until the turnips are light golden brown, 8 to 9 minutes.

2. Add the paprika, tossing to coat. Add the vinegar, bring to a boil, and cook until it has evaporated. Serve hot.

MARINATED ZUCCHINI
Concia di Zucchine

Summer squashes are an excellent vehicle for other flavors, and zucchini works perfectly here to carry a vinegary chile jolt into lunch or supper. It is important to get the zucchini crisp when you cook it; the trick is to move it very little when it first goes into the pan and to work in small batches.

MAKES 8 SERVINGS

¼ cup EXTRA-VIRGIN OLIVE OIL

3 medium GREEN ZUCCHINI (about 1 pound), trimmed and cut lengthwise into ¼-inch-thick slices

3 medium YELLOW ZUCCHINI (about 1 pound), trimmed and cut lengthwise into ¼-inch-thick slices

6 medium cloves GARLIC, finely minced

2 teaspoons RED PEPPER FLAKES

1 cup fresh BASIL, cut into chiffonade

2 tablespoons KOSHER SALT

2 tablespoons freshly ground BLACK PEPPER

¼ cup RED WINE VINEGAR

1. In a deep 10- to 12-inch sauté pan, heat the olive oil over medium heat until just smoking. Add 5 or 6 zucchini slices and cook, turning once, until golden brown, 3 to 4 minutes. Transfer to paper towels to drain. Repeat with the remaining zucchini.

2. In a small bowl, gently stir together the garlic, red pepper flakes, basil, salt, and pepper until well mixed. Line the bottom of a deep-dish pie plate with one quarter of the zucchini slices. Sprinkle evenly with one quarter of the herb mixture and drizzle or spritz with 1 tablespoon of the vinegar. Continue layering the remaining zucchini and herb mixture, with the remaining vinegar. Cover with plastic and refrigerate for 2 hours.

3. Serve chilled or at room temperature.

DOLCI

I had always accepted the idea that Italians do not care for sweets and went along with the business of my life. But recently, upon much closer observance of Italian dining and snacking habits, I have had a change of mind.

Italians do love sweets, and they make lots and lots of really good ones. From gelati to crumbly cakes to "spoon desserts" and fruit tarts and pies, Italy measures up pound for pound with France and Austria in the development and love of the sweeter comestibles. The real issue is, *when* do Italians eat them? They do not so much enjoy their desserts and sweets after a fine meal, but rather throughout the entire day. I have seen Italians slurping on a cone filled with two or three flavors of remarkable gelati on their way home to supper, or in the late morning on a coffee break. At breakfast time in Napoli, I have seen hundreds upon hundreds of *sfogliatelle*, thousands of brioche with honey, and baba after baba sliding over the counter with cappuccino, well before 10 a.m. In the late afternoon, I've seen older Italian men sipping on a glass of prosecco or *caffè corretto* and gambling on games of Briscola, with the wager nearly always either a slice of panettone or a *pan d'oro*, depending on the season.

So, Italians are not so inclined to eat a big plate of something sweet after a big meal, and the proper ending to a magnificent symphony in savory may simply be a piece of cheese, a pear and a couple of biscotti, or tiny chocolates with coffee. But for the rest of the whole day, the sweet stuff does find its way into the regular rhythm of life, and the sweet shops, gelaterie, and *pasticcerie* are continuously busy. The following are my faves, the kinds of desserts I like best—that is to say, mostly not too sweet, and most important, none too difficult or time-consuming to make.

CHERRY JAM TART
Crostata di Ciliegie

Jam tarts are a blast of summer when you enjoy them warm on a cold snowy winter day. Their success relies on the quality of the home-made jam. If you do not have homemade jam on hand, find a friend who makes it, or a farm-ers' market that has a good supply of it. Smucker's will not do.

MAKES 8 TO 10 SERVINGS

2½ cups ALL-PURPOSE FLOUR

½ cup SUPERFINE SUGAR

Pinch of SALT

Grated zest of 1 LEMON

½ pound (2 sticks) UNSALTED BUTTER, cut into ½-inch pieces and chilled

3 large EGG YOLKS

¼ cup cold VIN SANTO, plus the rest of the bottle for your friends

2 cups CHERRY JAM

2 or 3 turns of the PEPPERMILL

1. Combine the flour, sugar, salt, and zest in a food processor and pulse 2 or 3 times to mix. Add the butter and pulse until the mixture resembles coarse crumbs.

2. In a small bowl, beat the egg yolks together with the cold vin santo. With the machine run-ning, add to the flour mixture and process for 5 to 6 seconds, or until the dough comes together and leaves the sides of the work bowl. Turn the dough out, shape it into a disk, and wrap in plastic. Refrigerate for at least 30 minutes.

3. Preheat the oven to 425°F. Butter a large baking sheet or line it with parchment.

4. Thin the cherry jam with a teaspoon or two of hot water, stirring until smooth. Add a few grindings of pepper to heighten the flavor of the cherries and stir again. Set aside.

5. On a floured surface, roll out the dough to a circle about 12 inches in diameter. Transfer it to the prepared baking sheet. Leaving a 2-inch border uncovered, spread the cherry mixture over the dough. Fold the edges of the dough up over the jam, pleating it as necessary.

6. Bake the tart for 20 to 25 minutes, or until the pastry is deeply golden and the filling is glossy. Cool on a rack for several minutes, and serve warm with glasses of vin santo.

Photograph on page 454.

LEMON TART
Crostata di Limone

I love the warm glow this gives me, both in the making and the eating. This recipe can serve as the base for any citrus fruit. It's great with blood oranges.

MAKES 8 TO 10 SERVINGS

PASTRY

1¾ cups ALL-PURPOSE FLOUR

½ cup ground toasted ALMONDS

½ cup SUGAR

8 tablespoons (1 stick) UNSALTED BUTTER

1 large EGG

Pinch of SALT

FILLING

3 LEMONS

4 large EGGS, separated

¾ cup SUGAR

1. To make the pastry, toss together the flour, almonds, and sugar in a medium bowl. Cut in the butter until the mixture is the consistency of fine bread crumbs. Add the egg and salt and mix well, kneading gently. Form the pastry into a disk, wrap it in plastic wrap, and refrigerate while you make the filling.

2. Preheat the oven to 450°F. Butter a 9-inch fluted tart pan.

3. Grate the zest from 2 of the lemons. Squeeze the juice from all 3 lemons.

4. In a large bowl, beat the egg yolks and sugar with an electric mixer until very thick and pale. Beat in the lemon zest and juice. Transfer to the top of a double boiler, set over barely simmering water, and cook, stirring constantly, until the mixture becomes thick, 15 to 20 minutes. Remove from the heat and set aside to cool slightly.

5. Roll out the dough between two sheets of waxed paper into an 11-inch circle. Fit it into the tart pan and trim the excess dough. Prick the bottom of the dough all over with a fork, line with foil, and fill with dried beans, rice, or pie weights to keep the bottom from puffing. Bake for 10 minutes, then remove the foil and beans, and bake for an additional 5 minutes, or until pale golden.

6. Meanwhile, in a large bowl, beat the egg whites until they hold very stiff peaks. Fold them into the cooled lemon mixture.

7. Remove the tart shell from the oven and reduce the temperature to 325°F. Spread the lemon filling evenly in the tart shell. Bake for 10 to 15 minutes, until the filling is thoroughly set. Cool completely on a rack.

Photograph on page 454.

ALMOND TART
Crostata di Mandorle

The intensely nutty and deliciously chewy almond topping on this apricot jam tart makes it very different, satisfying in a macaroon kind of way. The pastry recipe makes enough for two tart shells, so you can freeze half for another day—or just make two tarts and pig out.

MAKES 8 SERVINGS

PASTRY

1¾ cups all-purpose FLOUR

½ cup finely ground TOASTED ALMONDS

½ cup SUGAR

Pinch of SALT

8 tablespoons (1 stick) UNSALTED BUTTER

1 large EGG

FILLING

3 large EGG WHITES

¾ cup SUGAR

2 cups finely ground TOASTED ALMONDS

½ cup finely chopped SEMISWEET CHOCOLATE

½ cup APRICOT JAM

1. To make the pastry, whisk together the flour, almonds, sugar, and salt in a bowl. Cut in the butter until the mixture is the consistency of fine bread crumbs. Add the egg and mix well with a fork. Turn the dough out onto a work surface and knead briefly. Divide the dough in half, form each piece into a disk, and wrap individually in plastic wrap. Freeze one portion, well wrapped, for another use and refrigerate the remaining dough for 30 minutes.

2. Butter a 9-inch tart pan with a removable bottom. On a lightly floured surface, roll out dough to an 11-inch circle. Line the tart pan with the dough and trim the excess dough. Refrigerate the tart shell for 30 minutes.

3. Preheat the oven to 375°F.

4. Line the tart shell with foil and fill with dried beans, rice, or pie weights. Bake for 15 minutes, then remove the foil and beans, and bake until the dough is set but has not begun to color, about 5 minutes longer. Remove from the oven and set aside on a rack. (Leave the oven on.)

5. To make the filling, in a large bowl, beat the egg whites until they are foamy. Gradually beat in the sugar, about 1 tablespoon at a time, then beat until the whites hold firm, glossy peaks. Gently but thoroughly fold in the almonds and chocolate.

6. Spread the apricot jam evenly over the bottom of the tart shell. Spread the egg white mixture over the jam and use a narrow spatula or the back of a spoon to make decorative peaks on top.

7. Bake the tart for 30 minutes, or until lightly golden brown on top. Transfer to a rack to cool briefly and serve warm, or serve at room temperature.

From top: Lemon Tart (page 453), Cherry Jam Tart (page 452), Almond Tart, and Orange Tart Capri-Style (page 460).

BITTER CHOCOLATE TART

Torta di Cioccolato Amaro

MAKES 8 SERVINGS

PASTRY

1½ cups ALL-PURPOSE FLOUR

½ teaspoon SALT

¼ cup CONFECTIONERS' SUGAR

½ teaspoon ground CINNAMON

9 tablespoons UNSALTED BUTTER, cut into ½-inch pieces and chilled

¼ cup SWEET DESSERT WINE, such as vin santo

FILLING

1½ cups HEAVY CREAM

10½ ounces EXTRA-BITTERSWEET CHOCOLATE, finely chopped

2 large EGGS

1 large EGG YOLK

2 tablespoons UNSWEETENED COCOA POWDER

1 teaspoon ANISE SEEDS, crushed

1 tablespoon ANISETTE

GLAZE

1 cup CONFECTIONERS' SUGAR

1½ tablespoons MILK, or as needed

2 teaspoons ANISETTE

1. To make the pastry, combine the flour, salt, confectioners' sugar, and cinnamon in a food processor and pulse 2 or 3 times to mix. Add the butter and pulse until the mixture resembles coarse crumbs. With the machine running, pour in the wine and process until the dough comes together. Place the dough on a sheet of plastic wrap, gently press it into a disk, and wrap tightly. Refrigerate for 30 minutes.

2. Butter a 10-inch fluted tart pan. Roll the dough out between sheets of plastic to a 12-inch circle about ¼ inch thick.

3. Preheat the oven to 400°F. Line the tart pan with the dough and trim the excess. Refrigerate until chilled.

4. Prick the shell and bake the tart shell for 12 minutes, or just until set. Set aside to cool. Reduce the oven temperature to 375°F.

5. To make the filling, in a medium saucepan, bring the cream to a simmer over medium heat. Remove from the heat, add the chocolate, and stir to melt. Transfer to a medium bowl and let cool for 20 minutes.

6. In a small bowl, lightly beat the eggs and egg yolk together. Whisk the cocoa and eggs into the chocolate mixture, then whisk in the crushed anise seeds and anisette. Pour the filling into the tart shell and bake for 15 minutes, or just until the filling forms a shiny skin and is slightly firm but still loose at the center.

7. Cool the tart for 15 minutes on a rack, then remove the sides of the pan and cool completely.

8. To make the glaze, in a medium bowl, beat the confectioners' sugar with the milk and anisette to a thin, pourable consistency; add a few more drops of milk if needed. Drizzle over the cooled tart with the glaze. Allow the glaze to harden before serving with anisette.

DOLCI

GRANDMA'S PINE NUT *and* RICOTTA TART

Torta della Nonna

This is the classic pine nut tart you will find in every bakery in every town of Italy—and for good reason. A cool afternoon softened with a slice of this torta and a glass of dry red wine, and the whole world comes into proper focus.

MAKES 6 SERVINGS

PASTRY

3 tablespoons UNSALTED BUTTER

3 tablespoons EXTRA-VIRGIN OLIVE OIL

2 cups ALL-PURPOSE FLOUR

1 large EGG

2 large EGG YOLKS

½ cup SUGAR

½ teaspoon SALT

½ teaspoon VANILLA EXTRACT

FILLING

2 cups fresh RICOTTA, preferably sheep's milk

½ cup PINE NUTS

½ cup SUGAR

Grated zest and juice of 1 LEMON

3 large EGGS

2 EGGS, beaten, for egg wash

1. Preheat the oven to 375°F.

2. To make the pastry, in a small saucepan, melt the butter with the olive oil; let cool. Put the flour in a medium bowl and make a well in the center. Put the egg, yolks, sugar, salt, vanilla, and butter mixture in the well, and gradually stir in the flour, bit by bit, until the liquid in the well is too thick to stir. Work the remaining flour in with your hands, then turn out onto a floured work surface and knead until the dough is smooth. Allow to rest for 10 minutes.

3. Meanwhile, to make the filling, combine the ricotta, pine nuts, sugar, lemon zest and juice, and eggs in a medium bowl and mix until smooth and creamy.

4. To assemble, divide the dough in half. On a floured surface, roll out one half to a 12-inch circle. Line the bottom and sides of a 10-inch quiche or springform pan with the dough circle. Spread the ricotta mixture evenly in the pan.

5. Roll out the remaining dough to a 12-inch circle, place over the filling, and pinch the edges together to seal. Brush the entire top with the egg wash.

6. Bake for 35 to 40 minutes, until the crust is golden brown. Let cool briefly on a rack, and serve warm or at room temperature, with vin santo.

DOLCI

ORANGE TART CAPRI-STYLE

Torta di Arancia Caprese

The combination of brown sugar and oranges did not particularly appeal to me at first, but now I love the exotic combination, especially with the tangy mascarpone as its counterpoint. American cream cheese works well as a substitute for the mascarpone, if you cannot find it.

MAKES 8 TO 10 SERVINGS

PASTRY

2 cups ALL-PURPOSE FLOUR

½ teaspoon SALT

2 tablespoons SUGAR

Grated zest of 2 LEMONS

12 tablespoons (1½ sticks) UNSALTED BUTTER, cut into ½-inch cubes and chilled

1 large EGG

1 large EGG YOLK

2 tablespoons ORANGE LIQUEUR, such as Grand Marnier

1 cup CONFECTIONERS' SUGAR

FILLING

Finely grated zest of 1 ORANGE

1⅓ cups fresh ORANGE JUICE

¼ cup packed DARK BROWN SUGAR

½ cup MASCARPONE

7 large EGGS

3 tablespoons ORANGE LIQUEUR

CONFECTIONERS' SUGAR, for garnish

1. To make the pastry, in a medium bowl, combine the flour, salt, sugar, and lemon zest. Cut in the butter until the mixture resembles coarse crumbs. In a small bowl, combine the egg, yolk, liqueur, and confectioners' sugar, then stir into the flour mixture with a fork until the dough just comes together. Turn out onto a floured board and gently knead until a smooth dough is formed. Press the dough into a disk about 6 inches across, wrap tightly in plastic wrap, and freeze for 15 minutes.

2. Butter a 10-inch fluted tart pan. On a floured surface, roll the dough out to a 12-inch circle. Fit the dough into the tart pan and trim the excess. Wrap the pan in plastic wrap and refrigerate for 30 minutes.

3. Preheat the oven to 400°F.

4. Prick the pastry shell all over with a fork. Line the shell with foil and fill with dried beans, rice, or pie weights. Bake for 10 minutes. Remove the foil and weights, reduce heat to 375°F, and bake for 10 to 15 minutes more, until golden. Remove from the oven and allow to cool on a rack. Reduce the oven to 350°F.

5. To make the filling, in a medium bowl, combine the orange zest, juice, brown sugar, and mascarpone and beat well with a mixer or whisk. Add the eggs one at a time, beating well after each addition. Beat in the liqueur.

6. Pour the filling into the pastry shell. Bake until the custard is set, about 45 minutes. Allow to cool, then dust with confectioners' sugar.

Photograph on page 454.

CHESTNUT CAKE *with* LEMON SAUCE

Castagnaccio

This is the traditional cake of the hills outside Bologna. During World War II, foodstuffs were scarce, with very little getting through the battle lines, so the local chestnuts became a primary ingredient and recipes were developed or adapted to use chestnut flour. It's a unique, oddly delicious cake, which is always served by the baker with a short disclaimer about its tradition during difficult times.

MAKES 8 TO 10 SERVINGS

2 tablespoons EXTRA-VIRGIN OLIVE OIL

2 cups CHESTNUT FLOUR

½ cup SUGAR

¼ cup coarsely chopped WALNUTS

2 cups very cold WHOLE MILK

2 tablespoons chopped fresh ROSEMARY

LEMON SAUCE

4 LEMONS, sliced paper-thin and seeds removed

1½ cups SUGAR

1 cup WATER

1. Preheat the oven to 375°F. Grease a 10-inch quiche pan with 1 tablespoon of the oil.

2. In a large bowl, combine the flour, sugar, and walnuts. Add ½ cup of the milk, stirring constantly, then slowly add the remaining 1½ cups milk, stirring constantly to prevent lumps.

3. Pour the batter into the prepared pan. Drizzle the top of the batter with the remaining 1 tablespoon olive oil and scatter the rosemary evenly over the top. Bake for 45 minutes, or until a toothpick inserted in the center comes out clean. Transfer to a wire rack.

4. Meanwhile, to make the lemon sauce, in a small saucepan, combine the lemons, sugar, and water over medium heat. Bring to a simmer and cook until the lemons are quite soft, about 20 minutes.

5. Serve the cake warm or cool with the warm lemon sauce.

EASTER GRAIN *and* RICOTTA PIE
Tortiera

Traditionally, in Campania, they would start soaking the grain on Holy Thursday in the morning, changing the water on Friday and Saturday, before assembling and baking the pie on Easter Sunday, to be served after the big family lunch. The grain does not need the whole religious thing to be just as tasty.

MAKES 8 SERVINGS

FILLING

8 ounces FARRO

2 cups SKIM MILK

Grated zest of 1 LEMON

1 teaspoon ground CINNAMON

1 cup SUGAR

1 pound fresh RICOTTA

4 large EGGS, separated

¼ cup ORANGE FLOWER WATER

DOUGH

2½ cups ALL-PURPOSE FLOUR

¾ cup SUGAR

12 tablespoons (1½ sticks) UNSALTED BUTTER, cut into chunks, at room temperature

3 large EGG YOLKS

3 tablespoons CONFECTIONERS' SUGAR

1. For the filling, put the farro in a large bowl and cover generously with cold water. Let soak overnight in the refrigerator.

2. Drain the grain, place in a medium saucepan, and cover with cold water. Bring to a boil over high heat, reduce to a simmer, and simmer until tender, about 25 minutes. Drain the farro and allow to cool.

3. Meanwhile, to make the dough, sift the flour and sugar together onto a wooden cutting board or work surface. Form into a mound and make a well in the center. Mix together the butter and egg yolks in the well. Being careful not to break through the outer walls of the well, gradually incorporate the flour mixture, then knead until the dough forms a homogenous mass. Knead for 5 minutes more, then wrap the dough in plastic wrap and let rest in the refrigerator for 30 minutes.

4. In a medium saucepan, heat the milk over medium heat to just under a simmer. Add the farro, half the lemon zest, ½ teaspoon of the cinnamon, and 1 tablespoon of the sugar and cook, stirring occasionally, until the milk is completely absorbed. Remove from the heat.

5. Place the ricotta in a large bowl. Using a wooden spoon, stir the ricotta until creamy. Add the remaining ½ teaspoon cinnamon, lemon zest, and sugar, the egg yolks, orange flower water, and farro and mix with a rubber spatula until well combined. Set aside.

6. Preheat the oven to 350°F. Butter and flour a 9-inch tart pan.

7. Cut the dough into 2 pieces, one slightly larger than the other. Using a lightly floured rolling pin, roll out the larger piece on a floured surface into a large circle about 11 inches in diameter and about ⅛-inch thick. Fit the dough into the tart pan, using your thumb and forefinger to tuck the dough into the bottom edges of the pan.

8. In the bowl of an electric mixer fitted with the whisk attachment, beat the egg whites until they form firm, glossy peaks. Using a rubber spatula, gently fold the egg whites into the ricotta mixture. Gently spread the filling into the lined tart pan.

9. Roll the remaining dough into a 10-inch circle about ⅛-inch thick. Using a sharp knife, cut the dough into 1-inch-wide strips. Arrange the dough strips on top of the filling to form a diagonal lattice.

10. Bake for 1 hour, or until the pastry on top is golden brown. Remove from the oven and let cool to room temperature on a rack. Dust with the confectioners' sugar before serving.

PEAR MARMALADE
Marmellata di Pere

MAKES 3 CUPS

2 pounds firm unripe PEARS, peeled, cored, and chopped into small pieces

1⅓ cups SUGAR

3 CLOVES

1 tablespoon freshly ground BLACK PEPPER

1. In a large bowl, mix the pears, sugar, and cloves together. Cover with a kitchen towel and set aside for at least 3 hours to let the juices start to run.

2. Transfer the pears and juice to a large nonreactive saucepan, bring to a simmer, and simmer gently, stirring frequently with a wooden spoon to prevent sticking, until the pears are tender. Remove from the heat, stir in the pepper, remove the cloves, and allow to cool. (The extra marmalade can be covered and refrigerated for at least a week.)

LEMON SPONGE CAKE *with* PEAR MARMALADE

Ciambella con le Pere

The cakes in the family of ring-shaped *ciambelle* are more often served in the late afternoon, when *nonna* needs a sip of sweet wine before the evening apertivo.

MAKES 6 SERVINGS

2½ cups CAKE FLOUR

½ teaspoon SALT

2 teaspoons BAKING POWDER

5 tablespoons EXTRA-VIRGIN OLIVE OIL

¾ cup SUGAR

3 large EGGS

Grated zest of 6 LEMONS

½ cup WHOLE MILK

¾ cup PEAR MARMALADE (opposite)

CONFECTIONERS' SUGAR, for garnish

1. Preheat the oven to 350°F. Butter and flour two 8-inch round cake pans.

2. In a medium bowl, toss the flour, salt, and baking powder with a fork to mix well.

3. In a large bowl, beat the olive oil and sugar together with an electric mixer until well blended. Add the eggs one at a time, beating well after each addition. Put the dry ingredients in a sifter and sift about one third onto the egg mixture. Add the lemon zest and fold in the flour and zest, then stir in about one third of the milk. Add the remaining flour and milk in two additions each, blending well.

4. Turn the batter into the prepared cake pans. Bake for 25 minutes, or until the cakes are beginning to pull away from the sides of the pans and spring back when pressed lightly in the center with a finger. Turn the cakes out onto a rack, and invert onto another rack to cool.

5. To assemble, place one cake layer on a serving plate and spread the marmalade over the top. Place the second layer on top and gently press the layers together. Sprinkle the top of the cake with the confectioners' sugar.

CHOCOLATE CAKE *from* ABRUZZO
Parozzo

This is an Abruzzese classic, served most often in the afternoon as a snack. It seems, and tastes, a lot more exotic than it sounds, and it takes less than thirty minutes to put together.

MAKES 8 SERVINGS

1½ cups sliced BLANCHED ALMONDS

¾ cup SUGAR

½ cup ALL-PURPOSE FLOUR

6 tablespoons CORNSTARCH

⅛ teaspoon freshly grated NUTMEG

7 extra-large EGGS, separated

5 tablespoons UNSALTED BUTTER, melted and cooled

GLAZE

6 ounces BITTERSWEET CHOCOLATE, finely chopped

2 tablespoons UNSALTED BUTTER

1. Preheat the oven to 375°F. Butter a 9-inch round cake pan.

2. In a food processor, grind the blanched almonds to a fine powder; add a little of the sugar if necessary to keep the nuts from becoming a paste. Set aside.

3. Sift together the flour, cornstarch, and nutmeg into a small bowl. Set aside.

4. In a large bowl, beat the egg yolks with an electric mixer until blended. Gradually add the ground almonds and the (remaining) sugar, beating until light and fluffy. Gradually add the flour mixture and then the cooled butter, beating well after each addition.

5. In another large bowl, beat the egg whites with clean beaters until they form stiff, glossy peaks. Fold them into the batter.

6. Pour the batter into the prepared cake pan. Bake for about 40 minutes, until the cake is firm to the touch and golden. Let cool in the pan for 15 minutes, then turn out of the pan onto a rack and let cool completely.

7. To make the glaze, in a small heavy saucepan, melt the chocolate and butter over very low heat, stirring frequently until smooth. Remove from the heat.

8. Place the cake on a serving plate. Pour the chocolate glaze on top and spread it over the top and sides with a spatula. Serve at room temperature.

DOLCI

OLIVE OIL *and* ORANGE CAKE

Torta di Arancia ed Olio

This simple cake is the kind of dry, not too sweet dessert that Italians really love in the late afternoon. You can dress it up with whipped cream or, even better, crème fraîche, or even the fancy Greek yogurt that is so thick and delicious.

MAKES 6 TO 8 SERVINGS

6 medium ORANGES

⅓ cup EXTRA-VIRGIN OLIVE OIL

4 large EGGS

½ teaspoon SALT

1 cup SUGAR

1¼ cups ALL-PURPOSE FLOUR

1 tablespoon BAKING POWDER

1. Preheat the oven to 350°F. Oil a 9-inch round cake pan.

2. Using a grater, zest all the oranges, and juice one of the oranges. (Reserve the fruit for another use.) In a small bowl, combine the zest, juice, and olive oil. Set aside.

3. In a large bowl, with an electric mixer, beat the eggs and salt until frothy and light, about 2 minutes. Slowly beat in the sugar, and continue to mix until pale and thick, about 2 minutes more.

4. Sift the flour and baking soda together, and gradually beat into the egg mixture. Fold in the citrus zest mixture just until incorporated.

5. Pour the batter into the prepared pan. Bake for 50 minutes, or until a toothpick inserted in the center of the cake comes out clean. Cool on a rack for 10 minutes, then remove from the pan and cool to room temperature.

PANETTONE

This is my easy, yeastless variation on the classic holiday cake from Milan. It does not have the kind of stretchy consistency traditional to a yeast bread, but a more cake-like crumb, similar to a coffee cake.

MAKES 8 SERVINGS

8 tablespoons (1 stick) UNSALTED BUTTER, at room temperature

2 large EGGS

3 large EGG YOLKS

3½ cups ALL-PURPOSE FLOUR

1 cup WHOLE MILK

1 cup SUGAR

½ cup dried CURRANTS, soaked in warm water for 1 hour and drained

Grated zest of 2 ORANGES

2 teaspoons CREAM OF TARTAR

1½ teaspoons BAKING SODA

1. In the bowl of a stand mixer fitted with the whisk attachment, cream the butter with the eggs and yolks until pale yellow, 3 to 4 minutes. Switch to the dough hook attachment and, with the mixer running, add half of the flour. Add half the milk and mix for 1 minute. Add the remainder of the flour, followed by the remainder of the milk and then all of the sugar and mix for 20 minutes.

2. Preheat the oven to 425°F. Butter and flour a 8-inch panettone mold or other deep cake pan, such as a charlotte mold.

3. Spread the dough out into a rough square on a floured work surface. Sprinkle with the currants, orange zest, cream of tartar, and baking soda and knead for 5 to 10 minutes to incorporate. Place in the prepared pan and bake for 35 to 45 minutes, or until a toothpick inserted in the center comes out dry. The top will be cracked. Unmold the cake onto a rack, then invert and allow to cool. Serve sliced into wedges.

RUM BABAS
Babas al Rum

These are the most delightful little bites of Napoli you will ever taste.

MAKES 6 SERVINGS

BABAS

1 envelope ACTIVE DRY YEAST

¼ cup WARM WATER

5 cups plus 2 tablespoons CAKE FLOUR

6 tablespoons UNSALTED BUTTER, at room temperature

½ cup SUGAR

¼ teaspoon SALT

5 large EGGS

2 large EGG YOLKS

RUM SYRUP

1 cup WATER

1 cup SUGAR

½ cup DARK RUM

UNSWEETENED WHIPPED CREAM for serving

1. Butter and flour a 12-cup muffin pan.
2. In a small bowl, stir together the yeast and warm water until the yeast dissolves. Add 2 tablespoons of the flour, stirring until a paste forms. Let stand for 10 minutes.
3. In the bowl of a stand mixer, beat the butter and sugar together with the paddle attachment until light and creamy, about 5 minutes. Switch to the dough hook, add the yeast mix-

ture, the remaining 5 cups flour, the salt, eggs, and yolks, and beat until the dough comes together and then pulls away from the sides of the bowl, 8 to 9 minutes.

4. Remove the dough from the mixing bowl and divide it into 12 equal parts. Place each portion into a muffin cup, cover with a towel, and allow to rise for 1 hour, or until doubled in size.
5. Preheat the oven to 375°F.
6. Place the cakes in the oven and bake for 20 to 25 minutes, until a toothpick inserted into the center of a baba comes out clean. Allow to cool in the pan on a cake rack for 20 minutes, then remove the cakes from the pan and place them on a rack on a baking sheet.
7. To make the syrup, in a small saucepan, bring the water and sugar to a boil, stirring to dissolve the sugar. Lower the heat to a very strong simmer and cook for 15 minutes. Remove from the heat, stir in the rum, and allow to cool for 5 minutes.
8. Poke the top of each cake with a popsicle stick or a skewer to make 8 to 10 holes. Spoon the rum syrup over the cakes, letting it drip into the holes. Repeat twice with the syrup that accumulates in the bottom of the baking sheet. Serve warm with whipped cream.

Note: As a gift, place babas in a wide-mouthed jar, cover with syrup, and seal tightly. These will keep for 2 weeks refrigerated.

CANNOLI

You can make all of the components the day before, but to enjoy truly crisp cannoli, you must serve them immediately after filling them with the ricotta cream.

MAKES 6 SERVINGS

SHELLS

2 cups ALL-PURPOSE FLOUR

¼ teaspoon ground CINNAMON

1 teaspoon SUGAR

1 tablespoon UNSWEETENED COCOA POWDER

2 tablespoons UNSALTED BUTTER

6 tablespoons MARSALA

FILLING

1 pound SHEEP'S MILK or COW'S MILK RICOTTA

½ cup SUPERFINE SUGAR

⅓ cup fresh LEMON JUICE

1 tablespoon VANILLA EXTRACT

¼ cup grated ORANGE ZEST, plus extra for garnish

¼ cup MINI CHOCOLATE CHIPS

1 EGG WHITE, lightly beaten

8 cups CANOLA OIL, for deep-frying

CONFECTIONERS' SUGAR, for dusting

1. To make the dough, in a medium bowl, whisk together the dry ingredients. Cut in the butter with two knives. Add the Marsala, stirring with a fork until the dough comes together. Shape the dough into a ball, wrap tightly in plastic wrap, and refrigerate. (The dough can be made up to 2 days ahead.)

2. To make the filling, in a large bowl, stir together all the ingredients until well combined. Cover and refrigerate. (The filling can also be refrigerated for up to 2 days.)

3. Divide the dough into 2 equal pieces. Using a rolling pin, roll one piece out on a floured surface to ¹⁄₁₆ inch thick. Using a large round cutter (or a sharp knife and a plate as a guide), cut the dough into 4-inch circles (you should have 6 rounds). Using a rolling pin, elongate the circles into ovals. Wrap the ovals around metal cannoli tubes. Using your fingertips, brush the seam with a little egg white and press to seal. Use your fingers to flare the ends open a bit.

4. In a large pot, heat the oil to 375°F. Carefully place the shells in the hot oil and fry until golden brown on all sides, 2 to 3 minutes. Using a slotted spoon, transfer the shells to a plate lined with paper towels to drain. When the shells are cool enough to touch, carefully twist the molds from the shells. Roll out the remaining dough and shape and fry the remaining cannoli. (The shells can be stored, uncovered, for up to 1 day.)

5. Just before serving, spoon the filling into a pastry bag fitted with a large plain tip. Pipe the cream into the shells. Dust with confectioners' sugar and garnish the cream with orange zest.

POTATO DOUGHNUTS
Bombe di Patate

Sweet potato bombs—what else can you say that would make me as happy? The idea of working potatoes into a dessert is possible only in the land where the inhabitants also coat eggplant with chocolate. . . . Ahhh, sweet, sweet Napoli.

MAKES 4 SERVINGS

1 pound RUSSET POTATOES, peeled and cut into chunks

1 cup WHOLE MILK

1 tablespoon ACTIVE DRY YEAST

4 large EGGS

¾ cup ALL-PURPOSE FLOUR, or as needed

1½ teaspoons SALT

¼ cup SUGAR

½ cup EXTRA-VIRGIN OLIVE OIL, plus 4 cups for deep-frying

2 tablespoons SWEET RED VERMOUTH

Grated zest and juice of 1 ORANGE

CONFECTIONERS' SUGAR, for dusting

1. Place the potatoes in a large pot, cover with water, and bring to a boil. Boil gently until tender. Drain and pass through a food mill or ricer into a large bowl. Let cool.

2. Meanwhile, in a small saucepan, heat the milk over low heat just until warm. Remove from the heat, sprinkle the yeast into the milk, and let sit for 15 minutes, or until foamy.

3. Add the eggs, flour, salt, sugar, the ½ cup olive oil, the vermouth, and orange zest and juice to the potatoes and mix well to combine. Add the yeast mixture and knead well, adding a little more flour if necessary if the dough is very sticky. Cover and let the dough rise in a warm place for 1 hour, or until doubled.

4. Divide the dough into 4 equal pieces. Roll each one into a 1½-inch-thick rope. Cut each one into 5-inch lengths and form into little doughnuts. Place the doughnuts on a well-oiled baking sheet, cover with a towel, and let rise for 45 minutes, or until doubled.

5. In a deep pot, heat the remaining 4 cups olive oil to 375°F. Working in batches, fry the doughnuts until golden brown, about 5 minutes per batch. Remove with a slotted spoon and drain on a plate lined with paper towels. Dust with confectioners' sugar and serve warm.

CHRISTMAS HONEY FRITTERS
Struffoli

A plate of these sweet bites on the coffee table means only one thing: Christmas week has arrived. I have modified my original recipe to make a softer, wetter dough, which makes these a little less crisp, but the dough is a lot easier to work with.

MAKES 8 TO 10 SERVINGS

3½ cups ALL-PURPOSE FLOUR

5 large EGGS

1 large EGG YOLK

Grated zest of 2 LEMONS

Grated zest of 1 ORANGE

½ teaspoon SALT

1 tablespoon LIMONCELLO or GRAND MARNIER

4 cups EXTRA-VIRGIN OLIVE OIL, for deep-frying

2 cups HONEY

Juice of 1 LEMON

CONFECTIONERS' SUGAR, for dusting

1. In a large bowl, combine the flour, eggs, yolk, half the lemon zest, the orange zest, salt, and limoncello. Stir with a wooden spoon to mix well, then knead into a firm dough, 8 to 10 minutes. Cover and allow to rest in the refrigerator for 30 minutes.

2. Cut the dough into golf ball–sized pieces. One at a time, roll each one into a ½-inch-thick rope, cut into ½-inch-long pieces, and roll each piece into a ball. Place on a floured tray.

3. In a large deep pot, heat the olive oil to 375°F. Working in batches to avoid crowding the pan, fry the balls until dark golden brown, using a slotted spoon to turn them often; they will puff up while cooking. As they finish, transfer them to a tray lined with paper towels to drain.

4. When all of the struffoli are cooked, combine the honey, lemon juice, and the remaining lemon zest in a wide 6- to 8-quart pot and heat until quite warm (about 150°F) and substantially thinner. Add the struffoli and stir carefully until well coated. Remove from the heat and allow to cool for 5 minutes in the pot, stirring frequently.

5. Pour out the stroffoli onto a large serving tray in the form of a pyramid or a ring. Sprinkle with confectioners' sugar, and serve.

APPLE FRITTERS
Fritelle di Mele

It may seem strange to fry desserts in extra-virgin olive oil, but it works brilliantly with apples. The scent as the sweet apples cook almost resembles that of the orchards themselves in the chilly autumn harvest.

MAKES 4 SERVINGS

2 large EGGS

¼ cup WHOLE MILK

1 cup ALL-PURPOSE FLOUR

¼ cup SUGAR

2 tablespoons KIRSCH

8 cups EXTRA-VIRGIN OLIVE OIL, for deep-frying

6 GREEN APPLES, such as Granny Smith, peeled, cored, and sliced into ½-inch-thick rounds

2 cups VANILLA GELATO (page 492)

CINNAMON, for dusting

1. In a medium bowl, whisk together the eggs and milk. Slowly add the flour, about 3 tablespoons at a time, whisking until incorporated. Stir in the sugar and kirsch. Allow the batter to stand for 10 minutes.

2. In a large deep pot, heat the olive oil to 375°F. Working in batches of 3 or 4, dip each apple slice into the batter, add to the hot oil, and cook until golden brown. With a slotted spoon, transfer to a paper towel–lined plate to drain.

3. Place 5 fritters on each of four plates, in an overlapping circle. Place a scoop of gelato in the center, sprinkle with cinnamon, and serve.

RUM *and* RICOTTA FRITTERS
Fritelle di Ricotta

These are easy to work with if the ricotta is very cold.

MAKES ABOUT 36 FRITTERS

2½ cups fresh RICOTTA, chilled

5 large EGGS, separated, yolks lightly beaten

¼ cup DARK RUM

2 tablespoons SUGAR

1⅓ cups ALL-PURPOSE FLOUR

1 tablespoon BAKING POWDER

4 cups EXTRA-VIRGIN OLIVE OIL, for deep-frying

CONFECTIONERS' SUGAR, for dusting

1. In a food processor, pulse the ricotta until it is smooth and creamy. Turn the ricotta out into a large bowl. Add the beaten egg yolks, rum, and sugar, beating well with an electric mixer. Sift together the flour and baking powder onto the ricotta mixture, and fold them in.

2. In a large bowl, beat the whites to stiff but not dry peaks. Fold them gently into the ricotta.

3. In a large deep pot, heat the olive oil to 370°F. Working in batches, form the fritters by dropping scant tablespoonfuls of the batter into the oil, and cook until golden on the first side. Carefully turn with a slotted spoon and cook until golden on the other side.

4. With the spoon, transfer to paper towels to drain. Dust with confectioners' sugar, and serve.

CHOCOLATE HAZELNUT FRITTERS

Fritelle di Cioccolato

This dough can work with almost any filling. The fritters are just as good served at room temperature, which makes them an excellent dessert for a party, when you'd rather be spending time with your guests than cooking.

MAKES ABOUT 18 FRITTERS

1 cup ALL-PURPOSE FLOUR

Pinch of SALT

2½ tablespoons SUGAR

Grated zest of 1 LEMON

¼ cup EXTRA-VIRGIN OLIVE OIL, plus 4 cups for deep-frying

2 to 3 tablespoons DRY WHITE WINE

½ cup roughly chopped BITTERSWEET CHOCOLATE

⅓ cup HAZELNUTS, toasted and coarsely chopped

½ cup APRICOT JAM

1 EGG, lightly beaten

HONEY, for brushing the fritters

CONFECTIONERS' SUGAR, for dusting

1. Mound the flour on a work surface and make a well in the center. Add the salt, sugar, lemon zest, the ¼ cup olive oil, and 2 tablespoons wine, and gradually mix in the flour. If the dough is very dry, add up to 1 more tablespoon wine. Then knead for 5 minutes, or until firm but tender. Wrap the dough in plastic and let it rest for 30 minutes.

2. In a small bowl, combine the chocolate, nuts, and jam and mix well with a spoon. Cover the filling and set aside.

3. On a floured surface, roll the dough out ¼-inch thick. Using a 3-inch round cookie cutter, cut out as many circles as possible. Place a dab of filling on each circle of dough, moisten the edges with a bit of beaten egg, and fold each round in half, pressing the edges with your fingertips to seal, or crimp with a fork.

4. In a large deep pot, heat the oil to 350°F. Working in batches, fry the fritters until they are deep golden brown. With a slotted spoon, transfer to paper towels to drain.

5. Brush each fritter with honey, and serve hot or at room temperature.

NEARLY AUSTRIAN STRUDEL

Gubana

The simple strudel dough recipe totally rocks and can be the basis of a thousand variations for both dessert and savory courses. I like to stuff it with prosciutto, walnuts, and Parmigiano and serve it with a stingingly cold bottle of my partner Joe Bastianich's wine called Vespa, which also goes quite well with this sweet version.

MAKES 8 SERVINGS

PASTRY

1 pound cold UNSALTED BUTTER, cut into bits

1 teaspoon SALT

3½ cups ALL-PURPOSE FLOUR

½ cup ICE WATER

FILLING

1 cup roughly chopped WALNUTS

½ cup roughly chopped HAZELNUTS

Grated zest of 1 LEMON

Grated zest of 1 ORANGE

¼ cup chopped CANDIED CITRUS PEEL (opposite)

¼ cup roughly chopped SEMISWEET CHOCOLATE

¼ cup dried CURRANTS, soaked for 1 hour in ½ cup Verduzzo or other Italian dessert wine

2 large EGGS, separated

¼ cup plus 3 tablespoons SUGAR

1. To make the pastry, in a food processor, combine a quarter of the butter, the salt, and 2½ cups of the flour and pulse until the texture of coarse crumbs. Slowly add the ice water, pulsing until the dough comes together. Remove and form into a ball, then roll out into an 8-by-10-inch rectangle; this is the *pasta* mixture. Place on a small baking sheet and refrigerate.

2. Combine the remaining butter and 1 cup flour in the processor, and process until well blended. Scrape out onto a work surface and, working quickly, form into a 4-inch square; this is called the *burro* mixture. Place in the refrigerator for about 30 minutes.

3. When the two mixtures are similar in texture, place the *pasta* mixture on a well-floured marble or other work surface. Place the *burro* mixture in the center and fold the dough up over it, like wrapping a gift. Flatten with a rolling pin and roll out to an 8-by-16-inch rectangle, flouring the work surface regularly. If any butter comes to the surface, flour the spot heavily and continue rolling.

4. Starting with a short end of the dough closest to you, fold the bottom third of the dough up over the center third and then fold the top third down to form a small package. Turn it 90 degrees, tap with the rolling pin so it adheres, and roll out to an 8-by-16-inch rectangle again. Repeat the folding process, and refrigerate for 30 minutes, wrapped in a moist cloth.

5. Repeat the rolling-and-folding process 3 times, chilling the dough for 30 minutes between each maneuver. The dough is now ready to use. (It will keep in the refrigerator for 2 days, wrapped tightly in plastic wrap.)

6. Preheat the oven to 375°F. Grease a baking sheet.

7. To make the filling, in a large bowl, combine the walnuts, hazelnuts, lemon zest, orange zest, candied citrus peel, chocolate, and currants with their soaking liquid, and stir to combine.

8. In a medium bowl, beat the egg whites until foamy. Gradually beat in ¼ cup of the sugar, and beat to stiff peaks. Fold the whites into the filling mixture.

9. On a floured work surface, roll the pastry out to a 10-by-16-inch rectangle, and position it with a long side parallel to the edge of the work surface. Spoon the filling evenly over the pastry, leaving a 2-inch border uncovered at the opposite side. Roll the pastry up like a jelly roll into a thick cylinder. Transfer seam side down to the prepared baking sheet and make a circle by attaching the two ends, like a wreath. Beat the egg yolks and brush the strudel with this egg glaze. Sprinkle with the remaining 3 tablespoons sugar.

10. Bake for 50 minutes. Allow to cool on a rack before cutting.

CANDIED CITRUS PEEL
MAKES ABOUT 1 CUP

1 cup large pieces ORANGE, GRAPEFRUIT, or LEMON PEEL

1 cup SUGAR, plus extra for coating

1 cup WATER

1. Put the citrus peel in a saucepan, add cold water to cover, and bring to a boil. Boil for 10 minutes. Drain, and repeat the process two more times.

2. Rinse the drained peel under cold water until cool. Scrape away the stringy white part of the peel, and slice into strips.

3. In a small saucepan, combine the sugar and 1 cup water and bring to a boil, stirring to dissolve the sugar. Add the peel, reduce the heat to very low, and cook slowly until all the syrup is absorbed. This may take several hours. Stir occasionally and watch carefully so the peel does not scorch.

4. Spread the peel on a wire rack set over a baking sheet, separating the pieces, and let cool.

5. Toss the candied peel with sugar to coat. Spread out on the rack again, and let dry overnight. Store tightly covered.

"CLOUDS ON CREAM"

Sciumette

The evanescent, milky sweetness is what makes this simple-to-prepare yet dramatic-to-serve dessert so much fun to eat. The cloud-like texture seems almost incapable of sustaining any taste at all, but the poaching milk adds something unexpected, while accentuating the elusive sweetness of the blood orange. These are reminiscent of floating islands, but are even lighter and less substantial.

MAKES 6 SERVINGS

4 cups WHOLE MILK

1 cup HEAVY CREAM

Grated zest and juice of 1 small BLOOD ORANGE or ORANGE

1½ cups CONFECTIONERS' SUGAR

5 extra-large EGGS, separated

2 tablespoons UNSWEETENED COCOA POWDER

1. In a 10- to 12-inch deep skillet, bring the milk and cream to a boil. Add the orange zest and ¼ cup of the confectioners' sugar, stir well, and lower the heat to a medium simmer.

2. Meanwhile, in a large bowl, beat the egg whites to soft peaks. Add ¼ cup of the confectioners' sugar and the orange juice and beat to stiff peaks.

3. Scoop up large tablespoons of the egg white mixture, 3 or 4 at a time, place in the milk mixture, and cook for 2 minutes. (Be careful not to let the milk boil.) Carefully flip the sciumette over with a large kitchen spoon and cook for 2 minutes more, then transfer to a large shallow bowl. Set the milk aside.

4. In a large heavy-bottomed nonreactive saucepan, beat the egg yolks with the remaining 1 cup confectioners' sugar until the mixture is thick and pale and forms a ribbon when the beaters are lifted. Add the warm poaching milk to the egg yolk mixture and cook over low heat, stirring constantly, until as thick as heavy cream. Transfer to a bowl set over an ice bath and whisk until cool.

5. Pour the cooled custard into a shallow serving bowl and top with the sciumette. Dust with the cocoa powder, and serve.

TIRAMISÙ

This coffee shop stalwart is actually very delicious if you use good mascarpone and serve it within a couple of hours of making it. If it sits overnight, the savoiardi become oversaturated and lose their texture.

MAKES 6 SERVINGS

½ cup strong ESPRESSO (or substitute 2 teaspoons instant coffee dissolved in ½ cup boiling water), cooled

¼ cup ITALIAN BRANDY

2 large EGGS, separated

2 large EGG YOLKS

2 tablespoons SUGAR

2 cups MASCARPONE

30 small SAVOIARDI (Italian ladyfingers), or 15 larger ones, broken in half

3 ounces BITTERSWEET CHOCOLATE, cut into ¼-inch pieces

3 ounces MILK CHOCOLATE, shaved or grated

1. In a small bowl, combine the espresso and brandy. Set aside.

2. In the top of a double boiler, beat the egg yolks and sugar with a hand-held electric mixer until the mixture is pale and thick and forms a ribbon when the beaters are lifted. Transfer to a large bowl and allow to cool for 5 minutes.

3. In a medium bowl, beat the egg whites to stiff peaks. Fold the mascarpone into the egg yolk mixture one quarter at a time. Fold in the egg whites and set aside.

4. Reserve 6 savoiardi, and line six large wine goblets with the remaining savoiardi. Using a pastry brush, paint the cookies with the espresso-brandy mixture. Fill each goblet one-third full with the mascarpone mixture, and sprinkle with the chopped chocolate. Lay 1 of the reserved savoiardi across the center of each and and paint with the espresso mixture. Fill the goblets with the remaining mascarpone mixture, and top with the shaved chocolate. Serve at room temperature, or refrigerate and serve chilled.

RICOTTA PUDDING CAKE

Budino di Ricotta

This is my variation on the traditional Roman ricotta cheesecake, which has all too often gotten far too souped up and filled with other stuff here in the United States. The only crazy thing going in this version is the cinnamon and candied orange—in other words, it's all about the ricotta.

MAKES 8 SERVINGS

1 tablespoon CONFECTIONERS' SUGAR

1 teaspoon ground CINNAMON, plus a pinch

1 pound fresh RICOTTA

5 large EGGS, 3 of them separated

1 tablespoon ALL-PURPOSE FLOUR

¼ cup SUGAR

2 tablespoons chopped CANDIED ORANGE PEEL (page 479)

Grated zest of 1 LEMON

2 tablespoons high-quality BRANDY or GRAPPA

1. Preheat the oven to 375°F. Grease and flour a 10-inch quiche pan.

2. In a small bowl, combine the confectioners' sugar with the pinch of cinnamon; set aside.

3. In a large bowl, combine the ricotta, the remaining 1 teaspoon cinnamon, the 2 whole eggs, the 3 yolks, the flour, sugar, candied orange peel, lemon zest, and brandy, and mix well.

4. In a medium bowl, beat the egg whites to stiff peaks. Fold the whites into the ricotta mixture.

5. Turn the mixture into the prepared quiche pan. Bake for 30 minutes. Turn off the heat and leave the cake in the oven for 5 minutes.

6. Turn the pudding cake out onto a serving dish, dust with the confectioners' sugar and cinnamon mixture, and serve immediately.

ITALIAN TRIFLE
Zuppa Inglese

This is my take on the Italian take on English trifle, which I have pared down by removing the day-glo colored liqueurs and odd schlumpy custards that have made this nearly inedible in many lesser trattorie all over Italy.

MAKES 8 SERVINGS

3¼ cups WHOLE MILK

Grated zest of 1 LEMON

1 VANILLA BEAN, split

7 large EGG YOLKS

½ cup ALL-PURPOSE FLOUR

1 cup SUGAR

5 tablespoons UNSWEETENED COCOA POWDER

1¾ ounces UNSWEETENED CHOCOLATE, finely chopped

24 small SAVOIARDI (Italian ladyfingers)

¼ cup LIMONCELLO or other sweet citrus liqueur

1. In a large heavy-bottomed saucepan, combine the milk and lemon zest. Scrape the seeds from the vanilla bean, and add the seeds and bean to the pan. Bring a very brisk simmer over medium-high heat; do not allow to boil.

2. Meanwhile, in a large bowl, combine the egg yolks, flour, and sugar and whisk until the mixture is pale yellow and forms a ribbon when the whisk is lifted from the bowl. Gradually pour half of the hot milk into the egg mixture, whisking constantly. Return the mixture back to the saucepan along with the remaining milk and cook over high heat, stirring constantly with a wooden spoon, until the pastry cream coats the back of the spoon. Remove the vanilla bean. Pour half the cream into a stainless steel bowl and set in an ice bath to cool. Stir the cocoa and chocolate into the remaining pastry cream, making sure that the chocolate is completely melted. Then pour the chocolate cream into another bowl and set over an ice bath to cool. Whisk the creams occasionally as they cool.

3. Split each ladyfinger in half. Sprinkle the cut sides with the liqueur. Place a layer of the soaked ladyfingers in a large glass serving bowl. Top with a layer of the vanilla pastry cream, another layer of ladyfingers, and a layer of the chocolate cream; repeat the layering until all ingredients are used. Cover and refrigerate for 1 hour before serving.

BITTERSWEET
CHOCOLATE PUDDING
Sanguinaccio

This intense chocolate pudding is based on an ancient Neapolitan recipe. It is at its most excellent if you serve it with unsweetened whipped cream along with the toasted pine nuts. And it is perfect for holiday parties because you can make it up to two days in advance and hold it, well covered, in the fridge.

MAKES 10 SERVINGS

1 cup UNSWEETENED COCOA POWDER

⅓ cup ALL-PURPOSE FLOUR

2 cups SUGAR

4½ cups WHOLE MILK

12 ounces SEMISWEET CHOCOLATE, grated

1 teaspoon VANILLA EXTRACT

1 teaspoon ground CINNAMON

5 tablespoons PINE NUTS, toasted

1. In a large bowl, whisk together the cocoa powder, flour, and sugar. Gradually whisk in just enough of the milk to form a paste, then slowly whisk in the remaining milk. Transfer to a large saucepan and slowly bring to a boil over medium heat, whisking constantly.

2. Remove from the heat, add the chocolate, vanilla, and cinnamon, and stir to blend and to melt the chocolate. Pour the pudding into ten 6-ounce ramekins. Allow to cool, then cover and refrigerate until cold.

3. Sprinkle the puddings with the toasted pine nuts, and serve.

PEACHES *in* PRIMITIVO
Pesche in Primitivo

Serving fruit with red wine is a big tradition in Puglia, where they often chill the raisiny red wines and simply pour them over sliced fresh peaches. I have spiced up the wine and also sweetened it a bit to create a more syrupy liquid. It also goes well with cherries. There will be some extra syrup, which is great on other fruits—or on French toast. Serve the peaches with Walnut Biscotti (page 493).

MAKES 4 SERVINGS

2 cups SUGAR

2 cups PRIMITIVO DI GIOIA (from Puglia) or other dry red wine

1 CLOVE

4 PEACHES

1. In a medium saucepan, combine the sugar, red wine, and clove, bring to a simmer, and simmer until reduced by half, about 30 minutes. Let cool, and remove the clove. (The syrup can be made ahead and refrigerated for up to 1 week.)

2. Peel and slice the peaches, and divide among four footed bowls. Pour ¼ cup syrup over each peach and serve.

ROASTED PEARS *with* CHOCOLATE

Pere al Cioccolato

Pears as dessert are always a hard sell at my restaurants, but in Italy they are hugely popular, probably because there they are used to eating them plain anyway. The chocolate sauce is a little tricky, but it is so darn good it is worth the minor effort involved.

MAKES 6 SERVINGS

6 ANJOU or other firm pears, peeled but stems left intact

1 cup VIN SANTO or DRY SHERRY

1 cup WATER

¼ cup HONEY

Pinch of ground CINNAMON

5 ounces SEMISWEET CHOCOLATE, chopped

4 tablespoons UNSALTED BUTTER, at room temperature

2 large EGGS, separated

1 tablespoon CONFECTIONERS' SUGAR

1.   Preheat the oven to 375°F. Grease a sauté pan just large enough to hold the pears upright.

2.   Cut a tiny slice off the bottom of each pear to make it stand upright, then place them in the sauté pan. Add the vin santo and water and bake the pears for 40 minutes, or until tender, basting 3 to 4 times with the pan juices.

3.   Carefully transfer the pears to a plate (leave the oven on), and pour the pan juices into a small bowl. Add the honey and cinnamon and whisk together until the consistency of a light dressing, adding a little hot water if necessary.

4.   Drizzle the pears with the mixture, return to the oven, and bake for another 5 minutes. Remove from the oven and set aside until ready to serve. (The pears can be made several hours ahead and kept at room temperature.)

5.   In the top of a double boiler, melt the chocolate and butter together, stirring until smooth. Transfer to a large bowl and set aside to cool to room temperature.

6.   Whisk the egg yolks into the chocolate until well mixed. In a medium bowl, beat the egg whites and confectioners' sugar to stiff peaks, then fold the whites into the chocolate mixture. The sauce should be used immediately, as it can harden.

7.   Place 1 pear on each of six dessert plates, and top with the chocolate sauce. Serve immediately.

CLEMENTINES *with*
BALSAMIC VINEGAR AND PEPPER
Mandarini al Aceto Balsamico

My grandma always sent us a couple of boxes of clementines with the Christmas cookies, and they were always one of the quickest things to go on Christmas morning as we unwrapped the presents. Now, while I still love them right out of the peel, I also love the combination of real aceto balsamico and black pepper for an adult take on their simplicity.

MAKES 4 SERVINGS

8 CLEMENTINES (or other small seedless citrus fruit), peeled and segmented

2 tablespoons best-quality AGED BALSAMIC VINEGAR

1 teaspoon SUGAR

Coarse BLACK PEPPER

1. In a large bowl, toss the clementines, vinegar, and sugar together well.

2. Divide the fruit among four martini glasses or small bowls, being sure to get all the vinegar out of the bowl. Crack fresh pepper over the top, and serve.

COFFEE GRANITA
Granita di Caffè

A traditional granita is made by scraping the coffee ice with a fork every twenty minutes or so as it freezes to create a lighter texture, but this quick and easy method is hardly a compromise. I like to serve it plain with a shot of cold milk for a quick bump on a hot summer afternoon when I am struggling to avoid my well-deserved nap.

MAKES 6 SERVINGS

4 cups freshly brewed ESPRESSO

½ cup GRANULATED SUGAR

1 cup HEAVY CREAM

½ cup VANILLA-FLAVORED SUGAR

6 tablespoons BRANDY or ANISETTE

1. Sweeten the coffee with the granulated sugar while it is still hot. Let cool, then pour into two ice-cube trays and freeze for several hours, or overnight.

2. In a large bowl, whip the cream to soft peaks. Gradually beat in the vanilla-flavored sugar, but do not overbeat.

3. Crush the iced-coffee cubes in an electric crusher or a food processor. Distribute evenly among six chilled martini glasses. Add 1 tablespoon brandy to each glass, and top with the whipped cream. Serve immediately.

VANILLA GELATO

Gelato is different from ice cream in that it has less fat and thus coats the tongue with less viscosity, allowing the true flavor to come through—that is, provided you *have* true flavor. Italians like to roast the heck out of nuts like pistachios or hazelnuts to extract their most resonant flavors and to use high proportions of cooked and raw fruits to create their incredible flavors. This is a base recipe for vanilla, using a pair of vanilla beans. You could substitute the grated zest of 8 lemons to make Lemon Gelato, ½ cup chopped roasted walnuts for Walnut Gelato, 2 tablespoons ground cinnamon for Cinnamon Gelato—and on and on. . . .

MAKES 3 PINTS

3 cups WHOLE MILK

1 cup HEAVY CREAM

1 cup SUGAR

2 VANILLA BEANS, split

14 large EGG YOLKS

1. In a large heavy-bottomed saucepan, combine the milk, cream, and ½ cup of the sugar. Scrape the seeds from the vanilla beans and add the seeds and beans to the pan. Bring just to a boil.
2. Meanwhile, in a large bowl, combine the egg yolks and the remaining ½ cup sugar and whisk until the mixture is pale yellow. Remove the cream mixture from the heat and slowly whisk about one third of it into the yolk mixture. Return this mixture to the saucepan, whisking well, and cook over medium heat, whisking constantly, until the mixture begins to thicken, 4 to 5 minutes; do not boil. Lower the heat to a gentle simmer and cook, whisking, for 2 minutes longer.
3. Strain the custard through a fine sieve into a clean bowl set in an ice bath. Chill until cold, stirring often.
4. Freeze the gelato in an ice cream machine according to the manufacturer's instructions. Transfer to a container just big enough to hold the gelato, cover tightly, and place in the freezer for 2 hours before serving.

WALNUT BISCOTTI

Biscotti ai Noci

MAKES ABOUT 32 BISCOTTI

2¾ cups ALL-PURPOSE FLOUR

2 cups SUGAR

1 teaspoon BAKING POWDER

3 large EGGS

4 large EGG YOLKS

3 tablespoons NOCELLO (walnut liqueur)

½ cup chopped WALNUTS

1. Preheat the oven to 350°F.

2. In a large bowl, stir together the flour, sugar, and baking powder. In a medium bowl, whisk together the eggs, yolks, and Nocello. Add to the dry ingredients and stir just until the dough comes together, about 1 minute. Add the walnuts and mix until just incorporated.

3. Divide the dough in half and shape each one into a loaf about 10 inches by 2 inches. Place on an ungreased baking sheet about 2 inches apart. Bake for 20 minutes, or until light golden brown. Remove from the oven and let cool slightly. Reduce the oven temperature to 275°F.

4. As soon as they are cool enough to handle, cut the loaves on a slight diagonal into ½-inch-thick pieces. Arrange cut side down on one or two baking sheets and bake for 20 minutes longer, or until crisp and dry. Allow to cool on a rack.

SARDINIAN RAVIOLI COOKIES

Sebadas

The idea of fried dessert may at first seem challenging, but these sweet Sardinian odes to ravioli are well worth the effort required to enter the domain of hot oil. Yogurt and honey are the showcased ingredients here, so take the time to find really distinct examples of both at a specialty store.

MAKES 10 RAVIOLI

½ cup WHOLE MILK

8 tablespoons (1 stick) UNSALTED BUTTER

1 cup ALL-PURPOSE FLOUR

1 cup SEMOLINA FLOUR

2 cups RICOTTA, preferably sheep's milk

Grated zest of 2 LEMONS

1 large EGG

1 cup YOGURT, preferably Coach Farm goat yogurt or fancy Greek sheep's milk yogurt

½ cup SUGAR

2 cups EXTRA-VIRGIN OLIVE OIL, for shallow-frying

CONFECTIONERS' SUGAR, for sprinkling

1 cup HONEY, warmed, for serving

1. In a small saucepan, combine the milk and butter and heat over low heat, stirring, until the butter is melted; let cool. In a large bowl, combine the flour and semolina and make a well in the center. Pour the butter mixture into the well and stir into the dry ingredients to form a dough.

2. Turn the dough out onto a floured work surface and knead for 1 minute. Form into a ball, wrap in plastic, and refrigerate for 1 hour.

3. In a medium bowl, stir together the ricotta, lemon zest, egg, yogurt, and sugar until well blended. Set aside.

4. In a 10- to 12-inch sauté pan, heat the olive oil to 375°F. Meanwhile, with a rolling pin, roll out the dough out on a floured surface to ¼-inch thick. Using a cookie cutter, cut twenty 3½-inch rounds out of the dough. Place 2 tablespoons of the cheese mixture on 10 of the rounds. Cover each one with another round, like a sandwich, and press the edges together to seal.

5. Working in batches, fry the cookies until golden brown, about 1 minute. Remove from the oil and drain on paper towels.

6. Arrange on a platter, sprinkle with confectioners' sugar, and serve with the warm honey.

GLOSSARY

ALMONDS   Two varieties of almonds are available in Italy: bitter almonds, which contain toxic hydrocyanic acid when raw but when cooked are used to make almond extract and amaretto; and sweet almonds, available raw or roasted, whole, sliced, or slivered, blanched or unblanched. They can be salted, smoked, or ground into almond paste. In America, only sweet almonds are available. Almonds should be purchased in their shells if possible; otherwise, choose those packed in tightly sealed bags, cans, or jars.

ANCHOVIES   These small, flavorful fish from the Mediterranean and southern Atlantic are eaten both fresh and preserved in salt or oil. In this country, we most often see the latter, but the best are packed whole in salt; they must be filleted and rinsed before using. The least desirable are made into a paste sold in tubes or jars. In a pinch the tube will do, but for superior flavor and sublime texture, the salt-packed ones are for you and me.

BALSAMIC VINEGAR   This deep, intensely flavored, complex vinegar is made exclusively in Emilia-Romagna from the unfermented juice of white Trebbiano grapes. The freshly pressed juice is cooked slowly overnight in copper cauldrons over open fires right in the fields of vines to form a thick syrup called *mosto*, or *saba*. This saba is first placed in giant wood barrels to begin the development of its acidity and is then aged in progressively smaller barrels of different woods over a period of twelve years or more to achieve a unique and complex flavor like nothing else. The finished product is then submitted to a consortium for tasting and, if approved, placed in bottles whose shapes indicate the place of origin, one for Modena and another for Reggio, the only two areas that can legitimately produce the real thing. True *aceto balsamico tradizionale* will cost you at least fifty dollars for a four-ounce bottle and should only be used to dress salads if you own the joint. The regular supermarket stuff sold in tall green bottles for $3.99 is made with caramel coloring and is fine for a change of pace in the salad dressing department, but is unacceptable in the world of anointing perfect meats or Parmigiano-Reggiano, where you want the real thing.

BUTTER   Always buy fresh unsalted butter, preferably from an organic farm within a hundred miles of your home. Keep it wrapped in plastic to prevent it from absorbing any strong flavors or odors from whatever else is in the fridge.

CACIOCAVALLO   This highly prized Sicilian cheese is made with cow's milk taken from a single milking and coagulated with kid's rennet in a wooden barrel. The characteristic shape of the cheese is quadrilateral, formed by using a traditional wooden tool called a *rotula*. Aged for three months, caciocavallo is used as an ingredient in dishes such as stuffed sardines (*sarde a* *beccafico*). It is also wonderful paired with fine Sicilian red wines.

CAPERS / CAPER BERRIES Capers are the flower buds of a crawling shrub called *Capparis spinosa* that resembles something from an exotic nursery in an expensive neighborhood. The unopened flower buds are picked daily during a very short season immediately prior to flowering. When packed in vinegar brine, they lose much of their subtle flavor, but will add a lot of magnificent acidity to your dish as a result of the formation of capric acid. I prefer capers that are packed in salt, which retain a sweet forest floor flavor as well as the more subtle sea breeze scent that is lost in the pickling process. The best capers come from the island of Pantelleria, off the coast of Sicily.

At the end of the season, the fruit of the bush develops in the form of a drupe, or berry, that kind of looks like a small tomatillo. These are also sold pickled or salted and make a great partner to any dish with capers in it, to accentuate your super-savvy Mediterranean pantry.

CHESTNUTS / CHESTNUT FLOUR Sweet chestnuts, *Castanea sativa*, grow in mild temperatures throughout Europe and the Americas on distinctive shade trees. They have long been considered the food of poverty due to their abundant supply and the fact that they keep well. The best chestnuts are bigger rather than smaller, have flexible brown or dark brown shells, and are soft when fresh. Dried, they can be ground into a flour that is nearly equal in dietary benefits to wheat flour, with the exception being a lack of gluten, which makes the flour difficult to substitute in bread recipes but excellent for pasta dough and cakes. The best chestnuts for eating out of hand are available in the late autumn and winter, and every town in Italy has several roasters hawking the *caldarroste* in every neighborhood around Christmastime.

CHICKPEAS Also called ceci beans or garbanzos, these legumes, *Cicer arietinum*, are almost always dried first and then soaked prior to cooking. A flour made from the ground beans is the main ingredient in *panissa*, a flat pancake served as antipasto or bread in Liguria, and in Sicilian *panelle* (see page 38). Always buy dried beans and other pulses from a store with good turnover. The older they are, the harder they are to get just right when cooking.

COTECHINO A heavily spiced pork sausage made from skin mixed with lean meat and lots of back fat, cotechino is the lead singer in bollito misto and one of the crown jewels, along with mortadella, of the Emilian sausages. They are imported from Italy precooked, but I prefer making my own or buying the fresh from Faicco's Pork Store in Greenwich Village (see Sources, page 504).

FARRO A staple in the cooking of the Etruscans, *farro* (called emmer in English), or *Triticum dicoccum*, has enjoyed a renaissance in Tuscan and Umbrian cooking in the last twenty years and is increasingly available in Italy and the United States. The grain has a great nutty flavor and makes an excellent substitute for rice in risotto recipes. It also does well as a side dish or a soup ingredient.

GORGONZOLA   This blue cheese, is often referred to as *erborinato* ("parsley" in Lombard dialect) in Italian because of its greenish striations. It is made from cow's milk that is pasteurized and heated before being inoculated with the *Penicillium gorgonzola* mold. It is drained and ripened in a heated, damp "purgatory" for four to five hours, then dry-salted. Gorgonzola is known for its creaminess and pungent bite.

MOZZARELLA DI BUFALA   Buffalo mozzarella is a snowy-white, semi-soft fresh cheese with a slightly stringy consistency resulting from the many layers that comprise it. It is made entirely of whole buffalo milk, which is inoculated with a starter culture of whey from the previous day's cheese making. After about thirty minutes, the milk begins to coagulate and the cheese maker breaks the curd into small pieces that are allowed to ripen for five hours. Then the curd is transferred to large vats of hot whey and kneaded and stretched into its final shape, either large balls or smaller ones called *bocconcini*. Some *caseificie*, or dairies, offer scamorza, a smoked version. No matter what form it takes, mozzarella di bufala has a slightly sour tang that is offset by its creamy, milky bite. Produced almost exclusively in Campania and Sicily, the cheese has been protected under DOP status since 1996. It is an essential part of the wood-fired *pizze* of Naples. It is also often served on its own, accompanied by a slice of grilled bread and perhaps a simple salad.

OLIVE OIL   The pressed and centrifuged extract of the fruit of the olive tree is produced in nearly every province in Italy. Each region has its own style and flavor, which in turn defines the style and flavor of the region's cooking. I recommend having two kinds of olive oil in the pantry: a boutique Tuscan or Ligurian extra-virgin olive oil, for anointing both raw and cooked foods at the moment they are served, and a less expensive extra-virgin oil from a larger producer, that is, a less-distinctive but still high-quality oil at a much lower price, for everything else, including frying. In my opinion, you simply cannot scrimp when buying extra-virgin olive oil. Choose one that you like and stick with it for general uses, occasionally trying bottles from other areas, particularly when cooking dishes from those regions. My personal favorites are Tenuta di Cappezana (western Tuscany), Castello di Ama (Chianti), and Da Vero, produced by my friends Ridgely Evers and Colleen McGlynn in California's Dry Creek Valley, from the fruits of trees transported from my grandfather's hometown of Segreminio, near Lucca. It has a rich and peppery intensity.

OLIVES   The fruit of the olive tree is cured and preserved for eating using salt, water, lye, or oil, or a combination of the four. Unprocessed olives contain a bitter component (called glycoside) that renders them inedible, but it is leached out in the curing process. All olives start green and eventually ripen to black or purple. Each olive-producing area in the world has its own type of olives and seasoning profile, and I love them all. My favorites include Gaeta, Kalamata, and Alfonso, but I am happy to try any and all olives. I cure my own each year for gifts to olive *appassionati* and for the restaurants.

PANCETTA   Italian bacon, pancetta is cured pork belly, available rolled (*rotolata*) or flat (*stesa*). If you are having trouble finding good pancetta, excellent substitutes are the artisanal American bacons available in many good markets; or, for an excellent source, see www. gratefulpalate.com.

PARMIGIANO-REGGIANO   The undisputed king of cheeses, Parmigiano-Reggiano is produced from both skim and whole cow's milk from the same herd every day in each dairy. In order to be considered true Parmigiano, the cheese must have been entirely produced in a restricted area that includes only the provinces of Modena, Parma, and Reggio-Emilia and parts of Bologna and Mantova. According to an Italian law passed in 1955, any cheeses made outside of this area can not be called Parmigiano. And the cheese should be impressed all over the rind with "Parmigiano-Reggiano." There are just over six hundred dairies authorized to make it, sometimes as few as two wheels of cheese per day, following the traditional method. Each cheese is made from a vat of about 160 gallons of milk, which is first heated and then separated with calf's rennet and a handful of the whey from the batch made the day before, and yields a roughly 80-pound wheel, which is floated in salt-saturated water for about three weeks. It is then stored in aging vaults for at least one and up to three years before being sold.

Many Parmigiano enthusiasts claim to prefer cheeses made in the late spring and summer months, when the feed is fresh grass and wheat. I like all of them, but I do prefer a younger cheese for eating plain or with balsamic vinegar and older cheeses for grating over my pasta and risotto.

PEPERONCINO   Hot peppers are used mostly in the southern parts of Italy and the type varies from town to town, but the word *peperoncino* generally refers to the crushed dried chile flakes we find at the pizzeria. Most of us know our own preference for heat content, but I like to use fresh chile peppers, especially the Mexican varieties like jalapeños, serranos, and even habaneros, in many Italian dishes.

PINE NUTS   Pine nuts are the seeds from the pinecones of a stone pine, *Pinus pinea*. The best are the longer oval-shaped ones from the Mediterranean countries; the more triangular variety from Asia is less desirable. Both are very susceptible to going rancid and should be stored in the freezer in a Ziploc bag or airtight jar.

POLENTA   Polenta is the Italian take on grits, although polenta is often yellow and grits are almost always bleached white. Polenta changes from region to region in the way that it is ground (rough or fine), the way it is cooked, and the way it is served. Although I sometimes recommend the longer-cooking variety versus the instant because its depth of rich corn flavor is unsurpassed, a good instant variety, as long as it is fresh, can be perfectly acceptable in many dishes. I do not recommend cooking polenta in anything but water, with a little salt, because I prefer the simple and pure corn taste to anything else.

PROSCIUTTO Italian hams from Parma, Friuli (San Daniele), and Le Marche (Carpegna) are the benchmark internationally and have achieved wide distribution almost everywhere in the United States. Domestic prosciutto is an unacceptable substitute, so bite the bullet and splurge. The most important tip is to buy your prosciutto from a shop that sells a lot of it—the less time between first cutting into the ham and eating it, the less the likelihood of oxidization or drying out. The second most important tip is to have it sliced on a good machine and to have the butcher layer it carefully, not overlapping, on wax paper, not parchment. Prosciutto does not hold well once it is sliced, even if done the right way, so just buy enough for a day or two—and return often to the shop, just to help the prosciutto itself.

PROVOLONE Provolone originally came from southern Italy. It is the Italian cheese with the greatest varieties of shapes and weights, reflecting its ancient origins and deep roots within Italy. Each local community where it is produced has its own characteristic shape. The flavor becomes tangier and the texture flakier as it ages. An excellent table cheese, it can be found in smoked versions as well. It is also a good cooking cheese because of its ability to stretch, melt, and flirt with other flavors in a dish.

RICOTTA Fresh ricotta is a dairy product more than a cheese; its name means "recooked," and it refers to the fact that it is made from whey that is heated a second time. The whey left over from daily cheese making is heated until its proteins separate out and form little clumps that rise to the surface. This ricotta is then skimmed off using a strainer and transferred to rush baskets to drain for a few hours.

Italian ricotta is made primarily from sheep's milk or water buffalo milk whey, though occasionally goat's or cow's milk whey may be used. It has a mild, nutty, and sweet flavor and a drier texture than most American-made ricottas. Ricotta is most commonly used in pasta dishes and desserts. In Italy, fresh ricotta is sold by weight and wrapped in paper. If possible, you should taste before purchasing to make sure it is fresh. If it feels prickly on the tongue or tastes sharp and/or fruity, it is no longer fresh.

SALT There are now hundreds of brands of great salt in the market. I use sea salt from Sicily and buy the coarse grind (chunky large grains) for finishing meat and fish, as well as for pasta water and for focaccia and similar breads.

SEMOLINA Semolina is ground from durum wheat, a hard wheat high in protein. It comes both coarsely and more finely ground; fine semolina is also referred to as semolina flour. Semolina is used to make pasta and a type of gnocchi; it is also sometimes used in desserts.

VIN COTTO *Vin cotto* translates literally as "cooked wine," and it is the cooked must of grapes. It falls somewhere between an aged balsamic and a syrup. The must is boiled and reduced to about one fifth of its initial volume. The syrup may used at that point, or it may be aged in oak barrels to develop more complexity, like wine. The result is a rich, smooth, syrupy liquid that can be enjoyed with sweet and savory foods and used in a variety of dishes.

ESSENTIAL EQUIPMENT
FOR A GREAT ITALIAN KITCHEN

A food processor—the largest you can afford

A KitchenAid mixer—splurge, it is amazingly useful

A pasta machine

A sausage-making device—I love the attachment to the KitchenAid mixer

A 12- to 14-inch sauté pan, heaviest gauge available

A 10- to 12-inch sauté pan, heaviest gauge available

An 8-inch nonstick skillet

A grill pan, with press

An 8- to 10-quart Dutch oven or other heavy-bottomed casserole with a lid

An 8- to 10-quart spaghetti pot, with a strainer insert

Two 4-quart saucepans with lids

Two heavy-gauge roasting pans, one large, one slightly smaller

One lasagne pan

A set of stainless steel bowls

1 copper bowl (for egg whites; optional)

Two heavy-duty baking sheets

A pizza pan

A 10- to 12-inch chef's knife

A boning knife

A paring knife

A serrated bread knife

Four wooden spoons, two wide, two deep

Four large metal spoons, two slotted, two plain

One metal spaghetti spoon

Two flexible metal turners, one large, one small

Two slotted metal turners, one large, one small

A carving fork

Two pairs metal tongs

One pair metal serving tongs

One metal lasagne server

Two whisks, one balloon, one egg

Two ladles, one 8-ounce, one 4-ounce

Two heatproof plastic spatulas

A slotted spatula

A silicone brush

An ice cream scoop (I like the Teflon-coated scoops)

A plastic counter scraper

A wooden rolling pin

A meat pounder

Three cheese graters of the rasp variety, one coarse, one medium, and one fine (for Parmigiano)

A mortar and pestle

A vegetable peeler

A garlic press

A citrus press

A pizza cutter

A ricer (essential for gnocchi)

A 2-cup liquid measuring cup

A set of measuring spoons

A set of solid measuring cups

Two colanders, one large and one small
     hand-held

One large (8-inch) strainer

A salad spinner

A meat thermometer

A fat skimmer

A squirt bottle

A large (24 inches by 36 inches) wooden cutting
     board

Two small (12 inches by 9 inches) plastic cutting
     boards for small jobs, and for moving stuff

A roll of butcher's twine

A box of parchment paper

NOTE:

For my absolute favorite stuff, please check out
my own personal equipment and kitchen tool
line at www.italiankitchen.com

SOURCES

ARMANDINO'S SALUMI
309 Third Avenue South, Seattle, WA 98104
(206) 621-8772
Cured meats made by my dad
www.salumicuredmeats.com

ARTHUR AVENUE CATERERS
2344 Arthur Avenue, Bronx, NY 10458
(866) 2-SALAMI / (718) 295-5033
www.arthuravenue.com
Cured meats, specialty items, and cheeses

BIANCARDI MEATS
2350 Arthur Avenue, Bronx, NY 10458
(718) 733-4058
Fresh meat, game, and house-cured meats

CITARELLA
2135 Broadway, New York, NY 10023
(212) 874-0383
www.citarella.com
Fish and shellfish of all types

CONCA D'ORO
72-02 51st Avenue, Woodside, NY 11377
(718) 446-4588
Italian cheeses, cured meats, olives, oils,
vinegars, pasta, and spices

D'ARTAGNAN
280 Wilson Avenue, Newark, NJ 07105
(800) 327-8246
www.dartagnan.com
Fresh game and poultry; truffles

DEAN & DELUCA
560 Broadway, New York, NY 10012
(800) 221-7714 / (212) 226-6800
www.dean-deluca.com
Cured meats, cheeses, olive oil, vinegar, blood
orange juice, and specialty produce

DIPALO
200 Grand Street, New York, NY 10002
(212) 226-1033
Italian cheeses (including eighty-five types of
pecorino), cured meats, olives, oils, vinegar,
and pasta

FAICCO
260 Bleecker Street, New York, NY 10014
(212) 243-1974
Cured meats, dry pasta, oils, and vinegar

FORMAGGIO KITCHEN
244 Huron Avenue, Cambridge, MA 02138
(888) 212-3224 / (617) 354-4750
Cheese, olive oils, vinegars, pasta, and
specialty foods

GRATEFUL PALATE
(888) 472-5283
www.gratefulpalate.com
Olive oil, vinegar, wine, and
Bacon-of-the-Month Club

MANICARETTI
Mail-order available through The Pasta Shop:
(888) 952-4005
www.manicaretti.com
Imports many of the specialty products used
at our restaurants, including bottarga, saba,
estate-produced olive oils and vinegars, high-
quality grains and rices, and superb pasta

MURRAY'S CHEESE SHOP
257 Bleecker Street, New York, NY 10014
(888) 692-4339 / (212) 243-3289
www.murrayscheese.com
Extensive cheese selection, as well as olives,
oils, pasta, vinegar, and other imported
specialty items

NIMAN RANCH
www.nimanranch.com
Free-range meats

TODARO BROS.
555 Second Avenue, New York, NY 10016
(877) 472-2767
www.todarobros.com
A wide variety of Italian products; chestnut,
chickpea, and semolina flour in small bags at rea-
sonable prices

VINO E OLIO
(877) 846-6365
www.vinoeolio.com
Beans, cheese, coffee, mushrooms, pasta,
truffles, oil, vinegar, and other specialty items;
cookware

ZINGERMAN'S
422 Detroit Street, Ann Arbor, MI 48104
(888) 636-8162 / (734) 663-DELI
www.zingermans.com
Cheese, olive oils, vinegars, produce, and other
specialty items

INDEX

514